OXFORD HISTORICAL MONOGRAPHS

The Detection of Heresy in Late Medieval England

IAN FORREST

CLARENDON PRESS · OXFORD

OXFORD
UNIVERSITY PRESS

Great Clarendon Street, Oxford OX2 6DP

Oxford University Press is a department of the University of Oxford.
It furthers the University's objective of excellence in research, scholarship,
and education by publishing worldwide in

Oxford New York

Auckland Cape Town Dar es Salaam Hong Kong Karachi
Kuala Lumpur Madrid Melbourne Mexico City Nairobi
New Delhi Shanghai Taipei Toronto

With offices in

Argentina Austria Brazil Chile Czech Republic France Greece
Guatemala Hungary Italy Japan Poland Portugal Singapore
South Korea Switzerland Thailand Turkey Ukraine Vietnam

Oxford is a registered trade mark of Oxford University Press
in the UK and in certain other countries

Published in the United States
by Oxford University Press Inc., New York

© Ian Forrest 2005

The moral rights of the author have been asserted
Database right Oxford University Press (maker)

First published 2005

British Library Cataloguing in Publication Data
Data available

Library of Congress Cataloging in Publication Data
Data available

Typeset by Newgen Imaging Systems (P) Ltd., Chennai, India
Printed in Great Britain
on acid-free paper by
Biddles Ltd., King's Lynn, Norfolk

ISBN 0–19–928692–2   978–0–19–928692–8

1 3 5 7 9 10 8 6 4 2

In memory of John A. F. Thomson

Preface

John Wyclif and lollardy have become a major scholarly industry in Britain and North America. For many years the subject was one of the few non-'political' topics studied by undergraduate historians, and more recently it has become a standard feature of courses in Middle English literature. Today, a growing corpus of edited Wycliffite texts is, it seems, continually being revisited in the light of a sometimes bewildering array of critical theories. This book is an attempt to step back from recent debates, and examine lollardy from a different, and really quite unfashionable, point of view: as a sin and a crime. The prosecution of heresy in medieval England is a neglected subject, but one that is fundamental to our appreciation of the records on which all new interpretations of lollardy are ultimately based. I have tried to look at the subject anew, from the outside, whilst integrating it with wider currents in social and legal history.

The doctoral thesis upon which this book is based was completed with the aid of four years of funding from the Arts and Humanities Research Board, and additional assistance from the Snell and Jowett Exhibitions at Balliol College, Oxford. I would like to thank the wardens and fellows of Merton and All Souls Colleges, Oxford, for providing me with the time and resources necessary to complete the further research and rewriting required before the thesis could become a book.

In the course of this work, I have received help and encouragement from many sources. The staff of the archives and libraries listed in the Bibliography provided exemplary guidance during many visits. Several very important references were provided by Paul Brand and Maureen Jurkowski. Richard Helmholz, Kantik Ghosh, Andrew Roach, and Norman Tanner read early drafts of single chapters. My greatest debts, however, are to my teachers and mentors over the years. At Glasgow University Alison Peden encouraged my early interest in lollardy, and suggested I speak to John Thomson, who then became my master's supervisor, jointly with Sam Cohn. After moving to Oxford, my work on lollardy was punctuated by letters from John and long discussions at conferences and Christmases, in which he continued to recall to my attention pieces of evidence I had forgotten, or ideas I had blithely discarded. His death just before the completion of this book is a great sadness to me.

In Oxford, my supervisors, Miri Rubin and Rees Davies, challenged me to develop what was really then a series of polemical ideas about other people's work, into a coherent and fully considered piece of my own work. Their questions and suggestions have shaped my outlook and understanding to a greater degree than they would acknowledge. Rees's involvement continued in the role of Advising Editor. My doctoral examiners, Anne Hudson and Margaret Aston, provided the tough criticism needed to tighten the argument and focus all my attention on the subject in hand. They have since been immensely supportive in reading every revised and rewritten chapter in great detail, and I hope they enjoy the finished product, even though we may disagree on some points. Any remaining errors and extravagancies are entirely my own responsibility.

Finally, I could not have devoted the attention to this book that I have been able to, without the loving support and encouragement of my wife Helen Brockett.

I.F.

All Souls College
2004

Contents

Abbreviations

ad v.	ad verbum
BL	British Library
Bodleian	Bodleian Library, Oxford
BRUC	*Biographical Register of the University of Cambridge to 1500*, ed. A. B. Emden (Cambridge, 1963)
BRUO	*Biographical Register of the University of Oxford to A.D. 1500*, ed. A. B. Emden, 3 vols. (Oxford, 1989)
CCR	*Calendar of Close Rolls*
CPL	*Calendar of Entries in the Papal Registers Relating to Great Britain and Ireland: Papal Letters*
CPR	*Calendar of Patent Rolls*
CUL	Cambridge University Library
CYS	Canterbury and York Society
d. a.	dictum ante
DDC	*Dictionnaire de droit canonique*, ed. R. Naz et al., 7 vols. (Paris, 1935–65)
DNB	*Dictionary of National Biography*
d. p.	dictum post
EETS	Early English Text Society
EHR	*English Historical Review*
Fasciculi zizaniorum	*Fasciculi zizaniorum*, ed. W. W. Shirley, Rolls Series (London, 1858)
Glos. ord.	*Glossa ordinaria* (to canon law texts)

Hudson, *Premature Reformation*	A. Hudson, *The Premature Reformation: Wycliffite Texts and Lollard History* (Oxford, 1988)
JEH	*Journal of Ecclesiastical History*
Norwich Heresy Trials	*Heresy Trials in the Diocese of Norwich, 1428–31*, ed. N. P. Tanner, Camden Society, 4th ser. 20 (London, 1977)
PRO	The National Archives: Public Record Office
Rotuli Parliamentorum	*Rotuli Parliamentorum ut et petitiones et placita in parliamento*, ed. J. Strachey, 6 vols. (London, 1767–77)
SCH	Studies in Church History
Statutes of the Realm	*Statutes of the Realm*, ed. J. Raithby and A. Luders, 9 vols. (London, 1766–1826)
TRHS	*Transactions of the Royal Historical Society*
Wilkins, *Concilia*	*Concilia Magnae Britanniae et Hiberniae, a synodo Verolamiensi, A.D. 446 ad Londinensem, A.D. 1717*, ed. D. Wilkins, 4 vols. (London, 1737)
ZRG Kan. Abt.	*Zeitschrift der Savigny-Stiftung für Rechtsgeschichte, kanonistische Abteilung*

Canon Law Citations

References to books of canon law follow the modern form of citation, proceeding from the largest unit to the smallest subdivision, as outlined in J. A. Brundage, *Medieval Canon Law* (London, 1995), 190–205. The capital letter 'X' refers to the *Liber extra*, 'VI' to the *Liber sextus*, 'Clem.' to the *Clementines*, and 'Dig' to the *Digest* of Justinian. Citations are from the *Corpus iuris canonici*, ed. E. Friedberg, 2 vols. (Leipzig, 1879–81; repr. Union, NJ, 2000).

Bishops' Registers

References are given in an abbreviated form identifying the bishop and diocese, with published registers in *italic type* and unpublished in roman type. Full bibliographical references can be found in the relevant section of the Bibliography. Thus 'Reg. Buckingham (Lincoln)' is the unpublished register of John Buckingham for the diocese of Lincoln; and '*Reg. Trefnant (Hereford)*' is the published register of John Trefnant for the diocese of Hereford. There have been a number of new editions, and changes to archival arrangements, since J. A. F. Thomson's major study of these records in *The Later Lollards, 1414–1520* (Oxford, 1965); for details of these changes see D. Smith, *Guide to the Bishops' Registers of England and Wales* (London, 1981), and *Supplement to the Guide to Bishops' Registers of England and Wales*, Canterbury and York Society (2004).

Introduction

This book is about the detection of heresy in England between the condemnation of John Wyclif and his followers in 1382 and the mid-fifteenth century. It is not in the first instance a book about heresy. I will not discuss Wycliffite theology or literature in any depth, and I will not engage with many of the familiar questions relating to the subject. The aim of the book is to enhance our understanding of how heresy was defined as a crime, and how its detection was achieved within the legal and social contexts of the time. Once heresy had been identified as a pressing social problem, spreading outwards from the lecture halls of Oxford, its detection became a major political issue for church and crown alike. However, heresy was counted as an occult or hidden crime, and so its detection was far from simple. It often happened in secret and its psychological roots were buried in the depths of the mind. Detection thus involved surmounting considerable epistemological and evidential problems, such as how one could know the internal workings of another's mind, and how material evidence could reveal beliefs.

It also required the avoidance of certain social and moral dangers associated with the involvement of the laity in prosecution, since the qualities of zeal and discernment required for the detection of heresy were only a short step away from the religious enthusiasm and unauthorized interpretation that characterized the Wycliffite heresy itself. Lay participation in anti-heresy work was necessary, but it created a conundrum that called for careful management on the part of the authorities directing the anti-heresy campaign. This book examines the relationships between all the different sections of society who had a role to play in the detection of heresy, from the formulation of legislation to its communication and finally its implementation.

The focus of the book may be sharpened with reference to a classic of the genre. Henry Charles Lea wrote in 1888 that 'when the existence of hidden crime is suspected there are three stages in the process of its suppression—the discovery of the criminal, the proof of his guilt, and finally his punishment. Of all others the crime of heresy was the most difficult to discover and prove.'[1] In this book I will be concerned for the most part with the first of Lea's stages: the discovery of the criminal, although in recognition of the difficulties involved and the strict rules governing proof, the more judicious term 'suspect' will be preferred to Lea's somewhat premature 'criminal'. I have chosen to concentrate on this pre-trial stage of the judicial process because knowing how the offence and the offenders were identified should be a first step in our study of heresy. The historiography and literary scholarship of heresy in medieval England has tended to focus on the beliefs, associations, and writings of the people who, I shall argue, are too uncritically called heretics and lollards. 'Heresy' and 'heretic' were legal categories of quite a precise nature, as well as being terms of social description, and we should do all we can to understand both usages. The exploration of how heresy and heretics were identified in the Middle Ages may be seen as an overdue, or perhaps overlooked, prelude to our own scholarly consideration of lollard or Wycliffite identity, a topic of some debate.[2]

The parameters of the subject as it is treated here require some explanation, if I am not to raise readers' expectations too high. Although the systematic prosecution of heresy in England began in 1382, Wyclif's ideas were first condemned in 1377 and there had been sporadic prosecution of other heresies over the preceding two centuries. This longer history will be addressed in Chapter 1, although on the whole 1382 is the start date for the study, being the point at which heresy began to be conceived as a social problem rather than an isolated or academic one. A very few documents and cases from the later fifteenth and the early sixteenth centuries will be adduced as comparative evidence, but my primary aim is to understand how the response to heresy developed during the first two to three generations to experience it on a wide scale. By the mid-fifteenth century anti-heresy procedures had acquired a settled pattern, and by the early sixteenth century, humanist learning on

---

[1] H. C. Lea, *A History of the Inquisition in the Middle Ages*, 3 vols. (London, 1888), i. 305.

[2] For assessments of lollard identity in social and theological terms see R. G. Davies, 'Lollardy and Locality', *TRHS* 6th ser. 1 (1991), 191–212, and K. Ghosh, 'Bishop Reginald Pecock and the Idea of "Lollardy"', in H. Barr and A. M. Hutchison (eds.), *Text and Controversy from Wyclif to Bale: Essays in Honour of Anne Hudson* (Turnhout, 2005), 251–65.

the part of the episcopate and the trickle of Lutherans crossing the Channel began to create new modes of heresy detection, and a new climate of fear, that deserve separate attention.[3]

Of course a great deal of what I have to say must be placed within a geographically comparative context, not least because canon law, the legal system by which heresy was defined and heretics formally condemned, had a good claim to be the universal law of the Latin Christian church, equally applicable in Iceland and Sicily, Lisbon and Lithuania, as in England. However, there are good reasons for focusing on the English experience of heresy as a case study in the application of that law. The two salient reasons are the remarkable wealth of documentation preserved in both episcopal and royal archival collections, and the empirically irresistible prospect of being able to chart the adaptation of the English church, crown, and people to circumstances which, although new to them, had been known in large parts of continental Europe for two centuries.

Thematically the major omission from this study is a detailed consideration of the detection of heresy in texts, as opposed to in people. Deciding whether certain written propositions represented error and heresy was of course closely allied to testing the suspicion of heresy that surrounded the author, writer, compiler, reader, or hearer of those words. The focus of this study, however, is on heresy and heresy detection as expressions of personal action and social relationships.[4] Because of this social and non-academic emphasis, the discovery of heresy within the universities will only be addressed insofar as it sheds light on the detection of heresy amongst the wider public.[5]

Consequently, the main sources for this study are the records produced by ecclesiastical investigators (whether bishops and their staff or specially

---

[3] See in particular C. D'Alton, 'The Suppression of Heresy in Henrican England', D.Phil. thesis (Melbourne University, 1999), and the new editions of two major prosecutions: *Kent Heresy Proceedings 1511–1512*, ed. N. Tanner, Kent Records, 26 (Maidstone, 1997); *Lollards of Coventry, 1486–1522*, ed. N. Tanner and S. McSheffrey, Camden Society, 5th ser. 23 (Cambridge, 2003).

[4] On the scrutiny of texts see R. Copeland, *Pedagogy, Intellectuals and Dissent in the Later Middle Ages: Lollardy and Ideas of Learning* (Cambridge, 2001); and K. Ghosh, *The Wycliffite Heresy: Authority and the Interpretation of Texts* (Cambridge, 2002).

[5] On heresy in Oxford University see J. I. Catto, 'Wyclif and Wycliffism at Oxford 1356–1430', in J. I. Catto and R. Evans (eds.), *The History of the University of Oxford,* ii: *Late Medieval Oxford* (Oxford, 1992), 173–261.

delegated inquisitors) and various branches of royal justice, most prominently Chancery and the court of King's Bench. The bulk of the ecclesiastical documentation is now contained in the registers that were compiled sometimes during, sometimes at the end of, the administration of individual bishops.[6] These survive in almost unbroken sequences for most English dioceses of the period, and have over the last century become more and more familiar to historians as numerous editions and calendars have been published. This familiarity may obviate the need for further explanation, but a few comments on the nature of the documents as they appear in the registers may be helpful. Medieval bishops' registers were collections of incoming and outgoing letters, mandates, statutes, and commissions, put together in the episcopal chancery by a member of the bishop's household staff, in some cases a registrar, in others a chancellor. In one sense then they were not original documents, but copies of original instructions and communications. In this respect they are similar to the copies of royal letters made onto the close and patent rolls in Chancery, and the two forms of registration have many similarities, as is to be expected given the clerical origins or future careers of many royal servants.[7]

The documents both in episcopal registers and on the rolls in Chancery may not be exact or full copies of the original documents received or sent out, since the bureaucratic record might be abbreviated or compiled from a number of original exemplars relating to the same case. In bishops' registers, a single entry frequently draws together the text of several separate documents, representing the successive stages of a judicial process carried out by a variety of officers. This often produces patterns of repetition and variation that allow us to reconstruct the texts of the original documents the registrar had before him, even though certain sections might be abbreviated with a terse *etc* once the nature of the repetition had been established. Characteristically, a register entry represents the final stage of a judicial process, such as a judgement, a sentence, or a certification that sentence had been carried out. In this way,

---

[6] For what follows see D. Smith, *Guide to Bishops' Registers of England and Wales* (London, 1981), pp. vii–xi, and C. R. Cheney, *English Bishops' Chanceries 1100–1250* (Manchester, 1950), 99–141.

[7] On royal records and their influence on ecclesiastical practice see M. T. Clanchy, *From Memory to Written Record: England 1066–1307* (2nd edn., Oxford, 1993), 57–68, 74–8.

much of our evidence relating to the early stages of trial—detection and proof—is recoverable only as traces left in documents that reflect outcomes. Such traces are sometimes reasonably full, such as the inclusion of an instruction to supervise penance within a certification of completed penance, but sometimes they have to be reconstructed from documents that have no interest in reproducing material that was not always seen as worthy of preservation. The choices made by registrars as to what merited inclusion in a register can sometimes seem eccentric, and varying practices between dioceses could mean that material thought important by one administration was discarded by another.

This was even more true when it came to decisions about the preservation of non-registered material. Very few 'court-books', kept separately from the main registers and recording the proceedings and decisions of episcopal or archidiaconal courts, survive, and it is likely that most of those that have been lost were destroyed as soon as the information they contained was not in regular use.[8] Anne Hudson has reasonably suggested on the basis of a few surviving court-books that contain heresy cases, uniquely or with other material, that many more such may once have existed.[9] When we know that a bishop proceeded against a suspect without recording the action taken in his register, this is especially plausible; but one may alternatively suggest that the survival of court-books containing heresy cases was due less to chance than to purposeful preservation, given the importance of their contents to bishops who wished to record heresy and their action against it, and to sixteenth-century reformers who saw their predecessors in these records.[10] Volumes such as the thirty-two-folio paper visitation book that furnishes the data for Chapter 8, were flimsy, carelessly written, and entirely routine documents, and there is usually a good reason for their survival beyond the limit of their immediate usefulness.[11]

---

[8] *Lower Ecclesiastical Jurisdiction in Late-Medieval England: The Courts of the Dean and Chapter of Lincoln, 1336–1349 and the Deanery of Wisbech, 1458–1484*, ed. L. R. Poos, Records of Social and Economic History, NS 32 (Oxford, 2001), pp. xi–xlv; C. Donahue Jr., *The Records of the Medieval Ecclesiastical Courts, Part II: England, Reports of the Working Group on Church Court Records*, Comparative Studies in Continental and Anglo-American Legal History, 7 (Berlin, 1994).   [9] Hudson, *Premature Reformation*, 34.
[10] J. A. F. Thomson, 'John Foxe and Some Sources for Lollard History: Notes for a Critical Reappraisal', in G. J. Cuming (ed.), *Papers Read at the Second Winter and Summer Meetings of the Ecclesiastical History Society*, SCH 2 (London, 1965), 251–7.
[11] Lincolnshire Archives, MS Vj/0.

Bishops' registers survived because they contained material relating to the rights and privileges of the diocese that had to be kept for legal purposes, but also because they were sturdy volumes of parchment within hard bindings, designed for archival and reference purposes. In contrast, perhaps 99 per cent of original writs, mandates, commissions, citations, and licences do not survive, because of their small size, their wide dispersal, and the fact that they were not documents of record. It is somewhat surprising that we have no extant examples of preaching licences, documents so central to the anti-heresy programme, but their wide distribution among itinerant clergy provides some explanation for the deficiency. Neither are any citations for heresy known amongst the collections in some diocesan archives, although poor historical and even archival knowledge of these in general means that some may yet be discovered. Copies of both citations and licences, however, survive in large numbers in the episcopal registers, but it is still worth remembering that these are duplicates of the originals. It is not the aim of this study to search out and itemize every mention of heresy in every class of document, nor to follow up every lead about the persons mentioned therein. Although it is likely that a number of new cases, procedural documents, and biographical details will emerge in time, the broad themes and arguments of the present book rely largely on material that has been used in some way by other historians in the past.[12] However, this material has never been used for a sustained systematic study of the activity to which it relates, namely the detection and prosecution of heresy.

In an activity that required collaboration between rulers and the ruled, ecclesiastical and secular authorities had to put in place procedures and personnel capable of deciding on the difficult matter of orthodoxy, while parish priests and laymen and women had to respond with reliable reports of suspected heresy. Consequently the plan of this book moves from the actions of the rulers to those of the ruled, and from the general to the specific. The first part of the book (Chapters 1, 2, and 3) is concerned with the legal response to heresy in England, the culture within which laws were formulated, and the intentions of legislators. Chapter 1 is an assessment of knowledge about heresy, setting the limits of historical inquiry within the context of

---

[12] Research in the PRO by Maureen Jurkowski has yielded particularly interesting items, such as an inventory of John Purvey's goods and the writ for the production of William Thorpe for trial. See her 'New Light on John Purvey', *EHR* 110 (1995), 1180–90; and 'The Arrest of William Thorpe in Shrewsbury and the Anti-Lollard Statute of 1406', *Historical Research*, 75 (2002), 273–95.

medieval and specifically English expectations of the law. Chapter 2 sets out the basic structures within which heresy detection took place, looking at the co-operation and conflicts of church and crown, and the conduct of investigations by bishops, inquisitors, royal justices, and other officers. Chapter 3 examines in detail the two main planks of detection—reporting and licensing—and episcopal expectations of popular participation are introduced. The central section of the book (Chapters 4, 5, and 6) deals with the communication of these new legal categories and procedures to the parish clergy and the laity, who were responsible for reporting their suspicions of heresy. Chapter 4 deals with the creation of new procedures through the adaptation of older models, and describes how statutes and other legal instructions were circulated within the governing class. Chapter 5 looks at the channels by which knowledge of these new procedures was communicated beyond the powerful and Latin-reading to the anglophone laity, and in Chapter 6 the creation of messages deemed suitable for lay duties and understanding is described. The third part of the book (Chapters 7 and 8) examines the results of legislation and its communication: implementation. Chapter 7's description of the reporting and detection of heresy, in general terms across England, is followed in Chapter 8 by a case study of how anti-heresy policy was implemented and the reactions to it in Leicester archdeaconry during the course of a single investigation.

Progressing from legislation to communication, and then on to implementation, permits exploration of the ways in which an essentially new phenomenon was faced, first by law makers, then by the wider public. However, there is a danger in this kind of approach that knowledge and practice are assumed to filter downwards through society from the powerful at the top to the powerless at the bottom. No such simplification is meant by the arrangement of this book. As a consequence of the social history boom of the past half-century and the interest in ideology and rhetoric now shown by many political historians, history from below can no longer be written to the exclusion of history from above. Indeed the interaction of governments with the people over whom they ruled, and vice versa, has arguably become the major feature of medieval historiography at the beginning of a new century of scholarship.[13] It is very much in that spirit that this book has been written.

---

[13] W. M. Ormrod, *Political Life in Medieval England, 1300–1450* (Basingstoke, 1995); J. Watts, *Henry VI and the Politics of Kingship* (Cambridge, 1996), 81–101.

While disputes between individuals are best suited to a litigant-focused analysis, this is only partially adequate when dealing with public prosecutions initiated by inquisition, a procedure that was designed to remove the need for private accusers, putting the church or the crown in their place.[14] Because prosecutions of heresy were directed and conducted by representatives of central authority, it is that authority—its intellectual traditions, practices, and personnel—which holds the key to understanding the subject. This does not mean that the people of parishes across the country who were prosecuted as heretics and/or co-opted as witnesses and informants do not matter: far from it. Public reaction to the designs of rulers determined their success or failure, and government had to be responsive to it in order to be effective. As we shall see, various aspects of the anti-heresy campaign were products of local experience turned into national policy.

[14] Litigant-focused study of inter-personal disputes is exemplified by W. Davies and P. Fouracre (eds.), *The Settlement of Disputes in Early Medieval Europe* (Cambridge, 1986); F. Pedersen, *Marriage Disputes in Medieval England* (London, 2000); C. Wickham, *Courts and Conflict in Twelfth-Century Tuscany* (Oxford, 2003). On the development of public prosecution through inquisition see Chapter 1 below.

PART I

LEGISLATION

1

Questions of Knowledge
and Ignorance

The investigation of heresy, whether by medieval inquisitors or modern historians, has always encountered problems of knowledge and ignorance. Both professions have asked who is and who is not a heretic, and what beliefs are and are not heretical. Although these questions have shaped our understanding of heresy, they cannot be answered with any certainty. Inquisitors and others charged with the detection of heresy had to identify heretics to the satisfaction of standards set by canon law, while historians have to satisfy their peers that their ideas are sufficiently plausible according to an arguably much less rigorous and well-defined code of professional standards. It is significant that neither medieval canon law, nor modern historical inquiry, has made any claims to absolute knowledge of the truth, albeit for very different reasons. Inquisitors were doubtful whether the information at their disposal could reveal the truth about heresy because final knowledge rested with God. Historical circumspection arises from problems of source analysis and the chronological remove at which we stand in relation to the past.[1]

Given this shared attitude to the truth, it seems natural that historians should ask how inquisitors went about gathering and interpreting their evidence, in addition to using their records to write histories of heresy. One might go so far as to say that the records produced by inquisitors are in the first instance evidence of anti-heresy, and any information on heresies and heretics that they provide is filtered through a distorting lens. Nevertheless, while some historians have studied the practices of inquisitors, others have concentrated on the heretics.

[1] Inquisitors and professional historians are seen as the earliest and latest interpreters of heresy, in a single chronological spectrum, in the influential A. Borst, *Die Katharer* (Stuttgart, 1953), 1–58.

In anglophone historiography these alternatives are exemplified by the work of Peter Biller and Robert Moore. For Biller the prime object of study is the heretic, individually and in his or her networks and groups. His many works on the subject show how the historian may use the literature of secretive, underground movements, and the 'texts of repression', to cast light on what it was that led people to hold dissenting opinions and form new collectivities for worship. He has long been interested in the question of how sources essentially hostile to heretics can be made to reveal facts about the people and beliefs they meant to suppress and even misrepresent. Whatever the technical and epistemological difficulties involved, for him the records of inquisition and repression are available to historians as they were to inquisitors, as sources for the study of heresy.[2] In his 1987 book, *The Formation of a Persecuting Society*, Moore took a very different approach. For him, the records of bishops, kings, and inquisitors are sources for the study of power. He uses them to tell a story of bureaucratic innovation and the centralizing ambitions of ecclesiastical and secular rulers, in which the phenomenon of heresy is produced, not discovered, by inquisitorial questioning. This approach and its implications have divided historians, highlighting the differences between the study of heretics and the study of inquisitors.[3]

The study of heresy in late medieval England has tended to concern itself with the study of the heretics. This was originally because of confessional sympathies between Protestant or Anglican historians and John Wyclif, who was seen as the 'morning star of the reformation'.[4] Latterly, this preponderance of interest in the heretic has been encouraged and facilitated by the editing and analysis of a large body of English-language

---

[2] Early articles are collected in *The Waldenses, 1170–1530: Between a Religious Order and a Church* (Aldershot, 2001); introduction to C. Bruschi and P. Biller (eds.), *Texts and the Repression of Medieval Heresy* (York, 2003), 3–19.

[3] R. I. Moore, *The Formation of a Persecuting Society: Power and Deviance in Western Europe, 950–1250* (Oxford, 1987). The variety of responses to Moore's work include J. B. Given, *Inquisition and Medieval Society: Power, Discipline and Resistance in Languedoc* (Ithaca, NY, 1997), 213–20; P. Strohm, *England's Empty Throne: Usurpation and the Language of Legitimization, 1399–1422* (New Haven, 1998), 222; more critically D. Nirenberg, *Communities of Violence: Persecution of Minorities in the Middle Ages* (Princeton, 1996), 4–5; and C. J. Nederman, 'Introduction: Discourses and Contexts of Tolerance in Medieval Europe', in C. J. Nederman and J. C. Laursen (eds.), *Beyond the Persecuting Society: Religious Toleration before the Enlightenment* (Philadelphia, 1998), 13–24.

[4] G. H. Martin, 'Wyclif, Lollards and Historians, 1384–1984', in F. Somerset, J. C. Havens, and D. G. Pitard (eds.), *Lollards and their Influence in Late Medieval England* (Woodbridge, 2003), 237–50.

texts written by Wyclif's followers.[5] Studies devoted to anti-heresy are more rare.[6] However, the two endeavours are related and must inform one another, always remembering that prosecuted heresy and religious dissent are not exactly the same thing, since dissent frequently eluded the machinery of its repression, and inquisitors often pursued people who were essentially orthodox but not easily accommodated within the structures of the church.[7] The heresy reported in legal records is a reflection of only a part of the enormously varied spectrum of dissent, some of which came to the attention of the authorities, some of which did not.

Besides those who study heresy and those who study anti-heresy, some historians of medieval religion have chosen to relegate the subject's importance or ignore it altogether. Their ideas deserve a brief comment at this stage, but really the whole of this book is designed as a riposte to the notion that the significance of heresy and anti-heresy can be measured by the (allegedly small) numbers of people concerned. Doubts about heresy's significance in late medieval English society and religion stem from the rediscovery of popular religion, based on the records of parochial Christianity which survive in particularly large numbers from England.[8] As John Bossy, Jack Scarisbrick, and Eamon Duffy mapped out this area of historical inquiry, their consternation grew that all historians of religion did not share their zeal for the study of the catholic majority. Why should time and energy be spent on studying a tiny, heretical, minority of the population? In Duffy's case, frustration at a historiography 'peopled largely by Lollards, witches and leisured, aristocratic ladies' led him to a portrayal of late medieval religion that, despite the richness of its

---

[5] *English Wycliffite Sermons*, ed. A. Hudson and P. Gradon, 5 vols. (Oxford, 1983–96); *Lollard Sermons*, ed. G. Cigman, EETS 294 (1989); *Two Wycliffite Texts: The Sermon of William Taylor 1406, The Testimony of William Thorpe 1407*, ed. A. Hudson, EETS 301 (1993); *The Works of a Lollard Preacher*, ed. A. Hudson, EETS 317 (2001).

[6] J. A. F. Thomson, *The Later Lollards, 1414–1520* (Oxford, 1965), ch. 11; A. Hudson, 'The Examination of Lollards', in *Lollards and their Books* (London, 1985), 125–40; M. Aston, 'Bishops and Heresy: The Defence of the Faith', in *Faith and Fire: Popular and Unpopular Religion, 1350–1600* (London, 1993), 73–94; A. K. McHardy, '*De heretico comburendo* 1401', in M. Aston and C. Richmond (eds.), *Lollardy and the Gentry in the Later Middle Ages* (Stroud, 1997), 112–26; D'Alton, 'Suppression of Heresy'.

[7] Hudson, *Premature Reformation*, 34; R. E. Lerner, *The Heresy of the Free Spirit in the Later Middle Ages* (Berkeley, 1972), 36–54; Thomson, *Later Lollards*, 241–2.

[8] For a discussion of churchwardens' accounts and other records of parochial religion, see C. Burgess, 'Pre-Reformation Churchwardens' Accounts and Parish Government: Lessons from London and Bristol', *EHR* 471 (2002), 306–32, and the ensuing debate in *EHR* 480 (2004), 87–116.

documentation, was a somewhat idealized picture of parochial harmony undisturbed by dissent, social difference, or regional variation.[9] One recent historian of heresy in England has gone even further by asking 'why we should bother with Lollards at all'. This comment was made, and answered in the negative, in a textbook on heresy.[10] Just as one cannot study heretics without studying inquisitors, so the study of heresy and orthodoxy are necessary bedfellows in any analysis of the religious life of the Middle Ages. Defining and pursuing heresy was after all one of the constituents of orthodoxy. The analogy between the doubts of inquisitors and historians reminds us that in order to dismiss the heretics from historical consequence, one must first know who they were. The recognition by most historians of heresy that inquisition, and indeed the historical enterprise itself, construct a picture of heresy and the heretic that may not reflect the reality of dissent and dissenters, means that such black and white reductionism is not tenable.

1. THE UNCERTAINTY OF MEDIEVAL KNOWLEDGE OF HERESY

No medieval bishop or inquisitor took the view that heretics were easily identifiable and thus wholly separable from the orthodox, in the way that Bossy and Duffy have suggested. This was because canonical jurisprudence was informed by doubt and circumspection, and because heresy was hidden from view. In its biblical Greek origins, heresy meant a choice or a thing chosen, and a heretic was someone who chose to remove himself or herself from the church, believing his or her own choices to be truer than God's revealed word.[11] Quite soon that choice came to have

---

[9] E. Duffy, *The Stripping of the Altars: Traditional Religion in England c.1400–1580* (New Haven, 1992), 2; J. Bossy, *Christianity in the West 1400–1700* (Oxford, 1985); J. J. Scarisbrick, *The Reformation and the English People* (Oxford, 1984). In response to this trend see D. Aers, 'Altars of Power: Reflections on Eamon Duffy's *The Stripping of the Altars*', *Literature and History*, 3rd ser. 3 (1994), 90–105.

[10] R. Rex, *The Lollards* (Basingstoke, 2002), p. xv. See also C. Burgess, 'A Hotbed of Heresy? Fifteenth-Century Bristol and Lollardy Reconsidered', in L. Clark (ed.), *The Fifteenth Century*, iii: *Authority and Subversion* (Woodbridge, 2003), 43–62.

[11] C. 24 q. 3 c. 27; Johannes Balbus, *Catholicon* (Lyon, 1492), alphabetically under *Heresis*; see also *Glos. ord.* to X 5.7.9. This etymology was current in fourteenth-century England when the canonist William Paul included it in his *Summa summarum*, V. X. q. 41 (Bodleian, MS Bodley 293, fo. 178ᵛ). It was also cited approvingly by Robert Grosseteste; R. W. Southern, *Robert Grosseteste: The Growth of an English Mind in Medieval Europe* (Oxford, 1986), 292–3.

the pejorative meaning of deviance from the church, as patristic writers and the early councils fought off the challenges of a variety of splinter groups. Each successive heresy brought a refutation that not only reaffirmed orthodoxy, but often redefined it at the same time.[12] Because orthodoxy was always changing, heretics could not be defined from century to century by a simple checklist of condemned beliefs. Also, no one could be expected to maintain orthodoxy without instruction. So it was that the early church adopted a practical approach to error and deviance that emphasized pastoral care and gave dissenters every opportunity to return to the church. In a text that was incorporated by Gratian into his *Decretum* in the 1140s, St Augustine of Hippo advised that a person who after careful questioning on the truth was prepared to submit to correction was not to be counted a heretic.[13] Only those who persisted in defending their error once they had been twice admonished for it were heretics.[14] It was the decision, or choice, to remain in error, having been given the opportunity to recant, that defined the heretic. Legally then, heresy was not a way of life, or even a set of beliefs, but a moment in a judicial trial when a suspect had to decide between returning to the church, or perversely turning his or her face against God.[15] This momentary decision was in addition a simplification, or a representation, of the sin of heresy, since deviance was understood as a tendency of character arising from concupiscence, an aberration of the will resulting from original sin. The criminal trial was designed to test for this aberration, which lay dormant in every man and woman. The will had to be turned towards God in order to prevent concupiscence being realized.

This made heresy an omnipresent and hidden danger that was difficult to discern. Writing in the mid-fifteenth century, the bishop of Chichester,

---

[12] H. Chadwick, *The Early Church* (Harmondsworth, 1967), 66, 80–3; J. McClure, 'Handbooks against Heresy in the West, from the Late Fourth to the Late Sixth Centuries', *Journal of Theological Studies*, NS 30 (1979), 193–6.

[13] C. 24 q. 3 c. 29 with *Glos. ord.* The composition of the *Decretum* is now attributed to two authors, Gratian 1 and Gratian 2, but it will not be necessary to distinguish between them here; see A. Winroth, *The Making of Gratian's* Decretum (Cambridge, 2000).

[14] C. 24 q. 3 cc. 31–2; *Summa summarum*, V. X. q. 8 (Bodleian, MS Bodley 293, fo. 178ʳ); G. Leff, *Heresy in the Later Middle Ages: The Relation of Heterodoxy to Dissent, c.1250–c.1450* (2nd edn., Manchester, 1999), 1–2.

[15] Hostiensis, *Summa aurea* (Venice, 1605), 1532: 'Ergo sola praesumptione, vel suspicione quamuis vehementi, non tamen probabili de tanto crimine non condemnatur quis, ex quo negat, et paratus est ecclesie obedire.'

Reginald Pecock, explained the opacity of heresy in terms of the relationship between speech, writing, and the will: 'an errour or heresye is not þe ynke writen, neiþir þe voice spokun, but it is þe meenyng or þe vndirstondyng of þe writer or speker signified bi þilk ynke writen or bi þilk voice spokun.'[16] Writing and speaking heretical things were only signs of heresy, which was constituted by intention, meaning, and understanding. Historians of heresy, like their inquisitorial forerunners, set themselves a difficult task if they wish to discover intention. More knowable are the methods used by inquisitors to narrow down the potential margin of error, remaining aware that pronouncements of heresy could never be definitive judgements. Judgement of final guilt or innocence belonged solely to God. On earth it was mankind's responsibility to protect the peace of the church by punishing the most dangerous examples of heresy, and tolerating those who could not be punished without causing scandal equal to the damage done by the crime itself.[17] The requirement for justice, to balance punishment with equity, meant that the whole canonical system was predicated upon indeterminacy and careful interpretation.[18]

In the period when the legislative framework for the inquisitorial method was being put in place, approximately between 1179 and 1231, the values of tolerance, circumspection, and equity seem to disappear from the minds of canonists and theologians as they respond to increasingly widespread heresies. Gratian had chosen to represent the indeterminacy of human judgement with an Augustinian homily on penance, writing that 'many are corrected, like Peter; many tolerated, like Judas; while many are not known until the coming of the Lord, who will illuminate the secrets of the darkness'.[19] Augustine, however, had famously changed his mind about the use of force against heretics when dealing with the Donatists in north Africa at the end of the fourth century. Consequently, the early thirteenth-century taste for a more combative

---

[16] Reginald Pecock, *The Donet*, ed. E. V. Hitchcock, EETS 156 (London, 1921), 4.

[17] C. 23 q. 4 cc. 18–19.

[18] On the toleration of suspected heretics see C. 23 q. 4 cc. 1–5, 15. On doubt, justice, and equity see B. E. Ferme, *Canon Law in Late Medieval England: A Study of William Lyndwood's* Provinciale *with Particular Reference to Testamentary Law* (Rome, 1996), 12; W. P. Müller, *Huguccio: The Life, Works, and Thought of a Twelfth-Century Jurist* (Washington, DC, 1994), 129.

[19] C. 2 q. 1 c. 18: 'Multi corriguntur ut Petrus; multi tollerantur, ut Iudas; multi nesciuntur, donec ueniat Dominus, qui illuminabit abscondita tenebrarum.' See I Cor. 4: 5.

jurisprudence could be justified from his writings as easily as the more tolerant attitude of the earlier period.[20] Gregory IX decided to let Augustine's statement on unrepentant souls set the tone for his treatment of heresy in the *Liber extra*: 'There is no doubt that all heretics and schismatics will burn in eternal fire with the devil and his angels.'[21] In a similar vein the conception of heretical agency was widened, treating simple followers of heretics in the same way as originators of heresy.[22] This new tone in anti-heresy law was symptomatic not only of fears about heresy out of control, but also of a shift in the conception of the role of law *per se*. From the mid-twelfth century onwards, canon lawyers were seeking new ways of dealing with problems such as clerical concubinage and heresy. The existing methods of reporting crime were proving inadequate and so new powers of inquiry for ecclesiastical judges were instituted. They were now allowed to instigate an *inquisition* on the basis of public fame, rather than relying on the formal accusations or denunciations of named, and thus vulnerable, witnesses.[23] This allowed the net of suspects to be cast very widely indeed, a necessary gain in the fight against crimes of thought and intention.

At first glance it seems as though the medieval church was turning its back on the circumspect attitudes of the past and embracing a future of moral clarity and harsh certainties. However, much in the new legislation was polemical hot air, intended to galvanize negligent bishops into action, and when they did act they were not meant to ride roughshod over the basic precepts of canon law.[24] In addition, as inquisitorial powers became a more familiar part of European life, reaching Languedoc and

[20] C. Gallagher, *Canon Law and the Christian Community: The Role of Law in the Church According to the* Summa aurea *of Cardinal Hostiensis* (Rome, 1978), 186–7; Nederman, 'Tolerance in Medieval Europe', 17.

[21] X 5.7.3: 'Firmissime tene et nullatenus dubites, omnem haereticum vel schismaticum... cum diabolo et angelis eius aeterni ignis incendio participandum.'

[22] X 5.7.5, 6 (families of heretics acquire guilt by association), X 5.7.8, 9 (receivers and helpers of heretics condemned), X 5.7.15 ('credentes' to be treated the same as heretics).

[23] W. Trusen, 'Der Inquisitionsprozess: Seine historischen Grundlagen und frühen Formen', *ZRG Kan. Abt.* 74 (1988), 168–230; on inquisition and *fama* see M. Lambert, *Medieval Heresy: Popular Movements from the Gregorian Reform to the Reformation* (3rd edn., Oxford, 2002), 106–7.

[24] B. Hamilton, *The Medieval Inquisition* (London, 1981), 41; G. G. Merlo, *Eretici e inquisitori nella società Piemontese del trecento* (Turin, 1977), 12, argues that tolerant and intolerant passages in legal documents reflect complementary procedural and polemical aims.

Italy in the thirteenth century,[25] Aragon and Portugal in the fourteenth century,[26] and the German lands, Bohemia, and the Low Countries between the thirteenth and fifteenth centuries,[27] successive popes took pains to limit the powers of inquisitors and prevent abuses. Decrees were issued instructing bishops, inquisitors, and judges to ensure there was no undue influence on the cases they tried, and it was made possible to conduct proceedings in private to protect the accused, or witnesses, from such influence.[28] What is more, thirteenth-century legal commentators advised judges to proceed 'with the love of correction and freedom, so that the guilty may be corrected and the innocent set free', and 'keeping equity in mind, always choosing the more humane course'.[29] So despite the more aggressive tone and new powers to round up suspects, heresy was still defined by a moment of choice in a trial, when the defendant opted to return to God or stubbornly to defend his errors. Widespread heresy also brought with it a political imperative for the circumspect approach. 'Bishops ought to be cautious,' wrote the canonist Hostiensis, 'and not excite their province because of heresy for nothing, nor invite complaints by which the province may be defamed.'[30]

For Gratian toleration had meant spiritual punishment. Quoting from Luke 9: 54, he said that physical punishment expressed a certainty that was out of step with the claims of human law, and that those who lived by the sword would perish by the sword.[31] Throughout the history of heresy and inquisition in medieval Europe, hope was maintained for the return

---

[25] Lea, *Inquisition*, ii. 7–8, 199–203.

[26] M. Escamilla, *Synthèse sur l'inquisition espagnole et la construction de la monarchie confessionnelle, 1478–1561* (Nantes, 2002), 28; Hamilton, *Medieval Inquisition*, 80; Borst, *Die Katharer*, 26.

[27] D. Kurze, 'Anfänge der Inquisition in Deutschland', in P. Segl (ed.), *Die Anfänge der Inquisition im Mittelalter* (Cologne, 1993), 131–93; R. Kieckhefer, *Repression of Heresy in Medieval Germany* (Liverpool, 1979); *Die Anfänge einer ständigen Inquisition in Böhmen: Ein Prager Inquisitoren-Handbuch aus der ersten Hälfte des 14. Jahrhunderts*, ed. A. Patschovsky (Berlin, 1975); Lerner, *Free Spirit*, 85–163.

[28] VI 5.2.8 § 3; Clem 5.31 § 4; VI 5.2.20.

[29] *Glos. ord.* to C. 23 q. 4; X 1.36.11; Hostiensis, *Summa aurea*, 331: 'iudex procedere debet aequitate seruata, semper in humaniorem partem declinando.' In private cases before ecclesiastical courts judges were similarly meant to encourage parties to use arbitration and reach compromises; J. E. Sayers, *Papal Judges Delegate in the Province of Canterbury, 1198–1254: A Study in Ecclesiastical Jurisdiction and Administration* (Oxford, 1971), 239–41.

[30] Hostiensis, *Summa aurea*, 1535: 'Episcopus autem debet esse cautus, quia non debet pro nihilo prouinciam praetextu heresis commouere, nec grauamen inferre.'

[31] C. 23 q. 4 c. 12.

of errant individuals to the faith, and even if punishment was administered, that in itself was not meant to be taken as a sure sign of guilt.[32] The aim of healing and the principle of uncertainty had been commonplace in medieval jurisprudence since Gregory the Great had written that justice should be medicinal.[33] Johannes Teutonicus (*c.*1170–1245) glossed 'medicine' in this case as 'correction', and elsewhere described excommunication as the medicine of the soul.[34] Innocent IV (d. 1254) also commented that 'excommunication is not guilt, but medicine or penance'.[35]

The careful avoidance of definitive judgements in all but manifest and dangerous cases is further explained by the distinction in canon law between heretics as persons and heresy as a crime. This separation between the crime and the criminal is clearly expressed in the ordinary gloss to the *Decretum*, where Teutonicus cites Augustine's view that while wrongdoers may be tolerated for the sake of peace and unity in the church, their deeds should be condemned nonetheless.[36] In canon law, heresy was the choice of disobedience over correction, and the actions which were evidence of this choice. So polemicists and propagandists could decry the evil of heresy, but when it came to actually finding out who was or was not a heretic, the distinctiveness of the category evaporated and the processes of detection proceeded hedged with safeguards and doubts. These general observations on the uncertainty of medieval knowledge about heresy may now be augmented with some more specific comments relevant to the English experience.

2. THE LIMITATIONS TO ENGLISH KNOWLEDGE OF HERESY

Before the 1380s England had seen no widespread heresy on the scale of Catharism in Languedoc or Waldensianism in the Alps, Germany, and

---

[32] On the medicinal nature of excommunication see R. H. Helmholz, 'Excommunication as a Legal Sanction: The Attitudes of the Medieval Canonists', *ZRG Kan. Abt.* 68 (1982), 202–18. On punishment not being a sign of guilt, see William Lyndwood, *Provinciale seu constitutiones Angliae* (Oxford, 1679), 340.

[33] C. 23. q. 4 c. 25.

[34] *Glos. ord.* to C. 23. q. 4 c. 25 ad v. *medicina*; *Glos. ord.* to C. 24 q. 3 c. 37 ad v. *disciplina*: 'Medicina animae est excommunicatio.'

[35] *Apparatus in quinque libros decretalium*, on X 5.39.6, quoted in E. Vodola, *Excommunication in the Middle Ages* (Berkeley, 1986), 45.

[36] *Glos. ord.* to C. 23 q. 4 c. 5.

Bohemia, and in the years before the 1381 revolt, there was no obvious reason for thinking that the country was on the brink of a worryingly popular heresy spreading outwards from Oxford. What then was the state of knowledge about heresy and anti-heresy law in England prior to 1380; from what sources had it come; and what were its limitations?

Although heresy was a 'mixed' case dealt with by both secular and spiritual jurisdictions, it was through the universal law of the church, canon law, that knowledge of the offence was disseminated across Europe. The study of canon law had had a long history in medieval England, becoming an integral part of the curricula of the universities in the first half of the thirteenth century.[37] The rise of canon law as a higher degree was driven by the needs of the expanding ecclesiastical courts, whose business increasingly demanded qualified lawyers, and royal and episcopal government, where their skills were much in demand.[38] The text of Gratian's *Decretum*, along with one or other of its accompanying glosses written between the twelfth and fourteenth centuries, was consequently very widely available in England.[39] Similarly, the collections of decretals (papal letters and conciliar decrees) that preceded Gregory IX's compilation of the *Liber extra* in 1234 are still to be found in English university and cathedral libraries, and we must assume that their numbers were once much more plentiful.[40]

Even more common, since their promulgation corresponded to the growth in legal studies in the thirteenth century, were the texts and major commentaries on the *Liber extra* (promulgated in 1234), the *Liber sextus* (1298), and the *Clementines* (1317), which contained the texts that formed the basis for the later medieval prosecution of heresy. English canonists, most

---

[37] L. E. Boyle, 'Canon Law before 1380', in J. I. Catto and R. Evans (eds.), *The History of the University of Oxford*, i: *The Early Oxford Schools* (Oxford, 1984), 531; D. M. Owen, *The Medieval Canon Law: Teaching, Literature and Transmission* (Cambridge, 1990), 3; R. H. Helmholz, *The Oxford History of the Laws of England*, i: *The Canon Law and Ecclesiastical Jurisdiction from 597 to the 1640s* (Oxford, 2004), 187–94.

[38] Owen, *Medieval Canon Law*, 10–16. On legal learning in cathedral schools, see D. Lepine, ' "A Long Way from University": Cathedral Canons and Learning at Hereford in the Fifteenth Century', in C. M. Barron and J. Stratford (eds.), *The Church and Learning in Later Medieval Society: Essays in Honour of R. B. Dobson. Proceedings of the 1999 Harlaxton Symposium* (Donington, 2002), 178–95.

[39] S. Kuttner, *Repertorium der kanonistik (1140–1234): Prodromus corporis glossarum*, Studi e Testi, 71 (Vatican, 1937), 22–30, 81, 96, 101, 105–6, 116, 125–67, 172, 192, 199, 205.

[40] Ibid. 274, 278–85, 288, 291, 294–8, 301, 303, 305, 311–13, 317–21, 333–5, 348–9, 361, 376, 383, 388, 394.

notably in the fourteenth century William Paul (also known as William of Pagula) and Thomas Chillenden, produced commentaries on these texts in common with their more famous continental colleagues. Paul's *Summa summarum* (1319–22), which exists today in thirteen manuscripts, covered every aspect of canon law in 'questiones' that address issues of definition and procedure, drawing on the *Decretum, Liber extra, Liber sextus,* and *Clementines,* as well as the major commentaries on these.[41] Bishops and lawyers looking for guidance as to how to deal with suspected heretics would have been well prepared by reading Paul's comments and following up some of his more accessible references. Chillenden's *Repertorium* of canon law follows the chapter divisions of the *Liber sextus* and the *Clementines,* referring the reader to the relevant portions of the *Decretum* and *Liber extra,* as well as to the standard glosses and commentaries.[42]

The work of these two English canonists formed part of a trend in legal literature towards the assimilation of the vast and growing body of decretals and commentaries into encyclopedias, providing practical instruction for priests, lawyers, and administrators. They had been preceded in this by Peter Quesnel, a Norwich Franciscan, who reportedly died in 1299. If this date is correct, then he was one of the most up-to-date canonists of his day, managing to incorporate extracts from the *Liber sextus,* promulgated in 1298, into his *Directorium iuris in foro conscientie et judiciali,* a digest of canon law on all aspects of church administration and justice.[43] Other works of the thirteenth and fourteenth centuries that distilled the accumulated interpretations of canon law were also available in England. The *Summa de casibus conscientie* of Bartholomaeus Pisano was a widely disseminated work that drew on some of the same sources as William Paul. It dealt with anti-heresy decrees and decretals in three chapters, similarly divided into practical 'questiones'.[44] Perhaps the most

---

[41] On Paul and his *Summa,* see L. E. Boyle, 'The *Summa summarum* and Some Other English Works of Canon Law', in *Pastoral Care, Clerical Education and Canon Law, 1200–1400: Essays by Leonard E. Boyle* (London, 1981), essay XV, 415–56. The section on heresy may be found in Bodleian, MS Bodley 293, fos. 178ʳ–180ʳ.

[42] For Chillenden's comments on heresy see Bodleian, MS New College 204, fos. 177ʳ–180ʳ (on the *Liber sextus*), 376ᵛ–378ʳ (on the *Clementines*).

[43] Merton College Oxford, MS 223, fos. 214ᵛ, 263ʳ–271ʳ (heresy); *DNB,* xvi. 542.

[44] BL, MS Royal 9 E X, fos. 48ᵛ–50ʳ. On 'Pisanus' see P. Michaud-Quantin, *Sommes de casuistique et manuels de confession au Moyen Âge* (Louvain, 1962), 60–2. Copies may be found in numerous fourteenth-century English manuscripts; T. Kaeppeli, *Scriptores ordinis praedicatorum Medii Aevi,* 4 vols. (Rome, 1970), i. 158–66.

voluminous, albeit unrepresentative, collection of canonical material in England was contained in the encyclopedia known as *Omne bonum*, compiled by an exchequer clerk called James le Palmere in the late 1360s.[45] The treatment of heresy begins with a summary of C. 23 and C. 24 of the *Decretum*, the decretal X 5.7.13, and Guido de Bayso's *Rosarium*, before excerpting parts of Hostiensis' *Summa aurea*, Paul's *Summa summarum*, William Durandus' *Aureum confessorium et memoriale sacerdotum*, and Johannes Balbus' *Catholicon*.[46] *Omne bonum* is an interesting text but it exists only in one copy, and the significance of encyclopedias in general is lessened by the fact that heresy was not accorded any special place in them.

Some more specific works on heresy were available, however. An abridged version of the *Tractatus de excommunicatione et interdicto* by Cardinal Bérengar Frédol, dealing with procedure against heretics, schismatics, and infidels, was copied by at least four English lawyers or ecclesiastical administrators in the early fourteenth century.[47] Frédol was the archbishop of Béziers in the south of France, and a renowned canonist who had been one of the editors of the *Liber sextus*. The appearance of his tract in England may be related to the trials of the Knights Templar between 1309 and 1311, or to Frédol's contacts with the general chapter of the English Carmelites in 1312.[48] In one of the manuscript books containing the Frédol tract, there is a text in the same early fourteenth-century hand by one William Roving, an otherwise unknown English writer, which uses parts of Frédol, supplemented by citations from Hostiensis and Goffredus de Trano, to show that heresy was a crime reserved for episcopal attention.[49]

In addition to legal texts, English chroniclers and historians of the twelfth and thirteenth centuries had written on heresy in southern

---

[45] On date and authorship see L. F. Sandler, *Omne bonum: A Fourteenth-Century Encyclopaedia of Universal Knowledge*, 2 vols. (London, 1996), i. 16–26.

[46] BL, MS Royal 6 E VII, fos. 200ʳ–205ʳ.

[47] BL, MS Royal 8 A XVIII, fos. 97ʳ–101ʳ and MS Royal 11 A XIV, fos. 15ᵛ–19ʳ. The unabridged text also occurs in BL, MS Cotton Julius D XI, fos. 60ʳ–84ʳ. For the text of this see *Le Liber de excommunicatione du Cardinal Bérengar Frédol*, ed. E. Vernay (Paris, 1912).

[48] M. Barber, *The Trial of the Templars* (Cambridge, 1978), 71, 74, 111, 234–5; *DDC*, v. 905–7; J. F. von Schulte, *Die Geschichte der Quellen und Literatur des canonischen Rechts, von Gratian bis auf Papst Gregor ix*, 3 vols. (Stuttgart, 1875–80), ii. 180–2; *Monumenta historica Carmelitana*, ii, ed. R. P. B. Zimmerman (Îles de Lérins, 1906), 228; J. H. Arnold, 'Lollard Trials and Inquisitorial Discourse', in C. Given-Wilson (ed.), *The Fourteenth Century*, ii (Woodbridge, 2002), 88.

[49] BL, MS Royal 11 A XIV, fos. 153ᵛ–154ʳ.

Europe, and collections of anti-heretical sermons, notably those of Bernard of Clairvaux, were common in English libraries.[50] This familiarity would suggest an extensive knowledge of the legal and theological position of the church against heretics; but without experience in applying that knowledge, no common body of procedure developed in either diocesan or provincial statutes.[51]

What practical experience the English church and crown had had of heresy before 1380 was limited and may be briefly summarized.[52] Despite the strengths of its church, England was not completely immune from the major heretical movements of continental Europe. Around 1166 a number of Rhineland Cathars were condemned and exiled at a provincial council in Oxford, and in the 1170s Peter of Blois wrote to the archbishop of York warning him of 'new and recent heresies'.[53] The early thirteenth century saw further prosecutions of heretics, in London in 1210, York in 1236, and Cambridge in 1240.[54] In addition, the high-profile crusade against the Cathars from 1208 to 1218 may have kindled a general suspicion of people from Languedoc. In 1236 a Périgueux wine merchant's goods were confiscated because of suspicions of heresy, and in 1241 a suspected heretic from Agen was freed only after showing testimonials of his orthodoxy.[55] Later in the thirteenth century a heretical Englishwoman is mentioned in a testimony given to Dominican inquisitors in Languedoc. Around the same time Archbishop Pecham condemned academic heresy at Oxford, and in the 1280s he insisted on his right to try all persons suspected of heresy.[56]

The fourteenth century saw an increase in recorded action against heresy, beginning with the proceedings against the Knights Templar.

[50] P. Biller, 'William of Newburgh and the Cathar Mission to England', in D. Wood (ed.), *Life and Thought in the Northern Church c.1100–c.1700: Essays in Honour of Claire Cross*, SCH Subsidia, 12 (Woodbridge, 1999), 12–15.

[51] F. Pollock and F. W. Maitland, *The History of English Law before the Time of Edward I*, 2 vols. (2nd edn., Cambridge, 1968), ii. 544, state that 'until Lollardy became troublesome there was too little heresy in England to beget a settled course of procedure'. This seems correct.

[52] See H. G. Richardson, 'Heresy and the Lay Power under Richard II', *EHR* 51 (1936), 1–4. [53] Biller, 'William of Newburgh', 11–30, 25.

[54] Richardson, 'Heresy and the Lay Power', 1–2; Biller, 'William of Newburgh', 27–8.

[55] Richardson, 'Heresy and the Lay Power', 2.

[56] P. Biller, 'The Earliest Heretical Englishwoman', in J. Wogan-Brown et al. (eds.), *Medieval Women: Texts and Contexts in Late Medieval Britain. Essays for Felicity Riddy* (Turnhout, 2000), 363–76; Richardson, 'Heresy and the Lay Power', 3.

Two papally appointed inquisitors arrived in England in 1309 and interrogated 144 suspects with the assistance of the archbishops of Canterbury and York and the bishops of London and Chichester, while church councils in both provinces deliberated on the threat of heresy and the crown prevaricated on the use of torture.[57] The large volume of these cases and their status as a *cause célèbre* must have stimulated public consciousness of heresy and institutional knowledge of anti-heresy law, although subsequent prosecutions show no perceptible sign of a direct influence. In 1315 Archbishop Greenfield of York heard a case of withheld offerings in which there was 'fermentum heretice pravitatis' and in 1319 Archbishop Reynolds of Canterbury dealt with a heretic in Milton Keynes.[58] A commission issued by Bishop Charlton of Hereford for the trial of a heresy suspect in 1336 suggests only a very general knowledge of anti-heresy law, asking the commissioners to proceed 'according to the type and nature of the case'.[59] This should not give the impression that isolated cases of heresy were not taken seriously. In 1355 news of heresy in the diocese of York reached even the papacy, and at the same time Bishop Grandisson of Exeter, who had studied under the French inquisitor Jacques Fournier, took great pains with a local heretic and sent to France for copies of sentences against two suspect Franciscans who had come to his attention.[60] Despite the gravity with which heresy was viewed, isolated incidents of prosecution were separated by years, often decades, and despite the sophistication of some individual responses, there does not seem to have been much development of a shared body of knowledge.

The sporadic attention that was given to heresy meant that it had little impact on ecclesiastical statutes, which were the basic tool of church government in the thirteenth and fourteenth centuries. Despite the fairly enthusiastic reception and adaptation of the decrees of the Fourth Lateran Council in England, heresy is one of several issues that made little impression on English bishops of the succeeding generations.[61]

---

[57] Barber, *Templars*, 195–204.

[58] *Reg. Greenfield (York)*, ii. 199; Richardson, 'Heresy and the Lay Power', 3.

[59] *Reg. T. Charlton (Hereford)*, 71: 'juxta ipsius negocii qualitatem et naturem'.

[60] *CPL 1342–1362*, 565; *Reg. Grandisson (Exeter)*, ii. 1147–9, 1179–81; M. Haren, *Sin and Society in Fourteenth-Century England: A Study of the* Memoriale presbiterorum (Oxford, 2000), 47.

[61] M. Gibbs and J. Lang, *Bishops and Reform, 1215–1272: With Special Reference to the Lateran Council of 1215* (Oxford, 1934), 113.

For example, in his statutes for Salisbury diocese issued between 1238 and 1244, Robert Bingham said that heresy had been growing in the area, but merely ordered that no heretic be made a priest, and that the clergy report any hint of it they heard in confessions.[62] While important constituents of the detection of heresy, on their own these two measures appear somewhat limited and suggest that although on the increase, heresy was not perceived to be endemic.

Another habit of the thirteenth and fourteenth centuries was to associate heresy with the fringes of Christendom, as in Alexander Stavensby's statutes for Coventry diocese issued between 1224 and 1237, where heretics are grouped with Saracens amongst the enemies of the church.[63] Similar perceptions may have been behind the petition for military aid sent to the 1322 Lincoln Convocation by the northern religious houses, who bolstered their plea with the claim that the Scottish nobles erred in the faith.[64] Apart from synodal constitutions issued by the bishop of Ossory in Ireland in 1320, the only other anti-heretical statute before the 1380s was issued by John Thoresby, archbishop of York, in 1367. This reforming and diligent bishop set out the circumstances in which cases in the ecclesiastical courts were reserved for his attention, a category of offence which included sins against the faith and receiving baptism or ordination from a heretic.[65] In 1368 the archbishop of Canterbury, Simon Langham, did issue a list of condemned opinions and order that they not be taught or discussed in Oxford; but no reference was made either to heresy or to anti-heresy law.[66]

Even when the Templar trials are taken into consideration, the volume of cases and the concomitant codification of statutes and practices in the Wycliffite period stand in stark contrast to the preceding two centuries. However, there does seem to have been a quickening of interest in heresy and an increase in the number of texts dealing with it in the pre-Wycliffite period. Although not a massive corpus, Quesnel's *Directorium*, the

---

[62] *Councils and Synods with Other Documents Relating to the English Church*, ii: *1205–1313*, ed. F. M. Powicke and C. R. Cheney, 2 vols. (Oxford, 1964), i. 371, cc. 14, 19. On heretics not being ordained see C. 23 q. 7 c. 3 and VI 5.2.2.

[63] *Councils and Synods*, i. 225. See also the legend of the heretical Lombard king in the fourteenth-century *Liber exemplorum ad usum praedicantium*, ed. A. G. Little (Aberdeen, 1908), 70.　　　　　　　　　　　　　　　　　[64] Wilkins, *Concilia*, ii. 517–19.

[65] Ibid. iii. 72–3. These issues are treated by Gratian in C. 24 q. 1 d. p. c. 39. For the Irish response to heresy see Wilkins, *Concilia*, ii. 501–6, 652.

[66] Wilkins, *Concilia*, iii. 75–6.

Summae of Pisano and Paul, Chillenden's *Repertorium*, le Palmere's *Omne bonum*, and Frédol's *Tractatus* suggest a shift from the mechanical copying of decrees and decretal collections, to the classification and distillation of such knowledge, and the beginnings of its use in actual cases. It therefore seems as though Wyclif's movement into ever greater disobedience, and the fears engendered by the 1381 revolt, came at a time when the English church was slowly becoming more alert to heresy and more alive to the techniques available for dealing with it. Some of the vigour with which Wyclif and his followers were then pursued may be explained by this heightened awareness of heresy in the immediate pre-Wycliffite period. Nevertheless, the state of legal writing on heresy before 1380 was such that we may treat England after that date as a case study in the reception, development, and application of anti-heresy law, as royal, provincial, and diocesan legislation was substantially augmented to deal with the threat.[67]

Given the doubts of medieval inquisitors and the lack of extensive experience on the part of the English episcopate, a cautious approach seems appropriate for historical analysis of how the investigation, reporting, and detection of heretics was achieved. Inquisitors and bishops operated in a system that drew back from categorical assertions of heresy or ortho-doxy, and in England they were learning the business of heresy detection as they went, although within the confines of what was compatible with canon law. It is not unreasonable that the historian should view the efforts and limitations of medieval churchmen sympathetically, and indeed embrace their doubts and their learning processes as an object of study. For a long time the historian's view of anti-heretical work has been expressed in the emotive language of repression, persecution, and the abuse of power. Lea described the 'cruel ferocity of barbarous zeal' wrought in the name of Christ; Moore spoke of a persecuting rather than a prosecuting society; and Henry Kelly and Paul Strohm describe how the odds were stacked against the accused, arguing that the heresy trial was

---

[67] The danger in assuming knowledge of anti-heresy canons on the basis of the existence of law books in English collections is illustrated by the omission of CC. 23 and 24 (the *causae* dealing most extensively with heresy) from the BL, MS Royal 9 A VIII *Decretum*, the omission of *Ad abolendam* from the copy of the decrees of the Third Lateran Council in BL, MS Royal 10 B IV, fos. 62^r–65^r, and the severely truncated texts of that canon and *Excommunicamus* in an abridged *Liber extra*, BL, MS Royal 11 A II, fos. 183^r–184^v.

a mere show of legal process.[68] Without descending into *apologia* for torture and execution it is possible, and desirable from the point of view of academic inquiry, to evaluate the efforts made by bishops and inquisitors not to condemn the innocent. It is important not to forget that inquisition was a legal process, governed by rules that bound all parties to certain standards.

[68] Lea, *Inquisition*, i. 233; Moore, *Persecuting Society*; Strohm, *England's Empty Throne*, 45–53; H. A. Kelly, 'Lollard Inquisitions: Due and Undue Process', in A. Ferreiro (ed.), *The Devil, Heresy and Witchcraft in the Middle Ages* (Leiden, 1998), 279–303.

2

The Investigation of Heresy

The task of dealing with heresy fell within the competence of a number of different jurisdictions in the Middle Ages. Deviation from the faith and disobedience to the church was primarily a concern of canon law, represented by the papal law books containing decrees and decretals, and the commentaries upon them. However, canon law was a much broader discipline, encompassing the provincial and diocesan statutes of the episcopate in addition to papal decrees. Provinces and dioceses were the jurisdictional units within which heresy cases were ordinarily judged, as is indicated by the phrase 'ordinary jurisdiction', and within these areas the archbishop or bishop had the authority to promulgate his own legislation. In addition to bishops and archbishops, specially delegated inquisitors could exercise their own jurisdiction within and across dioceses, with particular responsibility for heresy; self-governing corporate bodies such as universities were also expected to discover and deal with heretics. Despite the obvious spiritual nature of the crime, heresy was an offence that secular authority, in this case the English crown, had a duty to resist, as protector of the church and guarantor of peace between men. Lesser secular jurisdictions such as municipalities were naturally concerned with heresy in their localities, but they had no formal role in detection, so need not concern us here.[1] This chapter will address the question of who was responsible for directing investigations into heresy, and the following chapter will look at the detection techniques used in those investigations.

---

[1] On 7 December 1428 the Common Council of London decreed that no citizen was to employ anyone convicted of heresy; Corporation of London Record Office, Journals of the Court of Common Council, 2 (1425–8), fo. 127^r. Municipalities were limited by VI 5.2.9 which stated that the statutes of towns, castles, and villages must not hinder the work of inquisitors.

To begin with, a word must be said about the character of law in the Middle Ages, and particularly about the relationship between papal canon law and the statutes issued by English kings, archbishops, and bishops. In 1407 Archbishop Thomas Arundel and his lawyers formulated a series of constitutions for the defence of the faith and the extirpation of heresy. In the preamble to this famous collection of anti-heresy law, they complained that the laws promulgated against heresy to date had been little heeded: further legislation was therefore necessary to strengthen the *ius commune* in this matter.[2] If the *ius commune* was not sufficient, one is bound to ask what its role was in governing the English church. This was the question that became a point of controversy in the late nineteenth century between William Stubbs and F. W. Maitland. Indicating instances where English church law seemed to diverge from Roman canon law, Stubbs asserted that the latter was not binding on the English ecclesiastical courts. Arguing from the wealth of 'Roman' legal literature, terminology, and specific decisions clearly applied in those courts, Maitland countered that it was in fact binding. It is possible to see merit in both their premisses, but their conclusions are incompatible. English canon lawyers clearly worked within the system of the *ius commune*, basing their procedures and judgements upon those found in the *Corpus iuris canonici* and the major commentators, but at times they diverged from the precise letter of those texts. Historians therefore now agree that the Stubbs–Maitland dispute was based on a false dichotomy.[3]

The *ius commune* of the universal church was neither utterly binding on English courts, nor was it completely irrelevant to them. As a body of principles, canon law was 'a starting point for the analysis of legal problems', which did not pretend to provide a simple remedy for every ill.[4] Papal decrees were often responses to circumstances highly specific in time and

---

[2] Reg. Arundel (Canterbury), ii. fo. 10ᵛ: 'Prohibiciones et decreta canonum contra huiusmodi pestilentes seminatores proinde promulgatur minime ponderantes...in vberiorem fortificacionem iuris communis in hac parte editi.' *Ius commune* is a term often used to describe papally sanctioned canon law, which, in contrast to local statutes, was common to all Latin Christians.

[3] C. Donahue Jr., 'Roman Canon Law in the Medieval English Church: Stubbs vs. Maitland Re-examined after 75 Years in the Light of Some Records from the Church Courts', *Michigan Law Review*, 72 (1974), 647–716; *Select Cases on Defamation to 1600*, ed. R. H. Helmholz, Selden Society, 101 (1985), pp. xiv–xvi.

[4] R. H. Helmholz, *The Ius Commune in England: Four Studies* (Oxford, 2001), 13; Ferme, *Canon Law in Late Medieval England*, 11–12; M. Bellomo, *The Common Legal Past of Europe, 1000–1800* (Washington, DC, 1995), 79–83.

place, and so when they were put to more general use, they were meant only for guidance. Returning to Arundel's complaint of 1407, we can see more clearly what he meant by the fortification of the *ius commune*: more provincial legislation was needed to facilitate the enforcement of the decretals. His aim, however, was not merely to publicize papal letters and conciliar decrees more effectively, but to add material to their provisions that was specifically geared to English needs. Even without the extra material, reiteration necessarily involved a degree of interpretation, as well as a good deal of innovation. The constitutions, as they were eventually issued in 1409, contained much that was not specifically mentioned in the *ius commune*. From a wider perspective, one may even credit Stubbs's belief that the English church enjoyed a particular relationship with Rome, but he was only right insofar as *every* province of the medieval church had a particular relationship with Rome, based on the peculiar interpretations and additions to canon law that pertained in each place.[5] It is also worth reminding ourselves that despite the idea of the division of the two powers, to which I will turn shortly, secular rulers were also subject to the principles of canon law, especially on an issue so close to the church's heart as the defeat of heresy.

1. CHURCH AND CROWN

English royal government proved to be an enthusiastic ally of the church in the fight against heresy. On the face of it, king and Parliament had little choice in the matter, as successive canonists had decreed that it was the duty of every Christian prince to do the church's bidding when it came to the defence of the faith. Secular rulers, however, were not bound to the church in quite the same way as bishops, and some resistance to the ecclesiastical demands was envisaged in many of the relevant canons. Gratian had acknowledged that, although authorities could be produced to prove that force of arms may *not* be used to defend friends from harm,[6] to seek

---

[5] For example, in the decree *Ad abolendam* (X 5.7.9) clauses on secular–ecclesiastical co-operation refer to imperial statutes, which would not be relevant in the English case. The need to spell out the exact relationship between church and state in each province of the church is one reason why the *ius commune* should not be seen as a code of law complete in itself.

[6] C. 23 q. 3 d. a. c. 1: 'Quod uero iniuria sociorum armis propulsanda non sit, exemplis et auctoritatibus probatur.'

or to provide relief from an evil threat is both expedient and honourable as it brings peace to the church.[7] He supported this view with canons drawn from the fathers and early councils (C. 23 q. 3 cc. 2–11), ending with the assertion that secular aid is not only desirable, but required.[8] The obligation on secular rulers to assist the church in defeating heresy was taken up in a discussion of why the church might lawfully persecute heretics (C. 23 q. 4 cc. 37–49). The church was duty bound to ask secular rulers for help against heretics (C. 23 q. 4 c. 41), and those rulers were bound to provide such help, or else risk being forced out of the church.[9] The principle and the sanction were reiterated in the thirteenth-century *Glossa ordinaria* to Gratian, where excommunication was given as the punishment for failure to provide aid against heretics.[10] By this time, widespread heresy in the form of Catharism and Waldensianism had made the co-operation of church and state a more urgent matter than in Gratian's day.

The decree *Ad abolendam*, formulated at the Third Lateran Council in 1179 and promulgated in the *Liber extra* in 1234, stipulated that secular authorities should aid the church against heretics whenever required, obeying the mandates of church and empire. Rulers who did not co-operate would be excommunicated and their lands subject to interdict.[11] The deliberations of the Fourth Lateran Council in 1215 led to an even tougher statement of the necessity for secular rulers to help the church against heretics in the bull *Excommunicamus*. They were to be warned,

---

[7] C. 23 q. 3 d. a. c. 2: 'Petere autem uel prestare solacium, ut malis facultas delinquendi adimatur, ut ecclesia pacem adipiscatur . . . utile est et honestum.'

[8] C. 23 q. 3 d. p. c. 10.

[9] C. 23 q. 5 d. a. c. 26: 'secularium dignitatum administratoribus defendendarum ecclesiarum necessitas incumbit. Quod si facere contempserint, a communione sunt repellendi.' [10] *Glos. ord.* to C. 23 q. 3 c. 10.

[11] X 5.7.9: 'Statuimus insuper, ut comites, barones, rectores et consules civitatum et aliorum locorum, iuxta commonitionem archiepiscoporum et episcoporum, praestito corporaliter iuramento promittant, quod in omnibus praedictis fideliter et efficaciter, quum ab eis exinde fuerint requisiti, ecclesiam contra haereticos et eorum complices adiuvabunt et studebunt bona fide iuxta officium et posse suum ecclesiastica simul et imperiali statuta circa ea, quae diximus, exsecutioni mandare. Si vero id observare noluerint, honore, quem obtinent, spolientur et ad alios nullatenus assumantur, eis nihilominus excommunicatione ligandis, et terris ipsorum interdicto ecclesiae supponendis.' Hostiensis, *Summa aurea*, 1539, cites the rather confused story of Pippin III being deposed by Ludwig of Bavaria on these grounds, with the blessing of Pope Zacharias. In fact Zacharias was asked by Pippin to authorize the deposition of Childeric III in 751, and there was no mention of heresy; see E. James, *The Origins of France from Clovis to the Capetians, 500–1000* (London, 1982), 154–5.

induced, and, where necessary, compelled by ecclesiastical censure to publicly swear an oath for the defence of the faith, promising that they would cleanse their lands of heretics as and when indicated by the church.[12] The obligation to provide aid was repeated in the *Liber sextus*, given sharper teeth in the additional clause that any ruler failing to do his duty would himself be declared a heretic, and made more practical by allowing excommunicated rulers to participate in anti-heresy work.[13]

The threat was repeated in William Paul's *Summa summarum*, which may reflect a developing mood in fourteenth-century English government, later to be realized in the extraordinary energy of the English crown's anti-heresy activity.[14] Going far beyond the stipulation for action in response to a request from the church, Richard II's government launched a full-scale attack on heresy and the first two Lancastrian kings made occasional, highly publicized, contributions to anti-heresy policy.[15] There was also a great deal of day to day co-operation between the king and his archbishops, between Parliament and Convocation, and on the ground between diocesan officials and the sheriffs and justices of the royal administrative machine. This was made easy and inevitable by the ubiquity of officials at all levels who had held office in both episcopal and royal administrations, something to which Wycliffites particularly objected.[16]

The prosecution of heresy may be thought of as having four stages. They are detection, arrest, trial, and punishment. In a model that fits most anti-heresy campaigns from the twelfth to the sixteenth century, the church oversaw detection, the secular arm dealt with the arrest of suspects who were then handed over to the church for trial, to be relinquished to

---

[12] X 5.7.13: 'Moneantur autem et inducantur, et, si necesse fuerit, per censuram ecclesiasticam compellantur saeculares potestates, quibuscunque fungantur officiis, ut, sicut reputari cupiunt et haberi fideles, ita pro defensione fidei praestent publice iuramentum, quod de terris suae iurisdictioni subiectis universos haereticos, ab ecclesia denotatos, bona fide pro viribus exterminare studebunt'; see also *Glos. ord.* to X 5.7.13 (kings who do not have the fear of God before their eyes).

[13] VI 5.2.18; VI 5.2.6, and *Summa summarum*, V. X. q. 60 (Bodleian, MS Bodley 293, fo. 179ʳ). See Hamilton, *Medieval Inquisition*, 32–3, on church–state co-operation in the late twelfth and early thirteenth centuries.

[14] *Summa summarum*, V. X. q. 55 (Bodleian, MS Bodley 293, fo. 178ʳ).

[15] W. R. Jones, 'Relations of the Two Jurisdictions: Conflict and Co-operation in England during the Thirteenth and Fourteenth Centuries', *Studies in Medieval and Renaissance History*, 7 (1970), 80.

[16] A. Hudson, '*Hermofodrita or Ambidexter*: Wycliffite Views on Clerks in Secular Office', in Aston and Richmond (eds.), *Lollardy and the Gentry*, 41–51.

the secular arm once again for punishment. The transfer of suspects between the powers necessitated co-operation, and the practical considerations of this were spelled out in legislation such as the parliamentary statute of 1414. 'Since the cognizance of heresy, errors, or lollardies appertains to the judges of Holy Church and not to secular judges, indicted persons shall be delivered by indenture to the ordinary of that place or his commissary within ten days of their arrest, or sooner if possible, to be acquitted or convicted by the laws of Holy Church.'[17] As will become clear, jurisdictional boundaries were not always respected, something which may explain the frequency with which they were defended by canonists. For example, the ordinary gloss to the *Liber sextus* stated that secular powers were to 'obey and assist inquisitors or bishops in the investigation, capture, imprisonment, and punishment of heretics, but since some aspects of heresy only pertain to the church, they must have no role in judging or discerning heresy, notwithstanding any secular laws to the contrary'.[18] The opinion that the discernment of heretics was a matter solely for the church was asserted, with a caveat, by Hostiensis, who thought that 'the cognition, examination, and condemnation of this crime belongs *principally* to the ecclesiastical judge'.[19] The possibility that a secular judge may try a case of heresy seems to be allowed here, but Hostiensis does not give it any further treatment. In fact he later goes beyond the words of the canons, arguing that the examination, amercement (*mulctacio*), and punishment of here are all the responsibility of the church, not of the secular arm.[20] However, he was not proposing an ecclesiastical encroachment on the state's responsibilities, merely observing that the judgement of mortal sins should be directed by the church.[21]

---

[17] *Statutes of the Realm*, ii. 182–3: 'Et pour tant que la conusance des Heresies errours ou Lollardries apperteignent as Juges de Seinte Esglise et nemye as Juges seculers, soient tieux enditeez livres as Ordinaries des lieux ou a lour Commissaries per endentures entre eux affairez dedeinz x. jours apres lour arest ou pluis tost si ceo pourra estre fait pour ent estre acquitez ou convictz par les leies de Seinte Esglise.'

[18] *Glos. ord.* to VI 5.2.18: 'rectores locorum parere inquisitoribus ordinario vel alteri eorum inuestigatione, captione, custodia et punitione hereticorum et fautorum suorum, eorum proclamationibus vel appellationibus non obstantibus, itacumque de illo crimine cum sit mere ecclesiasticum nec iudicent nec cognoscant.'

[19] Hostiensis, *Summa aurea*, 1533: 'cognitio, examinatio et condemnatio istius criminis ad ecclesiasticum Iudicem pertinet principaliter, non ad secularem.' See also X 2.1.13 and J. A. Watt, *The Theory of the Papal Monarchy in the Thirteenth Century: The Contribution of the Canonists* (London, 1965), 41–4.

[20] Hostiensis, *Summa aurea*, 1535.   [21] Watt, *Papal Monarchy*, 127.

Whatever emphasis a canonist or legislator put on the relative authority of church and state, some kind of separation of the powers of judgement and force was always accepted.

After a trial had been conducted, and if a guilty verdict was reached, the condemned heretic was to be handed over to secular officers present at the hearing. If the offender was a cleric, he was first to be degraded of his status.[22] Relinquishment was a normal part of canonical procedure, and there is no need to attribute the presence of royal servants in the wings of William Sawtry's 1401 trial to Lancastrian conspiracy, as Paul Strohm does.[23] As the legitimate agent of judicial force, the state took responsibility for punishing offenders, as instructed by the church,[24] with execution and the confiscation of goods being accepted by the canonists as the correct punishments for heretics.[25] The formulation of a parliamentary statute providing for the burning of heretics in 1401, and the detailed itemization of confiscation in 1414, have in this light seemed unnecessary to some historians; but their manifest importance in the legislative programmes of Henry IV and Henry V is a further indication that local (that is English) legislation was needed to facilitate the universal principles of the *ius commune*.[26] Not being a modern code of positive law, the legal validity of canon law cannot be separated from the political circumstances in which it was applied. The division between the powers was reiterated at the punishment stage, with canonists stipulating that the goods of heretics are not to be confiscated until the verdict has been decided by the church, as that would constitute pre-judgement of the case and action in excess of the state's authority.[27] Henry V agreed and on 11 January 1414, the day after the Oldcastle revolt, he ordered the sheriff of London to proclaim against greedy people who had been taking the goods of heretics on the pretext of punishing them.[28]

---

[22] X 5.7.13, 5.7.15: 'Damnati vero per ecclesiam saeculari iudicio relinquantur'; X 5.40.27: 'per ecclesiasticum iudicem degradatus . . . saeculari potestate praesente'; Hostiensis, *Summa aurea*, 1531, 1538; *Summa summarum*, V. X. q. 98 (Bodleian, MS Bodley 293, fo. 180ʳ). [23] Strohm, *England's Empty Throne*, 43. [24] X 5.7.13: 'ab ecclesia denotatos.' [25] Burning was widely understood to be the punishment implied by X 5.7.9, based on the Roman decree Dig. 48.19.28. See *Summa summarum*, V. X. q. 12 (Bodleian, MS Bodley 293, fo. 178ʳ), and R. H. Helmholz, *The Spirit of Classical Canon Law* (Athens, Ga., 1996), 362. Confiscation was introduced by X 5.7.13. [26] McHardy, '*De heretico comburendo* 1401', 117–19. [27] VI 5.2.19; *Summa summarum*, V. X. q. 86 (Bodleian, MS Bodley 293, fo. 179ʳ). [28] PRO, C 54/263, m. 8d (*CCR 1413–19*, 109–10). It is also clear that Henry did not wish to see popular action take the place of royal justice.

The practical distinction between the powers regarding arrest was blurred almost as soon as heresy became politically significant in England. In May 1382 Richard II instructed sheriffs and other royal officers to capture suspected heretics who had already been cited by their bishop and had failed to appear.[29] The aim of this was to enable bishops to force suspects to appear, which could prove difficult for an overstretched and understrength diocesan administration. In the case of serious spiritual crimes, it was not uncommon for a suspect to move outside the jurisdiction of his or her ordinary, at best postponing apprehension or at worst making it impossible. In 1382 it is probable that the bishop of Lincoln's difficulties in citing William Swinderby had triggered the royal action.[30]

The May 1382 commission began the process of incorporating and accommodating the precepts of the *ius commune* with English common law and the canon law of the two English provinces. However, the principle that the crown was required to assist the church in defeating heresy was quickly modified by another royal letter in June 1382, licensing bishops to make arrests themselves and keep the suspects in their own prisons while they awaited trial.[31] It seems that the session of Convocation that had condemned twenty-four opinions of Wyclif on 30 May 1382, and instructed the episcopate to proceed against heretics in their dioceses, had deemed the royal initiative insufficient, if initially helpful.[32] What the June licence suggests is that the crown wished to retain oversight of the use of force (arrest) within its realm, just as Hostiensis wished the church to direct the punishment of heretics without actually carrying it out. The actual division of labour in detecting and arresting heretics remained open to choice according to what was deemed most likely to succeed in any given case. At Reading in 1396, for example, the bishop of Salisbury informed the king that there were heresy suspects in the town. Richard responded by instructing the local bailiffs, along with the abbot of Reading, to arrest them.[33] The opportunity presented by the June 1382 licence for the episcopal arrest of suspects seems to have been declined,

[29] 5 Rich. II, st. 2, c. 5. In cases already under way, the ordinary could seek a writ of *de excommunicato capiendo* in Chancery, for the arrest of a contumacious suspect; F. D. Logan, *Excommunication and the Secular Arm in Medieval England: A Study in Legal Procedure from the Thirteenth to the Sixteenth Century* (Toronto, 1968), 68–71.

[30] Reg. Buckingham (Lincoln), fo. 236ᵛ.

[31] PRO, C 66/313, m. 35 (*CPR 1381–85*, 150); Reg. Courtenay (Canterbury), i. fo. 31ʳ.

[32] Reg. Courtenay (Canterbury), fos. 25v–26ʳ. On the Blackfriars council see Hudson, *Premature Reformation*, 69. [33] PRO, C 54/238, m. 28 (*CCR 1396–99*, 9).

with Bishop Mitford asking the king for help. Mitford's decision to act according to the May letter rather than the June one may have been because he did not wish to step on the toes of the abbot of Reading, who effectively had sole secular jurisdiction over the town.[34]

In those instances where detection and arrest were divided between the two powers, ecclesiastical weaknesses were probably responsible for the division of labour as often as was legal theory. The crown could step in where the church's lack of coercive power left it wanting. A good example of this is provided by a case which is startling in its incidental details. On 8 March 1389 the king and council ordered the sheriff of Northampton to cite forty-six suspected supporters of the heretic John Wodeward in Chipping Warden in the diocese of Lincoln. This order came after the bishop of Lincoln, John Buckingham, had been unable to cite the offenders. William Sligh, the dean of Brackley, and William Stoke, a chaplain of Brackley, had been sent to Chipping Warden sometime in the autumn of 1388 to cite Wodeward's supporters on charges of receiving and aiding a heretic, but when they arrived in the village, certain unknown and armed persons attacked them and forced them to flee to the parish church for safety. Their attackers, 'moved by the spirit of the devil and not fearing God', broke into the church and seriously injured the chaplain, spilling his blood on the consecrated ground. They then stole the dean's and chaplain's horses and cut off their tails, presumably in symbolic reply to the episcopal mandate. On 20 December 1388 the local clergy were instructed by Buckingham to pronounce the excommunication of the offenders, inquire as to their identities and cite them to appear before the bishop, or his commissary Richard Kyllom, in Sleaford. This second attempt failed as well, and so Buckingham reported his suspicions and investigations to the king. Co-operating with the crown in this way, the church was able to restart an investigation that had ground to a halt because of local resistance and the limitations of ecclesiastical power. Two days after the sheriff had been called in, Buckingham issued a new mandate to proceed against the Chipping Warden group, apparently safe in the knowledge that they had been apprehended.[35]

---

[34] *Reading Abbey Cartularies*, ed. B. R. Kemp, 2 vols., Camden Society, 4th ser. 31, 33 (1986–7), i. 17.

[35] Reg. Buckingham (Lincoln), fo. 357; PRO, C 54/229, m. 9d. (*CCR 1385–89*, 667–8); K. B. McFarlane, *Lancastrian Kings and Lollard Knights* (Oxford, 1972), 194–5.

The jurisdictional caesura between investigation and arrest continued into the fifteenth century. In May 1413, for example, Edmund Stafford, the bishop of Exeter, was requested to inquire into heresy in his diocese, and concurrently the sheriff of Devon was asked to arrest any suspects who were uncovered.[36] For all that they seem to be a model of church–state co-operation, the 1413 investigations in the south-west were initially ordered by the crown. This was a fairly common situation in the English struggle against heresy, especially under Richard II, and it can be read as an assertion of royal control over the whole process. For a papal theorist like Hostiensis, such a claim would be unacceptable, given that 'God is the origin of all power, and so therefore is his vicar'.[37] In his relations with the church's jurisdiction, Huguccio had earlier claimed that the secular ruler could achieve nothing unless called upon to do so by the church.[38] This view was certainly current in late medieval England, where an anonymous poet had versified a fake papal bull, arguing that the church had power over 'all temperelte', and identified all who disagreed as lollards.[39] This was the great irony of the two powers debate in late medieval England: while the crown wished to take control, or be seen to be taking control, of anti-heresy policy, Wyclif himself had argued that an errant church should be chastised and controlled by the crown.[40] Consequently, an over-enthusiastic crown ran the risk of being associated with the very threat it was trying to combat.

In 1399 a complaint to the king from Convocation had called for infringements of the church's rights and liberties by 'lollards in the present Parliament' to cease, illustrating this very problem.[41] However, this claim was made in the course of an appeal to the king to protect the church, which shows the relationship between church and crown to be far from reducible to theoretical extremes. For example, the bull *Excommunicamus*, a source of so much anti-heresy law, was one of the strongest statements of ecclesiastical superiority in the whole Middle Ages, and yet its requirement that secular powers obey the direction of

[36] Reg. Stafford (Exeter), i. fo. 182, ii. fo. 321; PRO, C 66/389, m. 29d (*CPR 1413–16*, 34).
[37] Hostiensis, *Summa aurea*, 1533: 'Deus est omnibus praeponendus... ergo et est eius vicarius.'   [38] Müller, *Huguccio*, 125.
[39] BL, MS Additional Charter 12794.
[40] M. Wilks, '*Reformatio Regni*: Wyclif and Hus as Leaders of Religious Protest Movements', in D. Baker (ed.), *Schism, Heresy and Religious Protest*, SCH 9 (Cambridge, 1972), 109–30.   [41] Reg. Arundel (Canterbury), i. fo. 51ʳ.

churchmen is betrayed by the quite evident reliance of the church on those who wielded political power.[42] The English crown made full use of this ambiguity, casting itself as saviour of a church beset by heresy. In 1389 a commission expressed the king's wish to see heretics get their just deserts, and in 1395 king and council asserted themselves to be zealous in the faith, 'the defenders of which we have been made by God'.[43] Again in 1395, in an order to the chancellor of Oxford University to suspend heretics who were spreading their errors among the people, the king and council asserted that this would sadly continue, unless quickly resisted by the royal majesty.[44] Such self-promotion, when it came with practical help, was accepted by the church, whatever reservations there might be about the crown's actions in other respects. At times, Convocation even appealed to the crown in exactly the same terms, hinting at catastrophe for the church if the king did not help defeat heresy.[45]

The crown proved itself quite a skilful manager of impressions and expectations in its presentation of anti-heresy activity. In a commission of 16 October 1397, the king expressed his wish to purge the diocese of Chichester of heresy, ordering the bishop to arrest all such persons and imprison them 'until we shall take order for their punishment'. In this beautifully crafted piece of political rhetoric—'quousque pro eorum punicione aliter duxerimus ordinandum'—the king's dependence on the bishop's decision as to punishment is disguised by expressing in an active form of the verb *duco* a relationship between king and bishop that would be better described by the passive form: 'until we are instructed as to their punishment.'[46]

The willingness of the church to allow the crown to direct anti-heresy activity at certain periods opened the door to secular encroachment upon the areas of heresy prosecution identified by the canonists as pertaining solely to the church. In terms of investigation, the key point at which the boundaries between the jurisdictions could be blurred was the distinction

---

[42] Watt, *Papal Monarchy*, 42–3.

[43] PRO, C 54/230, m. 31 (*CCR 1389–92*, 4): 'volentes ipsos . . . iuxta eorum demerita castigari'; PRO, C 54/237, m. 20 (*CCR 1392–96*, 437–8): 'Nos zelo fidei catholice cuius sumus et erimus deo dante defensores.'

[44] PRO, C 54/237, m. 24 (*CCR 1392–96*, 434): 'nisi brachio regie magestatis cicius resistatur.'

[45] Reg. Clifford (London), fo. 152ʳ; *Reg. Repingdon (Lincoln)*, ii. 362–3.

[46] PRO, C 54/240, m. 18 (*CCR 1396–99*, 158).

between inquiring into the whereabouts of suspects with the aim of arresting them, and inquiring into the substance of the heresy of which they were suspected. In cases where commissions were open-ended, it is possible to see how an even greater degree of judgement could creep into the secular remit. The status of the court to which suspects were sent for judgement also raises the possibility of encroachment. In an age when the same individual could hold high office in both church and state, this is unsurprising. It was perhaps only natural that the politically stronger power, the crown, would arrogate to itself some of the duties of its theoretically superior, but practically weaker, partner. That is not to say that this would always be acceptable to the church, and the dictum that the secular arm ought not to encroach upon the church and its jurisdiction was remembered even in an episcopate dominated by royal appointments.[47]

Some of the evidence is indistinct in this respect. For example, what was the purpose of the 1397 instruction to the sub-chamberlain that all the lollards in his custody were to be brought before the king? Was it for punishment, delivery to an ecclesiastical judge, examination, or judgement? Richard II's desire to control anti-heresy activity is confirmed, but we are left unsure as to the level of the crown's engagement.[48] Similar doubts must be entertained about the case of John Croft, who made a renunciation of heresy apparently before the Privy Council in 1395. A letter in French describing the form of the renunciation was sent to Bishop Trefnant of Hereford, but no further action against him is recorded in an episcopal court.[49] Croft may have been caught and examined by the committee of laymen appointed in 1393 to prevent interference in the trial of Walter Brut, a straightforward secular process, but what the Privy Council's involvement was is unclear, as it was not a body capable of hearing abjurations of spiritual offences.[50]

There is, however, a good deal of evidence to suggest that as the campaign against heresy progressed, successive governments managed to increase the amount and the significance of the investigative activity carried out by royal officials. Whether this was by design or whether it was an unintended result of seeking more effective methods of investigation is not always clear, and varies from one case to another. The first noticeable instance of possible

---

[47] Hostiensis, *Summa aurea*, 1535: 'nec debet ecclesiam vel iurisdictionem ecclesiasticam impugnare.' See also VI 5.2.18.   [48] PRO, C 54/238, m. 10 (*CCR 1396–99*, 37).
[49] *Reg. Trefnant (Hereford)*, 147–50.
[50] Ibid. 410–11. I owe this reference to Anne Hudson and Maureen Jurkowski.

encroachment is the potential for secular inquiry suggested by the 1388 commissions to search for heretical books. In March that year the mayor and bailiffs of Nottingham, together with the knights Rado of Crombewell and John Lekee, were commissioned to search for 'libros, libellos, cedulas et quaternos diuersas' written by Wyclif or Nicholas Hereford. They were to investigate and arrest any persons owning such material and deliver them to the council for examination.[51] This was followed in April by another commission for the knights John Godard and John Hochom, and the sheriff of York, William of Riseby, in much the same terms.[52] By May 1388, what had first been perceived as a local problem seems to have become a matter of national concern, as commissions were sent to Leicester, Salisbury, Norwich, Lincoln, and, for a second time, Nottingham.

In these the offences of buying, selling, reading, and writing condemned books were specified and, crucially, churchmen were named as commissioners alongside the knights, sheriffs, and bailiffs. In Leicester Thomas Brightwell, the dean of Newarke College, and William Chisulden, prebendary of the same; in Salisbury John Norton, the chancellor of the cathedral; in Norwich the bishop; in Lincoln Thomas of Owneby, a suffragan bishop; in Nottingham the prior of Thurgarton and the official of the archdeacon of Nottingham.[53] What the initial commission of March and April had failed to appreciate was the difficulty for knights and sheriffs, no matter how literate, to investigate works according to either their authorship or their orthodoxy. Identifying the author of a work by recognizing his arguments or citations was generally a skill peculiar to those with an up-to-date scholastic training. Secular officers did, however, have some experience of investigating and seizing ecclesiastical documents and making judgements about their provenance. In the 1360s and 1370s crown officers were implementing the 1343 Ordinance of Provisors which required them to search for written documents emanating from the papal court that were prejudicial to the king's interests. Some kind of judgement as to what was prejudicial is implied in this instruction, although the bearers of the letters and their seals were probably evidence enough for an indiscriminate seizure.[54] This precedent may have encouraged the crown to instigate

---

51 PRO, C 66/325, m. 20 (*CPR 1385–89*, 430).

52 PRO, C 66/325, m. 22 (*CPR 1385–89*, 427).

53 PRO, C 66/325, mm. 20, 26d, C 66/326, m. 20d, C 66/327, m. 3 (*CPR 1385–89*, 468, 536, 550).

54 A. D. M. Barrell, 'The Ordinance of Provisors of 1343', *Historical Research*, 64 (1991), 265, 276.

searches by laymen for heretical books, but the mistake was quickly realized and remedied in the succeeding commissions.

In 1406 a parliamentary statute was passed which significantly extended and made explicit such qualitative investigative activity by secular officers. Alongside ecclesiastical judges, justices of King's Bench, justices of the peace, keepers of the peace, justices of assize, sheriffs, mayors, bailiffs, and other ministers of the crown were given 'poaire & auctoritee . . . enquirer & enquestes prendre en celle partie par virtue de mesme l'estatuit saunz aultre commission . . .'[55] By making inquiry into heresy an integral part of these officers' duties a very bold claim was being made for the secular investigation of a spiritual crime. Previous *ad hoc* co-operation between secular and ecclesiastical investigators was capable of justification on the grounds that a diocesan staff had begun a case and then handed over names of individuals to secular officers for arrest. This statute went much further by empowering secular officers to instigate and conduct inquiries themselves. In this new role, men without a theological or canon law training would need to exercise a certain degree of judgement, and apply a good deal of discernment, the 'cognizance' of which the canons speak. The statute goes on to state that suspects uncovered by such inquests were to be delivered to Chancery and produced in Parliament to receive such judgement as they deserved. At no point are the church courts or their authority to judge heresy mentioned, pushing the crown's claims far across the traditional division between the powers.

There are two possible reasons for this intrusion, one general, the other specific. The secular role must be seen within the context of a more general extension of the role of justices of the peace between the Ordinance of Justices in 1346 and the confirmation in 1394 that they could determine cases as well as hear them. The impetus to award justices the power to investigate heresy may well have been a product of this trend as much as it was an encroachment on the liberties of the church. In the later fourteenth century justices of the peace and peace commissions were slowly becoming the main organ of royal justice in the provinces.[56]

We must also pay attention to the driving force behind the 1406 statute, which was, ironically perhaps, Thomas Arundel the archbishop

---

[55] *Rotuli Parliamentorum*, iii. 584.
[56] A. Musson and W. M. Ormrod, *The Evolution of English Justice: Law, Politics and Society in the Fourteenth Century* (Basingstoke, 1999), 50–4, 174.

of Canterbury. Arundel was aware that within a matter of months he would be chancellor again, an office he had held at several points from the late 1380s onwards. It is therefore likely that he wished to centralize under his own direction the investigation and prosecution of heretics, by the church as archbishop and by the justices as chancellor. Maureen Jurkowski suggests that he was exploiting the fact that his authority straddled the institutions of church and state to strengthen the laws against heresy.[57] In other words this was not a piece of ideological aggression against ecclesiastical rights, but the pragmatic step of a politician whose personal embodiment of both church and state power was an example of a shared governmental culture.[58] The same policy had been tried before when in 1388 people discovered buying and selling Wycliffite books in Nottingham had failed to appear before the ecclesiastical court designated to them, and were consequently ordered to appear in Chancery.[59] The missed appointment was in all likelihood to have been before Arundel as archbishop of York, the suspects' ordinary, and the subsequent appearance would have been before Arundel as chancellor. At the same time a heretical chaplain was mainprised from Nottingham gaol to appear either before his ordinary or before council.[60] Again, both possibilities involve Arundel. However, that this mode of proceeding was only adopted in difficult cases is suggested by the smooth transferral of John Bradburn to Arundel as archbishop of York in 1388.[61]

It was not in fact unheard of for the royal council to hear and determine upon matters of spiritual concern. In 1382 Prior Francis of Montacute was pronounced free from any heresy by the council after he complained that he had been pronounced a heretic by unnamed churchmen for his wrongly alleged support for the antipope Robert of Geneva.[62] In matters of international relations the crown was happy to see itself as an agent of canon law, in its character as a *ius commune* upon which Christian rulers could draw in their domestic acts. Extrapolating from Arundel's actions in 1388 and 1406, it would seem as though he also took this line, seeing

[57] Jurkowski, 'Arrest of William Thorpe', 284, 293.
[58] On Arundel as chancellor see M. Aston, *Thomas Arundel: A Study of Church Life in the Reign of Richard II* (Oxford, 1967), 336–73.
[59] PRO, C 54/229, m. 42 (*CCR 1385–89*, 519).
[60] PRO, C 54/229, m. 38 (*CCR 1385–89*, 529).
[61] PRO, C 54/229, m. 28 (*CCR 1385–89*, 550). Calendar has m. 27 incorrectly.
[62] PRO, C 54/223, m. 6 (*CCR 1381–85*, 271).

his dual powers as governed by a single body of law, and certainly not as detrimental to the church. It might also be said, and this may have under-lain contemporary thinking, that a bishop was usually in possession of the chancellorship, and bishops also played a role in Parliament, making any objection to the judgement clause on jurisdictional grounds redundant. However, the canonists had been clear that the secular arm was to have no part in the judging or discerning of heresy. It was not enough simply for ecclesiastics to be present: secular authority was to be excluded. As it turned out, the 1406 statute fell out of use fairly swiftly, being cited only in the 1407 inquiries in Coventry, where the prior of St Mary's and two clerics took action alongside the mayor and bailiffs, and in Shrewsbury, where the bailiffs acted alone.[63] The reasons for its lapse are unclear, but may have included difficulties of the kind experienced in 1388 when secu-lar officers were given responsibility for questions beyond their expertise.

The greatest challenge to the traditional division of the powers in the investigation of heresy came in response to the revolt allegedly led by Sir John Oldcastle on 10 January 1414.[64] The spring and summer of 1413 had been a time of growing unease about heresy, with investigations across the country discovering heretics of every social class, including Oldcastle himself.[65] Royal investigations into unlicensed preaching were carried out by sheriffs and officials of the Duchy of Lancaster. Although checking licences was a task that required some knowledge of ecclesiast-ical diplomatic, no theological training was necessary, and no specialized discernment involved. However, these commissions also ordered sheriffs to investigate persons suspected of unlicensed preaching or harbouring such preachers, something which was closer to cognizance than simple stop-and-search procedures, as it involved the evaluation of suspicions about heresy.[66] The feeling in royal government that its officers were

---

[63] PRO, C 66/377, m. 20d (*CPR 1405–08*, 476); Jurkowski, 'Arrest of William Thorpe', 293.

[64] For general analyses of the revolt see Strohm, *England's Empty Throne*, 65–86; E. Powell, *Kingship, Law, and Society: Criminal Justice in the Reign of Henry V* (Oxford, 1989), 141–67. For preliminary research on the participants in the revolt see C. Kightly, 'The Early Lollards: A Survey of Popular Lollard Activity in England 1382–1428', D.Phil. thesis (University of York, 1975), and M. Jurkowski, 'Lawyers and Lollardy in the Early Fifteenth Century', in Aston and Richmond (eds.), *Lollardy and the Gentry*, 155–82.

[65] Reg. Arundel (Canterbury), ii. fos. 25ᵛ, 27; Reg. Stafford (Exeter), i. fo. 182, ii. fo. 321; Lincolnshire Archives, MS Vj/0, fos. 1–31ᵛ.

[66] PRO, C 54/263, m. 22d (*CCR 1413–19*, 86).

uncovering something more than the low-level lollard activity of the preceding generation reached a climax in the early days of 1414, when two men were rewarded for reporting plotting by heretics, and information about illegal gatherings was extracted from 'lollardi vulgariter nuncupati iam tardi capti'.[67] Three days after this last piece of information was relayed to sheriffs around the country, the large gathering of armed insurgents outside London that has become known as the Oldcastle revolt was repressed by the combined efforts of Henry V's military and judicial machinery.

The immediate response, on the very day of the revolt, was to order the mayor of London and several prominent nobles to investigate 'many subjects of ours commonly known as lollards, and others who have treacherously plotted our death against their due allegiance, and many others who have planned the destruction of the catholic faith and the lords and magnates of the realm, both spiritual and temporal'.[68] The sheriffs and bailiffs of London and Middlesex were instructed to assist in the inquiries. This commission revitalized to some degree the claim that secular officers were capable of investigating heresy, although the language suggests that it was treason committed by heretics, rather than heresy itself, which was to be investigated. The offenders were already known to be lollards and their heresy was not in doubt. Like many royal commissions against lollards, this geographically focused order was followed by a more general one which both widened the search for rebels and added some polemical words justifying the action being taken. In this respect, the assertion that Henry V wished to act as a true Christian prince according to his oath may be read as a response to critics of secular encroachment.[69] Any criticism there might have been was quickly made irrelevant by the statute passed in April 1414 at the Leicester Parliament, which had been prorogued from January in order to allow the county commissions to report.[70] This statute provided for justices of the King's

---

[67] PRO, C 66/393, m. 22 (*CPR 1413–16*, 157); C 54/263, m. 6d (*CCR 1413–19*, 114–15).

[68] PRO, C 66/393, m. 30d (*CPR 1413–16*, 175): 'quamplures subditi nostri lollardi vulgariter nuncupati ac alii, mortem nostram contra ligeanciam suam debitam proditorie imaginauerunt, ac quam plura alia tam in fidei catholice quam status dominorum et magnatum regni nostri Anglie tam spiritualem quam temporalium destruccionem proposuerunt.'

[69] PRO, C 66/393, m. 23d (*CPR 1413–16*, 177–8).   [70] Powell, *Kingship*, 150.

Bench, justices of the peace, and justice of assize to have full power to inquire into all persons holding any errors or heresies, such as lollards, as well as those who were their maintainers, receivers, and favourers. People who supported the writers of suspected books and sermons were to be investigated, as well as those who facilitated their schools, conventicles, congregations, and confederacies. This clause was to be written into the commissions of justices of the peace, and if anyone was indicted on any of these points, the justice had the authority to issue a writ of *capias* against that person, and the sheriff would then arrest him or her.[71]

This was essentially a restatement of the lapsed provisions of 1406, made palatable by the threat of insurrection, and made possible by eliding the distinction between heresy and treason. Justices could easily assimilate the detection of heresy to their duties if heresy were defined as participation in armed uprising against the church and crown. Certainly there were strong reasons for extending the state's power in this respect that were purely a product of political nervousness after the first Lancastrian succession, but it is also probable that Arundel had been hoping and working towards the resurrection of the 1406 statute for some time before his death in February 1414.[72] Whatever the reasons for its drafting, the 1414 statute itself contains a suggestion that the issue of encroachment was important. In a passage already quoted, it states that the cognizance of heresy, errors, and lollardy pertains to the judges of the church and not to secular judges. Consequently, indicted persons were to be delivered by indenture to their ordinary or his commissary within ten days of arrest, to be acquitted or convicted by the laws of the church. This was to be so unless the suspect was also indicted of any offence that was within the jurisdiction of a secular judge, in which case he or she was to

---

[71] *Statutes of the Realm*, ii. 182: 'Et outre ceo que les Justices du Bank le Roy et Justices du Pees et Justices dassises prendre eient pleine poair denquerer de toutz yceux que teignent ascuns errours ou heresies come Lollardes, et queux sount lour maintenours recettours fautours susteignours communes escrivers de tieux livres, sibien de lour sermons come de lour escoles conventicles congregacions et confederacies; et que ceste clause soit mys es Commissions des Justices de la Pees; et si ascuns persones soient enditez dascuns des pointz suisditz eient les ditz Justices poair de agarder vers eux Capias, et soit le Viscount tenuz darrester la persone ou persones ensy endite ou enditeez si tost come il les purra trover par luy ou par ses Officers.'

[72] Aston, *Arundel*, 376; *The Chronicle of Adam Usk*, ed. C. Given-Wilson (Oxford, 1997), 248, reports that Arundel had sought assurances from the new king that royal justices would be given the authority to make inquiries and issue indictments for heresy.

be judged on those counts first, and then delivered to the bishop. The potential for secular judgements to prejudice, and thereby encroach upon, ecclesiastical judgements in such cases was recognized and a remedy provided. Any indictment before a secular judge was not to be taken in evidence by an ecclesiastical judge, except as information, and the trial in the church court was to proceed as if there were no indictment, having no regard for any such indictment.[73]

This clause reveals the crown's main concern to have been treason rather than heresy. Heretics seemed most interesting or threatening when they might be treasonous rebels.[74] Despite early approbation from preachers and poets, Henry V's anti-heresy activity petered out fairly quickly.[75] Over forty pardons for involvement in the revolt were issued between June and December 1414 as a result of the county commissions begun before Parliament sat. Those investigations, which had mopped up most of the rebels apart from Oldcastle and a few others, had been conducted without the sanction of the new statute and indeed little use was made of it after it had been promulgated.[76] In 1415 Bishop Repingdon of Lincoln cited it in his proclamation of the purgation of Thomas Novery, who had been indicted according to its provisions by royal officers, and around the same time, Repingdon also mandated the abbot of Osney to receive lollards indicted before royal justices.[77] Either the reluctance of justices to use their new powers, or the hostility of bishops to the jurisdictional challenge they presented, or both, are illustrated in two later mentions of the 1414 statute. In 1427 a royal commission for the arrest

---

[73] *Statutes of the* Realm, ii. 183: 'en cas que yceux persones ne soient enditez dautre chose dcount la conusance appertient as Juges et Officers seculers; en quell cas apres ceo qils soient acquitez ou deliverez devant Juges Seculers de tiel chose appurtenant as Juges Seculers, soient envoiez en seure garde as ditz Ordinaries ou a lour Commissaries et a eux liverez par endentures come desuis, pour yestre acquitez ou convictz dicell Heresies errours ou Lollardries come avant est dit selonc les leies de Seinte Esglise, et ceo deinz le terme suisdit. Pourveu que les ditz enditementz ne soient prisez en evidence si non pour enformacion devant les Juges espirituelx encountre tieux enditez, mesque les Ordinaries commencent lour process envers tieux enditez en mesme la manere come null enditement y fuisse, eiantz null regard a tielx enditementz.'   [74] Powell, *Kingship*, 153.
[75] R. M. Haines, ' "Our Master Mariner, our Sovereign Lord": A Contemporary Preacher's View of King Henry V', *Mediaeval Studies*, 38 (1976), 90; Bodleian, MS Bodley 649, fo. 130ʳ; BL, MS Cotton Cleopatra B 1, fo. 173.
[76] *CPR 1413–16*, 237, 250, 261–2, 271. The 1414 statute was copied into at least four episcopal registers: *Reg. Chichele (Canterbury)*, iii. 358–60; Reg. Kempe (London), fos. 211ʳ–212ʳ; Reg. Wakeryng (Norwich), fos. 1ᵛ–2ᵛ; Reg. Stafford (Exeter), ii. fos. 322ʳ–323ᵛ.   [77] *Reg. Repingdon (Lincoln)*, iii. 70–1, 73–4.

of a heretic in Hampshire cited the statute, although it was Bishop Beaufort who had made the initial investigation, and in 1428 it was recommended to Convocation as a useful tool merely for the arrest of suspects.[78] The new powers of secular detection had lapsed once again, leaving the investigation of heresy firmly in the church's hands.

2. BISHOPS AND INQUISITORS

The events of 1413–14 had provoked a major change in the way it was thought heretics should be investigated. Hitherto, most inquiries had been reactive, investigating a few named persons, or unknown persons in a specific locality; but the sweeping inquiries launched in the wake of the Oldcastle revolt seem to have precipitated a more pre-emptive strategy. The parliamentary statute of 1414 was at the forefront of this change, as the product of the fertile relationship between Archbishop Arundel and the Lancastrian monarchy. When Henry Chichele succeeded to the see of Canterbury, a different relationship between church and crown was inevitable. Chichele was by no means antipathetic towards Henry V, nor indeed to Henry VI, but he was a lawyer by training and this may have caused him to re-examine the procedures then in place for dealing with heresy.[79]

Chichele's instincts in terms of anti-heresy policy were to trust to the episcopal administrators whose talents and character he knew, rather than to rely on the machinery of royal government. Within two years of the ground-breaking 1414 statute, the new archbishop had issued his own statute to introduce large-scale pre-emptive inquiries into heresy, effectively making his predecessor's secular statute obsolete, or at least hastening its demise. The statute promulgated on 1 July 1416 drew extensively on the investigative clauses of the bull *Excommunicamus* (1215), which in turn had taken over some of the terms of *Ad abolendam* (1179). Chichele thus brought England broadly into line with inquisitorial practice as it had existed on the continent for two centuries.

[78] PRO, C 66/421, m. 19d (*CPR 1422–29*, 546–8); Hudson, 'Examination of Lollards', 137.

[79] E. F. Jacob, *Archbishop Henry Chichele* (London, 1967); R. G. Davies, 'Martin V and the English Episcopate, with Particular Reference to his Campaign for the Repeal of the Statute of Provisors', *EHR* 92 (1977), 309–44.

We ordain that every bishop and archdeacon in the province of Canterbury, either himself or through his officials or commissaries throughout his jurisdiction, must make inquiries at least twice a year in every deanery into persons suspected of heresy. And in each deanery or parish where heretics are rumoured to live, three or more men of good witness are to swear on God's holy gospel whether there are any heretics, any persons holding secret conventicles, any persons differing in life and morals from the behaviour of the faithful, anyone holding errors or heresies, anyone owning suspicious books written in English, anyone receiving persons suspected of errors or heresies or their favourers, or anyone in the area who has had communication with them or visited them. Such persons, along with every circumstance by which they are suspected, are to be denounced and revealed in writing to our bishops or their archdeacons or commissaries as soon as possible and transmitted to the diocesan.

Mirroring the earlier parliamentary statute, suspects detected in this way were to be delivered to the next session of Convocation for judgement, unless they had already been relinquished to the secular arm for punishment.[80] The intention of this statute was much the same as that of 1414: to make the investigation of heresy an ongoing and pre-emptive activity, rather than a sporadic and reactive one. The changes from 1414 were that church officials not secular officers were to make the inquiries, and that investigation was to be a regularly repeated process rather than merely a constituent of a justice's general duties. Chichele's statute differed from its 1215 model only to make its provisions more stringent, ordering inquiries not once but twice a year, and specifying in detail the information which was to be gathered. It was envisaged that heresy inquisitions would become a regular fact of life in England.

---

[80] *Reg. Chichele (Canterbury)*, iii. 18–19: 'statuimus ut singuli confratres nostri suffraganei singulique archidiaconi nostre Cantuarien' provincie per se aut suos officiales sive commissarios in singulis suis jurisdiccionibus, in quolibet decanatu rurali ad minus bis in anno, de personis de heresi suspectis diligenter inquirant, ac in singulis decanatibus hujusmodi singulisque parochiis in quibus fama est hereticos habitare, tres vel plures boni testimonii viros ad sacra dei evangelia jurare faciant, ut si quos hereticos sive occulta conventicula celebrantes aut a communi conversacione fidelium vita et moribus discrepantes, heresesve aut errores tenentes, sive libros suspectos in lingua vulgari anglicana conscriptos habentes, aut personas de heresibus sive erroribus suspectas receptantes, eisdemve faventes, aut infra loca hujusmodi habitare conversari sive ad eadem recursum habere sciverint, ipsas personas cum singulis circumstanciis de quibus habentur suspecti, eisdem nostris suffraganeis, archidiaconisve aut eorumdem commissariis quam cito commode poterint in scriptis denuncient et relevent, ipsique archidiaconi singulique commissarii supradicti nomina hujusmodi personarum denunciata unacum singulis circumstanciis eorumdem diocesanis locorum sub suis sigillis secrete transmittant.'

There were some precedents for this decisive change of direction in anti-heresy policy, particularly with regard to the universities. Perceived as the source of lollardy, Oxford University came under particular scrutiny after 1382, as successive attempts were made to force it to accept some form of external supervision. The unwillingness of the university to accept this intrusion led to the concession of various 'episcopal' powers to the chancellor, such as the right to signify excommunicates himself in 1393, and the instruction to proceed against heresy 'per inquisitionem vel alio modo legitime' in 1395.[81] This culminated in Arundel's stipulation in his 1407 constitutions that wardens and provosts of Oxford halls and colleges must conduct investigations into the beliefs of their members at least once a month, under pain of excommunication.[82] Given Arundel's attempt to visit the university in person in 1411 it is doubtful whether this constitution was adhered to, but the intention indicates a desire to prevent heresy from spreading, even if it was only within the confines of the university.[83] We have no record of such monthly inquiries, and it is easy to see why they might not have been implemented, given the time and money they would consume. What then became of the proposed twice-yearly inquiries of 1416?

The short answer is that this statute was never fully implemented in the terms in which it was promulgated. Diocesans interpreted the statute either as adding heresy to the list of offences to be investigated during their ordinary triennial visitations, or as encouraging sweeping but still reactive extraordinary inquisitions. This dilution of Chichele's measure is perceptible almost immediately. In September 1416, Bishop Repingdon of Lincoln issued a mandate to the archdeacon of Leicester to inquire into heresy according to 'the holy canons and the provincial constitution that ordered every bishop to inquire into heresy in his diocese'.[84] This would seem to be the conscientious implementation of the July statute, but Repingdon went on to instruct his commissaries to inquire into plurality, non-residence of the clergy, unlicensed celebration of divine services, and the unlawful farming of benefices, as well as heresy, saying that it was by

---

[81] PRO, C 66/337, m. 1 (*CPR 1391–96*, 288); C 54/237, m. 24 (*CCR 1392–96*, 434).

[82] Reg. Arundel (Canterbury), ii. fo. 12ʳ, constitution 11.

[83] Hudson, *Premature Reformation*, 102–3.

[84] *Reg. Repingdon (Lincoln)*, iii. 157: 'sacros canones constitucionesque provinciales in hoc casu editas proinde sit statutum ut singuli episcopi in suis diocesibus contra hereticos ... diligenter inquirant.'

ordinary visitation that these vices were to be uprooted. The use of ordinary visitation continued, with Bishop Nevill of Salisbury ordering the examination of heretics discovered during a visitation of Berkshire archdeaconry in 1428, and Bishop Spofford of Hereford commissioning the chancellor of Hereford cathedral, the rector of Pembridge, and the vicar of Leominster to inquire into heresy suspects revealed 'in nostra visitacione ordinaria triennali' in 1433.[85]

Other records from the 1420s and 1430s suggest the use of the 1416 statute to implement large-scale *extraordinary* inquisitions, outside the run of either triennial or semi-annual investigations. In 1427 Nevill had instructed the abbots of Reading and Abingdon, the prior of Wallingford, and the archdeacons of Berkshire and Buckingham to inquire into heresy, repeating the formulae of 1416. The choice of agents, including one from outside the diocese, indicates that this was not part of a regular diocesan activity.[86] In 1435 Thomas Brouns, the bishop of Rochester, also interpreted 1416 as an order for extraordinary inquisitions.[87] Many records of post-1416 inquiries are somewhat deficient as evidence for the nature of the investigation undertaken, especially if only the trial or purgation documents survive. However, the irregularity of heresy cases in the courts, and the lack of any other indication of semi-annual investigations, suggests that the frequency envisaged by Chichele was nowhere achieved.

It is possible that the full implementation of the statute had always been more than Chichele had hoped for. This is suggested by his first unilateral action against heresy as archbishop in June 1414, which had been to instruct the keepers of the vacant see of Coventry and Lichfield to investigate heresy as part of their ordinary duties.[88] They put this into practice the same month, sending out a mandate to the archdeacon of Stafford to conduct a visitation to inquire about non-residence, the farming of benefices, the retention of property in breach of last wills and testaments, and anyone preaching heresies contrary to sound doctrine, amongst other crimes, defects, and excesses.[89] The midland region had seen how a heresy investigation annexed to an ordinary visitation could work only the previous summer, when Repingdon had visited Leicester

---

85 Reg. Nevill (Salisbury), part 2, fo. 77ᵛ; *Reg. Spofford (Hereford)*, 152–3.
86 Reg. Nevill (Salisbury), part 2, fo. 28ʳ. See Chapter 4 for inter-diocesan co-operation.
87 Reg. Brouns (Rochester), fos. 1ᵛ–2ʳ.
88 *Reg. Chichele (Canterbury)*, iii. 294–5.   89 Ibid. 295–7.

archdeaconry and uncovered seventeen instances of suspected heresy amongst the more usual offences.[90] Besides these examples, the incorporation of heresy into visitation articles at this particular time may have been influenced by developments on the continent, where the chancellor of Paris University, Jean Gerson, had recently advocated precisely such a course of action in his treatise *De visitacione prelatorum*.[91] This innovation effectively reunited inquisition with the ordinary episcopal jurisdiction out of which it had developed in the twelfth century.[92]

The major procedural benefit of using ordinary visitation instead of inquisitions specifically into heresy was that inquiries into one crime might reveal suspicions of another. The bishop who was interested in combating heresy was no less enthusiastic about the more general moral reformation of his diocese, and if evidence of clerical negligence arose during an inquiry into heresy, it was desirable to be able to deal with it there and then, rather than to have to instigate a fresh inquisition. This would be necessary since one of the safeguards against the abuse of inquisitorial procedure was that information uncovered in one inquiry could not be used in the prosecution of a different crime.[93] This is reflected in the stipulation that inquisitors could not judge sorcery or divination.[94]

It might be objected that bishops were not inquisitors. That is a question to which I will turn shortly. At this point it will suffice to say that inquisition was a procedure, not an office, and as such it was governed by rules just like any other judicial procedure, whether engaged in by bishops or inquisitors. By acting against heretics in ordinary visitations, where the actual procedures were in any case based upon inquisitorial technique, bishops could in theory avoid embarrassing and dangerous technical oversights, letting heretics slip through the net. Besides the legal restrictions on effectively implementing Chichele's policy, there were strong practical reasons for using ordinary visitation. The episcopal or archidiaconal visitor was restricted in what he could achieve by the cost of

---

[90] Lincolnshire Archives, MS Vj/0. See Chapter 8 for a detailed analysis.

[91] Jean Gerson, *Œuvres complètes*, ed. P. Glorieux, 10 vols. (Paris, 1960–73), viii. 50.

[92] Trusen, 'Der Inquisitionsprozess', 229; E. Brambilla, *Alle origini del Sant' Uffizio: Penitenza, confessione e giustizia spirituale dal Medioevo al XVI secolo* (Bologna, 2000), 93–7.

[93] Tancred, *Ordo iudiciarius*, pars 2, tit. 7, § 3, in *Pillii, Tancredi, Gratiae libri de iudiciorum ordine*, ed. F. Bergmann (Göttingen, 1842), 154 (all subsequent references to this edition).   [94] VI 5.2.8.

the activity and the time taken to complete it satisfactorily. Medieval episcopacy, for all that it was a sophisticated governmental machine, was not capable of increasing its workload sixfold, from one visitation every three years, to two each year.[95] Even if it is allowed that archdeacons and commissaries could do the work independently, not even the largest dioceses had the manpower to undertake what would in effect be continuous visitation.

Let us take the example of Repingdon's 1413 visitation of Leicester archdeaconry, the results of which are the subject of a more detailed study in Chapter 8. After an initial tour of the archdeaconry by the bishop lasting two weeks, David Pryce and Thomas Brouns took another fortnight to follow up the *comperta* and *detecta*, things found and discovered. About 10 per cent of these cases were only concluded at a further session in the episcopal manor of Sleaford seven months later, by which time, under Chichele's provisions, the next visitation would have begun. We may add to this the time taken to prepare for an investigation, sending out citations and instructions to archdeacons, rural deans, parish priests, and lay juries, whose reports had to be collected and collated before the visitation proper began. The time spent on this would take away resources from the regular workings of the consistory court and other administrative business. Medieval dioceses worked on the basis of a steady income from property, rents, and tithes, and there was little room for manoeuvre. Procurations, the payments made to the visitor by the parishes being visited, had been capped in the twelfth century, and so extra funds could not be squeezed out of the parochial economy.[96] It seems that this was simply not a price the bishops were willing or able to pay, even in the defence of the faith.

The character of episcopal jurisdiction and its relationship with inquisition brings us to the question of whether or not there was ever an inquisition in England. Frequent mention has already been made of inquisitions into heresy and inquisitorial activity, but nothing has been said of inquisitors in an English context. Was this because there were no inquisitors, and no 'inquisition'? Henry III had, after all, banned Bishop Grosseteste from using inquisitorial techniques in 1252, complaining that fields were left untilled during his visitations.[97] As has already been

---

[95] R. M. Haines, *The Administration of the Diocese of Worcester in the First Half of the Fourteenth Century* (London, 1965), 148–64, describes a much less intensive programme of visitation.

[96] X 3.39.6; C. R. Cheney, *Episcopal Visitation of Monasteries in the Thirteenth Century* (2nd edn., Manchester, 1983), 104–6.   [97] *CCR 1251–53*, 224–5.

suggested, the question is slightly misleading. If by inquisition we mean a group of professional heresy hunters with their own institutional structure, hierarchy, and personnel, then the answer must be a qualified no, but if we mean a set of legal techniques and investigative practices, then we are closer to the mark. Delegated inquisitors could be appointed by either a bishop, a secular ruler, or the pope. Alternatively bishops could use inquisitorial procedures themselves while remaining within the bounds of their ordinary jurisdiction.[98] In England the usual practice was for bishops to implement inquisitorial procedures themselves, a situation which was encouraged by the relative wealth and organization of episcopal administration in England when compared with the rest of Europe, as well as by a domestic tradition of episcopal responsibility for heresy in canon law.

On 20 March 1388 several heresy suspects had been arraigned before an ecclesiastical tribunal which included William Bottlesham, bishop of Llandaff, among its number. 'On sight of the bishop the Lollards declared that they were not bound to appear or make any answer before that tribunal, which did not contain any judges, since the bishop was a friar and an apostate and the rest not qualified to hear them or to determine the matter.'[99] The defendants' view seems to have been that no one might judge them, but on closer inspection their objection is to Bottlesham's membership of a religious order, which they believe disqualified him from being a bishop. In fact this story shows that properly ordained bishops were the only judges popularly thought capable of determining a case of heresy. This view was not without foundation. In a country which had never had extensive experience of heresy or the apparatus of papally appointed inquisition, canonical texts that connected heresy with episcopal jurisdiction were commonplace. For example, even though Boniface VIII's canon *Ut commissi* had given delegated inquisitors the authority to issue citations and determine sentences, James le Palmere's *Omne bonum* argues that only a bishop may excommunicate a heretic, and William Paul's *Summa summarum* says that only a bishop may reconcile a heretic.[100] Another fourteenth-century English collection of canon law texts contains two treatises which discuss heresy only insofar as it is

[98] Clem. 5.3.2.

[99] *The Westminster Chronicle 1381–1394*, ed. L. C. Hector and B. F. Harvey (Oxford, 1982), 319–21.

[100] VI 5.2.12; BL, MS Royal 6 E VII, fo. 200ᵛ; Bodleian, MS Bodley 293, fo. 178ʳ.

a crime reserved for episcopal attention. These were William Durandus' *Repertorium* and William of Roving's tract on *casus reseruati*.[101]

In some areas of Christendom, such as Languedoc in the thirteenth century, mendicant inquisitors virtually controlled anti-heresy activity, with bishops playing a supporting role, if any at all. In other times and places, bishops acted against heresy without the presence of inquisitors, as in the diocese of Utrecht in the early fourteenth century, the archbishopric of Prague between 1344 and 1361, and the diocese of Magdeburg in the 1380s.[102] If the phenomenon of heresy is looked at across the European Middle Ages, a pattern emerges of experimentation with episcopal inquisition giving way to the use of specially delegated inquisitors. In Languedoc and Italy, for instance, the rather lacklustre campaigns against heresy by local rulers and bishops gave way in 1231 to the papally appointed Dominican inquisition.[103] Nevertheless, inquisitors were not given completely free rein in any region, being required to co-operate with the local bishop, each keeping the other informed of their activities, and acting jointly whenever possible. This co-operation could lead to conflict, and so legally defined standards of communication and reciprocation were introduced in the later thirteenth century.[104] The model of bishop and inquisitor working together became more prevalent after these changes, and was common in the Italian and German states during the fourteenth and fifteenth centuries.[105] This co-operation itself became unwieldy as time went on, and in places gave way to an inquisition run by the secular authorities, as in England for a time, but more definitely in Spain after 1478.[106] This long-term trend towards a specialized inquisition was aided by legislation allowing for unsuccessful or incompetent episcopal inquisitors to be deposed and replaced by more energetic or amenable men, a proposal which was mooted by Oxford University in

[101]　BL, MS Royal 11 A XIV, fos. 149ʳ–150ʳ, 153ᵛ–154ʳ.

[102]　Lerner, *Free Spirit*, 67; R. Zeleny, 'Councils and Synods of Prague and their Statutes (1343–1361)', *Apollinaris*, 45 (1972), 475–6; D. Kurze, *Quellen zur Ketzergeschichte Brandenburgs und Pommerns* (Berlin, 1975), 71–3.

[103]　Lambert, *Medieval Heresy*, 108–9; M. D'Alatri, *Eretici e inquisitori in Italia: Studi e documenti*, 2 vols. (Rome, 1987), i. 118.　　　　　　　　　　[104]　VI 5.2.17.

[105]　Merlo, *Eretici e inquisitori*, 128; H. Grundmann, 'Ketzerverhöre des Spätmittelalters als quellenkritisches Problem', *Deutsches Archiv für Erforschung des Mittelalters*, 21 (1965), 535–50; P. Gios, *L'inquisitore della Bassa Padovana e dei Colli Euganei, 1448–1449* (Candiana, 1990), 71 ff.

[106]　Escamilla, *Synthèse sur l'inquisition espagnole*, 27.

1414, and attempted in 1411 by an Ely Dominican who was disappointed by Bishop Fordham's lack of anti-heretical energy.[107]

The enthusiasm and ability of most English bishops contrasted with this picture of Fordham, which may itself have been nothing more than an accusation born of some other dispute. The hierarchy and structures of a widespread papally delegated inquisition were not introduced in the 1380s, as they had been temporarily in the early fourteenth century to deal with the English Templars, because the bishops could do their job. The canon *Per hoc* of Boniface VIII had urged that when heresy was dealt with by someone delegated by the papacy to a province, city, or diocese, *or by a bishop*, whether in his capacity as ordinary or with specially delegated powers, and that person proceeded with vigour, his responsibility should not be taken away.[108] If episcopal inquisition was successful there was no need for special delegations. That canon also emphasized that inquisition was a set of procedures constituting a special jurisdiction, not an office, and that a bishop could himself act against heresy as diocesan ordinary or as a delegated inquisitor. In this light it is worth investigating further the question of whether there were inquisitors working in England.

At the end of May 1382, Convocation issued a mandate to the bishops of the province ordering inquiries into heresy. The terms of the mandate suggest that inquisitors may have been working in England: 'according to the relevant canons anyone who is an inquisitor into heresy in his city and diocese should inquire carefully and diligently into these presumptions and proceed against them according to his particular office, so should you [each bishop] who are similarly placed also inquire and proceed, to the praise and honour of the name of the crucifix and for the salvation of the orthodox faith.'[109] This refers to the clause of *Per hoc* that states, 'if bishops proceed by ordinary or delegated power, they are to observe all in the

---

[107] Hostiensis, *Summa aurea*, 1534; 'Articles for the reform of the church' c. 43 in Wilkins, *Concilia*, iii. 365; *CPL 1404–15*, 299. Bishop Fordham's register contains a copy of *De heretico comburendo*, but no evidence of any investigation.

[108] VI 5.2.17: 'Per hoc, quod negotium haereticae pravitatis alicui vel aliquibus ab apostolica sede generaliter in aliqua provincia, civitate vel diocesi delegatur, diocesanis episcopis, quin et ipsi auctoritate ordinaria vel delegata, si habent, in eodem procedere valeant, nolumus derogari.'

[109] Reg. Courtenay (Canterbury), fo. 26: 'cum iuxta sacrorum canonum instituta quilibet eorundem in suis ciuitatibus et diocesibus heretice prauitatis inquisitor existat ac vos in vestris similiter existatis de huius presumptoribus sollicite et diligenter inquirant et inquiratis ac contra eos iuxta officii sui debitum cum effectu procedant et similiter procedatis ad laudem et honorem nominis crucifixi et saluacionem fidei ortodoxe.'

ius commune that applies to inquisitors, and all special instructions from the apostolic see.'[110] There is some evidence to suggest that occasionally the English bishops did act as delegated inquisitors, beyond the limits of their ordinary jurisdiction. In 1392 Bishop Trefnant of Hereford was having trouble laying hands on the fugitive William Swinderby, who had moved from the diocese of Lincoln to the border lands of the Welsh Marches and the limits of English common law. Perhaps in the false belief that the king's justices could not reach him if he hopped into Wales, Swinderby, his associate Stephen Belle, and other unnamed accomplices also moved outside the ordinary jurisdiction of the bishop of Hereford.[111] In order to pursue them, the bishop required special authority, which he received from the king in a letter of 9 March. The royal letter repeated the formulations of the 1382 licence for the episcopal arrest of offenders, explaining that a new letter was necessary because 'the vigour of our letters does not extend there'.[112] Although this was primarily an extension of the royal writ into Wales, Trefnant was also being asked to operate outside his diocese, making this an example of inquisitorial jurisdiction delegated by the crown.

A bishop could also be delegated as an inquisitor by a fellow bishop. This happened in December 1428 when Bishop Alnwick of Norwich called in Henry Beaufort, the bishop of Winchester and cardinal of St Eusebius, to investigate and judge reports of heresy in Bury St Edmunds. This delegation was necessary for two reasons. At the time Alnwick was busy overseeing heresy trials elsewhere in the diocese, and the reports from Bury were irritating because the town was exempt from episcopal jurisdiction. Beaufort was called in to assist the abbot of Bury, who had initially been instructed to carry out the investigation. Alnwick's choice of Beaufort may have been determined by the cardinal's high profile in anti-heresy work, having recently been put in charge of organizing the crusade against the Hussites.[113]

---

[110] VI 5.2.17: 'Sive autem ordinaria sive delegata episcopi potestate procedant: illum in procedendo modum observent, quem inquisitores possunt et debent per iura communia, vel per speciales concessiones seu ordinationes sedis apostolicae observare.'

[111] On Swinderby's opinion of royal justice see S. Jenks, 'Die Rolle von König und Klerus bei der Häretikerverfolgung in England', *Zeitschrift für Kirchengeschichte*, 99 (1988), 23–46.

[112] PRO, C 66/334, m. 20 (*CPR 1391–96*, 40–1): 'ad quas vigor dictarum litterarum nostrarum nullatenus se extendit.'

[113] Reg. Alnwick (Norwich), fos. 108ʳ–109ᵛ; G. Harriss, *Cardinal Beaufort: A Study of Lancastrian Ascendancy and Decline* (Oxford, 1988), 174–6.

A more problematic case concerns the jurisdiction of Walter Skirlaw and William Grene in Calais. Skirlaw was the bishop of Durham from 1388 to 1406, but also commissary for the English possessions in Calais and the surrounding area, which was nominally at least within the diocese of Thérouanne. Grene was the rector of St Mary's church in Calais.[114] Around 1401 Skirlaw was ordered to proceed against named persons suspected of heretical and erroneous wickedness, apostasy, and diverse crimes and enormities in the area. In January 1404 a further mandate was sent from Canterbury to William Grene, as warden of the spirituality of Calais, and friar John Wrotham, to make inquiries into the same problem.[115] These commissions reflect a special delegation from Canterbury which had been in effect since the treaty of Brétigny in 1360, and had been authorized by a papal grant in 1379. Both Grene and Skirlaw were exercising ordinary jurisdiction in the area, which in Skirlaw's case qualified him to act against heresy, since he was a bishop elsewhere. Grene, however, was not a bishop, and as such had to be delegated as an inquisitor in order to investigate and judge heresy. He and Wrotham were thus inquisitors into heresy, appointed by Archbishop Arundel.

Other non-episcopal churchmen were delegated by bishops as inquisitors. As archbishop, Arundel was very active in issuing these commissions himself. Around 1400 he delegated the prior of St Bartholomew's hospital in Smithfield, London, to investigate reports of heresy in his own institution, and William Melton, the archbishop's registrar, to investigate lollardy and other abuses in St John's hospital in Bristol.[116] In 1427 Thomas Bekynton, who was archdeacon of Buckingham in Lincoln diocese, was appointed by the bishop of Salisbury to assist with the investigation of heretics on the border of Lincoln and Salisbury dioceses on the Thames south of Oxford. As with Trefnant in Wales, delegated inquisitorial jurisdiction was necessary because the two ordinaries could not operate in each other's diocese. Bekynton's authority in Berkshire only extended to heresy cases, in line with the restrictions of *Ut commissi* and *Per hoc* outlined above.[117] Ordinary jurisdiction covered all offences within a geographical area, while inquisitorial jurisdiction covered a single

[114] I. J. Churchill, *Canterbury Administration: The Administrative Machinery of the Archbishopric of Canterbury Illustrated from Original Records*, 2 vols. (London, 1933), i. 510–11.   [115] Reg. Arundel (Canterbury), i. fos. 105ʳ, 138.
[116] Ibid., fos. 105ʳ, 125ʳ.   [117] Reg. Nevill (Salisbury), part 2, fo. 28ʳ.

offence, similarly within a defined region. The detection of heresy in England was carried out by bishops with the assistance of specially delegated inquisitors, who might be bishops themselves, but were sometimes diocesan officials or heads of religious houses. Without episcopal authority, the status afforded by the bishop's commission was for them a necessary precondition to their investigation of heresy.

It may seem as though there was no papally appointed inquisition in England, but this may well be a trick of the sources, since most cases of heresy that have come to the notice of historians were those that survived in bishops' registers or their court-books. However, there are some sources that suggest this is not the whole story. The passage in the Westminster Chronicle discussed above mentions that in 1388 Bottlesham was part of a heresy tribunal headed by the pope's sub-collector in England, Master Thomas Southam. Southam was a bachelor of canon law and since 1383 had been the deputy of the papal nuncio, Cosmato Gentili de Sulmona. He was appointed to the tribunal by Parliament, where rumours of four lollard preachers had caused an uproar.[118] This would make him an inquisitor delegated by the secular authority, but an entry in the papal registers suggests that he or his superior may also have been a papally appointed inquisitor. Southam's tribunal met in March and April 1388, and in May Pope Urban VI appointed James Dardani, a clerk of the papal court, to replace Cosmato Gentili as nuncio and collector and receiver of the papal revenues in England, Scotland, and Ireland, with special authority to hear the accounts and receive the dues of inquisitors into heresy.[119] It is possible that the pope considered Southam to be an inquisitor, which may in turn suggest that he had been papally appointed. It was certainly quite normal in other areas of Europe for inquisitors to act alongside bishops, and in fact the distinction between the two jurisdictions could become quite blurred.[120]

In addition to these traces there are a few more concrete references to papally delegated inquisitors. In 1423 Pope Martin V delegated the bishop of Trieste to reconcile heretics and schismatics in England and absolve them from excommunication, and in 1444 similar duties were given to Baptisma de Padua for England, Scotland, Ireland, Germany,

---

[118] *Westminster Chronicle*, 319; *BRUO*, iii. 1733.   [119] *CPL 1362–1404*, 267.
[120] L. A. Anaya Hernández, *Judeoconversos e inquisición en las Islas Canarias (1402–1605)* (Las Palmas, 1996), 169.

and Holland, perhaps lumping the English Wycliffite 'lollards' with the continental Beghard 'lollards'.[121] The assumption that there was no inquisition in England must, it seems, be abandoned. There were both English inquisitors, delegated by popes, bishops, archbishops, and the crown, and foreign inquisitors, direct agents of papal authority with jurisdiction over *ecclesia anglicana*. Although we do not know whether Baptisma de Padua ever came to England, the possibility that he and the other papal inquisitors were appointed in response to perceptions of English negligence is sobering in the light of the reputations of Richard II, Henry V, and archbishops Arundel and Chichele as scourges of heretics. In 1395 Boniface IX had warned the archbishops of Canterbury and York (Courtenay and Arundel) that they risked severe penalties if they did not act immediately against heresy. No English bishop was ever deposed for being lukewarm in the anti-heresy cause, but the possibility of papal action is still worth pondering alongside Stubbs's view of English particularism.

England was integrated into a juridical culture that covered all of Christendom, but the investigation of heresy in late medieval England was peculiar to that time and place. The particular relationships between successive kings, archbishops, Parliaments, and Convocations served to create a pattern of investigation that was unique. At the same time it was thoroughly grounded in canon law and would have been recognizable to any papal appointee, wherever he came from. Churchmen took their responsibilities under the *ius commune* very seriously indeed, as did the crown, especially under Richard II. This brought the two powers into occasional conflict, but the dominant theme was of co-operation, with lapses in enthusiasm on both sides from time to time. This then was the shape of heresy investigation. How detection was to be achieved within it is the subject of the next chapter.

---

[121] *CPL 1417–31*, 13; *CPL 1427–47*, 297. On Beghards and Beguines described as lollards from 1300 onwards see Lerner, *Free Spirit*, 40.

3

The Techniques of Detection

Because heresy was a diffuse category of sin that was defined by such inscrutable aspects of personality as choice, will, and conscience, and because the legal category of *heretic* was created only at the moment a suspect was condemned, the techniques of detection were meant to reveal signs of heresy rather than clues about heretics. As we have seen there was considerable debate over who exactly was qualified to judge heresy, and this question had a bearing on detection since the evaluation of suspicion naturally involved a degree of judgement. The techniques of detection had to reflect the difficulty of knowing for sure who was or was not a potential heretic, a difficulty that was considerably magnified when the detecting relied in part upon the involvement of the unschooled: the parish clergy and the laity. Consequently the signs of heresy had to be simplified. This was achieved through licensing, which made suspicion subject to a simple documentary check, and reporting, which allowed the unschooled to make their suspicions known to a better-educated judge.

1. LICENSING

Heresy was feared most as a social problem, spread by word of mouth. Although books emanating from universities were crucial to the spread of Wycliffite ideas, the dreaded popularization of those ideas occurred through preaching, an activity that had always been restricted, even for those privileged by status or learning. On certain occasions bishops could preach in their own cathedrals only at the will of their chapters; parish priests were limited to their own churches; and in university towns academic sermons had to be delivered in Latin to prevent their comprehension by the laity. Other classes of preacher were even more heavily circumscribed, in accordance with the frequently cited question posed by St Paul: how may they preach unless they are sent?[1] Sending, or authority to preach, was a hotly contested issue throughout the Middle Ages, with controversy centring on whether that authority could come directly from God or whether it had to be mediated by some temporal authority. Heretics, Wycliffites included, often fell into the former camp, claiming inspiration or a divine calling to the task of preaching. The response of ecclesiastical authority was to tighten up the regulations governing preaching, asserting the principle of sending by temporal authorization. Historically only priests had been allowed to preach,[2] but by the late twelfth century Thomas of Chobham was pointing out that the number of sufficiently educated priests was too small and the word of God was not being properly proclaimed to the laity. In his *Summa de arte praedicandi* he proposed that 'literate men who are not priests or even perhaps deacons may preach the word of God in churches and instruct the people, but, however, they ought not to do this unless asked by the priest or prelate of the church in question'.[3] Thomas's literate men were most probably university graduates who had not taken priestly orders. His comment was a liberal interpretation of Clement III's instruction that any secular priest or member of a religious order who held a licence from the bishop was to be accepted as a preacher.[4] The implication of this was that those without such a licence should not be accepted.

In two cases pre-dating the problem of heretical preaching in England, the possession of licences became a major issue. When heresy moved to the fore of the political agenda these earlier experiences naturally informed the response. The first group of preachers to be restricted by licences had been persons collecting alms for charitable purposes, often the building of a great church or shrine, at home or abroad.[5] In return for

---

[1] Rom. 10: 15. On preaching in general see H. L. Spencer, *English Preaching in the Late Middle Ages* (Oxford, 1993).   [2] C. 16 q. 1 c. 19.

[3] Thomas of Chobham, *Summa de arte praedicandi*, ed. F. Morenzoni, Corpus Christianorum Continuatio Mediaevalis, 82 (Turnhout, 1988), 59: 'uiri literati, quamuis non sint sacerdotes nec forte diaconi, predicent uerbum Dei in ecclesiis et instruant populum, sed tamen hoc non debent facere nisi rogati a sacerdotibus uel a prelatis illarum ecclesiarum in quibus predicent.'

[4] X 5.6.10: 'indulgemus, ut quicunque religiosi seu clerici . . . requisita et habita praelatorum suorum licentia, tibi voluerint adhaerere.'

[5] R. N. Swanson, *Treasuring Merit/Craving Indulgence: Accounting for Salvation in Pre-Reformation England* (Birmingham, 2003).

alms they would preach and confer indulgences granted by the pope, playing on people's desire for salvation in the afterlife as well as their desire for news and information in this life. The word of God, however, was not to be sold but freely given, leading to the restriction of alms collectors' activities in two thirteenth-century papal decrees.[6] Such legislation was open to reinterpretation in the light of the Wycliffite problem in the fourteenth century. In 1386, for example, the bishop of Exeter issued a decree against the preaching of false alms collectors, who were 'sowing [*seminantes*] many excesses, abuses, and errors through the city and diocese'. In large part this was a reissue of a statute drafted for Exeter diocese in 1287 by Peter Quivel, except for the image of preachers sowing error, which may have been a response to an as yet ill-defined fear of heresy in the diocese.[7]

Alms collectors aroused the suspicions of ecclesiastical authorities because they were not part of the parish system, which allowed a modicum of control over the preaching done in parish churches. Other itinerants who upset the stabilities of thirteenth-century settled society included the mendicant friars, especially the Franciscans and Dominicans. These two orders had been given a general licence in 1300 by Boniface VIII to preach freely except in parish churches or at times when the local clergy customarily preached, otherwise than by special licence.[8] Two licences were thus envisaged: one general and pertaining to the whole order, the other specific and subject to the relationship between individual friars and the ecclesiastical hierarchy. In England the interpretation of this canon tended to be hostile to the friars, with individual licences being issued where Boniface's general one was, strictly speaking, sufficient.[9] The English dioceses indeed had a record of legal hostility to the friars going back to the first appearance of Franciscans in the 1220s, when the bishop of Winchester and a provincial council at London reiterated the principle that no one should preach unless he possessed a special licence identifying him as an 'authentic' person sent by the bishop or archdeacon.[10] The Statutes of Chichester of 1289 eschewed this coyness, overtly naming and condemning mendicant preaching.[11]

---

[6] Thomas of Chobham, *Summa*, 60; X 5.38.14 (*Cum ex eo*) and Clem. 5.9.1 (*Abusionibus*).

[7] *Reg. Brantyngham (Exeter)*, ii. 607–8; *Councils and Synods*, ii. 1043.

[8] Clem. 3.7.2.

[9] B. Z. Kedar, 'Canon Law and Local Practice: The Case of Mendicant Preaching in Late Medieval England', *Bulletin of Medieval Canon Law*, NS 2 (1972), 17–32.

[10] *Councils and Synods*, i. 128, 648.   [11] Ibid. ii. 1088–9.

The peculiar requirement that friars have individual licences to preach meant that the legislation against them, like that against alms collectors, was available as a model to later bishops legislating against heretical preaching. Legal continuity, together with a recurring difficulty in perceiving differences between radical Franciscans and Wycliffite preachers, meant that some English anti-heresy legislation was interpreted as having an anti-mendicant intention.[12] In particular, shortly after Arundel's 1409 prohibition of unlicensed preaching (which will be discussed in more detail below), the archbishop received reports that certain bishops had wrongly interpreted it to include all mendicants, against the clear intention of the statute.[13] Lyndwood felt the need to clarify this matter further in the 1420s, when he glossed Arundel's constitution with the comment that 'Dominicans and Franciscans are authorized by the *ius commune* to preach freely according to the form and limitations of the canon *Dudum a Bonifacio*'.[14] Familiarity with preaching licences and a willingness to use them, albeit on occasion rather too enthusiastically, made this an effective tool in the detection of heresy.

The practical usefulness of preaching licences lay in the prospect of being able to tell who was a heretic by a simple documentary check. Philosophically the possession or lack of a valid licence symbolized whether the preacher possessed divine authorization. The disparity between checking papers and checking a divine sending was lessened by the fact that preachers lacking the proper licence were only made suspect of heresy; they were not made heretics. An episcopal judge or inquisitor would subsequently give his attention to the case, and come to a decision based on whatever further information his investigations turned up. Despite Arundel's concern that friars should not be tarred with suspicion, if they were preaching unlicensed in a place or at a time that was restricted, suspicion could legitimately fall upon them. The same was

---

[12] On confusion between friars and lollards see R. N. Swanson, 'The "Mendicant Problem" in the Later Middle Ages', in P. Biller and B. Dobson (eds.), *The Medieval Church: Universities, Heresy and the Religious Life*, SCH, Subsidia, 11 (Woodbridge, 1999), 224–6; L. M. Clopper, 'Franciscans, Lollards, and Reform', in Somerset et al. (eds.), *Lollards and their Influence*, 177–96.

[13] Reg. Arundel (Canterbury), ii. fo. 119ʳ: 'sinistre interpretari nituntur . . . contra mentem ipsius statuti manifestam.'

[14] Lyndwood, *Provinciale*, 289, v. *auctorizatus est*: 'fratres praedicatores et minores auctorizati sunt de iure communi, ut possint libere predicare secundum formam eis limitatem in c. dudum.'

true for alms collectors, or indeed for anyone preaching without authorization.

In twelfth- and early thirteenth-century legislation against heresy, no mention was made of how a system of licensing should operate, although the principle that no one may preach unless sent was frequently reiterated. In 1184 Lucius III inveighed against preachers without proper authorization, and in 1199 Innocent III heard that lay men and women in the city and diocese of Metz had been translating the Gospels, Paul's letters, the psalter, and Gregory the Great's *Moralia in Job* into 'gallico' and using these as preaching material. Parish priests were reported to have collaborated with them, but no provision for checking licences was suggested as a result. Gregory IX likewise stipulated that no lay person should preach, but offered no remedy if they were found doing so.[15] It is likely that some system of checking licences was assumed in these papal pronouncements, probably by whoever of the clergy suspected the authorization of a preacher in their locality. In the second half of the thirteenth century Hostiensis concluded that the parish clergy were responsible for preventing the laity from preaching, for checking the licences of clergy seeking to preach, and for allowing bishops to preach in their churches.[16]

When the English episcopacy came to use preaching licences to control and detect heresy there was initially some confusion or disagreement about exactly how they should be checked. The statute promulgated by William Courtenay on 30 May 1382 spoke of the archbishop's desire to halt the spread of the lethal contagion of heresy that was slaying many souls, and ordered that no one preach without proper authority and no one hear or listen to the sermons of an unlicensed preacher or help him in any way. Instead they were to flee him on pain of excommunication as if he were a venomous snake emitting poison.[17] With the emphasis on the responses of the sermon audience to an unlicensed preacher, no provision was made for detecting such preaching before it happened. A similar lack of practical sense is found in a mandate issued nine days before Courtenay's statute by Bishop Wykeham of Winchester. Citing 'holy

---

[15] X 5.7.9, 12, 14.   [16] Hostiensis, *Summa aurea*, 1542.

[17] Reg. Courtenay (Canterbury), fo. 26ʳ: 'quod tam perniciosum malum quod in plurimos serpere poterit eorum animas letali contagione necando . . . ne . . . aliquem predicantem audiat vel ascultet seu ei faueat vel adhereat publice vel occulte sed statim tanquam serpentem venenum pestiferum emittentem fugiat et euitet sub pena excommunicacionis maioris.'

canons in which it is found that no one, unless sent, may take upon themselves the office of preaching in a church or other public place', Wykeham prohibited the admission of Nicholas Hereford and others to preach in the diocese, but did not take any wider steps to stop unlicensed preaching by others in the future.[18] In contrast, Thomas Arundel's anti-heresy mandate for Ely diocese, issued one day before Wykeham's, did specify who was to check preaching licences. The mandate states that 'each and every one of our subjects, ecclesiastical and secular of both sexes, should on our behalf prevent, just as we ourselves in the present document prohibit you to admit or permit, anyone to preach in their churches, chapels, oratories, cemeteries, cities, villages, or other places whether sacred or profane, unless they are constituted by a letter of admission or our special licence.'[19] When compared with the archiepiscopal measure released ten days later, this one seems much more practical and far-sighted. Perhaps we have an indication here, at the very beginning of anti-heresy activity in England, of the vigour by which Arundel's later career was to be characterized. The contrast between the Ely and the Canterbury measures may be explained by the possibility that Arundel was absent from the crucial sessions of Courtenay's Convocation at London Blackfriars, and not able to influence the decisions taken.[20]

Even so, what exactly was meant or envisaged by these three measures is not necessarily immediately clear from the texts as they stand. Wykeham's is the most straightforward, dealing with named and known heretics, but can we really believe that the archbishop of Canterbury in 1382 would have hoped to defeat heresy by ordering people to run away from it? It is likely that Courtenay's statute was meant for guidance only, and since it was directed to the bishops of the province, we may suppose that it was they who would arrange for checks on the licences of suspect itinerant preachers. That this was the situation throughout the province

---

[18] *Reg. Wykeham (Winchester)*, ii. 337–8: 'Et evidenter in sacris canonibus est repertum, quod nullus, nisi qui mittitur, debeat in ecclesia Dei vel aliis locis publicis sibi predicacionis officium usurpare.'

[19] Reg. Arundel (Ely), fos. 41ᵛ–42ʳ: 'mandamus quatinus omnibus et singulis subditis nostris ecclesiasticis et secularibus vtriusque sexus ex parte nostra interdicatis et inhibeatis, interdici et inhiberi efficaciter faciatis quibus nos etiam tenore presencium interdicimus et inhibemus ne aliquos ad predicandum in eorum ecclesiis capellis oratoriis cimiteriis ciuitatibus villis seu plateis aut locis aliis sacris seu prophanis admittant . . . aut eos predicare permittant nisi tales sunt de quorum admissione littera seu licencia nostra speciali legitime constiterit.' [20] Aston, *Arundel*, 147n.

is suggested by a comment in the Wycliffite sermon cycle, whose production Hudson and Gradon date to the late 1380s: 'þus axen prinsis of prestis today, whanne men tellen by þe gospel þe defautis þat ben in þes princes, "Who yaf þe leeue to preche? Y suspende þee wiþoute my leeue to preche in my diosise".'[21] 'Princes' here are princes of the church, meaning the bishops, and they are caricatured in the process of personally challenging the sending of a preacher. However, as a caricature it is a polemical point against bishops, and may not indicate actual practice. Arundel's mandate is more detailed, and it seems to suggest that all persons in the diocese, clerical and lay, are responsible for making checks. That may be too general an interpretation, as the pronoun 'their' preceding the list of places indicates that it was persons in positions of authority over these places who were to check the licences of anyone wishing to preach there. However, the range of places listed would extend the category of 'persons in authority' from abbots, abbesses, rectors, and patrons to, possibly, village elders, manorial officials, churchwardens, and so on. On the other hand the phrase 'on our behalf' may indicate that only those whose office linked them directly to episcopal authority were expected to make the checks. This interpretation is encouraged by there being only a single instance, in 1413, when secular officers were instructed to check preaching licences, despite their experience in checking other ecclesiastical documents.[22] In any case, Archbishop Courtenay does not seem to have caught up with his more progressive suffragan until 1391 when he issued a mandate to the bishops of Llandaff and St David's to prevent their subjects from *admitting* William Swinderby to preach.[23]

The anti-heresy statute of 1401, *Contre les lollardes*, more widely known by the name of the writ *De heretico comburendo* associated with it, was not drafted with detection in mind. Burning and confiscation are the major areas of innovation, and very little is said about preaching licences, or indeed about inquiries, beyond a reiteration of the canonical limitations. Interestingly, after his thoroughgoing measures for Ely in 1382, Arundel, now archbishop, reverted to the sense of Courtenay's 1382 statute in prohibiting the act of preaching without a licence, rather than the act of admitting the unlicensed preacher. Faced with Wycliffites

---

[21] *English Wycliffite Sermons*, iii. 251.
[22] PRO, C 54/263, m. 22d (*CCR 1413–19*, 86).
[23] Reg. Courtenay (Canterbury), fo. 338ʳ.

committed to preaching without licences, this was of little value. Real strengthening of the legal position with regard to licensing did not come until 1409, when Arundel's constitutions formulated two years earlier were finally promulgated. The first constitution concerns the licensing of preaching, and although the wording is not obviously derivative of earlier measures taken in this area it must be read in the light of twenty-seven years of searching for unlicensed heretical preachers, and two centuries of regulating other kinds of preachers by licence. Helen Spencer has indeed argued that 'as far as preaching went, the new provisions either reaffirmed pre-existing restrictions, or gave legal force to well-understood principles'.[24] We have seen that the exemption of the friars from these restrictions was well understood neither before nor after Arundel's legislation; but still the place of 1409 in a long tradition is very clear. To begin with, the duty of checking licences was allocated to parish priests, which may be seen as potentially less effective than the Ely mandate, but much more specific than the previous provincial legislation on the topic. In addition licences were required to be carried and exhibited 'realiter', which Lyndwood understood to mean that the vicar of the place must be able to see, read, and understand it. The process of issuing licences was also regulated, with provision made for the examination of preachers' morals, knowledge, and honesty, interpreted by Lyndwood to mean that the orthodox preacher should be upright, discrete, modest, and sufficiently experienced as a preacher. In knowledge he should be competent rather than eminent, and as for honesty, that meant blamelessness, usefulness, and fitness for the job.[25]

The efficacy of licences as a way of discovering heretical preachers also depended on the church's definition of preaching. The normal understanding was that preaching was public and distinguished from teaching, which was private. Spencer points out that teaching in private homes was an activity whose legitimacy, content notwithstanding, could be invoked to defend against charges of unlicensed preaching. Conversely it is clear from subsequent practice, as well as the restrictions on teaching itself in the fifth constitution of 1409, that bishops and inquisitors were quite prepared to conflate the two categories for judicial purposes.[26] Licensing was also used in the tenth constitution, in order to control unbeneficed

---

[24] Spencer, *English Preaching*, 164.
[25] Reg. Arundel (Canterbury), ii. fos. 10ᵛ–11ʳ; Lyndwood, *Provinciale*, 289.
[26] Spencer, *English Preaching*, 33–54.

chaplains celebrating divine services in dioceses other than that where they had been ordained. Such a chaplain was only to be admitted if he could exhibit his letters of ordination and letters of commendation either from his diocesan, or from the bishop of a diocese where he had lived for a long time.[27] These letters were to detail the habits and morals of the bearer and state whether he was suspected of any 'novel opinions' against the catholic faith, and whether he was free from suspicion.

Spencer's view of the constitution against preaching as derivative is correct, despite Arundel's assertion that these were 'nouellas constituciones', and despite the reaction of the Wycliffite author of the *Lanterne of Li3t*, who decried

þise *newe* constituciouns, bi whos strengþe anticrist enterditiþ chirchis, soumneþ prechours, suspendiþ resceyuours & priueþ hem þer bennefice, cursiþ heerars & takiþ awey þe goodis of hem þat forþeren þe precheing of a prest, 3he þou3 it were an aungel of heuene, but if þat prest schewe þe mark of þe beest, þe which is turned in to a *newe* name & clepid a *special lettir of lisence*.[28]

Novelty was a concept open to polemical use in two senses. Arundel used it to mean fresh and vigorous, while this author used it to mean unwarranted and illegal. In sympathy with these polemical views, recent scholarship on 1409 has tended, incorrectly, to see it as a complete break with the past.[29] All the details of this analysis of the canon law against heresy, however, have shown it to be cumulative and interpretative, rather than either wholly innovative or slavishly derivative.

2. REPORTING

Instances of preachers and celebrants without the proper documentation were one of the things that people were supposed to report to their ordinary

---

[27] Reg. Arundel (Canterbury), ii. fo. 12ʳ: 'Statuimus eciam et decernimus vt nullus capellanus admittatur ad celebrandum in aliqua diocese nostre Cantuariensis prouincie in qua oriundus siue ordinatus non fuerit, nisi deferat secum litteras ordinacionum suorum atque litteras comendaticias diocesani sui et nichilominus aliorum Episcoporum in quorum diocesi interim per magnum tempus conuersatus fuerit.'

[28] *The Lanterne of Li3t*, ed. L. M. Swinburn, EETS 151 (London, 1917), 17–18. My italics.

[29] N. Watson, 'Censorship and Cultural Change in Late Medieval England: Vernacular Theology, the Oxford Translation Debate and Arundel's Constitutions of 1409', *Speculum*, 70 (1995), 822–64.

as savouring of heresy, but we have seen that there was some ambiguity as to who was to check licences and, by implication, make such reports. In order better to understand how information about heresy was supposed to come to the attention of the episcopacy, we may examine the canons and English statutes on clerical and lay involvement in the detection of heresy. The questions of who should report heresy, and what they should report, will be addressed following an assessment of *how* reports of heresy were to be made.

In the fourteenth and fifteenth centuries the word *detectio* did not have the connotations of investigative police work or sleuthing that it has for us. Most frequently it meant reporting, informing, and discovering, with overtones of uncovering and revealing. When in 1414 Chichele ordered a visitation of the archdeaconry of Stafford *sede vacante* he instructed the keepers to cause 'men of unsound minds preaching hostile doctrines, sacrilegious heresies, and nefarious opinions contrary to sound teaching to be faithfully reported'.[30] In 1438 suspicions about the faith of John Brewer of Wiltshire were 'reported and informed upon to our official', and in 1430 Richard Herberd of Kent promised to 'trewely and faithfully detecte and discouer' persons suspected of heresy 'to you my worschipfull fader in god' the bishop of Rochester.[31] The act of reporting, rather than sleuthing, is suggested by detection *to* the bishop, a phrase which makes no sense in modern English. However, the way in which a case initially came to the attention of a bishop is not usually described in any detail in legislation. For example, the procedural instructions drafted at the 1428 Convocation tantalizingly begin: 'Firstly, after the heretic has been detected, denounced or informed against to the bishop . . .'[32] This is typical of the philosophical myopia that prevented canon lawyers from properly acknowledging or discussing the basis that many of their procedures had in public participation. Much was assumed by the bishops drafting this instruction, and this must be reconstructed from a range of canonical sources.

Cardinal Hostiensis explained that the bishop or inquisitor could proceed against heretics by accusation, denunciation, or inquisition.[33] Accusation and denunciation were modes of instance procedure, that is cases brought by private individuals or by corporate bodies, while inquisition, a procedure developed in the twelfth century as part of a shift

---

[30] *Reg. Chichele (Canterbury)*, iii. 297: 'fideliter detecturos'.

[31] Reg. Nevill (Salisbury), part 2, fo. 48ᵛ: 'officium nostrum detectum pariter et dilatum'; Reg. Langdon (Rochester), fo. 75Xᵛ.

[32] Hudson, 'Examination of Lollards', 137.   [33] Hostiensis, *Summa aurea*, 1530.

towards a more proactive jurisprudence, was instigated by a judge and was known as an *ex officio* procedure.[34] The manner in which crimes were reported varied according to the procedure being used. An accusation was a written statement by a named person that someone had committed an offence. The accuser was required to supply sufficient proof by two credible witnesses, or else risk being punished himself or herself for the crime in question. Denunciation allowed for anonymous and unwritten reports, but the same standard of proof was required, and the denouncer was expected to offer fraternal admonition to the offender before reporting him to a judge. Neither of these methods would recommend itself to the cowed or threatened witness. Inquisition differed in that it was begun by a judge and the burden of proof was public rather than private, reports could be anonymous and unwritten, no prior admonition was required, and the witness had only to report suspicion rather than verifiable evidence.[35] The problem for the historian is that unlike procedure by accusation, the notary recording reports made in response to an inquisition was only required to write down what was useful to the case.[36] In common with the 1428 procedural instructions, this meant that detection was often not described in any detail. This apparent regression in legal standards was tacitly acknowledged in the thirteenth-century saying that a judge proceeding *ex officio* should treat rumour as the accusation and outcry as the denunciation.[37] Nevertheless inquisition became the favoured, though not the only, method for the prosecution of heresy.

Procedure by inquisition was associated with a category of persons identified for their trustworthiness before the law, the implication being that it was reports from these men that would be sufficient to instigate judicial action. We can learn something of their qualities and duties from Chichele's 1416 statute on inquisitions, and the records of visitations, with which its provisions were so closely allied. Chichele ordered the questioning of 'three or more sworn men of good testimony from every deanery and parish where it is rumoured that heretics live'.[38] These sworn

---

[34] R. M. Fraher, 'Preventing Crime in the High Middle Ages: The Medieval Lawyers' Search for Deterrence', in J. R. Sweeny and S. Chodorow (eds.), *Popes, Teachers and Canon Law in the Middle Ages* (Ithaca, NY, 1989), 212–33; Trusen, 'Der Inquisitionsprozess'.

[35] Tancred, *Ordo iudiciarius*, 152–3, 157.   [36] Lyndwood, *Provinciale*, 302.

[37] X 5.1.24 (chapter eight of the Fourth Lateran Council).

[38] *Reg. Chichele (Canterbury)*, iii. 18: 'in singulis decanatibus hujusmodi singulisque parochiis in quibus fama est hereticos habitare, tres vel plures boni testimonii viros ad sacra dei evangelia jurare faciant.'

men of good testimony are often referred to in visitation articles as 'trustworthy men' or *viri fidedigni*. They were expected to be upright and honest, not suspected of any crime, and chosen without fraud, disregarding their popularity amongst the people of the parish.[39] They could number up to six or eight, and they were to be selected from across the parish so as better to inquire into the state of the whole community.[40] Not only were they to be 'upright and catholic men', as the bishop of Lincoln stipulated in a heresy investigation in 1393, but also respected within their community, 'good and substantial men'.[41] The Latin *bonos et graves* suggests that the social standing necessary for raising suspicions of heresy was in fact very similar to that required for upholding charges of other crimes based on speech and communication, such as defamation. Just as the imputation of a crime was not considered to constitute defamation unless the person imputed had enjoyed previously good fame in the opinion of good and substantial persons, so suspicions of heresy had to be reported by good and substantial persons in order to be taken seriously.[42]

This social group was defined by legal rather than economic status: they were trusted collaborators with the ecclesiastical courts and the local arbiters of moral boundaries. The concept of 'persons in authority', who Arundel had said should be responsible for checking preaching licences, may be useful for understanding reporting as well. In the case of the *fidedigni* 'authority' seems to have meant a person whose standing made them trusted in the eyes of the law, and of the community that they were supposed to represent.[43] How this trustworthiness should be understood in social terms naturally varies from one jurisdiction to another, as each has its own language and habits of mind.

[39] *Reg. Grandisson (Exeter)*, i. 382; *The Register of John Chandler Dean of Salisbury 1404–17*, ed. T. C. B. Timmins, Wiltshire Record Society, 39 (Devizes, 1984), 1; *Reg. Trilleck (Hereford)*, 30; *Summa summarum*, V. X. q. 94 (Bodleian, MS Bodley 293, fo. 179ᵛ).

[40] *Reg. Langham (Canterbury)*, 245–6: 'quatuor sex vel octo parochianos fidedignos secundum cujuslibet parochie amplitudinem per quos status tocius parochie melius inquiri poterit.'

[41] Reg. Buckingham (Lincoln), fo. 406ʳ: 'probos et catholicos viros'; Tancred, *Ordo iudiciarius*, 153: 'apud bonos et graves'.

[42] *Select Cases on Defamation*, pp. xxxiv–xxxvi.

[43] R. R. Davies, 'Kinsmen, Neighbours and Communities in Wales and the Western British Isles, c.1100–c.1400', in P. Stafford, J. L. Nelson, and J. Martindale (eds.), *Law, Laity and Solidarities: Essays in Honour of Susan Reynolds* (Manchester, 2001), 182: 'The local community was . . . the custodian of knowledge—of fact, contract and opinion. No law-worthy man could operate outside it.'

The Chancery proceedings against heresy occasionally alluded to a very broad constituency indeed of potential reporters. The phrase 'each and every liege and subject of our cities and their suburbs' is used in conjunction with instructions to avoid preachers, to assist justices, and to not assist unlicensed preachers.[44] It was echoed by the poet John Audelay, who urged that every Christian man was obliged to guard against heresy.[45] However, this very broad social profile may just have been a figure of speech when it came actually to reporting heresy. Crown investigations in 1414 for example used presentment juries made up of knights, trusted local officials, and other men who, with some allowance for linguistic differences between the jurisdictions, would fit the profile of the ecclesiastical *fidedigni* very well. Juries were to be comprised of 'free and law-worthy men from the better and more discreet sort'.[46] The canons upon which the investigatory clauses of the 1416 statute were based, namely *Ad abolendam* and *Excommunicamus*, also held out to the bishop the option of extending his questioning to 'all the neighbourhood, if he believes it will help', a clause which Chichele dropped, leaving the English diocesans with the select panel familiar to the late medieval governing class from visitations and common law juries.[47]

Reporters of heresy described as *fidedigni* or *bonos et graves* were augmented by other, less honest, upright and catholic classes of witness, namely excommunicates, perjurers, and condemned heretics. In the mid-thirteenth century Alexander IV had issued a number of decrees to inquisitors, expanding upon and delimiting their duties and responsibilities. Excommunicates, criminals, and perjurers were to be admitted as witnesses, within the jurisdiction of inquisitors into heresy, that is to say only in cases that proceeded by inquisition and not by accusation, and to the exclusion of any crime other than heresy.[48] The lack of social standing or any other normal legal qualification was waived as a special measure in the belief that any information on heresy was useful information. Protection for such witnesses, who we may assume were often subject to public

---

[44] PRO, C 54/263, m. 22d (*CCR 1413–19*, 86).

[45] *The Poems of John Audelay*, ed. E. K. Whiting, EETS 184 (London, 1931), 91: 'And be ware, vche Cristin mon, | Fore heretekis and renegatis þat vncriston be.'

[46] PRO, KB 9/204/1, m. 21: 'liberos et legales homines de melioribus et discrecioribus.'

[47] X 5.7.9: 'tres vel plures boni testimonii viros, vel etiam, si expedire videbitur, *totam vicinam* iurare compellat.'

[48] VI 5.2.5 with *Glos. ord.*; VI 5.2.8, § 3; see also Clem. 5.31, § 4.

disapprobation, was provided by the option of holding hearings in secret.[49] Most significant in terms of detection was the innovation that suspected and convicted heretics, as well as their helpers, favourers, and receivers, could act as witnesses. In Chapter 7 a number of examples of English heresy suspects being questioned on their contacts and influences will be dissected. It was a practice that was in accordance with Hostiensis' instruction to judges that they should always ask suspects where their opinions came from.[50] Such interest in the social dimension of heresy, in addition to its manifestation in individuals, demanded an epidemiological approach, tracing who had come into contact with whom. The maxim that *receptores et favores* were people without whom heretics could not stay hidden for long, gave the interrogation of this class of witness a great deal of urgency.[51]

Asking the parish clergy and the laity, not to mention criminals and excommunicates, to make reports of heresy to their ordinary opened the ecclesiastical justice system to all the politics and uneducated inconsistencies of the world outside the canon law schools. Furthermore, asking them to report their suspicions might seem to have been a rash invitation to the peddling of false and malicious information. However, once gathered, the information gained through *detectio* was subjected to the normal legal tests. That process will be examined in detail in Chapter 7. Even at the reporting stage the content and definition of suspicion was limited in such a way as to filter out unfounded or politically motivated testimony. Tancred's *Ordo iudiciarius* asserted this principle, stating that not only must suspicion, or *fama*, precede procedure by inquisition, but it must be frequent and not based on only a single occurrence.[52] Of course, those making reports could not always be relied upon to make this distinction. The role of the canon lawyers in the bishop's household was to vet reports according to Tancred's legal definition of *fama*, and filter them according to the nature of the crime. Reporting crime always requires the involvement of two parties: the person doing the reporting and the authority receiving the report. Consequently we should read reports of heresy as a collaboration between episcopal administration and popular participation.

The thirteenth constitution of Arundel's 1409 statute ordered that anyone defamed, detected, denounced, or vehemently suspected of anything

---

[49] VI 5.2.20.   [50] VI 5.2.5; Hostiensis, *Summa aurea*, 1533.

[51] Hostiensis, *In decretalium libri commentaria* (Venice, 1591), ii. part 2, fo. 39ʳ; *Glos. ord.* to X 5.7.13, v. *receptatores*: 'sine quibus heretici manere diu non possunt.'

[52] Tancred, *Ordo iudiciarius*, 153.

prohibited by the statute was to be reported to a bishop.[53] Lyndwood glossed this phrase by providing a list of actions and behaviour that should be reported as constituting 'vehement suspicion'. They were the knowing reception of heretics, listening to heretics' preaching, receiving condemned books, defending heretics so that trials failed, neglect amongst princes and prelates in punishing heretics, swearing to point out heretics but then concealing them, excusing known heretics by word or deed, bringing food to heretics, providing anything by which they might evade capture, praying for their release, being contumacious in a legal case relating to the faith, having continuous familiarity with heretics, going with them to secret meetings, differing in life and morals from the usual behaviour of men, and finally, obscuring the truth in *causa fidei*.[54] Clearly many of these relied upon the prior legal identification of heretics, and they relate to the information provided in trials by persons suspected of heresy or already condemned. In terms of the wider population of *fidedigni* and other heresy reporters, they were being encouraged to feel suspicious about their neighbours if they owned unusual books, attended sermons given by preachers of unknown provenance, or if they were thought to have unorthodox social contacts. The two clauses relating to trials in matters of the faith, *causa fidei*, imply the attention of lawyers rather than laity, and they need not have been cases of heresy. For example in 1411 the pope threatened that an English priory would be declared heretical if its representative failed to appear and make satisfaction in a dispute over temporal possessions.[55]

In 1416 Chichele's statute ordering twice-yearly inquiries instructed his bishops to question the 'boni testimonii viros' as to whether they knew of any heretics, whether there was anyone in their parish celebrating secret conventicles, anyone differing in life and morals from the behaviour of the faithful, anyone holding heretical or erroneous opinions, anyone owning suspicious books written in the vulgar English tongue, anyone receiving or favouring someone suspected of heresy or error, or anyone having conversation with suspected heretics or meeting them.[56] Any suspicion on these

[53] Reg. Arundel (Canterbury), ii. fo. 12ᵛ: 'diffamati, detecti, siue denunciati siue vehementer suspecti.' [54] Lyndwood, *Provinciale*, 302–3.

[55] *CPL 1404–15*, 279–80.

[56] *Reg. Chichele (Canterbury)*, iii. 18: 'hereticos sive occulta conventicula celebrantes aut a communi conversacione fidelium vita et moribus discrepantes, heresesve aut errores tenentes, sive libros suspectos in lingua vulgari anglicana conscriptos habentes, aut personas de heresibus sive erroribus suspectas receptantes, eisdemve faventes, aut infra loca hujusmodi habitare conversari sive ad eadem recursum habere sciverint.'

grounds was to be written down by the investigating official and relayed to the bishop as quickly as possible. Like Lyndwood's list, these instructions imply prior knowledge or suspicion of heretical persons, probably preachers identified by the content of their sermons or their lack of the necessary licence. As the public manifestation of a secret crime, heretical preachers were in the mind of Lucius III when he referred to the citation of 'anyone who is caught *clearly* in heresy'. This was glossed by Bernard of Parma as meaning caught in the act of publicly preaching heresy.[57] The prosecution of such a person would allow the subsequent reporting of anyone who had helped, received, fed, communicated with, or listened to him or her.

Some of these triggers for suspicion were straightforward, but on others there was not universal agreement. William Paul had argued in the mid-fourteenth century that those people who merely hear the sermons of a heretic without repeating them are not to be judged as if they were believers of heretics. Believers are those who proclaim their adherence to heretics.[58] However, in the fifteenth century it does seem as though the audiences of unlicensed preachers could be threatened with individual excommunication as well as the parochial interdict allowed for by Arundel's second constitution.[59] In Coventry in 1424 the disruptive, but probably not Wycliffite, preacher John Grace made sure to say in all his sermons that he was licensed to preach, reassuring his listeners that they would not be suspected of heresy. It was rumoured that the prior of St Mary's in Coventry had excommunicated his whole audience.[60]

If one's chance presence in the audience of a condemned preacher were enough to make one suspect of heresy, even greater latitude is suggested in the phrase 'differing in life and morals from the behaviour of the faithful', used by both Chichele and Lyndwood. Hostiensis had glossed this, with some ambiguity, as meaning simply suspected, but a more realistic interpretation is that ecclesiastical judges were interested in hearing about anyone who failed to conform to the outward requirements of the creed, described in the decrees of the Fourth Lateran Council. Someone who failed to attend annual confession or communion, who did not attend

[57] *Glos. ord.* to X 5.7.9, v. *deprehensi*: 'facti euidentia, puta que publice predicant heresim.' C. 23 q. 4 c. 19 states that manifest crimes ought to be punished.

[58] *Summa summarum*, V. X. qq. 50, 52 (Bodleian, MS Bodley 293, fo. 178ᵛ).

[59] Reg. Arundel (Canterbury), ii. fo. 11ʳ.

[60] *The Coventry Leet Book or Mayor's Register*, ed. M. D. Harris, 4 vols., EETS 134, 135, 138, 146 (1907–13), i. 97.

church on Sundays and feast days, or who did not pay tithes, was liable to be reported under suspicion of heresy if the action was repeated and frequent. This is not to say that everyone guilty of such infractions was held suspect of heresy: filtering by the bishop's officials and the later attention of an ecclesiastical judge would determine that. Nonetheless, such actions were thought of as signs of heresy, alongside refusal to swear oaths, refusal of meat apart from on fast days, and the freeing of vassals from their obligations without good reason.[61] Other signs of heresy could be less overt and much more difficult to discern. For example the canon that claimed heresy was made manifest through sophistry added nothing to the duties of the *fidedignus*, whose competency did not stretch to such scholastic discernment.[62] Nonetheless his duties were vital to the success of an anti-heresy campaign, since without reliable reporting prosecution could not proceed. The signs that the *fidedigni* and the other witnesses had to report were not sufficient to prove someone a heretic, being mere indications of suspected heresy. Unless proved by a judge, they would remain only suspicions.[63]

The detection of heresy was one of the areas of canonical jurisprudence where the theorizing of academics and the legislating of the episcopate met popular participation head on. The indispensability of laymen and the lower clergy to its success meant that the essence of the law had to be adequately communicated to them. The relative novelty of heresy and anti-heresy law in late medieval England gave this communication an added imperative. It also allows the historian to chart the methods and effectiveness of a shift from ignorance to knowledge. The next three chapters will examine this shift, looking at the circulation of knowledge within the episcopate and upper clergy, the channels by which it was communicated to the lower clergy and the laity, and the substance of that knowledge as it pertained to the detection of heresy.

[61] *Summa summarum*, V. X. qq. 15–17 (Bodleian, MS Bodley 293, fo. 178ʳ).

[62] C. 24 q. 3 c. 33.

[63] Innocent IV, *Apparatus super quinque libros decretalium* (Rome, 1511), De simonia, c. *Sicut simoniacam*.

PART II
COMMUNICATION

4

Statutes and the Circulation of Knowledge

There was no single legislative body in medieval England and no single path by which knowledge of the law came to those responsible for its enforcement. The archbishops of Canterbury and York could promulgate provincial statutes or constitutions but they could also exercise their metropolitan authority directly over dioceses perceived to be in need of special attention. Diocesan bishops could themselves formulate statutes for the area under their ordinary jurisdiction, and likewise issue specific mandates to deal with individual cases. Provincial statutes were often issued in the name of Convocation, although they would be formulated by an inner circle. Council, and to a lesser extent Parliament, played a similar role in the formulation of 'secular' anti-heresy policy, although statutes were issued in the name of the king. Whatever the influences upon a particular measure, the drafting of secular statutes, commissions, or writs such as *Venire facias* or *De heretico comburendo* took place in Chancery.

As we have seen in the preceding chapters, there was a good deal of overlap between these law-making bodies at the highest level, personified in Arundel as archbishop and chancellor. This overlap meant that Convocation could petition Parliament to act against heresy when it had decided that secular action was required and could expect its request to be understood. In 1401 a clerical petition resulted in the parliamentary statute *Contre les lollardes*, with minimal changes being made to the Latin text formulated in Convocation. The exchange of texts is matched by the interchange of personnel, with bishops sitting in both Convocation and Parliament, as well as on the king's council. Despite the removal of the lower clergy from Parliament in 1340, the communication of information about heresy and anti-heresy cannot therefore be divided into two hermetically sealed cultures of church and state.[1] Instead it must be seen within a common governmental culture embracing both 'secular' and ecclesiastical spheres. It was within this shared intellectual culture that an exchequer clerk, James le Palmere, wrote a major synthesis of canon law and theology, the *Omne bonum*, discussed in Chapter 1, and a Chancery clerk, Robert Ragenhill, could own copies of Bartolus of Sassoferrato, John of Legnano, Nicholas of Lyra, the *Clementines*, and the Old Testament. John Wakeryng was Keeper of the Rolls in Chancery before becoming bishop of Norwich in 1415, and the future bishop of Bath and Wells, Nicholas Bubwith, began his career as a Chancery clerk.[2]

This common culture did have its limits. The royal courts of justice were based on statute law and the writs of common law, texts which could be edited and modified by the clerks in Chancery, but whose substance was unalterable. By contrast the church courts interpreted and applied a vast body of instructions and commentary which was both international in its literature and extremely local in its practical realization. Individual bishops had wide discretion to issue statutes particular to their own dioceses, an option unavailable to sheriffs and justices of the peace. This was facilitated by the devolution of ecclesiastical authority, which was spread across the twenty-one diocesan administrations of England and Wales. Whereas the royal Chancery was a central government department, each bishop had his own chancery consisting of lawyers, notaries, and scribes, in addition to those of the archbishops.

By the late fourteenth century both provincial and diocesan legislation consisted mainly of statutes and mandates designed to meet specific problems, replacing the all-encompassing statutes of the thirteenth century, which have been edited up to 1313 by Christopher Cheney and Maurice Powicke. The last general programme of archiepiscopal legislation was in 1342 under Archbishop Stratford.[3] Arundel's 1407 constitutions, although detailed and ambitious, are highly specific by comparison, reflecting the belief that existing statutes were sufficient to deal with

[1] McHardy, '*De heretico comburendo* 1401', 116–17; Strohm, *England's Empty Throne*, 40–5; J. H. Denton and J. P. Dooley, *Representatives of the Lower Clergy in Parliament 1295–1340* (Woodbridge, 1987), 83–8.

[2] Sandler, *Omne bonum*, i. 131–3; M. Richardson, *The Medieval Chancery under Henry V*, List and Index Society, Special Series, 30 (Kew, 1999), 13–14, 40, 103–4.

[3] C. R. Cheney, *English Synodalia of the Thirteenth Century* (Oxford, 1941), 43; on Stratford's 1342 statutes see B. Bolton, 'The Council of London of 1342', in G. J. Cuming and D. Baker (eds.), *Councils and Assemblies*, SCH 7 (Cambridge, 1984), 147–60.

familiar questions, but that new problems like heresy required new measures. This chapter examines the incremental growth in knowledge about heresy within royal and episcopal government, based on interactions between legal texts and amongst the people who wrote and used them. By the mid-fifteenth century heresy was no longer a novelty and had become a familiar feature of the legal landscape.

1. INTER-TEXTUALITY

The processes of drafting, circulating, and copying ecclesiastical statutes against heresy are revealed to a certain extent in the texts of the documents themselves. By examining textual relationships between statutes and mandates we can see something of the patterns of knowledge transfer operating between centre and locality, as well as between and within those localities. The degree of centralized control may be measured by the extent to which diocesan mandates duplicated the text of provincial statutes. In some cases a bishop might simply reissue the text he received from Lambeth, but more frequently he would modify, edit, or combine it with other materials he had to hand. Writing about the copying of thirteenth-century statutes Christopher Cheney observed that 'some prelates seem content to copy them practically in their entirety, while for others they provide a store-house to plunder for particularly desirable chapters and well turned phrases.'[4] This underlines the criteria of local applicability and linguistic appeal that seem to determine the practice of late medieval episcopal chanceries. A set of case studies in how anti-heresy law was made will illuminate these themes.

In May 1382 Archbishop Courtenay issued a provincial statute against heresy, the receipt of which is noted in three episcopal registers.[5] This does not mean it did not reach other dioceses, since the decisions made by registrars as to what incoming and outgoing letters and documents were copied into a register, and which were filed elsewhere, are often difficult to penetrate.[6] One of the bishops whose copy of the statute survives, Henry Wakefield of Worcester, repeated much of its preamble and directive clauses

---

[4] Cheney, *Synodalia*, 62.
[5] Reg. Braybroke (London), fo. 269; *Reg. Wakefield (Worcester)*, 131–2; *Reg. Brantyngham (Exeter)*, i. 462–4.   [6] Smith, *Guide to Bishops' Registers*, pp. viii–xi.

in a 1387 mandate to prevent Wycliffites preaching in his diocese.[7] This is a rare example of almost verbatim repetition, but it is likely that the parroting of provincial legislation in specific cases was more common since much time and energy was saved thereby. Such direct copying may well be under-represented in the registers because no registrar would be willing to copy out the same text twice when he could record its transmission in a short note, such as that in Beaufort's Winchester register concerning Arundel's 1409 constitutions, or John de Bottlesham's memorandum on the receipt of Chichele's 1416 statute at Rochester.[8] Where local mandates are recorded, it is because their texts diverge from provincial and royal models to some degree.

The copying and modification of statutes produced recognizable families of texts, comparable to the *stemmata* by which literary scholars illustrate the redaction and alteration of prose and verse works. In anti-heresy legal texts these chains of modification drew in citations from decretals and earlier diocesan instruments, creating hybrid documents that are sufficiently distinctive to allow the identification of their derivatives in a number of different contexts. In particular, diocesan mandates often marry the pream-ble of a provincial statute to locally relevant directive clauses, in much the same way that provincial statutes themselves altered the detail of decrees and decretals while remaining within the spirit of the canon law. In 1394 Bishop Wykeham of Winchester began a mandate inhibiting the preaching of the withdrawal of tithes and oblations with the preamble of the 1382 provincial statute, which has a clear polemical appeal: 'Prelates of the church to whom the safety of the Lord's flock has been entrusted ought to turn their attention to the wolves, who in order to deceive them, fraudulently appear in sheep's clothing to ravage and disperse the flock.'[9] Wykeham's mandate then moved swiftly on to matters of peculiarly local concern, referring to a single deanery, in clauses which are perfunctory and not copied from Courtenay's original.

Another use of the provincial statute as an exemplar is evident in the man-date formulated by Bishop Buckingham of Lincoln for his archdeaconries in

---

[7] *Reg. Wakefield (Worcester)*, 150–2.

[8] Reg. Beaufort (Winchester), fo. 144[r]: the full text of the constitutions is entered at fos. 149[r]–151[v]; Reg. J. Bottlesham (Rochester), fo. 152.

[9] *Reg. Wykeham (Winchester)*, ii. 453, and Reg. Courtenay (Canterbury), fo. 25[v]: 'Ecclesiarum prelati circa gregis dominici sibi commissi custodiam eo vigilancius intendere debent quo lupos intrinsecus ouium vestimentis indutos ad rapiendum et dispergendum oues nouerint fraudulencius circuire.'

1388. This opens with a condemnation of unlicensed preaching copied from the canon *Excommunicamus*, referring to 'all those who have been forbidden to preach or are not sent, and yet dare publicly or privately to usurp the office of preaching without receiving the authority of the apostolic see or the catholic bishop of the place in question'.[10] It goes on to cite a statute promulgated at the Convocation 'recently held at Oxford', which must have been that convened at St Frideswide's in November 1382, before falling in with the text of the May 1382 provincial statute directing the laity not to listen to such preachers. We may assume from this comment that Courtenay's statute had been reissued in November when Buckingham and the other bishops were gathered together in Oxford.

Staying with Buckingham's Lincoln diocese, a series of mandates may be identified whose basic structure remains constant while specific details are altered to accommodate changes in the names, number, and location of the suspects being pursued. In 1381 Buckingham was much troubled by the itinerant preacher William Swinderby, who was suspected of preaching scandal and error to the people. At this point he was neither considered a heretic nor associated with the teachings of Wyclif, but the bishop still feared the influence he might have on the peace of his diocese. Twelve years later in 1392, by which time Swinderby was causing problems in Wales and Herefordshire, Buckingham was dealing with a major outbreak of suspected heresy in Northampton, where it seemed that the whole town was departing from orthodoxy under the malign influence of the mayor.[11] So the bishop sent a mandate to warn rectors, vicars, and parishioners there that they should not admit lollards to preach. Nearly all the preamble and about a quarter of the directive clauses are directly copied from the mandate against Swinderby from 1381. The adaptation of a tested formula to new circumstances is apparent in the changes to the identifying clauses. Passages from these are best cited in Latin so as to convey the altering and updating that they underwent. '[Q]uidam Willelmus hermita in capella St Johannis prope villam Leycestr habitans presbiterum

---

[10] Reg. Buckingham (Lincoln), fo. 349ᵛ, cf. X 5.7.13: 'omnes qui prohibiti vel non admissi preter auctoritatem ab apostolica sede vel catholico episcopo loci susceptam publice vel priuatim predicacionis officium vsurpantes.' On dating the mandate see A. K. McHardy, 'Bishop Buckingham and the Lollards of Lincoln Diocese', in D. Baker (ed.), *Schism, Heresy and Religious Protest*, SCH 9 (Cambridge, 1972), 135.

[11] McHardy, 'Bishop Buckingham and the Lollards', 136–42.

se asserens' in 1381 becomes 'nonnulli per orbem terrarum vagantes presbiteros se asserentes' in 1392. A general reference to the archdeaconry of Leicester was also altered, to read 'town of Northampton'.[12] In 1393 the original Swinderby mandate was again used as the model for a commission to inquire into the names of lollards and their followers in Northampton. By this time it had transpired that the preachers in the town professed to be graduates, in a mistaken attempt to legitimize their preaching, and so the identifying clause was altered once more to read 'nonnulli pseudo prophete per orbem terrarum vagabundi presbiteros et aliter graduatos se asserentes'.[13] Around these empirical changes in detail the texts of the three documents remain remarkably similar, revealing what we might term a Lincoln chancery style, developed from a single exemplar and modified over time as and when the need arose. The image of Buckingham's registrar reaching into a muniment chest or consulting his personal formulary for a suitable model on which to base a new text is a compelling and plausible one. The mechanics of this will be explored later in this chapter.

Of course the reuse of old formulae meant that new problems were to some extent assimilated to previous experience on a 'best fit' basis. We must assume that decisions on using an exemplar were taken with its utility and applicability in mind, but a perfect match between legal text and social circumstance was unlikely. One effect of a chancery style determined by precedent, as at Lincoln, was the creation of an artificial continuity with the past that elided differences between the events of the 1380s and the 1390s. This is especially striking in respect of the three Lincoln documents under discussion, and in particular a change made to the passage in which unlicensed preachers were compared with ravening wolves, their actions described as scandalous and their words as weeds sown in the minds of the faithful. To the 1381 phrase narrating how Swinderby 'venit superseminare zizania spiritu ducti nequissimo fideli populo predicare et exponere', the author of the 1392 document added 'ad modum lollardorum' after the word 'predicare'. Since 1381, when the word lollard was hardly used if it was known at all, the teachings of Wyclif had been connected with unlicensed preaching and popular rebellion, all of which was encapsulated in the word lollardy. Just as in Knighton's chronicle account of Swinderby's preaching, written in the 1390s, these

---

[12] Reg. Buckingham (Lincoln), fos. 236ᵛ, 398ʳ.   [13] Ibid., fo. 406ʳ.

judicial documents associate him with Wyclif and lollardy retrospectively. One recent scholar has called this rhetorical process the 'back formation' of lollardy: creating a history for a social category that only gained widespread currency in the later 1380s.[14] Whatever the combination of politics and expedience that gave rise to this phenomenon, the importance of textual transmission in lending cohesion and momentum to anti-heresy legislation seems clear.

In royal government chains of modification such as those common in episcopal administration are confined to the Chancery, where documents were drafted and modified under a single central authority. The texts of the anti-heresy commissions that emanated from Chancery between 1382 and 1414 are frequently derived from a common exemplar such as the 1382 licence for the episcopal arrest of heretics or the 1388 instruction for secular officers to search for books. Both of these spawned a series of variant commissions sent to places where suspected heretical activity continued to cause problems after the original commission had run its course.[15] In response to particular circumstances a Chancery clerk could also combine the texts of exemplars, as in the 1388 commission for Worcester and that of 1389 for Hereford, both of which combined the 1382 and 1388 letters on arrest and heretical books in a single text.[16] The royal commissions also exemplify a most significant textual practice in terms of developing an appropriate response to heresy: that of piloting a new measure in one locality before launching it as a national policy. Examples of this include the Nottingham commission to discover heretical writings in 1388 and the 1414 post-revolt commission for London and Middlesex, both of which were discussed in Chapter 2. Chichele's experimentation with visitation during the Coventry and Lichfield vacancy of 1414, prior to the promulgation of this as provincial policy in 1416, was also examined in Chapter 2.

In a hierarchical organization such as the late medieval church or English royal government, one might assume with some justification that

---

[14] A. Cole, 'William Langland and the Invention of Lollardy', in Somerset et al. (eds.), *Lollards and their Influence*, 45.

[15] For variants of the arrest licence between 1382 and 1394 see PRO, C 66/318, m. 7 (*CPR 1381–85*, 487); C 66/321, m. 12 (*CPR 1385–89*, 145–6); C 66/322, m. 37 (*CPR 1385–89*, 200); C 66/334, m. 20 (*CPR 1391–96*, 40–1); C 66/339, m. 10 (*CPR 1391–96*, 414). For variants of the instruction to search for books 1388–9 see PRO, C 66/326, m. 20d (*CPR 1385–89*, 550), C 66/327, m. 3 (*CPR 1385–89*, 536).

[16] PRO, C 66/325, m. 10 (*CPR 1385–89*, 448); C 66/329, m. 21 (*CPR 1388–92*, 172).

new legislation would be formulated at the top and transmitted downwards to those responsible for its implementation. However, the devolution of legislative authority and writing expertise within the church begs the question of whether or not provincial policy could be influenced by the unilateral decisions taken by diocesans in their struggles against heresy. In some cases the proposition is made highly unlikely by a marked lack of vigour in anti-heresy matters, and everywhere the losses of documentation make relative assessments of one bishop's zeal as compared with another's very difficult. However, in one notable case there is compelling evidence to suggest that legal innovation could begin in the localities before being subsequently taken up by central authority.

The diocese in question is again Lincoln, during the episcopacy of Philip Repingdon, and the period in question is a crucial one for the development of anti-heresy policy, 1413. I have already discussed the change from reactive to proactive investigations that came to fruition in Chichele's 1416 statute, but movement towards this had begun in 1413. The story is quite a complex one, made difficult to follow by a lacuna in the archiepiscopal register for that year. However, in piecing together the course of events from other sources, our attention is forcibly shifted away from Lambeth and the central bias inherent in the archiepiscopal records. In November 1413 Convocation promulgated a circular letter to the diocesans detailing the trial and sentencing of John Oldcastle. The letter is copied into Arundel's archiepiscopal register, as well as those of Lincoln, Winchester, Chichester, Hereford, and Bath and Wells.[17] There is, however, no complete record of what happened at that November Convocation, as there is for almost every other such gathering in the late Middle Ages. We know that Convocation was called 'to discuss the unity and reformation of the English church' and to petition the king for aid against heresy, because the summons is preserved in a number of diocesan registers, but on the basis of the Lambeth register we do not know what was decided, nor whether any decisions were promulgated.[18] However, action taken against heresy by Repingdon, probably in December 1413, provides some clues as to the content of the discussions of the November

---

[17] Reg. Arundel (Canterbury), ii. fos. 142ᵛ–145ᵛ; *Reg. Repingdon (Lincoln)*, iii. 10–13; Reg. Beaufort (Winchester), fos. 175ᵛ–177ᵛ; *Reg. Rede (Chichester)*, i. 151–6; *Reg. Mascall (Hereford)*, 116; *Reg. Bubwith (Bath & Wells)*, i. 154–65.

[18] Reg. Clifford (London), fo. 152; *Reg. Repingdon (Lincoln)*, ii. 367–9; *Reg. Rede (Chichester)*, i. 156–7; *Reg. Bubwith (Bath & Wells)*, i. 151–4.

Convocation. The Lincoln records are also suggestive of how such discussions could be influenced by the judicial practice and political skills of a particularly innovative bishop.

On 14 December Repingdon cited the official of the archdeacon of Huntingdon to answer the charge that he had failed to execute the writ summoning the November Convocation. In a paraphrase of the original summons, Repingdon bemoaned the occlusion of the English church by a misty and heretical blindness that was settling in the minds of the people. He explained that Arundel had called Convocation to find a remedy for this lest more people were infected with the stinking plague of heresy, and confirms that he and the other bishops and clergy (apart from the representative of Huntingdon, one assumes) did indeed attend.[19] Further details of the deliberations at St Paul's in November are provided by another document in the Lincoln register, which although undated, can be firmly connected with this Convocation by its repetition of the language in the summons and the citation of the negligent official. This document is a mandate from Repingdon to his archdeacons ordering them to inquire into heresy in accordance with the decisions of the recent Convocation. After long deliberation and the winnowing of different possibilities, Repingdon reports, Convocation decided that each bishop of the province should make general inquisitions in his city and diocese and in every borough and deanery, through literate men of good fame, good conscience, and equal sufficiency.[20] They should aim to discover whether anyone was defamed or suspected of heresy or error, whether anyone was suspected of being a receiver or favourer of heretics, whether any religious were apostate, whether the numbers of chaplains, paupers, and the infirm in hospitals conformed with the founder's charter, whether there were any clerical concubines, whether married men exercised any jurisdiction that rightly belonged to the sphere of apparitor, official, commissary, or scribe, and finally whether there was any unauthorized absenteeism amongst the clergy. The archdeacons were to proceed with the aid of a theologian, and to certify to the bishop the names and details of all

[19] *Reg. Repingdon (Lincoln)*, ii. 365–7.

[20] Ibid. 371: 'diffinitum extitit finaliter et conclusum, ut singuli episcopi provincie antedicte cum suis civitatibus et diocesibus ac singulis burgis et decanatibus eorundem de et super articulis materias heresum errorum et aliorum defectorum quorum tenores inferius describuntur fieri faciant inquisiciones generales per viros litteratos bone fame bone consciencie et satis sufficientis.'

those detected, delated, and denounced. In other words, they were to annex the detection of heresy to their ordinary visitatorial duties, the policy that was adopted in 1416. This was not, however, the policy direction indicated in the initial summons to Convocation, which had spoken of a petition to the king for aid. The outcome of that was the 1414 royal statute on secular investigation, but one bishop at least felt that the discussions on episcopal visitation should not go to waste.[21]

Is this evidence of a previously unknown provincial statute against heresy? The answer is not quite as simple as one might imagine. Repingdon certainly claimed to be acting in accordance with the decisions of Convocation, but that is not the same as carrying out provincial legislation. We can be fairly certain that no statute was promulgated, as it would have left some trace in at least one episcopal register. It seems that Repingdon's decision to treat the conclusions of November 1413 as binding was unilateral. This leads us to ask why he alone took this route. The immediate context for his action in December is his visitation of Leicester archdeaconry in May and June 1413, which uncovered seventeen reports of heresy alongside the usual range of offences, excesses, and defects that make up the business of such courts.[22] This combination of heresy inquisition with ordinary visitation was, as we have seen, ahead of its time. On this evidence it seems that the bishop of Lincoln was more than just the keen executor of a sidelined or forgotten provincial policy. His enthusiasm for the proposals of the November Convocation and his previous utilization of the methods it came to advocate suggest that Repingdon was a formative influence on provincial policy as it developed over the next three years. So much might well be expected from a man whose deeds were imbued with the zeal of the reformed heretic, of whom Arundel is alleged to have said, 'noo bischop of þis londe pursueþ now scharplier hem þat holden þat wei þan he doiþ', an accolade for which the unrepentant Wycliffite William Thorpe believed Repingdon to be an enemy of Christ.[23]

Although this evidence of local practice influencing putative provincial policy casts Repingdon in the active role, the relationship between the individual bishop and archiepiscopal legislation was in reality never so simple as either the downwards *or* the upwards movement of ideas within

---

[21] See Chapter 2 above.

[22] Lincolnshire Archives, MS Vj/0; see Chapter 8 below for a full discussion of the visitation. [23] *Two Wycliffite Texts*, 42.

the hierarchy. The movement of ideas was frequently circular in motion. For example, the impetus for Repingdon to take the course he did in 1413 may well have come from the discussions of the Convocation that met in March that year, when Oldcastle and his chaplain John Lay were questioned and a heretical tract examined and burnt. At this time Arundel also issued a series of provincial constitutions that included a clarification of his 1409 constitution on interdict, an order to observe the constitutions of the papal legate Otto of 1237, a reassertion of canons nine and ten of Archbishop Pecham's 1281 Council of Lambeth relating to the education of the clergy (*Ignorantia sacerdotum*), the publication of the general sentence of excommunication, and an exposition of the canonical basis for visitation.[24] The connections between vigorous episcopal visitation and the detection of heresy are unarticulated but clearly implied. Repingdon may have taken the idea for his May–June visitation from here, after which his local innovation became provincial policy.

This example raises an important question concerning the authorship of statutes. The convention applied in this book has been to attribute statutes, mandates, and commissions to the archbishop, bishop, or king in whose name they were promulgated. However, without explanation such an approach runs the risk of simplifying the formulation of legislation by attributing it to a small number of men who in some cases may have had very little involvement in the process. The chancellor, keeper of the rolls, and the preceptor were often the key figures in drafting royal and parliamentary measures in Chancery, while bishops kept from their diocesan business by diplomatic missions and counselling the king were assisted by the lawyers, theologians, and notaries who made up their households. That is not to say no bishop ever took an interest in the documents issued by his chancery. Indeed the detection of heresy was an issue that one might expect to have enjoyed the bishop's attention, given that his judicial involvement was demanded in canon law. Nevertheless, we may assume that the more involved and the more learned a bishop was, the better the quality of legal and theological learning he was likely to have in his household.[25] This is particularly exemplified by the scholars and administrators gathered around Repingdon at Lincoln. The bishop himself was a doctor of theology, but he was supported by a range of

---

[24] Reg. Arundel (Canterbury), ii. fos. 25ᵛ–27ᵛ.
[25] Richardson, *Medieval Chancery*, 13–14, 20; Cheney, *Synodalia*, 49.

expert civilians and canonists, all of whom would have had a knowledge of both branches of the learned law.[26]

The civil lawyer John Southam was a highly experienced ecclesiastical administrator, having been keeper of the vacant see prior to Repingdon's accession, and archdeacon of Oxford from 1404 until his death in 1441. As the bishop's official between 1412 and 1417, his advice and learning would have been crucial to Repingdon's anti-heresy policy. From his donation to the newly founded, avowedly anti-heretical, Lincoln College (1427) in Oxford, we know that he owned a copy of Durandus' *Rationale divinorum*, indicating a reading knowledge of canon law in addition to his Roman law background.[27] It is possible that he had also acquired a working knowledge of heresy law from his uncle, the canonist and papal official Thomas Southam, who had tried a number of lollards in 1388. Although not preserved in this case, pre and post-mortem bequests of legal notes and literature between uncles and nephews were quite common in the period.[28] As a canon of Lincoln cathedral, Southam formed part of Repingdon's inner circle alongside the chancellor of Lincoln Thomas Duffield, a doctor of theology. These two men came to be supervisors to a younger generation of lawyers recruited by Repingdon between 1405 and 1412 that included the doctor of laws Thomas Brouns, and the bachelor of laws David Pryce. Pryce was vicar-general in 1413, a position which made him responsible for the judicial actions of the bishop in his absence.[29] Other eminent men on whose expertise Repingdon may have been able to draw included the bachelor of civil law Richard Courtenay who was chancellor of Oxford University in 1413 and soon to be elevated to the see of Norwich from the archdeaconry of Northampton, and the bachelor of canon law Henry Welles who was archdeacon of Lincoln from 1407 to 1431. More suggestive in terms of the legislative initiatives in 1413 was the presence of William Milton as archdeacon of Buckingham from 1402 until 1424. Milton was registrar to Archbishops Arundel and Chichele, and therefore intimately acquainted with the course of policy deliberations and with the textual materials available for drafting new statutes and mandates.[30] In many ways it is no surprise that legislative innovation came from Lincoln.

[26] Boyle, 'Canon Law before 1380', 539; M. Archer, 'Introduction', to *Reg. Repingdon (Lincoln)*, i. p. xx.   [27] *BRUO*, iii. 1732–3.

[28] Owen, *Medieval Canon Law*, 31.   [29] *BRUO*, i. 281–2, 549–50.

[30] *BRUO*, i. 500–2, ii. 1283–4; *BRUC*, 625–6.

2. INSTITUTIONAL STRUCTURES AND INDIVIDUAL CAREERS

The careers of men such as Thomas Brouns and David Pryce, from the law faculties of Oxford and Cambridge, through the offices of diocesan, provincial, and royal government, ending for some in a bishopric of their own, were vectors for the transmission of legal knowledge about heresy. Margaret Aston has suggested that 'one of the questions we have to face in considering the English church's response to the development of heresy, is the manner and stages by which the hierarchy ordered and pooled its experience.'[31] In her analysis Chichele's statute of 1416, and the 1428 attempts to regulate the interrogation and abjurations of offenders, were the key moments in a trajectory of legal progress. To some extent experience could be ordered and pooled by institutional structures, and those two dates do indeed represent significant milestones; but the standardization of practice equally depended on personal relationships and the course of individual careers. To understand how the English church moved from a position of relative ignorance about the laws against heresy to one of experience requires an analysis that integrates the institutional and the personal, building on the textual evidence of legal development described above.

Knowledge about heresy circulated within the governmental class, made up of canon lawyers, bishops, diocesan administrators, Chancery clerks, and royal councillors. As the collective experience of heresy investigations and trials was augmented year on year, the volume of information about heresy in circulation increased and, feeding on itself, grew at an exponential rate. This alone would explain why between 1416 and 1428 anti-heresy procedures were to a large degree standardized: the volume of knowledge had reached a critical point at which separate and divergent practices had borrowed and bastardized each other to such an extent that they coalesced into increasingly similar forms. It could be argued that Chichele was merely recognizing and codifying this process in the 1416 and 1428 Convocations. If career development and education are added to this model, then standardization between one and two generations after the first anti-heresy measures of the 1380s points to the

---

[31] Aston, 'Bishops and Heresy', 75.

importance of training and staff replacement within Chancery and the dioceses. This section will look at the formal and informal routes by which knowledge of anti-heresy law circulated within the governmental class, focusing on the copying of statutes, the sharing of documents and personnel, education, diocesan and personal record keeping, attendance at trials, and Convocation.

Provincial statutes, once formulated, were sent to the bishop of London who, as dean of the province of Canterbury, had copies made and sent to all the diocesan bishops under Canterbury's jurisdiction. In the northern province, where a much smaller volume of anti-heresy statutes and mandates was issued, the circulation of legal texts was executed by the residentiary canons of York Minster who formed the archbishop's chancery.[32] Royal commissions were recorded on the patent and close rolls in the form of an exemplar, to which is often added the note that copies were sent out to all sheriffs, and in some cases the chancellor of the Duchy of Lancaster as well.[33] Upon receipt of such letters, a diocesan registrar would make a good copy of the text, and in some cases he would copy it into the bishop's register, as well as making further copies for circulation amongst those parties indicated in the original instruction. David Smith shows that many bishops' registers were compiled at the end of a bishop's tenure, but the creation of heresy 'reference sections' by some, especially in the 1410s and 1420s, suggests that unbound quires might be actively used by the diocesan administration before the register, as we have it today, was created.[34] For example, John Kempe, bishop of London from 1422 to 1425, had the texts of the 1401 statute *Contre les lollardes*, the 1414 parliamentary statute, and abridged versions of Arundel's 1409 constitutions and Chichele's 1416 provincial statute written down and bound into an end section of his register.[35] Edmund Stafford, bishop of Exeter from 1395 to 1419, had a copy of the 1416 statute in the first volume of his register and a collection of Arundel's constitutions, a number of royal commissions, and the text of the 1414 statute in Latin in the second. The latter entry is augmented by the complete text of the

[32] Churchill, *Canterbury Administration*, i. 355–9; R. B. Dobson, 'The Residentiary Canons of York in the Fifteenth Century', in *Church and Society in the Medieval North of England* (London, 1996), 214.

[33] See for example the commission to investigate heresy in 1413: PRO, C 54/263, m. 22d (*CCR 1413–19*, 86).   [34] Smith, *Guide to Bishops' Registers*, pp. ix–xi.

[35] Reg. Kempe (London), fos. 211ʳ–213ᵛ.

Leicester Parliament, including the heresy statute, written in French on a separate quire inserted to follow the other heresy statutes.[36] John Wakeryng, bishop of Norwich from 1416 to 1425, had the texts of 1401 and 1414 copied onto the first few folios of his register, presumably at the beginning of his episcopacy, signifying a clear intention to be an active opponent of heresy.[37]

The prominence of parliamentary statutes in these collections is perhaps explained by the background of these three bishops, all of whom had moved between royal and ecclesiastical government service. Kempe was a civilian by training who before his translation to London had been examiner general and dean of the Court of Arches, commissary general of Canterbury's overseas jurisdictions, bishop of Rochester, and keeper of the Privy Seal.[38] Stafford was also a civilian who had been dean of the archbishop's court at York, king's clerk, and keeper of the Privy Seal before becoming the bishop of Exeter.[39] Both men subsequently served as chancellor. Wakeryng's early career took a slightly different course, beginning in the early 1380s as a Chancery clerk and rising to become keeper of the rolls in 1405 and keeper of the Privy Seal in 1415. He was promoted to Norwich the following year.[40] It is very likely that Chancery officials promoted to the episcopate would have kept with them privately owned registers of writs including exemplifications from parliamentary statutes. These may have helped them to copy relevant items into their registers. Similar collections of royal commissions were made by some sheriffs and justices as reference books for their judicial work. One such from Worcestershire contains a writ of *Venire facias* served in accordance with the 1414 statute.[41] The terminal date of this book is 1422, which echoes the compilation of statute collections in episcopal registers around the same time.

Diocesan and provincial legislation was sometimes recorded in separate statute books, in which episcopal and archiepiscopal decrees were collected over time. Because of improvements in diocesan registers and a slowing in

---

[36] Reg. Stafford (Exeter), i. fo. 224 (1416); ii. fos. 318ʳ–321ʳ (1409 and royal commissions), fos. 322ʳ–323ᵛ (1414 in Latin), fos. 324ʳ–330ʳ (1414 in French).

[37] Reg. Wakeryng (Norwich), fos. 1ʳ–2ᵛ.   [38] *BRUO*, ii. 1031–2.

[39] *BRUO*, iii. 1749–50.   [40] Richardson, *Medieval Chancery*, 72.

[41] *Early Treatises on the Practice of the Justices of the Peace in the Fifteenth and Sixteenth Centuries*, ed. B. H. Putnam, Oxford Studies in Social and Legal History, 7 (Oxford, 1924), 276–7.

the promulgation of provincial legislation from the mid-fourteenth century onwards, most surviving examples deal mainly with thirteenth- and early fourteenth-century statutes, although some include later statutes, of which a few are relevant to heresy. Of these, four collections include only Arundel's 1409 constitutions.[42] Three further manuscripts also contain a reissue of the 1401 statute made by Chichele in October 1414.[43] This reissue was one of several constitutions promulgated at a Convocation in that month, the records of which do not survive, including one on bigamous laymen and married priests.[44] An additional manuscript contains the 1409 constitutions and Chichele's 1414 statement on bigamy but not the 1401 reissue.[45] It was a statute book such as this that was the source for Lyndwood's commentary on provincial laws from the council of Oxford in 1222 to Chichele's constitution on bigamy. His *Provinciale* was compiled to benefit 'the less well-informed and well-equipped students, who presumably had no access to large libraries and needed a gloss not only to discuss the law but also to define the terms'.[46] In its scope and learning, this work may be seen as the most important expression of the legal codification that was being undertaken by the generation of 1420. The incorporation of anti-heresy statutes into collections of provincial legislation shows that the detection of heresy had become an integral part of the canon lawyer's duties.

The production of well-drafted and appropriate mandates by diocesan lawyers depended, as we have seen, on the availability of source texts in the shape of provincial statutes or earlier diocesan instruments. It is fair to assume that whoever drew up the series of Lincoln documents discussed earlier in this chapter was in the habit of referring to Buckingham's register, and that Bishop Brantyngham's repetition in 1386 of a diocesan statute against false alms collectors from 1287 necessitated a search

[42] Hereford Cathedral Library, MS P. vii. 7, fos. 155^r–158^r; Bodleian, MS Rawlinson C. 100, fos. 158^v–163^r; Exeter College, Oxford, MS 41, fos. 206^r–208^v; BL, MS Harley 3705, fos. 109^r–117^r.

[43] CUL, MS Gg. 6. 21, fos. 80^v–88^v, 95^r–102^r; BL, MS Harley 335, fos. 98^r–103^r, 105^v–107^v, where Chichele's reissue of 1401 in 1414 is misdated to 1413; All Souls College, Oxford, MS 42, fos. 257^v–262^r, 266^v–268^r. The latter MS does not specify 1401 as a Chichele reissue, but as it does contain his contemporary statute on bigamy at fo. 296^r, we may include it in this group. It also contains a copy of the 1414 parliamentary statute.

[44] See Jacob's introduction to *Reg. Chichele (Canterbury)*, i. p. cxliv.

[45] Balliol College, Oxford, MS 158, fos. 187^r–190^r.

[46] C. R. Cheney, 'William Lyndwood's *Provinciale*', in *Medieval Texts and Studies* (Oxford, 1973), 161.

through the diocesan muniments at Exeter. The marginal note 'bona forma' alongside a certain phrase in the abjuration of John Edward in Arundel's Canterbury register may well have been made by someone undertaking just such an exploratory exercise. However, that this search was not systematic is suggested by the occurrence of exactly the same phrase, unnoticed, in Repingdon's much earlier abjuration recorded in Courtenay's Canterbury register.[47]

The other source of exemplars available to lawyers was the formulary or precedent book into which notable and typical examples of various ecclesiastical instruments could be copied. Several examples survive of these highly personal collections, culled from the acts of courts and jurisdictions where the books' compilers had worked. A well-known example containing copies of documents relating to heresy trials is that made by John Lydford, a canon lawyer from Devon whose career took him from the chancellor's court at Oxford University and the Court of Arches, to the papal court at Avignon, and home to be official of Winchester and archdeacon of Totnes.[48] As one of the assessors of Wyclif's work at the Blackfriars Council in 1382 he had become interested in heresy. His formulary includes the 'frivolous appeal' to Rome made by Hereford and Repingdon following Wyclif's condemnation, a series of interrogatory articles drawn up for the bishop of London's trial of William Thorpe, and Thorpe's response to them.[49] As in some episcopal registers, the heresy-related texts are grouped together, presumably for ease of reference. Indeed, the similarity of purpose and form between formularies and diocesan registers means that in some cases they are not easily distinguishable. A register is essentially a diocesan formulary.[50]

When a register does not account for all of a bishop's activities, formularies are one of the sources we can turn to for information. Not much is known about the anti-heresy work of Richard Fleming, another youthful adherent of Wycliffism who shook off the taint of heresy to become bishop of Lincoln from 1420 to 1431.[51] What little we do know may be

[47] Reg. Arundel (Canterbury), i. fo. 390ʳ; Reg. Courtenay (Canterbury), fo. 34ᵛ.
[48] *John Lydford's Book*, ed. D. M. Owen, HMC, Joint Publications, 22 (London, 1974), 7–11.   [49] Ibid. 108–17.
[50] Owen, *Medieval Canon Law*, 33, describes a York formulary which is catalogued as Episcopal Register 13 in the Borthwick Institute.
[51] Catto, 'Wyclif and Wycliffism', 243–4; Thomson, *Later Lollards*, 102–3; Hudson, *Premature Reformation*, 101–2.

augmented from the pages of a formulary compiled by Master William
Symond, a bachelor of canon law who became official to the archdeacon
of Oxford and commissary for Oxford and Buckingham archdeaconries
in the 1440s.[52] The manuscript, British Library, MS Harley 670, fos.
37^r–198^r, contains notes on two heresy cases. One is a copy made from
the register of John Buckingham of the sentence against the heretical vil-
lagers of Chipping Warden, who in 1388 had mutilated the horses of the
bishop's commissaries.[53] The other is a letter from bishop 'R' of Lincoln,
who must be Fleming, testifying to the good fame and freedom from suspicion of one Richard 'D' from parish 'A' in the Chilterns, possibly
Amersham, who had been examined on charges of heresy.[54] Symond may
have copied this document because of the importance of getting the form
of such an important letter exactly right. Letters testimonial certifying
freedom from suspicion of heresy had potentially life-saving qualities.
Unfortunately we do not know whether either Symond or Lydford ever
had further cause to use these formulae in their diocesan work, as later
registers from Lincoln and Exeter do not mention them.

    One formulary that certainly was used by lawyers dealing with heresy
is Ely Diocesan Registry MS F/5/32, which has a terminal date of about
1439. It was compiled by a lawyer who had worked at both Ely and York,
and contains a copy of a commission from Archbishop 'R' of York initiat-
ing procedures against heretics in town 'N'.[55] Much of the preamble to
this York commission is taken from Arundel's 1382 mandate against
unlicensed preaching in Ely diocese, beginning with the characteristic
phrase 'Splendorem solitum fidei catholice per actus indiscretos et perversa
reproborum quasi tenebrosi fumi caligine vidimus obfuscari', and borrowing many other images besides.[56] This phrase is itself unmistakably a
modified version of the opening of Clement V's canon *Nolentes splendorum* from the Council of Vienne, 1311–12.[57] The archbishop in question
could be either Robert Waldby (1397) or Richard Scrope (1398–1405),
and town 'N' is likely to be Nottingham. Unfortunately neither of their

[52] On Symond see H. G. Richardson, 'An Oxford Lawyer's Notebook', in *Formularies
which Bear on the History of Oxford c.1204–1420*, ed. H. E. Salter, W. A. Pantin, and
H. G. Richardson, 2 vols., Oxford Historical Society, NS 4, 5 (1942), ii. 453–6.
    [53] BL, MS Harley 670, fos. 134^v–135^v. For the Chipping Warden incident see Chapter 2.
    [54] BL, MS Harley 670, fos. 152^v–153^r. For possible heresy in this area in 1415–16 see
Thomson, *Later Lollards*, 54.   [55] CUL, Ely Diocesan Registry, MS F/5/32, fo. 14^r.
    [56] Reg. Arundel (Ely), fo. 41^v.   [57] Clem. 5.3.2.

registers contains the original from which the formulary entry was copied. Although individual notaries or bishops were quite capable of using similar phrases independently of each other, the fact that the Ely and York documents alter the words of *Nolentes splendorum* in exactly the same way strongly indicates that the latter was drawn up with the former to hand. This suggests two movements of texts and people: someone copied the York text into the formulary now Ely Diocesan Registry F/5/32, and brought it south, prior to which someone else, or the same person, had taken a copy of Arundel's 1382 commission north to York. There are two possible explanations for the movement north, behind both of which lies a canonist's interest in a diocesan mandate so clearly superior to the provincial statute it pre-dated by a few days.

Arundel of course was translated to York in 1388, and many of his Ely staff moved with him, presumably taking boxes of legal documents with them. These men included John Newton, who was the official of Ely and then Arundel's vicar-general at York from 1388, and Thomas Dalby, archdeacon first of Ely and then of Richmond from 1388 until his death in 1400, a date which takes us into Scrope's episcopacy.[58] If the York document was indeed associated with Scrope rather than Waldby, another candidate for its transmission northwards is Scrope himself, chancellor of Cambridge University 1378–9 and official of the bishop of Ely from 1375 to 1379. He was a distinguished canonist who had served as papal chaplain and auditor of causes, and who owned copies of the *Liber sextus* and the *Clementines* as well as various glosses and commentaries, all of which he bequeathed to his nephew Stephen Scrope, who in turn left them to William Alnwick, later the bishop of Norwich.[59] If he was not only the vehicle for the transmission of a useful precedent northwards, but also the author of the formulary under discussion, that formulary may have found its way back to East Anglia by the same route as his other books.

Other pieces of anti-heresy legislation journeyed around the dioceses in a similar way, movements which are only explicable by the practice of note taking and copying by canon lawyers whose careers took them to new jobs and different courts where their cumulated expertise would be

---

[58] Aston, *Arundel*, 390–4; *Fasti Ecclesiae Anglicanae 1300–1541*, vi: *Northern Province*, ed. B. Jones (Oxford, 1967), 26.

[59] *BRUC*, 513–14; Owen, *Medieval Canon Law*, 13; M. Harvey, *The English in Rome 1362–1420: Portrait of an Expatriate Community* (Cambridge, 1999), 135.

much in demand.[60] Lost formularies are thus likely to lie behind many instances of textual transmission for which we have no more evidence than the similarity between two texts and speculation about the career paths that might connect them. One such example takes us from London in 1386 to Lincoln in 1405 and Rochester in 1435, with the possibility of two lost formularies having been used. What link these times and places are excerpts from a mandate issued by Robert Braybroke in November 1386 prohibiting the admission of John Aston and Nicholas Hereford to preach in the archdeaconry of London. Braybroke specified that preaching licences should only be recognized if they post-dated his mandate, and that according to the canon *Dudum a Bonifacio*, mendicant friars were exempted from the requirement for individual approval.[61] This mandate drew heavily upon Courtenay's 1382 statute on unlicensed preaching, but went into much more detail in this particular clause. The second appearance of Braybroke's London measure occurred in April 1405 when Philip Repingdon charged the official of the archdeacon of Huntingdon and the abbot of Notley to direct the clergy not to admit preachers without the bishop's licence.[62] Both mandates repeat the combination of clauses from Courtenay's statute and the references to mendicant exemption and *Dudum a Bonifacio* that characterize the London text.

There were many middle- and high-ranking clergy whose movements between London and Lincoln might have involved the copying and transmission of this text, but prominent among them are Braybroke himself, who had been a canon of Lincoln since 1378, and Thomas Stow, a doctor of civil law who was commissary to the bishop of London in 1385, then archdeacon of London from 1397 to 1400, dean of St Paul's from 1400 to 1405, and archdeacon of Bedford in Lincoln diocese from 1388 until 1405.[63]

---

[60] *Lydford's Book*, 16–17: For canonists 'the difficulties of the English hierarchy are . . . a series of problems in the drafting of documents, the arranging of compositions, the invocation of ecclesiastical censures'.

[61] Reg. Braybroke (London), fo. 372ᵛ: 'ne dictos Nicholum et Johannem aliquemve seu aliquos alios cuiuscumque condicionis vel preeminencie existant, fratribus mendicum ordinum iuxta formam constitucionem Clementis dudum exceptis, in ecclesiis seu capellis archidiaconate vestri supradicti ad predicandum admittant nisi litteras nostras post datum presencium eis concessis exhibuerint.' For *Dudum a Bonifacio* see Clem. 2.1.1.

[62] *Reg. Repingdon (Lincoln)*, i. 7–8, 48–9.

[63] *BRUO*, i. 254–5; *Fasti Ecclesiae Anglicanae 1300–1541*, v: *St Paul's London*, 6, 8, and i: *Lincoln*, 16; Boyle, 'Canon Law before 1380', 548.

At Lincoln the text appears to have been jotted down by the young Thomas Brouns, whose advancement through the legal profession took in the archdeaconries of Stow and Berkshire and the archbishop's court of audience, where he was auditor of causes and chancellor, before becoming bishop of Rochester in 1435 and bishop of Norwich in 1436.[64] During his brief tenure at Rochester Brouns used the text of the London 1386/Lincoln 1405 mandate to prevent unlicensed preaching in the deaneries of Dartford and Rochester. It is probable that he copied it not from Repingdon's register, but from a lost original in the Lincoln chancery, because his rendering of the preamble is closer to the 1386 version than to the 1405 registered version.[65] Given his long experience of dealing with heresy, on the ground in visitations and theoretically in Convocation, his resort to a fifty-year-old legal instrument to deal with a current problem, when many more recent models were available, cannot be dismissed as unimaginative repetition. We should see this as an informed choice, but one which nevertheless adds a caveat to the general theme of the increasing standardization of formulae. The combination of personal and institutional record keeping could perpetuate oddities as well as iron out differences.

A number of lawyers, theologians, and other persons interested in heresy made concerted efforts to gather material that would facilitate the refutation or detection of Wycliffites. Bishop Reginald Pecock's ill-fated project to engage systematically with English heretical texts is well known, and similar research had been undertaken by Thomas Netter into Wyclif and Purvey's Latin works in the preparation for his *Doctrinale antiquitatum fidei ecclesiae catholicae*.[66] Netter's work is also likely to have drawn upon the collection of anti-heretical documents known as *Fasciculi zizaniorum*, which was compiled by successive priors provincial of the English Carmelites from the 1380s to the 1430s, and included material from trials and the royal statutes of 1401 and 1414 in addition to theological refutations and documents relating to earlier academic

---

[64] *BRUO*, i. 281–2; Thomson, *Later Lollards*, 132, 177, 225.

[65] Reg. Brouns (Rochester), fo. 3ᵛ.

[66] Aston, 'Bishops and Heresy', 83–93; M. Bose, 'Reginald Pecock's Vernacular Voice', in Somerset et al. (eds.), *Lollards and their Influence*, 217–36; Ghosh, *Wycliffite Heresy*, 174–5; A. Hudson, 'Lollard Book Production', in J. Griffiths and D. Pearsall (eds.), *Book Production and Publishing in Britain 1375–1475* (Cambridge, 1989), 125.

heresies and to the Hussites.[67] Some of the items in *Fasciculi zizaniorum* are related to entries in another book that has the appearance of a dedicated heresy formulary, but which was probably a research tool made by someone involved in the dispute over the archiepiscopal visitation of Oxford between 1407 and 1412. It contains documents relating to the examination of Wyclif's works, possibly intended to prove the university's conscientious activity against heresy, and a copy of Arundel's 1409 constitutions, which stipulated the wide-ranging anti-heresy responsibilities of the university.[68] A book which contains different texts but exhibits the same anti-heretical zeal is All Souls College MS 42, in which the statutes of 1401, 1409, and 1414 are accompanied by a tract on the veneration of images, and a *Confutacio lollardorum* by John Barton, who in 1416 had purged himself of heresy and suspicion of heresy.[69]

Research into heresy and anti-heresy law was made possible by the multiplication of legal texts as they were copied and passed from diocese to diocese. Naturally Oxford was a centre for the accumulation of information on the subject, but other places such as the Carmelite library in London also became repositories. The Benedictine monks at Reading were another focus for information gathering, probably as a result of their involvement in heresy detection in 1396 and 1427.[70] A copy of William Paul's fourteenth-century *Summa summarum* owned by the abbey has a fifteen-column refutation of the Wycliffite belief that images should not be worshipped, and a copy of the conclusions of Walter Brut, added to the end leaves in a much later hand.[71] Brut, condemned by Bishop Trefnant of Hereford in October 1393, is misidentified as *John* Brut, but nonetheless this does seem to be an attempt to update the major canon law reference

[67] Bodleian, MS e. Musaeo 86; J. Crompton, '*Fasciculi zizaniorum*', parts I and II, *JEH* 12 (1961), 35–45; and *JEH* 11 (1960), 155–66. For the theological and polemical anti-heretical writings of Carmelites, see R. Copsey, 'The Carmelites in England 1242–1539: Surviving Writing', *Carmelus*, 43 (1996), 192–3, 208, 211–13; and *Carmelus*, 44 (1997), 190.

[68] BL, MS Cotton Faustina C VII, fos. 131^r–187^r, printed with older foliation in *Snappe's Formulary and Other Records*, ed. H. E. Salter, Oxford Historical Society, 80 (Oxford, 1924), 90–193. Arundel's constitutions are at fos. 159^v–165^r. On the examination of Wyclif's works see A. Hudson, 'Notes of an Early Fifteenth-Century Research Assistant, and the Emergence of the 267 Articles against Wyclif', *EHR* 118 (2003), 685–97.

[69] All Souls College, Oxford, MS 42, fos. 257^v–314^r; for Barton's trial see *Reg. Chichele (Canterbury)*, iii. 15–16.

[70] PRO, C 54/238, m. 28 (*CCR 1396–99*, 9); Reg. Nevill (Salisbury), part 2, fo. 28^r.

[71] BL, MS Royal 10 D X, fos. 308^r–313^r.

work owned by the abbey.[72] In addition, marginal annotations to the canon *Multorum querela* in a Reading manuscript of the *Clementines* belonging to Prior Thomas Erleye (1409–29) may be connected to deliberations on the proposal put before Convocation in 1428 that religious houses should be responsible for incarcerating heretics.[73] These two manuscripts show that academic and practical interest in heresy were intimately linked, an impression which is reinforced by the extensive collection of heresy-related documents gathered together by the Augustinian canon Henry Knighton as sources for his chronicle.

Knighton made copies of statutes and mandates against heresy, inserting them into his narrative alongside the vernacular texts of Wyclif's alleged statements on the Eucharist, sermons by Purvey and Aston, and lists of the early opinions of his abbot, Philip Repingdon.[74] In making a judgement as to whether Knighton travelled to look at these documents, or whether they were sent to him at Leicester, we may consider the resemblance between his use of original sources in a chronicle and the Carmelite use of similar documents in the less elaborate narrative of *Fasciculi zizaniorum*. The latter had been compiled from documents sent to London Whitefriars by members of the order involved in anti-heresy activities. For example, as bishop of Hereford, the Carmelite friar Robert Mascall had submitted a copy of the letter concerning Oldcastle's trial that he received in 1413.[75] Knighton may have received similar extracts from Bishop Buckingham of Lincoln, or he might have made copies from the many texts in circulation. Because of a lack of surviving documentation, we know very little about the copying and recopying of episcopal instruments in the course of their execution, but because of the numbers of officers involved we may assume that it was voluminous.[76]

Besides the multiplication of documents as provincial and diocesan initiatives were communicated to officials, statutes and mandates were copied and experiences shared in the course of co-operation between different dioceses. Two bishops might exchange information on a case of mutual interest to their jurisdictions, as when details of William

[72] *Reg. Trefnant (Hereford)*, 359.

[73] BL, MS Royal 11 C XI, fo. 82ᵛ; *Reg. Chichele (Canterbury)*, iii. 192–3.

[74] *Knighton's Chronicle 1337–1396*, ed. G. H. Martin (Oxford, 1995), pp. xxxvi–xxxvii; *Selections from English Wycliffite Writings*, ed. A. Hudson (2nd edn., Toronto, 1997), 141–3.   [75] *Reg. Mascall (Hereford)*, 116; *Fasciculi zizaniorum*, 433–50.

[76] Compare with comments in Bellomo, *Common Legal Past*, 131–3 on academic literature.

Swinderby's arrest and trial in Lincoln diocese were copied in London in 1389 by a member of Trefnant's household, and taken to Hereford where he had once again become suspected of heresy.[77] The staff of a neighbouring diocese could be co-opted for an investigation, to provide local knowledge or to prevent suspects escaping to a jurisdiction where the instigating bishop's ordinary authority did not run. This was certainly the case in Bishop Nevill of Salisbury's 1427 inquisition in the far east of his diocese, when he commissioned not only the abbots of Reading and Abingdon, the prior of Wallingford, and the archdeacon of Berkshire, but also Thomas Bekynton, who was then archdeacon of Buckingham in Lincoln diocese.[78] The border between Salisbury and Lincoln dioceses to the south of Oxford had previously been the focus of joint action between Ralph Erghum and John Buckingham, at the instigation of Archbishop Courtenay, against idolatry in the Wycombe and Marlow area in 1385.[79] Covering such a vast area, the borders of Lincoln diocese were extremely difficult to police during visitations and inquisitions. In 1413 Repingdon tried to prevent jurisdiction-hopping by heresy suspects in Leicester archdeaconry by employing John Oudeby, the archdeacon of Derby from the neighbouring diocese of Coventry and Lichfield, as a proctor.[80]

Joint action of this kind was regulated by the decree *Per hoc*, which ordered bishops and inquisitors to co-operate when acting together and to communicate when acting separately.[81] This naturally involved the reciprocal transmission of documentation. External help could be sought from even further afield, as in the trial of Henry Taylor of Worcester diocese in 1421. He abjured heresy in the collegiate church at Stratford-upon-Avon in the presence of David Pryce, who is styled canon of Lincoln, although he was also by that time the chancellor of St Davids, and John Firton, a canon of Salisbury. Also present as witnesses were three men described as esquires, one 'litteratus', and 'other worthy men of Coventry and Worcester dioceses'.[82] What this collection of witnesses suggests is the latitude bishops enjoyed when choosing appropriate personnel for heresy investigations. It is tempting to think that Pryce was sought out for his experience in these matters.

---

[77] *Reg. Trefnant (Hereford)*, 231. Hudson, *Premature Reformation*, 125–6, gives later examples of information being exchanged between dioceses.
[78] Reg. Nevill (Salisbury), part 2, fo. 28ʳ; Thomson, *Later Lollards*, 53–7.
[79] Reg. Erghum (Salisbury), fo. 181.   [80] Lincolnshire Archives, MS Vj/0, *passim*.
[81] VI 5.2.17.   [82] Reg. Morgan (Worcester), p. 87.

Lawyers gained experience of the kind exemplified in Pryce's career by attending trials. In addition to the president of a court or the official conducting a visitation, who would always be well versed in either civil or canon law, other lawyers would often be present in an advisory or delegated capacity. To take the heresy trials in Norwich diocese between 1428 and 1431 as an example, we see that diocesan officials such as Richard Caudray, notary public and archdeacon of Norwich, took part alongside lawyers and theologians holding no formal position in the diocesan hierarchy.[83] Among the canon lawyers present Thomas Ludham held no post in the diocese at all, Thomas Ryngstede was dean of St Mary's in the Fields in Norwich, while William Bernham was a former official and vicar-general.[84] Civil lawyers such as John Sutton (identifiable as either a fellow of King's Hall or a notary public from Cornwall) and James Walsingham also sat on the tribunals,[85] as did theologians such as William Worsted, the Benedictine prior of Norwich, Robert Colman, a Norwich Franciscan, and the Carmelites John Thorpe and John Keninghale.[86] In another category altogether was William Aiscough, the royal servant and theologian whose meteoric rise was just beginning at this time.[87] This selection of men learned in scripture and the law was typical of the heresy panels of the later Middle Ages, which reflected the need for episcopal judges to have expert advisers. This expertise was acquired at university and honed in legal practice. The career of Richard Caudray, moving between diocesan posts, the chancellorship of Cambridge University, and royal service, is typical of that class of men for whom the lecture room and the courtroom were both familiar territory. Even as far from the universities as Hereford diocese, a theologian of the calibre of Richard Rotheram could be present at a heresy trial, advising the vicar of Leominster, a bachelor of canon law called John Vir who often acted as a commissary for the bishop, and preaching against the errors detected.[88] How well did the training received at university prepare these men for their involvement in heresy detection?

[83] *Norwich Heresy Trials*, 51, 60; *BRUC*, 126–7.

[84] *Norwich Heresy Trials, passim*; *BRUC*, 376 (Ludham), 499–500 (Ryngstede), 57–8 (Bernham).   [85] *BRUC*, 567 (Sutton), 613 (Walsingham).

[86] *BRUO*, i. 468 (Colman), ii. 1035–6 (Keninghale), iii. 2089–90 (Worsted); *BRUC*, 586 (Thorpe).   [87] *Norwich Heresy Trials, passim*; *BRUO*, i. 15–16.

[88] *Reg. Spofford (Hereford)*, 152–3. On Rotheram's learning see Lepine, 'A Long Way from University', 187–91.

An education in canon or civil law gave prospective lawyers a general knowledge of the principles underpinning both the Roman and papal systems. To some extent the incorporation of Roman into canon law from the twelfth century onwards meant that the study of either involved much common ground. For canonists, two years were spent attending lectures on the *Liber extra*, *Liber sextus*, and *Clementines*, organized over a recurring cycle. Books 1, 4, and 5 of the *Extra* were made compulsory, while lecturers could select from the remaining corpus so as to make their workload more manageable.[89] This would have meant that all students in the canon law faculty had studied the title *De hereticis* in Gregory IX's collection (X 5.7), but relied for their knowledge of the same titles in the later books on voluntarily given lectures and individual study. Civilians need not have had any contact at all with the details of procedural canon law. This placed a premium on the importance of practice and personal reading for learning about anti-heresy procedure. In England such reading was likely to be restricted to the great continental commentaries and glosses, although specialist texts such as Berengar Frédol's *Tractatus de excommunicatione et interdicto* were available to a few readers.[90] The lack of a strong domestic tradition of legal commentary did not hamper the English episcopate's ability to deal with heresy. Men such as Edmund Stafford and John Trefnant, both of whom made significant contributions to the anti-heresy cause, were eminent civilians, each writing *repetitiones* on the *Digest* of Justinian.[91] At the other end of the scale, men such as Thomas Brouns and David Pryce produced no academic work that survives, and yet their reputation as heresy hunters was formidable.

Less certain is whether the faculties of canon law at Oxford and Cambridge ever taught provincial constitutions as part of the curriculum. Their graduates certainly went on to staff the courts of dioceses, archdeaconries, and other ecclesiastical jurisdictions, but the prominence of civilians in the same posts suggests that procedural aspects of canon law could be learnt on the job. Dorothy Owen has argued that the glosses of

[89] Boyle, 'Canon Law before 1380', 547–8; J. L. Barton, 'The Legal Faculties of Late Medieval Oxford', in Catto and Evans (eds.), *Late Medieval Oxford*, 299.

[90] R. H. Helmholz, 'The Canon Law', in L. Hellinga and J. B. Trapp (eds.), *The Cambridge History of the Book in Britain*, iii: *1400–1557* (Cambridge, 1999), 391. For Frédol see Chapter 1.

[91] R. G. Davies, 'The Episcopate', in C. H. Clough (ed.), *Profession, Vocation and Culture in Later Medieval England* (Liverpool, 1982), 69; *BRUO*, iii. 1749–50. Stafford's *repetitio* is in Bodleian, MS New College 179, fos. 33^r–103^v.

John Acton and Lyndwood were not part of the formal curriculum, but were studied in private by many students, while Brundage has since argued that these may have been taught as 'extraordinary' texts in the same way as the *Sext* and the *Clementines*.[92] Whether formal or informal, the study of provincial legislation alongside the papal law books has left codicological and bibliographical evidence in academic collections which combine the two. For example, a fourteenth-century book containing Peter Lombard's *Sentences*, the *Liber sextus*, and the canons of the legatine councils of London, 1237 and 1268, belonged to the Hereford canonist Richard Rudhale in the mid-fifteenth century.[93] A similar miscellany in a Cambridge manuscript includes Archbishop Stratford's constitutions, an index to the *Liber sextus*, extracts from the *Decretum* and the *Summa aurea* of Hostiensis, and material for a confessor. Owen described this book as an 'aid to learning'.[94]

Common lawyers, justices of the peace, and Chancery clerks received an increasingly specialized education at the 'third university' of the Inns of Chancery and Inns of Court. The core of the curriculum was the study of original writs, attendance at the law courts, and detailed 'readings' of statutes very similar to the *lecturae* of the universities.[95] Registers of writs and statute books were both the basis of this curriculum and the means by which knowledge of procedure in the royal courts reached a wider audience, especially once English-language copies began to be made. Numerous Latin and French statute books contain copies of the 1401 and 1414 statutes against heresy, often with cross-references in their indexes between 'heresye' and 'lollard'.[96] Collections of writs could be more idiosyncratic, such as the Worcester collection including the writ of *Venire facias* citing the 1414 statute, and a roll of writs in the British Library that contains writs of *De heretico comburendo* relating to William Sawtry and John Oldcastle, a 1414 instruction for justices to inquire into preaching,

[92] Owen, *Medieval Canon Law*, 2; J. A. Brundage, 'The Canon Law Curriculum in Medieval Cambridge', in J. A. Bush and A. Wijffels (eds.), *Learning the Law: Teaching and Transmission of Law in England 1150–1900* (London, 1999), 188.

[93] Hereford Cathedral Library, MS P. ii. 2. On Rudhale see Lepine, 'A Long Way from University', 191–2.   [94] CUL, MS Mm. 4. 41; Owen, *Medieval Canon Law*, 15–16.

[95] P. Brand, 'Courtroom and Schoolroom: The Education of Lawyers in England Prior to 1400', in *The Making of the Common Law* (London, 1992), 57–8.

[96] BL, MS Lansdowne 470, fos. 180ʳ–181ᵛ (1401), fos. 209ᵛ–211ʳ (1414); BL, MS Harley 644, fos. 194ʳ–195ʳ (1401), 216ᵛ–217ᵛ (1414); Bodleian, MS Douce 312, fos. 108ᵛ (writ of *De heretico comburendo* derived from 1401 statute), 124ʳ–125ʳ (1414).

insurrection, and sedition, an order to make proclamations for the capture of Oldcastle, and a writ for Bishop Alexander Tottington of Norwich to arrest heretics.[97] Later fifteenth- and early sixteenth-century books for justices of the peace sometimes include an instruction for jurors to report heretics and lollards. Those citing the 1414 statute go a little further, ordering jurors to inquire into such persons.[98] Cross-referencing, glosses, and, in British Library, MS Harley 1777, the full text of the statutes cited, all suggest that such collections were educational as well as practical in purpose, perhaps produced at the Inns of Chancery.

If Chancery was the hub of secular law making and education in late medieval England, Convocation performed a similar role for the church. The control over anti-heresy policy sought by Arundel as chancellor in 1406, to have all cases of heresy certified to him in Chancery, was matched by Chichele in 1416 when he ordered that anyone strongly suspected of heresy was to be kept in prison until the next session of Convocation, when he or she should be brought before the prelates and clergy of the province, together with documentation pertaining to 'each and every circumstance of the case, especially any abjurations'.[99] This information was then to be inserted into the records of the court of Canterbury. The view that this was an attempt to set up a 'central register of offenders' is plausible and entirely consistent with the summarizing, collecting, and codifying of anti-heresy procedures that was happening at this time. Chichele's personal role, however, may be said to be crucial.[100] From this point onwards, his archiepiscopal register records the frequent and extensive examination of heretics in Convocation, occasions which provided the bishops, lawyers, and diocesan administrators present with unrivalled opportunities to see trials in process, hear learned lawyers such as Lyndwood in action, and participate in the exchange of texts and information with their fellows.[101] But one cannot

[97] *Early Treatises*, 276–7; BL, MS Additional 35205, mm. 7, 13d, 15d.

[98] Northamptonshire Record Office, Andrew (Harlestone), A. 98; BL, MS Harley 1777, fo. 84ᵛ: 'Fyrst ye shall inquire of all heretyke and lollardys and of all such as holde erroneous oppynyons and teche or preche the same contrarie to the faith and lawes of holy chirche and if there be eny such ye shall doo us to wete of there names and of ther oppynyons and hough longe they have contynuyd theryn.' I would like to thank Paul Brand for these references and his guidance.

[99] *Reg. Chichele (Canterbury)*, iii. 19: 'aliisque omnibus et singulis circumstanciis premissis quomodolibet concernentibus, ac persertim de abjuracionibus.'

[100] Aston, 'Bishops and Heresy', 80.

[101] Ibid. 76–7; Churchill, *Canterbury Administration*, i. 372–3.

ascribe all of this to the archbishop alone. Many minds were involved in this project, behind the scenes and in organizational roles. Both aspects are fully illustrated in the Convocations of 1428, when serious efforts were made to standardize the whole process of heresy detection and trial.

In May 1428 Convocation was called to meet that July to discuss 'the extirpation of heretical wickedness from the bounds of the faithful', in topographical terms that recall the instruction to secular princes in *Excommunicamus*.[102] Convocation met from 5 to 21 July, and again from 25 November to 4 December, during which time a number of measures for the detection and prosecution of heresy were discussed, and procedural documents drawn up. On 10 July, while Chichele was in conference with the royal council, Thomas Brouns, at this time Chichele's chancellor, was directed to nominate representatives from the prelates and the clergy to form a committee to decide on the best methods by which to proceed against heretics.[103] Once this was formed, Brouns read out 'certain constitutions' and a royal statute against heresy, so as to facilitate discussion by reminding the committee members of prior legislation on the subject.[104] On 14 July Brouns came before Convocation, chaired in Chichele's absence by Bishops Langdon of Rochester and Fleming of Lincoln, and reported on the committee's deliberations. He 'publicly produced and read a tract on the mode of proceeding against heretics and also a formula for the abjuration of errors and heresies'.[105] These were inspected by the gathered prelates and clergy, but little was changed or added. The records of Convocation do not note the promulgation of these decisions, but Anne Hudson has discovered that they were copied by some of those present. The register of Thomas Polton, bishop of Worcester, who was present at the July Convocation, includes a form of abjuration and procedural notes on recording the detection or denunciation in writing, on contumacy, interrogation, the imprisonment of

[102] Reg. Alnwick (Norwich), fo. 98ᵛ: 'ad extirpandam de finibus fidelium hereticam prauitatem'; *Reg. Chichele (Canterbury)*, iii. 184.

[103] *Reg. Chichele (Canterbury)*, iii. 186: 'communicarent et deliberate viderent quo modo et qua via esset melius et expedicius procedendum contra hereticos.'

[104] Ibid.: 'Thomas Brouns legit ibidem publice quasdam constituciones et eciam quoddam statutum regium contra hereticos edita, ut hiis visis et intellectis possent lenius et facilius procedere in materia antedicte.'

[105] Ibid. 187: 'Thomas Brouns . . . produxit ibidem in publicum et legit quemdam tractatum de modo procedendi contra hereticos ac eciam quandam formam abjuracionis errorum et heresum.'

offenders to secure their appearance before Convocation, and purgation.[106] At the end of these the name 'Brouns' is noted, suggesting that they represent the texts read out and seen in the 1428 Convocation. Another copy of the procedural material exists in a formulary compiled by someone with experience of the courts of London and Coventry and Lichfield dioceses, where it is followed by a record of a heresy trial conducted by a Bishop Robert (probably Braybroke) of London as well as constitutions eight to twelve of Arundel's 1409 legislation.[107] Rough copies of Brouns's notes on interrogation and contumacy were also made by someone in the service of William Gray, bishop of London. This person wrote his copies onto an empty leaf of Richard Clifford's London register, using a diocesan register as a notebook in much the same way as lawyers did their formularies.[108] Further copies were later made by the compilers of two more general collections of pastoral and legal works, and the form of abjuration indeed came to be very widely used.[109] The evidence for bishops and canonists applying procedures that had been agreed upon in Convocation but never formally promulgated by the dean of the province may be compared with that for Repingdon's unilateral action in 1413. In both instances the importance of Convocation as a forum for deliberation as well as an authority for rubber-stamping legislation is emphasized.

The following week in Convocation, on 21 July, Chichele reminded his diocesans of a central plank of the 1416 statute against heresy. He 'asked, exhorted, and requested his bishops that when making inquiries into heresy they inform him of everything they do, especially of the names of anyone detected'.[110] The partial success of the centralization of anti-heresy work

---

[106] Reg. Polton (Worcester), pp. 111–12, 115. For a transcription see Hudson, 'Examination of Lollards', 135–9.

[107] BL, MS Harley 2179, fos. 157ʳ–159ʳ; Hudson, 'Examination of Lollards', 127, 129.

[108] Reg. Clifford (London), fo. 188ᵛ; Hudson, 'Examination of Lollards', 139. On the copying of statutes at Convocation and synods, see Cheney, *English Synodalia*, 45. Procedural material and instruments from two inquisitorial registers were similarly made into a formulary in fourteenth-century Bohemia: *Anfänge einer ständige Inquisition*, ed. Patschovsky.

[109] Balliol College, Oxford, MS 158, fos. 190ᵛ–192ᵛ and All Souls College, Oxford, MS 63, fos. 120ʳ–122ᵛ; for the influence of the abjuration formula see Hudson, 'Examination of Lollards', 127.

[110] *Reg. Chichele (Canterbury)*, iii. 190: 'rogavit, hortatus est et requisivit reverendissimus pater et dominus predictus prefatos confratres suos ut in inquisicione fienda contra lollardos et hereticos hujusmodi diligenciam interim omnimodam quam poterant adhiberent, et cum revenerint quid contra eos fecerint ipsum plenius certificarent, et specialiter de illis quorum nomina sibi detecta.'

since 1416 is evident in the record of the 1428 Convocation, which heard the cases of at least eight serious offenders and saw Chichele frantically communicating with the archdeacon of Canterbury about a large group of suspects in Kent who could not be found.[111] However, the reiteration of this policy emphasizes the need for the regular renewal of the anti-heretical zeal that could ebb and flow among the episcopate. Convocation provided an ideal occasion on which to do this. The July gathering was prorogued until 22 November, on which date a second committee was formed to consider the problem of heresy, consisting of the bishops of Ely, Bath and Wells, Worcester, and Rochester. It seems that they were digesting and editing a list of questions drawn up by Lyndwood for the interrogation of heresy suspects, which has survived in Polton's register and the Lichfield formulary alongside the procedural instructions discussed in July.[112] Again there is no indication that the resulting two lists, one produced 'by a jurist' and the other 'by theologians', were promulgated as provincial policy, but Hudson has argued that they were used in inquiries at Norwich between 1428 and 1431, and in Bath and Wells in 1449.[113] Abortive attempts were also made to tighten up the procedures for imprisoning heresy suspects in religious houses, and a clarification of the method and formula for degrading heretical priests may be dated to the same period.[114]

The energetic codification and centralization of anti-heresy procedures around 1428 may be linked to a series of factors other than the legislative will of the archbishop, all of which relate to the common experiences of the ecclesiastical governing class over the preceding generation. Community of outlook, the sharing of knowledge and documents, and a willingness to co-operate in the detection of heresy, were all fostered by what Leonard Boyle has called the 'old boys network' of Oxford and Cambridge law graduates in the later Middle Ages.[115] The links forged at university were often augmented by early training and experience as part of the household, or *familia*, of a successful bishop, such as Courtenay's circle at Hereford, London, and then Canterbury which included a number of talented canonists from the west country such as John Lydford, Ralph Tregrisiou, John and Baldwin Shillingford, and

[111] Ibid. iv. 297–301: correspondence concerning Kentish suspects, June to July 1428.
[112] Ibid. iii. 191–2; Reg. Polton (Worcester), pp. 113–14; Hudson, 'Examination of Lollards', 133–5. [113] Hudson, 'Examination of Lollards', 127, 130–1.
[114] *Reg. Chichele (Canterbury)*, iii. 192–3; BL, MS Additional 6157 (Chichele's pontifical), fos. 6ʳ–8ʳ. [115] Boyle, 'Canon Law before 1380', 556.

Robert Braybroke.[116] Lydford, John Shillingford, and Tregrisiou were all assessors of Wyclif's errors in 1382. Similarly the involvement of the young Thomas Brouns and David Pryce in Repingdon's 1413 anti-heresy drive gave them unrivalled experience which they put to use in later life as members of Chichele's household. Other lawyers on Chichele's staff were brought with him from his own Devon origins, such as Lyndwood and William Medford.[117] This was a small world of personal contacts and manuscript knowledge, the copying and circulation of which proceeded at a pace dictated by the movement of generations of students through the diocesan and curial career structures of the time.

The reception of provincial legislation, attendance at Convocation, and high-profile heresy cases, such as those of Wyclif's immediate circle and John Oldcastle, were the events that punctuated their careers and stimulated renewed interest in the subject. The major experience that defined the 1428 generation of bishops and canonists was the Council of Constance, which sat from 1414 until 1418. This general council of the church was called in order to bring an end to the schism that had afflicted the Latin church since 1378. Besides its aim of achieving unity in a universally acceptable papacy, the council was much concerned with heresy. The errors of Wyclif were condemned and Jan Hus was burned, having been examined before the council along with Jerome of Prague. The English delegation supplied much information about Wyclif that was important in tracing his influence upon Hus. The accumulation of proscribed writings and opinions that went into this effort must have had a significant effect upon their vigilance over heresy in their own dioceses. If, however, the English bishops were mulling over domestic instances of heresy whilst at Constance, they did in it their own time and kept it to themselves. No matter how often they referred to heresy in their sermons and speeches, it was rare that they mentioned the current problem in England, preferring to direct the council's attention towards Wyclif's influence in Bohemia.[118] As well as condemning the heresies of Wyclif

---

[116] *Lydford's Book*, 6–11; Boyle, 'Canon Law before 1380', 555.

[117] Owen, *Medieval Canon Law*, 36–7, discussing their communal formulary: BL, MS Harley 862. For Medford see *BRUO*, ii. 1252–3.

[118] See for example Robert Hallum's 8 December 1415 sermon in *Acta Concilii Constanciensis*, ed. H. Finke, 4 vols. (Regensburg, 1896–1928), ii. 423–5; Richard Fleming's of 6 January 1417 in *Andreas von Regensburg: Sämtliche Werke*, ed. G. Leidinger (Munich, 1903), 253–6; and Henry Abingdon's in *Monimenta Medii Aevi*, ed. C. Walch (Göttingen, 1757), i. part 2, 182–5.

and Hus the council issued a 'method of questioning anyone suspected of heresy', which was subsequently recorded in the Carmelite collection *Fasciculi zizaniorum*. Although substantially different from the 1428 lists of questions, this text may have sown a seed in the minds of the English delegation that they put into practice once on home ground.[119] After Hus's execution the problem of the Hussites continued to stimulate the English bishops in their own anti-heresy work. It is surely no coincidence that the sessions of Convocation in July and November 1428 which saw the trial of so many heretics and deliberation over so many areas of policy were also attended by the papal nuncio Condo de Zwola, who was negotiating for a subsidy and the sale of indulgences to finance the Hussite crusade, and Alexander Ferentini, who delivered several papal bulls touching on resistance to heretics.[120]

A good proportion of the English higher clergy were present at Constance, making it a truly unifying experience for a whole generation. At one time or another Robert Hallum (bishop of Salisbury), Nicholas Bubwith (bishop of Bath and Wells), Henry Beaufort (bishop of Winchester and cardinal bishop of St Eusebius), John Catterick (bishop of St David's), Richard Fleming (future bishop of Lincoln), Robert Nevill (future bishop of Salisbury), Henry Abingdon (future warden of Merton College), Thomas Spofford (then abbot of St Mary's York), Thomas Polton and Philip Morgan (future bishops of Worcester), and Richard Clifford (bishop of London) were all present. One contemporary observer noted twelve theologians and no fewer than thirty licentiates or doctors of canon law in the English party that arrived in January 1415.[121] If this figure is juxtaposed with Richard Davies's calculation that between 1399 and 1443 the proportion of lawyers in the English episcopate rose from one-quarter to two-fifths, a change he describes as the most important one of the period in episcopal appointments, then the standardization of anti-heresy law and practice can be seen within a more general pattern of increasing importance for canon law in church government.[122]

---

[119] Hudson, 'Examination of Lollards', 130.

[120] *Reg. Chichele (Canterbury)*, iii. 185–6, 194–6; W. E. Lunt, *Financial Relations of the Papacy with England 1327–1534* (Cambridge, Mass., 1962), 125–30, 562–70.

[121] Jacob, *Chichele*, 34; Richtenal's *Chronicle of the Council of Constance*, in *The Council of Constance: The Unification of the Church*, ed. L. R. Loomis, J. H. Mundy, and K. M. Woody (New York, 1961), 104.   [122] Davies, 'The Episcopate', 63.

Such were the means and timing by which the English episcopate and their diocesan administrators moved from ignorance about heresy to an informed familiarity. By 1428 investigations were often proactive and centrally co-ordinated, and they operated according to an increasingly standardized pattern. However, in order to succeed in actually detecting heresy on the ground, a much wider public had to be engaged: that of the trustworthy laity and the lower clergy. The channels and content of the propaganda intended for them will be the subject of the next two chapters.

5

The Channels of Propaganda

Communication in the Middle Ages was conducted through writing, speech, ritual, and appearance. This last category is very rarely perceptible to the historian and is included here a little awkwardly, and yet its importance in explaining how sin (including heresy) was discerned will become clear in the next chapter. The other three methods may more confidently be called media, and whether written or not, are all transmitted to us in written records, a factor which must be borne in mind when assessing the quality of our historical knowledge about the communicative event in question. Nonetheless, the voice, in the form of sermons and legal pronouncements, is fairly well attested in these records, and aspects of the visual scene may also be imaginatively reconstructed from literary and material evidence. Of course, there are difficulties in recreating past instances of communication, and the precise words of a sermon or the exact behaviour of a penitent are ultimately unknowable, but the potential for understanding remains greater than the historian can afford to ignore.

Three main classes of communication channel, or media, will be examined here: preaching and pastoral instruction, administrative or judicial *acta*, and public events. All communicative events (we may isolate 'events' from the constant continuum of communication in this case since they were largely formal occasions) naturally combine these media, besides gesture and body language, and so some of the classification is imposed purely for the sake of clarity. Propaganda, it should be noted, is used here in its neutral sense, with no connotation of lies, deceit, cynicism, or malice, although the sense of aiming to mould public opinion is retained. As a category of communication, the *propagation* of information reflects very well the medieval concept of centrally directed knowledge transfer, but our analysis cannot be so one-sided. The relationship between the propagator and the receiver of information was not a dichotomy between knowledge and ignorance, and the cultural divide between elite and 'popular' was not the chasm that it has sometimes been described as. Audiences of propaganda are of course fed with information and impressions, but the responses of those recipients in turn inform the propagandists about which media and messages are succeeding.

When we examine the channels by which knowledge of anti-heresy law and procedure was communicated to the laity and lower clergy, we must therefore bear in mind the total structure in which that communication took place. A great deal of information about heresy, and familiarity with the media in question, was derived from the systems of canon law, ecclesiastical government, and literary culture, and was not peculiar to heresy itself. For example, the methods of reporting serious spiritual crime and of checking licences were commonplaces of the church courts. So when a bishop came to instruct his diocese in the methods of heresy detection, he could rely upon his audience having a degree of fluency in the technical language he was using. Anti-heresy propaganda operated within an ecclesiastical culture that was in some measure common to all.

1. LICENSED PREACHING AND PASTORAL INSTRUCTION

Although a common culture, there were social distinctions in medieval Christianity, most notably between those who had access to the Latin word of God, and those who did not. Even by the late Middle Ages, by no means all of the parish clergy possessed sufficient Latin to be considered *litterati*. This was thought to be a serious limitation to the informed moral guidance the clergy were able to provide, and so, beginning in 1356 with John Thoresby's vernacular translation of the 1281 decree *Ignorantia sacerdotum*, English-language guides to the creed and pastoral duty were encouraged. These were one of the major conduits of information on sin and justice in the period, and despite being a highly derivative genre, the ideas they contained were vital to the detection of heresy. There is a pitfall of circular reasoning to be avoided when evaluating vernacular pastoral literature as an anti-heretical medium: all orthodoxy is non-heretical, so far as such absolute standards can be applied, but not all is directly anti-heretical. Some which was, such as Nicholas Love's *The Mirror of the Blessed Life of Jesus Christ*, licensed by Arundel in 1410 'for the edification of the people and the confutation of heretics or lollards', presented the anti-Wycliffite case to the reading public.[1] Not all the public was able to read, however, and pastoral literature was intended to serve as the basis for oral instruction.[2]

The Wycliffite heresy was in part a product of the same movement of pastoral reform that sought to educate the laity in the basics of the faith by providing the parish clergy with the literary and intellectual means to preach to them on the ten commandments, the creed, sin and virtue, the sacraments, and the essentials of canon law. Simon Forde has argued that Wyclif and his academic followers were conservative, if unusually idealistic, heirs of this preaching tradition.[3] As they moved towards an increasingly oppositional stance and their orthodoxy was called into question, that old tradition of pastoral instruction and lay education had to be revived by the episcopate, in competition with the Wycliffites, if heresy was not to be allowed to infect the whole community. By the early to mid-fifteenth century this repositioning of orthodoxy had led to 'a powerful new consensus, focused on the pastoral and evangelical dynamic of an educated, propertied clergy', coupled with 'vigilant orthodoxy' in the universities.[4] The growing perception that Wycliffite preaching exposed the laity to ideas and material only suitable for a clerical audience led to a vigorous restatement of the convention that sermon subject matter should be tailored to its audience.[5] In light of this, Arundel's constitutions proved to be a turning point both in stopping heretical preaching and in encouraging the organization of an orthodox preaching campaign that took proper account of the difference between lay and clerical audiences.

We have seen in Chapter 3 how Arundel hoped to stop heretical preaching in its tracks by making all preachers subject to a documentary check. In addition to enforcing this policy, diocesan bishops interpreted the legislation as the blueprint for a proactive campaign to license

---

[1] Ghosh, *Wycliffite Heresy*, 148.

[2] M. Aston, 'Devotional Literacy', in *Lollards and Reformers*, 125–7.

[3] S. Forde, 'Social Outlook and Preaching in a Wycliffite *Sermones dominicales* Collection', in I. Wood and G. A. Loud (eds.), *Church and Chronicle in the Middle Ages: Essays Presented to John Taylor* (London, 1991), 179–91; Hudson, *Premature Reformation*, 268–73.

[4] Catto, 'Wyclif and Wycliffism', 240; R. M. Ball, 'The Opponents of Bishop Pecok', *JEH* 48 (1997), 231.

[5] Reg. Arundel (Canterbury), ii. fo. 11ʳ, third constitution; Aston, *Faith and Fire*, 49 n.

orthodox preachers. This may well have been Arundel's unstated intention, as suggested by the entry recording the constitutions in Beaufort's Winchester register, where they are immediately followed by a general commission to his clergy to preach the word of God.[6] Preaching licences had been issued before 1409, including one to Thomas Wimbledon in 1385, which allowed him to preach in every church in Winchester diocese as long as he did not preach any heretical or erroneous conclusions, but after 1409 they are recorded with a much greater frequency in bishops' registers, especially those of Beaufort at Winchester, Repingdon, Fleming, and Alnwick at Lincoln, Stafford at Exeter, Lacy at Hereford and Exeter, Hallum at Salisbury, Polton at Worcester, Bubwith at Bath and Wells, and Arundel and Chichele at Canterbury.[7]

A licence granted in 1418 to Lewis Newchurch BA spells out the combative character that preaching had taken on in the wake of the Wycliffite challenge. Bishop Lacy wrote that since degenerate sons of the church, enemies and detractors under a simulated holiness, had newly and damnably been preaching and spreading bitterness, he deemed it most pious and meritorious to cause the true and divine seed to be preached to the people. To that end he announced to the abbots (as patrons of appropriated churches) and rectors of his diocese that he had licensed Newchurch to preach the word of God for the instruction of the people.[8] The metaphorical word, as a seed to be planted in the faithful, was contrasted with the bad seed of the heretical word. Commenting on Matthew 13: 24–30, one contemporary sermon writer explained that 'þer is grete vertu in þe worde of God. How so? For it turnythe a synfull man from his lyvyng . . . We þat ben sowers, þat is to sey, techars of Goddys law, we muste sow into youre sowlys þe sedys of the

---

6 Reg. Beaufort (Winchester), fo. 151ᵛ.

7 *Reg. Wykeham (Winchester)*, ii. 370–1: 'ad exercendum predicacionis officium, et proponendum verbum Dei in ecclesiis quibuscunque nostre diocesis . . . inhibentes tamen tibi expresse ne aliquas conclusiones hereticas seu erroneas, que statum nostre ecclesie Wyntoniensis . . . subvertere.' We have no extant examples of original preaching licences, the only copies being those entered in bishops' registers. Consequently the numbers that survive may under-represent numbers issued.

8 *Reg. Lacy (Hereford)*, 25: 'Cum utique post lollium jam noviter quod, proh dolor, in pluribus huius regni partibus per varios ecclesie catholice degeneres et privignos emulosque et detractores sub simulate specie sanctitatis Christicolas varios dampnabiliter seducendo nequiter sit aspersum et dogmatizatum, pium reputamus et meritorium semen verum et divinum in populo facere predicari.'

commowndementis of God.'⁹ Preaching was seen as a most powerful medium for instruction.

The majority of licensees were graduates, frequently masters of arts and theologians, and sometimes lawyers. Where lawyers were licensed it may be that anti-heresy law was being promulgated alongside theology, but instruction in the basic tenets of canon law was by no means beyond a theologian or master of arts. One theologian licensed to preach, Thomas Chace the master of Balliol, in fact owned a copy of the *Liber extra*, and another, Roger Huswyf, had trained in common law before becoming a bachelor of theology.¹⁰ The reforming bishops who appointed these preachers looked consciously to men whose talents and character were known to them. College fellows and local priests were the preferred choice, rather than the mendicant preachers who had been at the forefront of popular preaching in preceding centuries.¹¹ Clusters of these men indicate the conscious policy of the licensing bishop. For example, Repingdon and Bubwith each licensed three men who had been students or fellows at Merton in the first decade of the fifteenth century: John Duffield, Richard Eustace, and Richard Barron in Lincoln diocese, William Baret, John Peterton, and Thomas Cyrcetur in Bath and Wells.¹² Thomas Lute, fellow of Merton, was licensed in 1410 to preach in both Canterbury and Salisbury dioceses.¹³ In addition to his Merton appointments, Repingdon also appointed a pair of theologians from Pembroke Hall in Cambridge, John Thornhill and William Crosse, to preach in his diocese.¹⁴ Exeter College seems to have fostered a similar zeal and ability between 1400 and 1420, with William Grene licensed for Totnes archdeaconry in 1415 and Exeter diocese in 1421, Benedict Brent for the diocese in 1421, William Certeyn in 1422, and John Colyford in 1438.¹⁵ Edmund Lacy was keen to use Exeter College to support preaching in that diocese, but he also used a number of local men who were not

⁹ Bodleian, MS e. Musaeo 180, fo. 238ʳ, cited in C. J. Fraser, 'The Religious Instruction of the Laity in Late Medieval England with Particular Reference to the Sacrament of the Eucharist', D.Phil. thesis (Oxford, 1995), 66.

¹⁰ *BRUO*, i. 379–80 (Chace), ii. 990 (Huswyf).

¹¹ Catto, 'Wyclif and Wycliffism', 255.

¹² *Reg. Repingdon (Lincoln)*, i. 169, ii. 370; *Reg. Bubwith (Bath & Wells)*, i. 122, ii. 351; *BRUO*, i. 107–8, 115, 600, 653, iii. 1470. On Cyrcetur see R. M. Ball, 'Thomas Cyrcetur, a Fifteenth-Century Theologian and Preacher', *JEH* 37 (1986), 205–39.

¹³ Reg. Arundel (Canterbury), ii. fo. 123ᵛ; *Reg. Hallum (Salisbury)*, 146; *BRUO*, ii. 1180.

¹⁴ *Reg. Repingdon (Lincoln)*, iii. 145; *BRUC*, 169, 585.

¹⁵ *Reg. Lacy (Exeter)*, i. 11, 89–90, ii. 118; *BRUO*, i. 259–69, 378, 471, ii. 820.

graduates: Nicholas Selman, William Persons, John Trevelyan, Walter Stalworth, and William Berwick.[16] William Trebell, a bachelor of civil law and rector of Lanteglos-by-Camelford, was an unusually well-educated west country appointment.[17] Choosing men from the same region or the same college gave preaching licensees a group identity and may have been intended to keep the anti-heresy cause alive in the universities.

The qualifications of these preachers in terms of ability are beyond our reach, but a familiarity with heresy and anti-heresy may be inferred in some cases. The eleventh of Arundel's 1409 constitutions had required the heads of colleges and the principals of halls in Oxford to conduct monthly investigations into heresy amongst the masters and students, a responsibility which gave them practical familiarity with the thrust of anti-heresy law. Roger Whelpdale, provost of Queen's, Thomas Lute, sub-warden of Merton, Thomas Tankelden, principal of Hart Hall, John Possell, provost of Oriel, Thomas Chace, master of Balliol, Edward Upton, principal of St Edmund Hall, Robert Oppy, principal of St George's Hall, John Waryn, principal of Great and Little Lion Hall, and John Colyford, rector of Exeter, were all given licence to preach under the terms of the 1409 constitution.[18] Experience of heresy and anti-heresy could also be gained in other ways. Possell, for example, was one of the masters chosen to administer the June 1411 university oath to reject Wycliffite ideas. John Luke, licensed to preach in Salisbury and Exeter dioceses in 1410 and 1411, was on the committee appointed to examine Wyclif's works for errors;[19] Thomas Wyche, licensed for Lincoln diocese in 1445 is known to have owned Guido Terreni of Perpignan's *Summa de heresibus et earum confutationibus*, now Magdalen College, Oxford, MS lat. 4;[20] John Marshall, licensed for Lincoln diocese in 1416, was rector of Wistow in Leicestershire, where the parishioners had been investigated for admitting an unlicensed preacher in contravention of Arundel's constitutions in 1413.[21]

[16] *Reg. Lacy (Exeter)*, i. 13, 17–19, 24, 290.　　　[17] Ibid. 252; *BRUO* iii. 1891.

[18] *Reg. Hallum (Salisbury)*, 109–10, 146; Reg. Arundel (Canterbury), ii. fo. 123ᵛ; *Reg. Bubwith (Bath & Wells)*, i. 112; *Reg. Repingdon (Lincoln)*, iii. 165, 271; *Reg. Chichele (Canterbury)*, iv. 247–8; *Reg. Lacy (Exeter)*, i. 25, ii. 118.

[19] Catto, 'Wyclif and Wycliffism', 245–6; *Reg. Hallum (Salisbury)*, 109–10; Reg. Stafford (Exeter), i. fo. 122ᵛ.

[20] *BRUO*, iii. 2102; Reg. Alnwick (Lincoln), fo. 62ᵛ. I am grateful to Ralph Hanna for information on this manuscript.

[21] *BRUO*, ii. 1227–8; *Reg. Repingdon (Lincoln)*, iii. 142; Lincolnshire Archives, MS Vj/0, fo. 26ʳ.

A further category with experience of heresy were those university men who had dabbled in Wycliffite thought in their youth but capitulated to academic or judicial pressure after coming under suspicion of heresy. According to Hostiensis, clerics who had purged themselves of heresy were obliged to preach against other heretics as part of their penance.[22] It is quite possible that as a former sympathizer himself, Repingdon saw the potential for orthodox enthusiasm in Peter Partridge, a theologian who had toyed with Wyclif's ideas in the past, but who in 1413 was appointed to preach in the archdeaconry of Oxford.[23]

The geographical extent of preaching licences differed radically, reflecting the variety of aims within the policy. While most preachers were licensed for a single diocese or one or two archdeaconries, some licences focused on much smaller areas and some applied to the whole province. Local licences were granted to Nicholas Sydenham in 1411 for the parish church at Henley-on-Thames, to Thomas Joye in 1412 for the deaneries of Wycombe and Wendover in the Chilterns, to Alexander Curtis in 1412 and again in 1414 for the deanery of Trigg in Exeter diocese, to the monks of Ely studying at Cambridge in 1415 for Ely cathedral, to Benedict Brent in 1419 for the deaneries of Woodleigh and Plympton in Devon, to William Persons in 1421 for the deaneries of Penwyth and Keryer in Cornwall, and to Peter Fader in 1444 for the town of Boston.[24] Licences for limited areas may have been issued in order to correct failures of parochial preaching, with neighbouring clerics being chosen for their orthodoxy, oral skills, and local knowledge. Of these local preachers, only Brent had any kind of university education.[25]

Alternatively, limited licences could be the prelude to, or the result of, a more general licence, suggesting an experimental and empirical episcopal policy. Brent for instance was given the job of preaching throughout Exeter diocese, two years after his stint in Woodleigh and Plympton. Curtis's licence for Trigg deanery was preceded by one for the archdeaconries of Oxford and Buckingham two months earlier; John Luke and Roger Huswyf received licences for two different dioceses; Adam Redforth

---

[22] Hostiensis, *Summa aurea*, 1531.

[23] *BRUO*, iii. 1430–1; *Reg. Repingdon (Lincoln)*, ii. 294; Hudson, *Premature Reformation*, 99–100; Catto, 'Wyclif and Wycliffism', 241.

[24] *Reg. Repingdon (Lincoln)*, ii. 238, 274; *Reg. Chichele (Canterbury)*, iv. 126–7; *Reg. Stafford (Exeter)*, 37, 222; *Reg. Lacy (Exeter)*, i. 24; Reg. Alnwick (Lincoln), fo. 38ʳ.

[25] *BRUO*, i. 259–60.

was tried out in Oxford and Buckingham archdeaconries in 1412, then given the task of preaching in Oxford University in 1420; John Everdon graduated from Oxford and Northampton archdeaconries in 1418 to all of Lincoln diocese in 1420, while Roger Whelpdale and Thomas Lovecok moved on from diocesan and archidiaconal responsibilities to authorization to preach throughout the province.[26]

Other preachers licensed for the whole province include Thomas Wissenden in 1402 and William Lyndwood in 1418. In the latter case it is probable that Chichele wanted his highest official to have the freedom to preach against heresy wherever his judicial duties took him. Wissenden was a theologian, but his special talents remain intangible to us.[27] Preaching across the breadth of the province may not have been Lyndwood's primary responsibility in Chichele's administration, but extensive travel in the course of a preaching tour was by no means unusual. Between 1430 and 1436, for example, the Franciscan preacher Nicholas Philip travelled over 500 miles between Lynn in Norfolk, Oxford, Newcastle upon Tyne, and Lichfield.[28] Some of the licensed graduates in this survey may have undertaken similar journeys. All the licences described gave the bearer the right to preach in all churches within the specified area. In addition, preachers were often engaged to speak at the punishment or abjuration of heretics, such as Richard Rotheram's sermon in the nave of Hereford cathedral after John Woodhulle of Almeley had revoked his errors in the chapter house, and before he read out his abjuration publicly in the body of the church.[29] In 1405 John Edward's revocation of heresy took place in the 'Greenyard' in front of Norwich cathedral before a crowd which had allegedly gathered to hear the preaching of the archdeacon of Norwich, John of Darlington. Like St Paul's Cross in London, the Greenyard was a traditional site for preaching and the conclusion of judicial business, which frequently occupied the same stage.[30]

[26] *Reg. Repingdon (Lincoln)*, ii. 252, 270, iii. 254; *Reg. Hallum (Salisbury)*, 109–10; Reg. Stafford (Exeter), i. fo. 122ʳ; Reg. Alnwick (Lincoln), fo. 30ʳ; *Reg. Lacy (Exeter)*, ii. 195; Reg. Fleming (Lincoln), fo. 214ʳ; *Reg. Chichele (Canterbury)*, iv. 192, 248.

[27] *CPL 1398–1404*, 593; *BRUC*, 643; *Reg. Chichele (Canterbury)*, iv. 192.

[28] A. J. Fletcher, *Preaching, Politics and Poetry in Late Medieval England* (Dublin, 1998), 48–9.   [29] *Reg. Spofford (Hereford)*, 155–7.

[30] Reg. Arundel (Canterbury), i. fo. 390ʳ; P. J. Horner, 'Preachers at Paul's Cross: Religion, Society and Politics in Late Medieval England', in J. Hamesse et al. (eds.), *Medieval Sermons and Society: Cloister, City, University* (Louvain-la-Neuve, 1998), 264–8; A. Walsham, *Providence in Early Modern England* (Oxford, 1999), 281–325.

A great deal of the energy behind the fifteenth-century preaching campaign came from Philip Repingdon. In the wake of the Oldcastle revolt of 1413 and again following Chichele's 1416 statute, he gave fresh impetus to the licensing programme by ordering the examination of suitable preachers in Oxford. On 3 March 1413 he commissioned Richard Fleming and Richard Barrow, a licentiate in canon law, to inquire about honest persons who could be licensed to preach within the university. They were to investigate the preachers' behaviour, life, morals, and knowledge.[31] In November 1416 two theologians, John Castle and William Filham, were commissioned to do the same with a view to licensing preachers for the town and suburbs of Oxford.[32] This focus on Oxford as the wellspring of heresy was a necessary precaution given the ingrained notion that heresy spread outwards from a central source, but it also produced resistance and opposition from those who saw it as just another aspect of outside interference in the university. Benedict Brent, for example, had been an active opponent of external visitation, resigning his position as junior proctor in protest in 1412, and being one of the masters who appeared before Repingdon's visitation in 1414, in which Edmund Lacy, who later patronized him as a preacher, was a commissioner.[33] John Luke, together with three other masters, had made even more fundamental criticisms of the whole licensing programme in December 1409, presumably in the belief that the system would be administered so as to exclude many worthy preachers from the office. Nonetheless, he too was later licensed himself, and even appointed to the committee that scrutinized the works of Wyclif in 1412.[34]

At a more local level the policy also ran into the occasional difficulty. In July 1409 Bishop Hallum of Salisbury was forced to explain to the clergy of Shaftsbury deanery that a chaplain called William Smith was licensed to preach there. Since the usual practice was for the licensee to carry his letter for examination by the resident cleric, this intervention by the bishop suggests that some parishes were prepared to make their own, unauthorized, decisions as to who they would admit to preach.[35] A more widespread refusal to honour an episcopal licence hampered the preaching of William Certeyn in 1422. Bishop Lacy had to send a warning to the archdeacons of

---

[31] *Reg. Repingdon (Lincoln)*, ii. 293–4.   [32] Ibid. iii. 152–3.
[33] Catto, 'Wyclif and Wycliffism', 250, 253.
[34] Reg. Arundel (Canterbury), ii. fo. 127ʳ; Catto, 'Wyclif and Wycliffism', 245–6.
[35] *Reg. Hallum (Salisbury)*, 103.

Exeter, Taunton, Barnstaple, and Cornwall, as well as all rectors, vicars, and parochial chaplains, that Certeyn should be admitted to preach.[36] Problems notwithstanding, licensed preaching was a powerful medium by which anti-heresy messages could reach the lower clergy and laity.

2. LEGAL PROCLAMATIONS

The words spoken by preachers are difficult to recover by historical method, and were difficult to control by medieval government. The most frequent and easily controlled form of communication between church or crown and the English people was the official governmental act. The effective administration of justice in particular depended upon a huge volume of written and oral communication to maintain public awareness of its aims, procedures, and limits. Both royal and episcopal governance were based on the propagation of information on the nature of law, the role of the individual in its upkeep, and the particular problems facing crown or church at any given time. Naturally this included heresy, and by looking at the administrative documents relating to it we can see how an anti-heresy propaganda campaign was conducted by the agents of the crown and the church.

Heresy was in fact merely one of several issues on which the crown expended considerable energies. It has been suggested that during periods of war 'the course of current events as the government wished them to be understood would be clear to any man who attended consistently to the proclamations made in the county court.'[37] The same stratum of society would have become well acquainted with pronouncements against heresy. Royal orders for proclamations to be made against heresy contributed to a steady stream of writs and commissions which together constituted 'a significant medium of political communication'.[38]

[36] *Reg. Lacy (Exeter)*, i. 89–90.

[37] J. Maddicott, 'The County Community and the Making of Public Opinion in Fourteenth-Century England', *TRHS* 5th ser. 28 (1978), 34. See also A. K. McHardy, 'Liturgy and Propaganda in the Diocese of Lincoln during the Hundred Years War', in S. Mews (ed.), *Religion and National Identity*, SCH 18 (Oxford, 1982), 215–27.

[38] J. A. Doig, 'Political Propaganda and Royal Proclamations in Late Medieval England', *Historical Research*, 71 (1998), 255; see also A. Musson, 'Law and Text: Legal Authority and Judicial Accessibility in the Late Middle Ages', in J. Crick and A. Walsham (eds.), *The Uses of Script and Print, 1300–1700* (Cambridge, 2004), 95–115; and J. Masschaele, 'The Public Space of the Marketplace in Medieval England', *Speculum*, 77 (2002), 383–421.

In October 1399 and May 1400 the recently enthroned Henry IV issued orders for proclamations to be made against heresy in every city, borough, market town, or other place where heretics had been preaching against the giving of alms to mendicant friars. The crown officers were to do this whenever so required by the friars themselves.[39] This piece of political propaganda was short-lived in its impact due to the swift fall from favour that the Franciscan order suffered once it became associated with lingering allegiance to Richard II; but more lasting communication channels were opened through the questions regularly put to jurors by justices of the peace. Questions on heresy based upon the 1414 parliamentary statute were at the head of such lists from the late fifteenth to the early sixteenth century.[40]

The extent of the audience for proclamations of statutes and citations was determined by the distribution and mobility of government agents, but it was also defined by the needs of the judicial system, which required prominent laymen in the localities, the *fidedigni* described in Chapter 3, to be able to report their suspicions in a useful and legally admissible way. Fundamentally, although law was increasingly dependent on written records, it remained connected to the idea of spoken pronouncements. Many men accountable as *fidedigni* would possess a functional literacy or at least a familiarity with documentary culture, but only a few would be able to read about anti-heresy measures themselves.[41] Indeed the very word *iuris-dictio*: to speak the law, gives an indication of the link between oral proclamation and the extent of the law in geographical and social terms.

Oral proclamation was also the vital correction to illicit preaching and heretical proselytizing. Just as Wycliffites were reported in 1382 to be going from town to town, preaching wherever there were large gatherings of people, so royal officers were instructed to counter them wherever they appeared.[42] Because heretics preached 'in churches and open places and other profane sites' statutes for their arrest were to be promulgated to every parish priest.[43] Within those localities ecclesiastical and royal

---

[39] PRO, C 54/245, mm. 24, 38 (*CCR 1399–1402*, 1, 30).

[40] Northamptonshire Record Office, Andrew (Harlestone), A. 98; BL, MS Harley 1777, fo. 84ᵛ. See Chapter 4 for further discussion of these.

[41] Clanchy, *Memory to Written Record*, 234–40.

[42] 5 Rich. II, st. 2, c. 5 in *Statutes of the Realm*, ii. 25.

[43] Reg. Courtenay (Canterbury), fos. 25ᵛ–26ʳ. On heretical preaching see *Fasciculi zizaniorum*, 276, and Hudson, *Premature Reformation*, 69.

officers 'spoke the law' to a society of which it had a sophisticated understanding. In no sense did medieval government see itself as battling against a single, undifferentiated, and unwilling public. If we take just two examples—the revocations of heresy made at St Paul's Cross by Thomas Garenter and Richard Monk in 1428—we see that a multiplicity of divergent and overlapping publics were imagined by the people who drafted administrative *acta*. Repeating the words written for them, and standing before 'populi multitudine', Garenter and Monk addressed audiences both present and absent: 'my lord offe Canterbury and alle yow my lordys here being present . . . Crysten men . . . Cristes body . . . yowr council provincial . . . chirche of Rome . . . the oonhede of the chirche . . . parish of Melton Mowbray . . . comyte of Laicestre . . . diocese of Lyncoln . . . good men and worthy . . . trewe Cristen men.' Some are literal, some metaphorical, but all are in contrast to the 'pryve conventicles or assemblees' of the heresy they were rejecting.[44] We might consider that the most important publics addressed in such proclamations were not the lords of the church, but the parishioners of Melton Mowbray, or the inhabitants of London listening to the revocations, for it was they who had no access to more exclusive forms of communication, and they who would be required to report suspicions about their neighbours, families, and friends.

These manifold publics were addressed most formally through the proclamation of statutes, most of which were accompanied by some kind of instruction for their publication. These are often, however, rather vague, and actual practice was determined by administrative habit and long-established custom. Chichele's 1416 statute for example, was ordered to be published and observed in each cathedral and diocese, a very general stipulation, while Arundel's 1409 constitutions were required to be published in the synods and chapters of each diocese, according to canon law and provincial constitutions. We have a record of the execution of Arundel's mandate in Hallum's Salisbury register: Adam de Motram, the vicar-general, reported that he had publicized the constitutions in full consistory to the clergy and people gathered there, and then forwarded them to the archdeacons who publicized them in their chapters.[45] Although Arundel's instruction implies an exclusively clerical audience for his constitutions, de Motram's certification suggests that a wider public was reached.

[44] *Reg. Chichele (Canterbury)*, iii. 205–8.   [45] *Reg. Hallum (Salisbury)*, 141.

When Arundel referred vaguely to canon law and provincial constitutions he most likely had in mind the decree *Sicut olim* which ordered that constitutions decided upon in provincial and general councils should be publicized annually in diocesan synods, suggesting a similarly clerical audience.[46] Provincial constitutions on a variety of matters also contained injunctions for the promulgation of statutes, often with a lay public implicitly or explicitly identified. For example, in 1343 Archbishop Stratford ordered that the provisions of the Council of London be observed and that bishops cause them to be brought to public attention for the common good and the glory of Christ, while similar calls had been made by Archbishops Langham and Pecham, and the papal legate Ottobuono.[47] In addition, bishops could have had recourse to their own diocesan statutes for details of the mode of proclamation.[48] It is only with Courtenay's 1382 statute that we have an example of provincial legislation being accompanied by a clear instruction for its promulgation to the laity as well as the clergy,[49] and the laity's regular exposure to anti-heresy statutes can only be conclusively demonstrated by the inclusion of heresy in the list of crimes that incurred *ipso facto* excommunication.[50] This 'general sentence of excommunication' was to be read out three or four times a year in every parish church. The lack of recurrent descriptions of promulgation should not lead us to conclude that it was an exceptional practice. Lack of comment should rather be taken to indicate the norm.

However, the existence of an established system for the promulgation of statutes and mandates did not mean it always operated as intended. Three years before Chichele reissued the general sentence, he had been

---

[46] X 5.1.25: 'quae statuerint faciant observari, publicaturi ea in episcopalibus synodis annuatim per singulas dioceses celebrandis.'

[47] Lyndwood, *Provinciale*, 13–14, 18–22. In the thirteenth century we have evidence of rural deans promulgating statutes; see P. R. Hyams, 'Deans and their Doings: The Norwich Inquiry of 1286', in S. Kuttner and K. Pennington (eds.), *Proceedings of the Sixth International Congress of Medieval Canon Law* (Vatican, 1985), 636.

[48] *Councils and Synods*, i. 381, 559 (Salisbury); i. 463 (Chichester); i. 631 (Canterbury province); i. 137 (Winchester); i. 498 (Norwich); ii. 1058–9 (Exeter).

[49] Reg. Braybroke (London), fo. 269ʳ: the statute was to be promulgated by all bishops 'singuli in ecclesiis suis et aliis suarum ciuitatibus et diocesibus'.

[50] This was common from the early fifteenth century: see *Jacob's Well: Part One*, ed. A. Brandeis, EETS 115 (London, 1900), 13–21; *John Mirk's Instructions for Parish Priests*, ed. G. Kristensson, Lund Studies in English, 49 (Lund, 1974), 104–7; but it only became official policy in 1435 with the provincial decree recorded in Reg. Gray (Lincoln), fos. 172ʳ–173ʳ and *Reg. Stafford (Bath & Wells)*, ii. 170–2. The copy of this decree in *Reg. Chichele (Canterbury)*, iii. 257–8, is abbreviated and does not mention heresy.

forced to threaten with interdict parishes where it was not being read out.[51] Similarly in 1413 Repingdon had admonished the archdeacon of Huntingdon for failing to carry out the writ for summoning Convocation, and in 1440 Alnwick reprimanded the archdeacon of Lincoln for failing to publish certain unspecified constitutions.[52] It was also fairly common for defendants in ecclesiastical suits to use their ignorance of the law as an excuse for non-compliance. For instance in 1410 when the parishioners of Southpole in Exeter diocese were subjected to an interdict in accordance with the eleventh of Arundel's constitutions for admitting an unlicensed preacher, they argued that they had acted out of ignorance and not malice, and the interdict was lifted.[53] In Kegworth, Leicestershire, an interdict imposed for the same reason in 1413 was also lifted because the chaplain concerned had admitted the unlicensed preacher 'out of simple-mindedness and not out of corruption'.[54] However, these protestations of ignorance are not reliable evidence for a widespread failure in promulgating anti-heresy law. Since it was desirable for all parties—bishop, clergy, and parishioners—to see the end of an interdict, this formula offered a way out that was acceptable to everyone. The bishop was able to correct a defect and avoid prolonging a scandal, the clergy would regain their income from marriage fees and so on, and the parishioners would see the return of divine services. We may thus infer a qualified success for the promulgation of statutes as a channel of propaganda.

A great deal of education about the nature of heresy was inherent in the processes of justice, as every document and proclamation contained information on the crime and its detection. In any case begun by the bishop acting *ex officio*, the first act was the citation of the offender, either in person or, if that failed, in public. Public citations give us some idea of the geographic and demographic range achieved by the judicial process and thus its propaganda value. A good summary of the procedure of citation is given in the thirteenth constitution of 1409: anyone suspected of contravening the constitutions was to be cited 'by letters or by a sworn public messenger, or alternatively by edict at the home of the offender where he or she is commonly believed to live, and also publicly in his or

[51] *Reg. Chichele (Canterbury)*, iii. 223–4.
[52] *Reg. Repingdon (Lincoln)*, ii. 365–7; Reg. Alnwick (Lincoln), fo. 41ʳ.
[53] Reg. Stafford (Exeter), i. fo. 107ʳ: 'non ex contemptu set ex quadam simplici ignorancia.'
[54] Lincolnshire Archives, MS Vj/0, fo. 16ᵛ: 'ex simplicitate quadam et non ex vitiacionem.'

her parish church if the place of residence is certain, otherwise in the cathedral church of the diocese where he or she was born, and in the parish churches where the offender had preached and taught'.[55] Three citations might be issued, increasing in urgency, with the third, peremptory one threatening excommunication if the offender did not appear.[56]

When William Swinderby hid from the bishop of Hereford's apparitor in 1391, the citation was repeated with greater vigour. The rural dean of Leominster, together with the rectors of Croft, Almeley, and Whitney, the vicars of Kington, Yardley, Monmouth, Clifford, and of the altar of St John in Hereford cathedral, were ordered to attempt to cite him in person. If that failed and William went into hiding again, they were to cite him peremptorily in their own churches in a loud and clear voice, when the multitude of people were gathered for services.[57] In this mandate Trefnant aimed to achieve two things: the apprehension or denunciation of Swinderby, and an increased awareness among his flock of the dangers of heresy, aims which were obviously related. The addressees of the mandate were the clergy from those places where he was reported to have preached, so efforts were directly focused on the areas where they were most needed. News of the citation did indeed reach William and, we may also assume, the wider public of the region, for in lieu of a personal appearance he sent a written response to the bishop, which is recorded in Trefnant's register for the sheer audacity it demonstrated. 'It is, I do me to understonde, that ye have sende owte letters to sommone me for to appere byfor yow at Ledebury [Ledbury], the xx day of Julye, to answer to certeynes materes that touchen my feyth.' Swinderby was clearly either sitting at the back of one of the churches mentioned, or had heard news of his citation from someone who had heard it first hand. He continued: 'I bysyche yow meekly that ye hafe me excused of me commyng to Ledebury: for it is certifiede me be me frendes that I hafe many enemeyes that liggen in awayte for me, and also yt is told me that the kyngges

---

[55] Reg. Arundel (Canterbury), ii. fo. 12ᵛ: 'per litteras siue per nuncium publicum iuratum, sin autem per edictum ad locum habitacionis ipsius delinquentis vbi morari communiter consueuit, et in ecclesia sua parochiali si certum habuerit domicilium publice propositum, alioquin in ecclesia cathedrali loci originis sui et in ecclesia parochiali ipsius loci in quo sic predicarunt et docuerunt.'

[56] Sayers, *Papal Judges Delegate*, 72–4, 150–4.

[57] *Reg. Trefnant (Hereford)*, 251–2: 'in ecclesiis vestris, cum maior multitudo populi ibidem convenerit ad divina, et publice alta et intelligibili voce ipsum Willelmum peremptorie ad premissa citari.'

commyssion is ycommen for me and cried in townes, and baylefes charged to tak me yif thai mowen and puten me in prisone.'[58] Not only had the ecclesiastical citation reached him, but he had also heard about a royal commission for his arrest being proclaimed in local towns. Acting in concert, the authorities of church and crown had clearly spread information about his crimes fairly widely. These tactics were later used in the apprehension of John Oldcastle, whose public citation in November 1413 was matched by the issuing of royal writs to sheriffs for his arrest.[59]

Citation involved hybrid media, writing and speech in conjunction. In 1410 when Arundel had tried to cite Oldcastle's chaplain in Rochester diocese, he had had to make three attempts. First he was cited orally in the parishes of Hoo St Mary's, Hoo St Werburgh's, Halstow, and Cooling, then again in neighbouring parishes, and finally by affixing the written citation to the doors of those churches. The target publics for these communications were the 'notable' inhabitants of the parishes, and the suspect's own friends.[60] In a combination of writing and proclamation, Arundel hoped to bring sufficient social pressure to bear upon the suspect or his harbourers to ensure his appearance in court. The written word was also used in conjunction with speech in the citation of Friar William Russell, an outspoken critic of tithes, in 1425.[61] So serious was his preaching deemed to be that the initial citation was sent to all the rectors, vicars, chaplains, notaries public, clerks, and *litterati* of the province. This was to warn the general public. Chichele's mandate was then fixed to the doors of the London house of the Minorites and read out 'so that the clamour and noise of the citation comes to his ears'.[62] The combination of a publicly posted text and a proclamation was designed to persuade the Minorites not to harbour Russell within their walls.

[58] *Reg. Trefnant (Hereford)*, 252–3.

[59] Reg. Arundel (Canterbury), ii. fos. 142ᵛ–145ᵛ, and *Reg. Repingdon (Lincoln)*, iii. 185; BL, MS Cotton Cleopatra E II, fo. 332ʳ and MS Additional 35205, m. 15d.

[60] Reg. Arundel (Canterbury), ii. fo. 14ʳ: 'Vobis . . . mandamus quatinus ipsum dominum Johannem capellanum si personaliter tute valeat apprehendi alioquin in ecclesiis antedictis ac ecclesiis et locis conuicinis coram notis vicinis seu amicis suis ita quod huiusmodi citacio ad ipsius noticiam verisimiliter poterit peruenire publice citacionis edicto proposito copia publicancium in valuis ecclesiarum et locorum huiusmodi ad maiorem noticiam et ipsius pocius conuincendam maliciam patenter affixa citetis.'

[61] On Russell see C. A. Robertson, 'The Tithe Heresy of Friar William Russell', *Albion*, 8 (1976), 1–16.

[62] *Reg. Chichele (Canterbury)*, iii. 142: 'ita quod clamor et noticia dicte citacionis ad ipsius fratris Willelmi aures pervenit.'

There is a certification of Russell's public citation being proclaimed at St Paul's Cross, presumably by an archiepiscopal official or a specially appointed preacher. Similarly in 1409 the citation of William Taylor had been addressed to 'whoever is preaching the word of God at St Paul's Cross in London', with the instruction that he should read it to the gathered crowds.[63] We may be in no doubt as to the wide audience that citations for heresy achieved, but in order to assess the impact of the polemic and propaganda they contained, we need to know what form the oral proclamation actually took. Too often we have no record of the execution of a mandate for the citation of heresy suspects, only a registered copy of the mandate itself. If the practice of those delivering or proclaiming the citation was to gloss its contents or render them in simplified terms, then the propaganda value is difficult to gauge. This possibility was raised by Lyndwood when he described proclamations made 'in the common and mother tongue, that is English to an Englishman, French to a Frenchman: not literally, but so as to be understood by the vulgar people'.[64] However, his argument is merely for another form of translation, from sophisticated into simple language, which need not involve excessive abbreviation, and may in any case have resulted in a punchier, more accessible message. The English-language denunciation of Oldcastle as a heretic in November 1413 is fully comparable to Latinate analogues, however, and was ordered to be read out word for word in parishes across the province.[65] Indeed, the descriptive content of citations, relating to the case, the suspect, and procedure for reporting suspicions to the judge, was vital to the successful operation of the legal system.[66]

If citation failed and a suspect did not appear then he or she was considered contumacious, an excommunicable offence. When Repingdon

---

[63] Ibid, 126; Reg. Arundel (Canterbury), ii. fo. 118ᵛ: 'cuilibet verbum dei ad crucem Sancti Pauli London predicanti.' On the combination of written and oral communication see Aston, 'Devotional Literacy', 106–7.

[64] Lyndwood, *Provinciale*, 54: 'in lingua materna et vulgari—Anglica viz. Anglicus, Gallica Gallicus . . . id est non litteraliter sed ad intellectum vulgi.'

[65] *Reg. Repingdon (Lincoln)*, iii. 12: 'tenorem dictarum litterarum de verbo ad verbum alta et intelligibili voce et lingua materna prout superius est expressum publicari exponi intimari et declarari faciatis.'

[66] Compare the entry in Repingdon's register with Tancred, *Ordo iudiciarius*, 133: 'delegati iudices in prima citatione consueverunt tenorem commissionis sibi factae in literis citationis totum de verbo ad verbum inserere et reo, qui ad iudicium vocatur, transmittere, ut sciat, qui sunt, qui eum ad iudicem vocant, et cuius auctoritate. Et in literis citationis contineri debet, quod die tali, loco tali, tali actori, coram ipsis iudicibus responsurus accedat.'

and Hereford failed to appear before Courtenay in July 1382 after making an ill-advised appeal to Rome against their earlier treatment, mandates were sent to the bishop of London and the chancellor of Oxford ordering their excommunication to be declared.[67] This presented a further opportunity to publicize a notorious incident, and to strengthen the public's general knowledge about heresy. In this case we are fortunate to have a copy of the chancellor's certification that the mandate was carried out in Oxford. He states that the two suspects were declared excommunicate in St Mary's church and the university schools, and that he had attempted to cite them as the mandate required, but they had gone into hiding and were not to be found. Five days after receiving this, Courtenay issued another mandate in the same terms, now ordering their denunciation as excommunicates throughout the province. Just as in the citation process, excommunications involved hybrid media. In 1414, for example, Edmund Frith, who had been Oldcastle's butler, was absolved from the crime of tearing down from the doors of Rochester cathedral Arundel's notice regarding his master's excommunication. Frith's action underlines the communicative potential of displayed text, which could be read by the literate and heard by the illiterate if someone were to read it out to them.[68]

3. PERFORMANCE AND PARTICIPATION

Excommunication takes us beyond the scribal and oral communications of administrative *acta* and into the world of performance and ritual. Communicative events which combined not only the writing and hearing of the anti-heresy message, but also participation in its performance, were arguably the most likely to succeed in their propaganda aims. As discussed in Chapter 1, excommunication was not merely a punitive sanction but a medicinal one, in effect coercing the subject to return to the unity of the church and the community of the faithful. Symbolic and actual participation was essential to such judicial rituals, because not only was the unified social body of the church the ultimate symbol and standard of moral boundaries, but it also constituted, in the widest possible

---

[67] Reg. Courtenay (Canterbury), fos. 27ᵛ–30ᵛ.
[68] *Reg. Chichele (Canterbury)*, iv. 139–40.

sense, the audience with which the ecclesiastical hierarchy had to communicate and co-operate if heresy was to be discovered.

The major ritual performances of the judicial process were excommunication, interdict, penance, purgation, revocation, abjuration, and punishment. In cases of heresy these were accorded greater importance than in more familiar, everyday crimes, and so public involvement with the symbolism of ecclesiastical justice could be intensified at these specific moments. As insights into anti-heresy propaganda these ceremonies are invaluable because the documents recording them often tell us exactly what the bishop or judge intended to be heard and seen by the public. In many cases we remain sadly in the dark about whether a ceremony was carried out, but since enforcement and the certification of completed rituals was often specified by the original mandate, we need not discard this line of inquiry completely. For example, when Thomas Wade abjured on 1 April 1429, he was ordered to undergo the penance of being whipped three times before the solemn procession to Norwich cathedral on three separate Sundays, in addition to six whippings around his parish church and three around Norwich market place. His priest, William, was ordered to follow immediately behind him on each occasion, wearing his surplice and carrying a rod, so as to certify that the whippings took place.[69] Although we do not have a certification from William in this case, about half of the extant records of such judicial rituals do come from certifications of completed events. When John Russell of Stamford was ordered by Chichele to perform penance in his parish church of St Mary's, the rector, John Smythe, was sent a schedule containing the form of the abjuration Russell was to read out, and he was instructed to pay special attention to its recitation, making sure that nothing was missed out. Smythe was able to report to Chichele that the penitent had not omitted a single word.[70]

As with specially commissioned preaching and citations, ceremonies of penance and abjuration were carried out at the sites of heretical preaching, so the offender could purify the place as well as his or her person.

---

[69] *Norwich Heresy Trials*, 35–8, at 38: 'Vobis insuper ut supra mandamus quatinus, superpelico induti, virgam vestris manibus deferendo, singulis diebus memoratis tempore execucionis presencium dictum Thomam, ut premittitur, incedentem sequamini continue et immediate.'

[70] *Reg. Chichele (Canterbury)*, iii. 99: 'in vulgari revocavit juxta modum et formam in cedula hujusmodi plenius annotatos, nullum verbum in ipsa cedula contentum aliqualiter omittendo.'

In 1426 the abjuration which John Burgh had to read out before Bishop Langdon of Rochester included the promise that 'I ham and schall be redy for to mak [a revocation of my errors] in my paroch' chyrch of Adyngton forsayd and in all oder plasys of yowr diocesy wher as it may be likely supposyd that my evyll communicacion hath hyndred crystene pepell.'[71] Undoing the work of evil communication was also the intention behind the penance enjoined upon William Swinderby in 1382. On the Sunday following his admission to purgation he was to read out a revocation of his errors and heresies in Lincoln cathedral, and then in turn at the prebendal church of St Margaret, the church of the Blessed Mary in Newark, and the parish church of St Martin in Leicester, besides the parish churches of Melton Mowbray, Hallaton, Market Harborough, and Loughborough on successive Sundays.[72] These were allegedly the sites of his heretical preaching in 1381, and the penitential journey would have taken him eight weeks.

It was hoped that such repetition would restore orthodoxy in each place, and allow the greatest number of people to hear the proclamations. John Seynour of Donington in Leicestershire abjured heresy around 1403 in Canterbury cathedral on the patronal feast day of St Alphege (19 April), between the celebration of masses, when the church could be expected to be filled with people. In a similar sequence to Swinderby, he was then to revoke his errors and heresies in words provided in a prepared schedule, in those places 'where he first preached, taught, or held' those beliefs.[73]

Each record of abjuration or revocation includes some comment on the number of people present, and instructions for these events often stipulate the need for maximum publicity in phrases such as 'before the said lord and a great multitude of people' and 'before many other witnesses'.[74] This was not simply adherence to traditional sentencing: in 1382 Repingdon had abjured in Convocation, which, although a highly theatrical venue where the minds of the higher clergy could be focused on the threat of heresy, was not the public sphere indicated in later cases.[75] It is possible

---

[71] Reg. Langdon (Rochester), fo. 58ʳ.   [72] Reg. Buckingham (Lincoln), fo. 243ᵛ.

[73] Reg. Arundel (Canterbury), i. fo. 411ᵛ: 'vbi eas primitus predicauit, docuit vel tenebit, reuocaret.'

[74] *Reg. Trefnant (Hereford)*, 145: 'coram dicto patre et magna multitudine populi'; Reg. Nevill (Salisbury), part 2, fo. 57ᵛ: 'coram . . . multis aliis testibus'.

[75] Reg. Courtenay (Canterbury), fo. 34ᵛ.

that in those early years of academic Wycliffism the archbishop did not believe he was facing a problem that would grow beyond the clerical sphere. There may also have been a feeling that the body hindered or scandalized by Repingdon had been clerical and scholarly, rather than the universal social body alluded to in more public abjurations. Just as with preaching, distinctions were commonly made as to what audience was appropriate for an abjuration. Such proclamations may be seen as attempts to reverse the penitent's influence on the specific public that had been harmed or offended by the original crime. For example, the text of the abjuration written for the Dominican John Beket in 1400 was sent to the four mendicant orders in London, perhaps to satisfy them that he had been dealt with and to encourage vigilance, but perhaps also to prevent news of heresy among the religious from reaching a wider public.[76] Publicizing anti-heresy measures and techniques could, of course, have the undesired effect of publicizing, and popularizing, the heresy. The language of the Beket text is also of a noticeably different register from that of documents aimed at the laity or secular clergy, including a great deal of polemic against the stupidity and temerity of those who condemn the powers of the church, and complex reflections on the gravity of penance and contrition, values particularly associated with the friars.[77]

The judicial event that achieved the most in terms of audience participation and attention was perhaps the parochial interdict, imposed from 1409 upon parishes that had admitted an unlicensed preacher.[78] The specificity of Arundel's initial enactment was, however, too vague to be effective, since it was found that unnamed bishops were subverting the spirit of the constitution by imposing the interdict only on the exact site of the illicit preaching, allowing the business of divine service and parochial life to continue. Lyndwood, who reports this in his *Provinciale*, argued that if illegal preaching had occurred in any church, cemetery, or other place 'within the boundaries

[76] Reg. Arundel (Canterbury), i. fos. 407ᵛ–408ʳ.

[77] K. J. Jansen, 'Mary Magdalen and the Mendicants: The Preaching of Penance in the Late Middle Ages', *Journal of Medieval History*, 21 (1995), 1–25.

[78] Reg. Arundel (Canterbury), ii. fo. 11ʳ: 'nullus clerus aut populus cuiuscumque parochie aut loci nostre Cantuariensis prouincie aliquem in ecclesiis cimiteriis aut locis aliis quibuscumque ad predicandum admittat nisi prius de auctorizacione priuilegio aut missione eiusdem . . . Alioquin ecclesia cimiterium seu locis quiscumque in quo sic predicatum fuerit ipso facto ecclesiastico subiaceat interdicto sique maneat interdictus quousque ipsi sic admittentes seu predicari permittentes se congrue emendauerint et per loci diocesanum seu alium superiorem ipsum interdictum optineant in debita iuris forma relaxari.'

and limits of the parish', then not only those sites but also 'the whole of that parish' would incur the interdict. To understand place narrowly in terms of church, cemetery, some other holy site, or farm, field, or house, was derisory and useless. Instead he believed that place ought to be understood as meaning the borough, castle, municipality, vill, village, or parish in which the offending persons lived.[79] These clarifications were necessary because the purpose of interdict was to communicate with the people of the parish as well as purify the exact site of the heretical preaching. The sanction could be used extensively, as happened in Bath and Wells diocese around 1412, when Bishop Bubwith placed twelve parishes under interdict for admitting John Bacon to preach without licence, or it could be used against a single parish, as Hallum did with Heytesbury, also in 1412. In both examples parish chaplains, by implication the people held responsible for admitting the unlicensed preachers, were required to abjure heresy themselves before the interdict could be lifted. In Heytesbury the chaplain was to perform penance on the day after the interdict was lifted, approaching the host, taking off his vestments apart from the chasuble, and genuflecting to the font saying seven penitential psalms and the litany. He was then to rise and proclaim to the parishioners that he had erred, presenting a living example of the anti-heresy message and reinforcing local knowledge of the new limits of orthodoxy.[80]

The drama and visual display of this ceremony was a familiar feature of medieval communication, which had much in common with staged drama, both liturgical and civic. Much has been written on the supposed lollardy of civic drama, but the critical manoeuvres necessary to make this kind of analysis belie the ubiquity and overt message of anti-lollard drama and orthodox visual culture.[81] The ceremonies of penance and purgation,

[79] Lyndwood, *Provinciale*, 294: v. *quicumque locus*: 'sive sit ecclesia, sive coemeterium sive locus alius. Sed hic est advertendum quia intelligendo de loco alio ab ecclesia sive coemeterio, vel alio loco sacro utputa platea vico, prato, campo, agro, fundo aut domo ut si talis locus dicatur interdictus modica foret pena et quodam modo inutilis et derisoria. Et ideo in tali casu intelligere debes locum: id est burgum, oppidum, castrum, vicum, municipium, villam, villatam sive parochiam vt sic appelatione *loci* contineantur homines talem locum inhabitantes.'

[80] *Reg. Bubwith (Bath & Wells)*, i. 115–16; *Reg. Hallum (Salisbury)*, 221–3.

[81] R. D. Kendall, *The Drama of Dissent: The Radical Poetics of Nonconformity 1380–1590* (Chapel Hill, NC, 1986); A. E. Nichols, 'Lollard Language in the Croxton *Play of the Sacrament*', *Notes and Queries*, 36 (1989), 23–5; R. Nisse, 'Staged Interpretations: Civic Rhetoric and Lollard Politics in the York Plays', *Journal of Medieval and Early Modern Studies*, 28 (1998), 427–52.

for example, were the symbolic mirrors of those relating to excommunication, dramatizing the subject's passage from a state of exclusion to one of inclusion. Excommunications were made with candles extinguished and dashed to the ground, bells rung, and sometimes even spitting being used to express the expulsion of the subject from the community.[82] Readmission to the church likewise required a certain level of publicity, and theatricality was central to achieving this. In the heresy trials recorded in William Alnwick's court-book for Norwich, 1428–31, public whipping was enjoined as a penance in many cases, much more often than in other sets of trials.[83] Typical was the penance enjoined upon Richard Fleccher of Beccles on 27 August 1429. He was sentenced to be whipped a number of times around the cemetery at Beccles in front of a solemn procession with bare head and feet, wearing only breeches and carrying a candle weighing one pound, in a penitential manner. He was then to do the same around the local market place. As a longer-term, more private penance, he was to fast on bread and water every Friday for a year in repentance for his heretical assertion that it was licit to eat meat during Lent and on saints' days.[84] The procession, whipping, and undress represent what was known as public penance, a ritual which in other cases might combine the theatrical with the oral, as the penitent recited and denounced his crimes in church, and his priest explained the reason for the penance.[85] This varied propaganda assault was meant to educate the public about the nature of heresy and anti-heresy, and create enough publicity to ensure that the penitent was prevented by social pressure from returning to his or her crime.

In more serious cases 'solemn penance' could be ordered. This was carried out in the cathedral rather than the parish church, with the symbolic expulsion of a group of penitents on Ash Wednesday and readmission to the physical church and the body of the faithful on Maundy Thursday.[86]

---

[82] For spitting see *John Mirk's Instructions*, 107.

[83] For this comparison see N. Tanner, 'Penances Imposed on Kentish Lollards by Archbishop Warham 1511–12', in Aston and Richmond (eds.), *Lollardy and the Gentry*, 229–49.　　　　　　　　　　　　　　　　　[84] *Norwich Heresy Trials*, 89.

[85] Lyndwood, *Provinciale*, 339; R. M. T. Hill, 'Public Penance: Some Problems of a Thirteenth-Century Bishop', *History*, 36 (1951), 218. For the public recitation of crimes as part of penance see Reg. Langdon (Rochester), fo. 75X[r].

[86] C. 26 q. 6 c. 14; Lyndwood, *Provinciale*, 339–40; *Councils and Synods*, ii. 899–900 (Council of Lambeth 1281, c. 7); M. C. Mansfield, *The Humiliation of Sinners: Public Penance in Thirteenth-Century France* (Ithaca, NY, 1995), 92–3. For details of the ceremony see T. Bailey, *The Processions of Sarum and the Western Church* (Toronto, 1971), 19–21.

These were major occasions in the liturgical calendar and times when a cathedral church could be expected to be full. Out of the fifty-one suspects tried by Alnwick between 1428 and 1431, sixteen were ordered to perform solemn penance, of whom nine were named in a note listing penitents who were to appear at Norwich cathedral on Ash Wednesday 1431, along with six persons guilty of other offences.[87] This list was necessary in order to record absentees such as John Fynche of Colchester, who may have returned to his home town across the border with London diocese to escape Alnwick's jurisdiction.[88] In three of the Norwich cases only one year's attendance at the ceremony was required, but in others two or three annual trips to the cathedral were imposed. By repeating the penance at the fulcrum of the liturgical calendar in successive years, Alnwick hoped to hold the attention of the citizens of Norwich and his cathedral clergy for the anti-heresy cause.

The choice of a major liturgical occasion as the vehicle for propagandizing against heresy is also apparent in the case of John Walcote of Hazelton in Gloucestershire, although its significance is not immediately apparent from the episcopal documentation alone. He was brought before Bishop Morgan of Worcester in October 1425 at Winchcombe abbey, publicly taken for a lollard and reputed to have held erroneous opinions. The case was prorogued for deliberation and on 29 March 1426, Walcote duly appeared before the bishop in the choir of Worcester cathedral. Asked whether he wished to abjure he said that he did, and kneeling before the bishop's feet he swore that he would never again hold any error or heresy and he would be bound by the determinations of the church, after which he kissed the Gospels, venerated the crucifix, which was being held aloft by two monks of the cathedral, and crawling on his belly, barefoot and bareheaded, he followed the cross around the church, kissing it at various points on the journey.[89] In the record of this case no explicit mention is made of any lay attendance: only the presence of the bishop, the chancellor, a professor of theology, the monks of the cathedral, and various canons is noted. However, since 29 March in 1426 was Good Friday we can be fairly sure that the anonymous others present 'in multitudine magna' included numerous laymen. The penance which Walcote underwent was clearly an augmented version of the traditional

---

[87] *Norwich Heresy Trials*, 194–5.   [88] Ibid. 188–9.

[89] Reg. Morgan (Worcester), pp. 168–70.

'creeping to the cross', in which many other people would have been taking part on that day. Much greater pomp, psalmody, and ceremonial, not to mention audience, than that referred to in the bishop's register, may thus be assumed.[90]

The form of ecclesiastical propaganda most closely associated with civic drama was the procession, which demanded extensive participation, and thus attention, from the laity. Because of the popularity and frequency of civic, liturgical, guild, and parochial processions, the episcopacy was able to manage and manipulate familiar forms of communal activity in support of current or pressing problems. Indeed in some cases it is difficult to differentiate the scheduled procession from the exceptional, but in these cases its effectiveness as propaganda may be increased rather than diminished.[91] Processions could be used to draw attention to new legislation against heresy or to heresy investigations, and to realize the dramatic potential of abjurations and penances. On the same day that Courtenay issued his mandate against heresy in 1382, he ordered processions to be organized around the country 'for the peace of holy church and its king and for fine weather'.[92] Although no specific mention was made of heresy on this occasion, the contiguity between the legislation and the processions indicates a clear wish to embrace the new problem of heresy within perennial concerns about church, kingdom, and the elements.

By the second decade of the fifteenth century the propaganda of church unity and anti-heresy had become more sophisticated. One of the final acts of Arundel as archbishop was to order processions against heresy on 21 January 1414, eleven days after the Oldcastle revolt had been put down.[93] The mandate begins with a polemical preamble describing how enemies try to replace church with synagogue, faith with schism, wheat with tares, and catholicism with heathenism. Henry V is praised as 'most victorious prince' in his defeat of Oldcastle and his accomplices, but the celebration is not all that it at first seems. Under the guise of national rejoicing,

---

[90] Duffy, *Stripping of the Altars*, 23, 29–31; Bailey, *Processions*, 21.

[91] J.-A. Derens, 'Pouvoir consulaire, espace urbain et cérémonies religieuses à Montpellier à la fin du Moyen Âge', in G. Cholvy (ed.), *Espaces religieux et communautés méridionales* (Montpellier, 1994), 75; Duffy, *Stripping of the Altars*, 39; C. Phythian-Adams, 'Ceremony and the Citizen: The Communal Year at Coventry 1450–1550', in P. Clark (ed.), *The Early Modern Town: A Reader* (London, 1976), 57–85; Bailey, *Processions*, 12.

[92] Reg. Braybroke (London), fo. 270ʳ: 'pro pace sancta ecclesie ac regni sui et aeris temperie.'   [93] Reg. Clifford (London), fos. 155ᵛ–156ᵛ.

Arundel was using public display and devotions to try to determine the course of future policy. On 24 September 1413, processions had been ordered to encourage Henry so that he might in future defeat heresy, and that mandate refers to a previous one along the same lines. The accompanying prayers were to implore God to protect the king and bring back the hearts of the lollards to the church, a formulation that implies the king to be an agent of God's will. However, the preceding comment, that lollardy 'will grow ever stronger unless opposed by our most Christian prince and our noble king', confirms that although the prayers were offered to God, their intended audience was the king.[94] The use of processions in 1382 and 1414 was thus very different. Whereas Courtenay had seen them as a medium for communicating urgent new fears and new laws to the population at large, Arundel had tried to use public action as an indirect means of petitioning the king to *make* new laws. His was a more sophisticated use of processions, using public opinion as a lever to governmental action, while simultaneously trying to influence opinion.

The use of processions as a means of building publicity and stimulating public awareness was also adopted by bishops acting against heresy in their dioceses. In November 1413 when Repingdon ordered his officials to conduct a general inquisition into heresy, he stipulated that it be accompanied 'by processions and sermons to the people, which should explain the reason for the inquisition'.[95] This is a rare example of an episcopal document explicitly referring to the necessity of a well-informed laity, something which was usually glossed over due to the lack of a canonical vocabulary for discussing it. A similar tactic was used by Robert Nevill in June 1428 when he forwarded a papal mandate for prayers against the Husssites on the same day as he ordered an investigation into heresy. Prayers against Bohemian heresy may have acted as a catalyst to episcopal action, but Nevill may well have also seen the papal mandate as an ideal opportunity to give extra weight and international significance to his own efforts in rural Berkshire.[96] The publicity needs of both pope and bishop were well served by this combination. In Norwich the same papal letter is

---

[94] Reg. Clifford (London), fo. 152ʳ; *Reg. Repingdon (Lincoln)*, ii. 362: 'Et quia tam plus solito invalescit mortalitas hominum ac pestis illa execrabilis Lollardrie . . . nisi se ex adverso opponeret Christianissimus in Christo princeps et Rex noster nobilissimus.'

[95] *Reg. Repingdon (Lincoln)*, ii. 371: 'cum processionibus procedentibus et sermone ad populum quo publice exponantur cause inquisicionum earundem.'

[96] Reg. Nevill (Salisbury), part 2, fo. 78ʳ.

recorded in Alnwick's register on 10 June 1428, about three months before the first dated heresy case in the Norwich court-book, and therefore around the time when those suspects would have been first detected and delated to the bishop.[97] Just as the presence of Cardinal Condo de Zwola at the 1428 Convocation added an international dimension to the anti-heresy deliberations there, so prayers and processions invoking concerns common to all Christendom were meant to stir up popular knowledge of and support for campaigns against heretics at home.

Processions also preceded the staged sentencing, penances, and punishments of heretics, a fact which draws the study of English heresy into the heady air of theatricality surrounding continental heresy trials, especially those of the fifteenth, sixteenth, and seventeenth centuries. The *auto da fé*, as it was known in Portugal and Brazil (*auto de fe* in Spain and Mexico), was 'a public presentation of abjuration, reconciliation and punishment' that showed the condemned and the penitent heretic to the public in a procession of spiritual and secular power, sporting the symbolic props and accoutrements of inquisition.[98] In England our descriptions are much less vivid than those that allow us to visualize the later phenomenon, but certain vital similarities are clear. When Repingdon accepted the abjurations of two anonymous suspects, J.B. and N.B., he ordered them to appear barefoot and bareheaded in procession in Lincoln. Carrying lit candles they were to precede the first friar in procession and walk to the cathedral where they were to wait in the middle of the nave by the pulpit while the rest of the congregation filed past them. There they were to remain while a sermon was preached, repeating in English the reason for their penance.[99]

In 1418 John Bath of Salisbury diocese was required to walk before a procession of the monks of Sherborne, and to throw into a fire the condemned books he had owned.[100] Richard Herberd of Kent was ordered to walk before the procession to Rochester cathedral, wearing only shirt and breeches, carrying a candle. Then he was to do the same around the churches of Hadlow, Tonbridge, and Malling.[101] In 1413 Richard Devenish

---

[97] Reg. Alnwick (Norwich), fo. 99ʳ.

[98] F. Bethencourt, *L'Inquisition à l'époque moderne: Espagne, Italie, Portugal XVe–XIXe siècle* (Paris, 1995), 249: 'une *présentation* publique de l'abjuration, de la réconciliation et du châtiment.'   [99] *Reg. Repingdon (Lincoln)*, iii. 169–70.

[100] Reg. Chaundler (Salisbury), ii. fo. 18ʳ.

[101] Reg. Langdon (Rochester), fo. 74Xᵛ.

was made to appear in procession on Whit Sunday at Holy Cross parish church in Bristol, where he had previously affixed 'a notorious libel of the lollards' to the choir stalls. While the Gospel was being read to the parishioners he was to stand barefoot and bareheaded, holding a candle. One may speculate that the subject of the sermon bore some relation to the living example of error presented to the people in the church. After the service Devenish was to offer the candle at the high altar.[102]

These kind of penances had been commonplace on the continent for some time, notably among inquisitors in southern Bohemia in the 1330s. Leo of Čáslav had been compelled to stand in front of his parish church on seven Sundays while the weekly procession entered the church. On the seventh occasion he was to appear barefoot, carrying a rod with which anyone who wished to do so might beat him.[103] Alžběta of České Budejovice had to appear in procession every Sunday for a whole year, wearing a yellow cross on her chest and back.[104] The encounter with one's neighbours in procession, filing past one by one, was meant to shame the penitent and illustrate the depravity of heresy. Distinctive penitential clothes were less common in England, where some degree of undress was the normal way of denoting the condemned or repentant heretic, although badges became more common from the late fifteenth century, perhaps adopting the practice of the newly formed state inquisitions of Rome and Spain.[105]

The horrific and spectacular conclusion of the *auto da fé* was the burning of the unrepentant heretics. Burnings occurred in England as well, but they were not so common as one might expect. Thomson calculates that between 1414 and 1522 only thirty-three out of 545 heresy cases resulted in execution, that is 6 per cent.[106] Although one cannot escape the conclusion that post-reformation martyrology has cast a long shadow over the historiography of heresy in England, execution by burning still speaks to our consciences, and was seized upon by chroniclers in the fifteenth century as the dramatic dénouement of the folly of heresy. Of course, only a few executions were needed to impress upon the public the dangers of heresy, and symbolically 'burning was the most effective

---

[102] *Reg. Bubwith (Bath & Wells)*, i. 144–5.
[103] *Anfänge einer ständige Inquisition*, ed. Patschovsky, 132.   [104] Ibid. 203.
[105] *Lollards of Coventry*, 298, 303; Bethencourt, *L'Inquisition*, 261–2; Moore, *Persecuting Society*, 10–11.   [106] Thomson, *Later Lollards*, 237–8.

method of cauterizing the poisoned limb, and society—the corporate body whose health was at risk—had to participate in the healing process.'[107]

As channels of propaganda, processions and other performative media gave an added, visual dimension to written and oral communication, but how should we assess their success or failure? To a medieval bishop, such ceremonies were designed to 'drive out of the community the evil spirits who created division between neighbours and sickness in man and beast' or to define 'a space that had to be purified, sanctified, and protected from evil forces'.[108] Measuring success in these terms is outside the historian's remit, although the currently popular anthropological notion of a community made whole by ritual can be equally intangible. We must content ourselves in this instance with an assessment more firmly grounded in political and social life. How effective were ritual and performance as channels of propaganda? Some historians have been fairly optimistic about the effectiveness of propaganda in sending messages to mass audiences, and this positive view is, I believe, well founded.[109] Almost all the cases of heresy extant in judicial records began with an accusation, a denunciation, or a response to an inquisition, all of which detective acts had to be informed to some degree by the nature of the crime and the procedure for reporting it. The spread of this information during the first two generations to experience heresy in England had to have come from somewhere, and the propaganda discussed here was intended as that source. Alison McHardy has suggested that 'if mandates to say prayers were indeed obeyed . . . then a sizeable proportion of England's population ought to have been informed'.[110] The problem of course surrounds that word 'if'.

If our knowledge of anti-heresy propaganda came only from mandates and instructions for proclamations, judicial *acta*, and so on, we would have no idea of whether such instructions were ever carried out. But we are lucky in having large numbers of certifications that proclamations were made, abjurations read out, penances completed. We also have a number of reports of the less successful execution of anti-heresy propaganda, illustrating the problems common to all governmental action. In

[107] Aston, *Faith and Fire*, 300.

[108] Duffy, *Stripping of the Altars*, 136; Derens, 'Pouvoir consulaire', 78: 'à travers un espace que l'on entend purifier, sanctifier et/ou protéger des forces du mal.'

[109] D. d'Avray, *Medieval Marriage Sermons: Mass Communication in a Culture without Print* (Oxford, 2001), 29–30. [110] McHardy, 'Liturgy and Propaganda', 217.

August 1416 Chichele sent a letter to his diocesans complaining that his mandates of 9 April and 7 June 1415 for processions for the peace, unity, and tranquillity of the church, the prosperity of the realm, and mild weather, to be accompanied by chanting, litanies, masses, and a special collect, with mention to be made of Emperor Sigismund's efforts against the Hussites, had not been obeyed.[111] He had heard that the devotion of the clergy and people for this had become lukewarm. By way of encouragement he went on to cite examples of the success of prayer in scripture and in history, but the results fell short of his expectations and in May 1417 he had to issue a further mandate for the completion of the processions and prayers.[112] Chichele's problems were echoed elsewhere in his church. Even a conscientious bishop like Repingdon had difficulties mobilizing the people of his cathedral city in processions, as on the occasion in 1418 when he lamented the sloth of the citizens and ordered pronouncements in English to explain the reasons for processions, instructing the dean of Lincoln to notify him of anyone who remained in contempt of the order. Around the same time Repingdon also issued a warning to the cathedral and city clergy to take part in *Corpus Christi* processions without irreverence or negligence.[113]

It has been suggested that religious processions were naturally the scene of tumult and disorder, but it is clear that their organizers saw this as a sign of failure.[114] However, mandates complaining about non-compliance with episcopal propaganda programmes should be understood as the fastidious exceptions that prove the general rule of successful event management. Information about anti-heresy procedures had only to reach a certain level and a certain number of the population, and public opinion had only to be pushed in the right direction for anti-heresy policy to be successful. Local difficulties were more alarming as challenges to episcopal authority than as propaganda failures, and so they need not cloud our assessment of anti-heresy communication.

---

[111] *Reg. Chichele (Canterbury)*, iv. 123–4, 127, 158–9.

[112] Ibid. 167–8.

[113] *Reg. Repingdon (Lincoln)*, iii. 215–16, 278. Duffy, *Stripping of the Altars*, 559, discusses the failure to attend processions in Marian England being used as evidence of heresy.

[114] J. Chiffoleau, 'Les Processions parisiennes de 1412: Analyse d'un rituel flamboyant', *Revue historique*, 284 (1990), 37–76.

6

The Content of Propaganda

There was a close relationship between the production of anti-heresy messages across different media, so that the thrust of a sermon might be supported by inferences in the judicial process, and the generic languages used by lawyers and homilists might cross-fertilize. Because it drew on common sources, the anti-heresy propaganda of law, theology, and what we call literature was rarely totally original, but even if its ideas and images were not new, unique emphases and combinations made it peculiar to its time and place. Such nuance and subtlety was possible because the people who were expected to report their suspicions of heresy would already have had a degree of familiarity with the moral, social, and legal ideas common to late medieval Christian culture.

One of the most popular literary strategies used in the English anti-heresy campaign, and deserving special mention at the outset, was to reconfigure existing debates, which was easier than fashioning new ones for a public who had no history of exposure to anti-heretical arguments. This strategy involved changing the focus of a particular moral discourse while retaining its basic structure and content. Two stock characters of late medieval legal and moral literature, the deceptive mendicant and the sinful priest, were especially well suited to this technique, since they possessed attributes that could be transferred wholesale to the new public enemy, the lollard. The stereotypical lollard was something of an amalgam of the unregulated itinerancy of the mendicants and the malign pastoral influence of sinful priests. We have already noted the expropriation of anti-mendicant legislation as a model for anti-heresy statutes, but the transfer of metaphor and stereotype from one to the other was not confined to the law.

The process of reconfiguration is most evident in the chronicler Henry Knighton's use of the anti-mendicant work *De periculis novissimorum temporum* by William of Saint-Amour, in his descriptions of the early Wycliffites. For Knighton the lollard was merely the most recent manifestation of a misguided urge to change the understanding of scripture, a charge William had levelled at the mendicant orders. William's prophecy concerning the friars is said by Knighton to 'better apply to those new people, the lollards', in what is a very self-conscious adaptation of an existing model.[1] Like Knighton, the Augustinian canon John Audelay wanted to extend latent suspicion of mendicants to heretics, whilst maintaining the force of the original polemic. Audelay's desire that his reader beware false prophets, both mendicant and lollard, is indicative of the early fifteenth-century atmosphere in which anti-heresy legislation could be misinterpreted as pertaining to the friars.[2] Even though mendicancy was looked on more favourably and received greater official protection when the opprobrium it had once attracted was transferred to heresy, the association with heresy meant that friars were not wholly freed from public suspicion.

The failings of the sinful priest were likewise easily transposed from a general critique of the clergy to a specifically anti-heretical genre from about 1380 onwards. The metaphors of pastoral care were homely and familiar, with the good priest cast as the shepherd, protecting his flock from danger in the guise of the wolf, and the bad priest imagined as negligent. The heretic could be represented as either the ravening wolf attacking the flock from outside, or the sinful priest allowing his attacks to take place. In this homiletic example he takes both roles: 'he [the wolf or heretic] is aferd to openly come among stedfast men in bileve, and therefore he awaiteth whan men berken nought agens synne and false techyng, but slepen in sinful lustis of flesshe, or if he se shepardis slowe, or absent from trewe techyng of her sheep.'[3] Like anti-mendicancy, the criticism of negligent clergy was not insulated from the effects of being connected with the anti-heresy cause; and briefly in the fifteenth century it became difficult to criticize a sinful priest without raising suspicions of heresy. These processes of cultural borrowing and modification permeate anti-heresy propaganda as lawyers and polemicists describe the danger of heresy, heretical doctrine, crimes analogous with heresy, the character and appearance of heretics, and the reporting of heresy.

[1] Knighton, *Chronicle*, 248–9: 'magis tamen congruunt istis nouis populis lollardis qui mutauerunt euangelium Cristi in euangelium eternum.'
[2] *Poems of John Audelay*, 28, 34.   [3] BL, MS Harley 2276, fo. 113^r.

1. THE DANGER OF HERESY

Heresy was presented to the public as an insidious and hidden danger, frequently through the metaphor of the wolf in sheep's clothing, which is reflected in the homily quoted above.[4] The image of the wolf provided notaries and polemicists with an evocative means of referring to heretics and the danger they posed in a readily understood shorthand. For example, in 1405, John Edward of Brington in Northamptonshire was tried before Bishop Despenser of Norwich, and made to abjure 'the ravening and roaring wolf' of his heresy and return to mother church. Similarly the Dominican writer Roger Dymmok described lollards as wolves who tore at their mother the church with sharp claws.[5] As well as attacking the flock from outside, the picture of a rapacious enemy expressed the psychological basis of heresy, located in the heart or will of every person. Lyndwood's formulation that heresy could exist 'in heart or in speech or in deeds' reflected a commonplace of judicial procedure, which, for example, was articulated by the public admission of Isabel Pruste in 1397 that she confessed her errors 'with her heart and voice'.[6] The fear of a hidden danger could thus be employed by propagandists to mean either that the heretic was the unknown 'other', or that the potential for heresy was hidden within each individual.

Both messages were necessary for the detection of heresy, but which was more important? If the *fidedigni* described in Chapter 3 were to have any chance of making valuable reports of their suspicions, it was vital that the rather diffuse crime of heresy was associated with a social category of heretics, even if that category were fictitious and meant purely for guidance. On the other hand, the church wished the danger of heresy to be on every individual conscience, because susceptibility to it was universal and it was a public crime that injured everyone.[7] Heretics as a discrete social group were most clearly depicted in ceremonies such as the exclusion of

[4] Matt. 7: 15.

[5] Reg. Arundel (Canterbury), i. fo. 390ᵛ: 'lupus rapax et rugiens'; *Rogeri Dymmok Liber contra XII errores et hereses Lollardorum*, ed. H. S. Cronin (London, 1922), 13.

[6] Lyndwood, *Provinciale*, 55, v. *Haeresis universa*: 'consistit in corde aut in ore vel in operi'; *Reg. Trefnant (Hereford)*, 145: 'corde et ore confiteor.'

[7] Hostiensis, *Summa aurea*, 1535: 'quia haereticus omnes offendit, quod enim in religionem diuinam committitur, in omnium fertur iniuriam, et ideo publicum crimen dicitur.'

offenders from the church during solemn penance, or the segregation of the penitent heretic beneath a pulpit or in procession. The possibility of heresy afflicting the whole community was most powerfully expressed through the interdicts used to coerce parishes that had permitted unlicensed preaching to submit to the authority of the church. Of course, the themes of the isolated heretic and the community susceptible to heresy were frequently mingled in propaganda. As part of his penance, John Edward was made to stand on a specially built stage and listen to his errors read out by a notary. As the embodiment of heresy he stood alone and despised, and yet it is surely significant that he stood 'in the midst of all the clergy and people', who were as passive as he in the judicial drama.[8] In the same way, the adapted ritual carried out by John Walcote in Worcester cathedral on Good Friday 1426, creeping to the cross, identified him with the lay public and made him the quintessence of their own sinfulness. The expiation of a heretic's sins in conjunction with those of the whole town was a potent symbol of the collective responsibility of every Christian for deviant belief, in oneself as well as in others. Neither conception of the danger of heresy was sufficient in itself for the needs of an anti-heresy campaign.

As Isabel Pruste's statement suggests, an individual's adherence to incorrect beliefs only came to light when he or she spoke or acted upon them, but even this did not constitute heresy in strict legal terms. The decision to remain in error after being given the opportunity to recant, or the relapse after abjuration, was the canonical definition of heresy, and this, it seems, was a message the hierarchy saw fit to communicate to the wider public. In John Seynour of Castle Donington's revocation around 1403, he announced to his audience that 'if, God forbid, I relapse into any condemned heresy or error, or any such opinion or article contrary to the determinations of the church and this my present oath, I observe, wish and seek that I come to be condemned as a manifest and notorious heretic without any hope [of remission]'.[9] Similarly, when Robert Hooke the rector of Braybroke appeared before Chichele after a lengthy trial in 1424, he was ordered to read out a prepared abjuration in the cemetery of

[8] Reg. Arundel (Canterbury), i. fo. 390ʳ: 'in medio tocius cleri et populi'.
[9] Ibid., i. fo. 411ᵛ: 'si quod absit in aliquam heresim aut errorem dampnatum vel opinionem seu articulum huiusmodi contra determinacionem ecclesie et presens iuramentum meum relapsus seruo volo et peto me tanquam hereticum manifestum et notorium sine quacumque spe venie condempnari.'

St Paul's and again in Northampton, a penance to which he had been assigned by Repingdon in 1405, 'the whiche penaunce I perfourmed nat as I was enjoyned, for the whiche cause and my rebellion in that caas I was by the auctorite of the forsayde bisshop accursed and openly denunced'.[10] Hooke was not denounced as a heretic for holding condemned beliefs, but for rebelling against the bishop's authority. This seemingly abstruse principle of canon law was a necessary part of anti-heresy propaganda because it indicated that the identification of heresy was an episcopal task, reminding *fidedigni* and other detectors of heresy that their reports of suspicion did not identify the heretic with any kind of finality. Two political aims might be served by this: preventing the laity from assuming their own authority to be sufficient in judging heresy, and reassuring the nervous that their reports would not necessarily lead to the punishment of an innocent but suspicious neighbour.

2. HERETICAL DOCTRINE

Despite the preliminary nature of reported suspicion, it was desirable that the lower clergy and laity be sufficiently well informed about heretical doctrine to be able to suspect it when they heard it. Indeed, the concept of heresy as incorrect belief was as common in the Middle Ages as it is among historians today, legalistic definitions of heresy notwithstanding. 'Both lollard and heretykys þus may be knowen: þay halde all hollely [that] are advers owre faythe', was how one polemical writer put it.[11] This was certainly the view that Roger Dymmok took in his refutation of the 'twelve conclusions', treating every permutation of Wycliffite belief to the same stinging and virulent polemic. However, the identification of wrong belief was not a simple matter; nor was the educational process that would teach people how to do it. Craig Fraser has observed that 'those [sermons] which touch on the heterodox challenge tend to sneer at Lollards rather than engage them in debate.' This tendency was due to a conflict between the need to point out heresies and the stipulation made to preachers in 1409 to avoid difficult theological subjects such as the Eucharist.[12] In the

[10] *Reg. Chichele (Canterbury)*, iii. 111. For Braybroke as a centre of heresy see Hudson, *Premature Reformation*, 206–7.   [11] BL, MS Additional Charter 12794.
[12] Fraser, 'Religious Instruction', 72, 82, 104.

wake of Arundel's constitutions, preachers and the episcopate had to find safe and controlled ways to educate people about heretical doctrine.

As Lyndwood had indicated in his discussion of what constituted suspicion of heresy, beliefs could be inferred from practices. Persons 'differing in life and morals from the behaviour of the faithful' were those who failed to confess and come to communion, to pay tithes, and so on. A similar inference of heretical belief from practice was recommended by the poet Audelay:

> ʒif he withdrawe his deutes fro hole cherche away,
> And wyl not worchip þe cros, on hym take good eme,
> And here his matyns and his masse apon þe haleday,
> And beleuys not in þe sacrement, þat hit is God veray,
> And wyl not schryue him to a prest on what deþ hedye,
> And settis noʒt be þe sacrementus, soþly to say,
> Take him fore a loller, Y tel ʒou treuly.[13]

In this formulation the withholding of tithes, refusal to worship the crucifix, absence from matins and mass on Sundays and feast days, denial of the real presence, refusal of confession, and denial of sacramental efficacy were reliable signs of heresy. Lists of such condemned beliefs, discovered in the hearts of captured heretics, were common features of the proclamations accompanying judicial *acta*. In 1413 for instance Oldcastle's heresies were read out across the province in English 'so that these erroneous opinions may be publicly annulled before the people, who otherwise would firmly understand these things to be the truth'.[14] It seems that the potential for the spread of heretical doctrines by the very method of their repudiation, public proclamation, was a risk that was willingly taken in order to counter their already strong grasp on the public mind.

To prevent such inadvertent contamination occurring, penitents could be made to repeat a denunciation of their previously held views as they were read out to them. In Norwich John Edward was made to repeat after each article of his abjuration, 'I sey þat this article is fals and erronee and by fals informacion y held it, the wheche y being beter enformed at this tyme by clerkes þat cunnyn more the lawe and the holy doctrine of god thanne y, renounce and aske foryeuenesse ther of and swere to these holi

---

[13] *Poems of John Audelay*, 34.
[14] *Fasciculi zizaniorum*, 448: 'ut sic opiniones erroneae populi, qui aliter concepit forte in hac materia quam se habet rei veritas, hac declaratione publica rescindantur.'

euangelies by me bodily touched þat fro þis tyme forward y shal it never prechin techin ne holdyn priueliche ne in apert.'[15] Thomas Hellis emphasized how he detested and despised his errors and heresies, and John Woodhulle's abjuration ended with the comment that 'the whiche wordes was never sayde for no sooth, ne to entent that man schuld holde them for no trewthe. Wherfor all those opinions and all conclusions and tales herafor rehersid I forsake.'[16] An alternative approach is signalled in the case of Robert Holbeche, a chaplain in the household of John Oldcastle, tried for heresy in July 1416. Instead of proclaiming the views he was repudiating, Holbeche was made to assert the orthodoxy of a series of positions that were the opposite of those he had held. For instance he was to say: 'I confess that pilgrimages to the relics of saints and holy places are not prohibited nor are they to be condemned by catholic men, but rather they are useful for the remission of sins, are approved by holy fathers and deserve to be commended.'[17]

We must also remain aware that the condemned beliefs read out by penitent heretics would not have been taken down verbatim during their trials, but extracted from what had been said during interrogation, itemized into separate and distinct articles, and presented in such a way as to emphasize their heresy and depravity. Abjured beliefs thus represent a caricature of heretical doctrine drawn up by lawyers whose only concern was to prevent them from having any appeal to whatever audience the abjuration might reach. This extension of the scholastic urge to itemize and classify was resented by those who were subjected to it under interrogation. One Wycliffite author mocked 'þes prelatis þat wolde wrynge oute anoþer absolute answere' from a suspect who presumably wished to equivocate as much as possible.[18] An especially potent technique for ridiculing the beliefs being abjured by a penitent heretic was to create a dramatic disjuncture between the words spoken and the visual scene witnessed. To return to John Edward's revocation at Norwich in 1405, we see him abjuring the opinion that 'no pope, prelate or bishop is able to compel a person to swear by any one of God's creatures or on the gospels',

[15] Reg. Arundel (Canterbury), i. fo. 390ʳ.

[16] Reg. Langdon (Rochester), fo. 75Xʳ; *Reg. Spofford (Hereford)*, 155.

[17] *Reg. Chichele (Canterbury)*, iv. 157: 'Item confiteor quod peregrinaciones ad reliquias sanctorum et loca religiosa non sunt prohibite nec a viro catholico contempnende, sed sunt in remissionem peccaminum utiles et a sanctis patribus approbate et merito comendande.'

[18] *Select English Works of John Wyclif*, ed. T. Arnold, 3 vols. (Oxford, 1869–71), iii. 426.

while he was doing exactly that.[19] Alnwick's trials a generation later used the same method: following a course of fustigation and public humiliation, penitents abjured the beliefs that 'censures and cursynges of bisshopes and prelates ar not to be drede ne pondred', and 'it is no synne to doon agayn the preceptes and lawes of holy churche', assertions which were rendered somewhat ridiculous by the context in which they were made. Education about, and condemnation of, heretical doctrine took place simultaneously.

3. HERESY DESCRIBED BY ANALOGY

In trying to convey the essential character of heresy, preachers and lawyers frequently resorted to analogy. By comparing heresy with other, more familiar crimes, key aspects of anti-heresy policy could be publicized. The three main categories of crime with which heresy was associated were treason, defamation, and lechery. The last of these was used purely as a metaphor by which ideas about the transmission of heresy, the secrecy of its gestation, and the use of inquisition in its detection could be explained. Treason and defamation were also used as metaphors, but their connection with heresy was much closer than that of sexual sin because they were themselves constituents of the crime of heresy. Treason and heresy had been intimately linked since Innocent III's decree *Vergentis* of 1199, which proposed that punishments for treason should also be applied to heresy, since attacking the majesty of Christ was in fact worse than attacking the majesty of a secular ruler.[20] This link made an enormous difference in bonding spiritual and secular powers together in the fight against heresy. After the Oldcastle revolt lollardy also became, in some instances, almost a synonym for treason, and the 1414 parliamentary

[19] Reg. Arundel (Canterbury), i. fo. 390^r: 'Item quod pape nec aliquis prelatus neque ordinarius potest aliquem compellere ad iurandum per aliquam creaturam dei nec ad sancta dei euangelia.' Hostiensis, *Summa aurea*, 1533, wrote that someone who argues against the power of the church or ecclesiastical judges is *ipso facto* a heretic.

[20] X 5.7.10: 'Quum enim secundum legitimas sanctiones, reis laesae maiestatis punitis capite, bona confiscentur eorum . . . quanto magis, qui aberrentes in fide Domini Dei filium Iesum Christum, offendunt, a capite nostro, quod est Christus ecclesiastica debent districtione praecidi, et bonis temporalibus spoliari, quum longe sit gravius aeternam quam temporalem laedere maiestatem?' Compare with the comment in *Glos. ord.* to VI 5.2.2, v. *filii*: 'hoc etiam procedit in crimine lese maiestatis, quod est minus hoc crimine que leditur eterna maiestas.'

statute assumed that people arrested for one offence would swiftly be indicted for the other as well.

Heresy's relationship to treason lay in their both being based on harm done to the 'majesty' of authority. In the case of treason this often meant armed rebellion, but it was increasingly understood as the utterance of words injurious to the king.[21] The idea that words could have a real detrimental effect upon a person's standing was also central to the crimes of defamation, slander, and scandal, which, like treason, contributed elements to the polemical and legal construction of heresy. Heresy was both 'treason against God' and 'a slander to the church'.[22] For instance, Dymmok described blasphemous bills distributed by the lollards as scandalous to the church and harmful to mankind, while their words were said to lacerate the church like the claws of wild beasts. Knighton made a similar link, writing that 'by the bitterness of their denunciations they rend and devour those who do not cleave to them', and the Benedictine sermon writer of MS Bodley 649 claimed that 'these lollards shot many small words at the poor friars', implying that the insults of heretics pierced mendicant honour like arrows.[23]

Scandal was understood as words or actions which created an impediment to the proper execution of an office. In the secular sphere the crime of 'scandalum magnatum', usually translated as the slander of lords, assumed that great men could be materially harmed by hostile words, and in the church courts a suit of defamation could be brought for falsely imputing to a person a crime causing harm to his or her reputation.[24] In 1382 Courtenay implied that the church was itself an entity capable of being harmed by the words of heretics, which were said to effect the 'subversion and enervation of the estate of the church and the tranquillity of the realm'.[25] In 1381, before he became known as a Wycliffite and lollard, William Swinderby was publicly cited for preaching 'many great errors

[21] J. G. Bellamy, *The Law of Treason in England in the Later Middle Ages* (Cambridge, 1970), 116–18.   [22] Trusen, 'Der Inquisitionsprozess', 220.

[23] Dymmok, *Liber*, 15: 'Qui libellus manifestam continet blasphemiam diuine magestatis et gloriose matris eius et scandalum ecclesie sacrosancte, et tocius generis humani dedecus et iniuriam manifestam'; Knighton, *Chronicle*, 300–1: 'detraccionum acerbitate eis non adherentes indesinenter lacerent et cruentant'; Bodleian, MS Bodley 649, fo. 35^r: 'isti lollardi sagittauerunt plura parua verba ad pauperos fratres.'

[24] 3 Ed. I, c. 34, and 2 Rich. II, st. 1, c. 5, in *Statutes of the Realm*, i. 35, ii. 9; Helmholz, *Select Cases on Defamation*, pp. xiv–xli.

[25] Reg. Braybroke (London), fo. 269^r: 'statum tocius ecclesie nostreque prouincie Cantuariensis et tranquillitatem regni subuertere et eneruare nituntur.'

contrary to the catholic faith, derogatory of the estate of the pope and other prelates, abusive to the whole clergy, scandalous and contemptuous of the universal church'.[26] By their injurious words, heretics slandered the church and caused scandal in the sense of creating impediments to salvation. At Exeter, Bishop Brantyngham described the preaching of John Edneves as 'enormities and ills [aimed at] the denigration and enervation of the estate and dignity of Pope Urban VI and King Richard II and the English bishops'.[27] The defamation of bishops was itself one of only three spiritual crimes for which a degraded cleric could be relinquished to the secular arm, the other two being the forgery of papal letters, and heresy itself.[28]

This connection between heresy and false speech was dealt with by the authors of pastoral literature under the second commandment, not to take God's name in vain. The *Memoriale credencium* compares heresy and slander in this context: 'Þe secunde heste is þu schalt not nempne þi lordis name in ydull. In thulke heste is forbode al manere heresie þat is for to do oþer maynteyne eny poynt aeyne þe bileue of holy churche and al manere sklaundre and vnreuerence to god and to holy seyntes.'[29] *Dives and Pauper* meanwhile groups heresy with the sin of pride: 'And al swyche takyn Godis name in ydilchepe þat techyn ony errours or eresyys aȝenys þe feyth & aȝens God or prechyn or techyn þe trewþe only for couetyse or for envye or for veynglorie and nout for ȝel of manys soule ne for þe worchepe of God.'[30] Such literary ubiquity allowed the link between heresy and defamation to be exploited by anti-heretical writers as well. In the Franciscan responses to the author of the Wycliffite poem *Jack Upland*, charges and counter-charges of slander were frequent. The verse retaliation known as *Friar Daw's Reply* complains that 'of felony thou felly us empechest', while William Woodford repeatedly stated that the *Upland* author 'falsely imputed' many crimes to friars.[31] Woodford's Wycliffite opponent accused the friars of turning a blind eye to lechery

---

[26] Reg. Buckingham (Lincoln), fo. 236ᵛ: 'quamplura erronea enormia catholice fidei contraria in Romani pontificis et ceterorum prelatorum status derogacionem tocius cleri opprobrium et vniuersalis ecclesie scandalum et contemptum.'

[27] *Reg. Brantyngham (Exeter)*, i. 160.

[28] Hostiensis, *Summa aurea*, 1538. See X 5.20.7 for forgery, and C. 11 q. 1 c. 18 for calumnious accusations against bishops.

[29] *Memoriale credencium: A Late Middle English Manual of Theology for Lay People*, ed. J. H. L. Kengen (Nijmegen, 1979), 41–2.

[30] *Dives and Pauper*, ed. P. H. Barnum, 2 vols., EETS 275, 280 (Oxford, 1976–80), i. 222.

[31] *Friar Daw's Reply*, in *Six Ecclesiastical Satires*, ed. J. Dean (Kalamazoo, Mich., 1991), 166.

and dishonesty in their pastoral care of the wealthy, to which Woodford countered that 'in this question, not only the poor friar, but also the lords and ladies are subjected to a defamation'.[32] These descriptions of heresy as a defamation served to familiarize the laity and lower clergy with the character of the new offence they were now being called upon to report. The implication is that they were to pay attention to words and their effect on reputations, specifically those of prelates and of the church in general.

At first glance it seems as though the connection made between heresy and sexual sins was meant to achieve the same kind of analogous responses. Paying attention to hidden crimes and reporting them in the same way would, after all, be consonant with fornication and heresy having been the twin stimuli to the development of inquisitorial procedure in the twelfth century. However, adultery, fornication, incest, and clerical concubinage were very common offences and a simple message advocating a heresy–sex equivalence would have resulted in many more speculative reports of heresy than the episcopate ever envisaged or desired. The connection was not so simple.

Nor was it always made obvious. The author of a series of sermons now in Worcester cathedral library alluded to the unmentionable vices of heretics: 'For þer was a lollard at Oxenfort but awhile agon þat for-suk al his errours & al his misleuyng & turnyd agen to þe leuyng of oþer good cristenmen, & tan a told certeyn rytes & doyng of hem, ye, so cursed & so oreble to her, þat e good feyth, ich am greuyse for to telle hem.'[33] Never one to be so coy about the depravity he was condemning, Roger Dymmok described the lollard doctrine of *coitus necessarius*, alleging that they permitted no woman to abstain from the lusts of any man.[34] The sexual allegation against heretics was not the sole preserve of literary polemicists or exaggerating moralists, keen to rubbish the arguments of radicals or to change attitudes to illicit sex by tarring it with the brush of heresy. It sprang from the fundamental theology of the fall that placed the

---

[32] E. Doyle, 'William Woodford O.F.M. (c.1330–c.1400): His Life and Works together with a Study and Edition of his *Responsiones contra Wiclevum et Lollardos*', *Franciscan Studies*, 43 (1983), 180–1: 'Respondeo hic et dico primo quod in quaestione supponitur diffamatio non solum fratrum pauperum, sed etiam dominorum et dominarum.'

[33] *Three Middle English Sermons from the Worcester Chapter Manuscript F. 10*, ed. D. M. Grisdale (Leeds, 1939), 65.   [34] Dymmok, *Liber*, 79, 275, 305.

aberrant will, concupiscence, at the root of all sin, but most directly the root of sex engaged in for the sake of pleasure rather than reproduction.

Concupiscence was also the impulse behind the malignant choice of heresy. The essential connection between sex and heresy was given a semblance of empirical verification when Reginald Pecock referred to his experiences as a bishop dealing with both categories of offence: 'sotheli y haue mad inquisicioun therto sufficient and diligent, and y am certified at fulle that among the holders of this . . . opinion [i.e. heretics] summe ben founde and knowun openli among hem silf and of othere neiȝboris to be greet lechouris, summe to be auoutreris in greet haunt and contynuaunce, summe to be theefis.'[35] The mention of inquisition and certification give this an air of legal verisimilitude, but given the ubiquity of the stereotype and the loss of Pecock's register it is difficult to confirm. Heretics as adulterers and seducers appear in many other, and earlier, sources, making the connection a very easy one to make. For example, the description of lechers in *Dives and Pauper*, who 'gon & rydyn fro town to town to getyn women at her lust', has significant structural similarities with Knighton's account of John Aston 'visiting churches all over the country . . . so that by breeding false doctrines and promoting his sect he might claim and seduce them'.[36] In *Friar Daw's Reply* heretics 'make men breke her matrimonye and leeve her wyves, | And whan the gode man is oute, pleye thei god rode'; they also rape the Eucharist, an accusation which goes beyond anything levelled at the Jews.[37] The theme was taken up in a prophecy that recurs in several works of pastoral theology, and was attributed variously to Boniface the Martyr and Pope Boniface III. It held that because the English were an adulterous nation, they would become feeble in the faith, weak in battle, dishonoured among men, and unloved by God.[38] This story made a causal link

[35] Reginald Pecock, *The Repressor of Over Much Blaming of the Clergy*, ed. C. Babington, Rolls Series, 19 (London, 1860), 103.

[36] *Dives and Pauper*, ii. 87; Knighton, *Chronicle*, 284–6: 'ecclesias regni . . . indefesse cursitando uisitauit . . . ut cum usuris insane doctrine et incrementis secte sue postea exigere posset . . . seductos.'

[37] *Friar Daw's Reply*, 160, 176; M. Rubin, *Gentile Tales: The Narrative Assault on Late Medieval Jews* (New Haven, 1999).

[38] Richard Lavynham, *A Litil Tretys on the Seven Deadly Sins*, ed. J. P. W. M. van Zutphen (Rome, 1956), 23; *Dives and Pauper*, ii. 63–4; *Jacob's Well*, 161; BL, MS Harley 1197 ('The Pore Caitif'), fos. 26ʳ–27ᵛ. For more details of this prophecy see I. Forrest, 'Anti-Lollard Polemic and Practice in Late Medieval England', in L. Clark (ed.), *The Fifteenth Century*, iii: *Authority and Subversion* (Woodbridge, 2003), 67–8.

between sexual incontinence and heresy based on the notion of concupiscence. What stories of this kind were intended to achieve was not the wholesale indictment of sexual offenders as heretics, but rather the activation of a particular kind of response from the clergy and laity. As secret crimes both fornication and heresy were dealt with by inquisition, a process whose rules were as well known to *fidedigni* as they were to judges and lawyers. Describing heresy in terms of sex was a way of managing reports, and was therefore meant to reduce wild accusations, rather than encourage them.

The reader of, or listener to, anti-heresy statutes or sermons could not help but imbibe the idea that heresy, as well as having similarities with other crimes, was a disease. Analogies of contagion, infection, botanical invasion, and poison were pervasive in anti-heretical texts in all periods and places, late medieval England being no exception. The medium which perhaps best exemplifies the degree to which thinking in natural symbols was habitual is the procession. Blurring the boundaries between what we would classify as political and natural, during the processions ordered to coincide with the signing of the truce of Leulinghem in 1389, people were directed to pray not only for lasting peace, but also for seasonal weather, a good harvest, and the conversion of heretics and schismatics. In 1413 processions were ordered that would secure peace, freedom from pestilence, and the extirpation of heresy.[39] We know from canonists and judges that heresy was not seen as a force of nature but a human weakness, so what purpose could this grouping of social dangers serve?

Moore contends that the image of heresy as a disease 'helped puzzled observers . . . to create an explanation' for its dynamic character.[40] Although heresy was the product of the individual will, it was nonetheless a social ill, spreading from person to person at a seemingly exponential rate. Metaphors of disease and invasion were familiar and straightforward ideas which could be used as shorthand for this attribute of heresy. In 1386 for example, after several earlier attempts to bring Nicholas Hereford to justice had failed, Archbishop Courtenay simply warned people to avoid him 'lest he deceive simple souls with his profane preaching and teaching, and infect the Lord's flock with the noxious pestilence

---

[39] *Reg. Waltham (Salisbury)*, 15; *Reg. Repingdon (Lincoln)*, ii. 362–3.

[40] R. I. Moore, 'Heresy as Disease', in D. W. Lourdaux and D. Verhelst (eds.), *The Concept of Heresy in the Middle Ages* (Louvain, 1976), 11.

of his words'.[41] This alarmist policy of isolating the person infected with heresy had begun in 1382 with Courtenay's instruction to 'flee and escape the unlicensed preacher as if he were a venomous snake spitting poison'.[42] Despite the ubiquity of equity and mercy in canon law, black and white segregation was sometimes urged, partly out of practical necessity, but partly as a polemical expedient. The more dangerous Wycliffites, those who made the longest preaching journeys and had most contacts with groups of dissenters around the country, had to be cut off from their adherents and from the as yet unaffected public.[43] On the other hand, if false and malicious accusations were to be kept to a minimum, the message that reported suspicions did not necessarily lead to a conviction had to be promulgated as well. Although virulent, heresy was curable.

The message that heresy was not confined to an identifiable social group was hinted at in the disease metaphor. Although the poisonous heretic figure presupposes the public to be the passive victims of his infection, medieval medical theories of contagion were based upon the idea that seeds of disease activated an innate predisposition to a particular illness. These seeds, transmitted from person to person by breath, sight, and touch, could in some cases be avoided, but a predisposition (to heresy if we extend the metaphor) could not.[44] Ideas about the transmission of disease and heresy thus had much in common, and as a result of observing the spread of pestilence from the mid-fourteenth century onwards, they may have been fresh in the minds of anti-heresy writers and legislators in late medieval England. The chronicler Jean de Venette described plague 'advancing town by town, street by street, and finally from house to house, or rather, person to person', phrases which are echoed in the 1382 royal statute against heresy, citing the danger of Wycliffites 'going from county to county and from town to town' spreading their errors

[41] Reg. Courtenay (Canterbury), fo. 65ᵛ: 'ne prefatus Nicholus simplicium animas sua prophana predicacione et doctrina decipiat et dominicum gregem inficiat labe sue pestifere communicacionis.'

[42] Reg. Braybroke (London), fo. 269ʳ: 'tanquam serpentem venenum pestiferum emittentem fugiat et euitat.'

[43] P. Ormerod and A. P. Roach, 'The Medieval Inquisition: Scale-Free Networks and the Suppression of Heresy', *Physica A*, 339 (2004), 645–52.

[44] V. Nutton, 'The Seeds of Disease: An Explanation of Contagion and Infection from the Greeks to the Renaissance', *Medical History*, 27 (1983), 1–34. See also *The Middle English Translation of Guy de Chauliac's Treatise on 'Apostemes'*, ed. B. Wallner (Lund, 1988), 152.

wherever large groups of people were gathered.[45] This piece of polemic stressed the danger of heresy, its social as well as its personal dimension, and indicated the need for the swift identification of suspected heretics. However, it also reassured the heresy-reporting *fidedignus* that were he or someone else in his community to become infected, a cure might be possible. His reported suspicions would be treated with the medicine of correction (see Chapter 1), and only cut off from the social body if incurable.

The parable of the wheat and the tares, which became closely associated with Wycliffism because of the connections between flour, bread, and the Eucharist, postpones the excision of the irredeemable until judgement day, when God will gather the corn into his barn and burn the weeds. Distinguishing the weed from the crop before they are fully grown cannot be achieved with any degree of certainty.[46] It is possible that the word 'lollard' acquired the currency that it did, both in the Low Countries from 1300 onwards and in England from the 1380s, because of the false, but appealing, etymology from the Latin 'lollium', meaning darnel or tare. The image of the lollard as a vigorous yet poisonous weed was most useful as an allegory for the spread of heresy sown by preaching. In 1381 for example, Swinderby 'came to spread weeds' among the faithful people of Leicester. In 1395 the University of Oxford was ordered to expel heretics who 'spread weeds among the people', and in 1397 a writ sent to the bishop of Chichester for the arrest of lollards used exactly the same phrase.[47] Although peculiarly associated with Wycliffites because of the title *Fasciculi zizaniorum* given to the Carmelite collection of anti-heretical materials, these weeds sprang up in a variety of different contexts, and so we must be careful not to infer an exclusive connection with lollardy. In 1392 the bishop of Exeter described people trafficking in benefices as 'zizania', and in 1409 the followers of Pope Eugenius XII were called 'spreaders of weeds' in the proclamation of Alexander V's election.[48] A fourteenth-century alphabetical guide to canon law written on the end leaves of a manuscript containing Thomas Chillenden's *Repertorium* applies the terms 'lollia' and 'zizania' to mendicant friars in the context of

[45] *The Chronicle of Jean de Venette*, in *The Black Death*, ed. R. Horrox (Manchester, 1994), 56; 5 Rich. II, st. 2, c. 5, in *Statutes of the Realm*, ii. 25: 'alantz de countee en countee et de ville en ville.'   [46] Matt. 13: 25–6.
[47] Reg. Buckingham (Lincoln), fo. 236ᵛ; PRO, C 54/237, m. 24 (*CCR 1392–96*, 434); C 54/240, m. 18 (*CCR 1396–99*, 158).
[48] *Reg. Brantyngham (Exeter)*, ii. 656–7; Reg. Fordham (Ely), fos. 115ᵛ–116ᵛ.

preaching licences, suggesting that the two words were more generally connected to preaching as a medium of illicit communication than they were with heretics as such.[49] The challenge of preachers sowing weeds among the corn would have to be defeated by the wholesome seed sown by orthodox preachers, but also, as in the parable, by the servants of the Lord who ran to tell him there were weeds in the fields and then obeyed his somewhat counter-intuitive order to let them grow until judgement day.

4. THE CHARACTER AND APPEARANCE OF HERETICS

The image of weeds springing up in the corn is one example of the medieval belief that sin could manifest itself materially or in such a way as to be recognizable. Anti-heresy propaganda often seems to be saying that heresy manifested itself not only through words and actions, but also through the character and appearance of the individual sinner. A range of facial, bodily, social, and moral characteristics of heretics were regularly indicated as being signs of heresy, although these were not meant to be taken as definitive any more than listening to a heretical sermon was understood to be a sure sign of heresy. The following depictions of heretics were intended only to give the would-be heresy reporter grounds for suspicion, which could then be tested by a judge.

In judicial performances such as the abjuration of heresy the enforced visual appearance of the penitent, half-undressed or wearing a distinctive badge, was an uncomplicated assertion of the principle that sin was made real in the world. In the polemical literature against heretics, however, it was not possible to say that seeing was believing, because that position had been tainted by its association with Wycliffite thinking. For Wyclif the Eucharist, even when consecrated by a moral and properly ordained priest, remained bread. What looks like bread, smells like bread, and tastes like bread, must be bread. The simplicity of this view had a dangerous appeal, and the assumption that sense perception was a reliable guide to a substance's or a person's true nature was not easily jettisoned. In order for the laity and lower clergy to point out possible heretics, the episcopate

[49] Bodleian, MS New College 204, fo. 420[r].

had to suggest some means of doing so. One way around the problem was to urge the identification of a character trait, hypocrisy, that was deemed to have recognizable manifestations and be typical of heretics, but which configured the link between appearance and sin in such a way as to avoid simplistic conclusions.

Hypocrisy was a variant of pride, and the crime of heresy was in part defined by excessive spiritual pride, trusting too much in one's own inspiration. It was therefore common to portray heretics as taking pains to appear more pious than they were, with one sermon writer calling lollards 'disguised messengers' who try to appear 'wrapped in holiness', while another author accused lollards of 'Sterching your faces to be holden holi'.[50] Some treatments of hypocrisy, such as that in *Jacob's Well*, could refer equally well to heretics, sinful priests, or deceptive mendicants 'spekyng holy wordys, doyng holy werkys, schewyng holy signes & spekyng of chastyte, of clennesse, of devocyoun, to wryen þerwyth þi wyckydnesse'.[51] The pliability of the hypocrisy model did indeed make it extremely useful to polemicists. However, while the recognition of hypocrisy and its association with heresy is urged, people liable to be deceived by heretics are told that visual appearance is a deceptive indicator of virtue. 'For we se now so miche folk & specialiche þes lollardes, þay go barfot, þei gon openhed, ye, þei wassche soþylike hir cloþes withowten with teres of hir eyen þat miche of þe peple is fowle blynded & deseyuyd bi hem.'[52] Although the very fact that people are being deceived is presented as evidence that heretics are at work, the epistemological problem posed by hypocrisy prevented incautious and simplistic connections being made between appearance and heresy.

The techniques of deception employed by lollards were said to be revealed in their speech and bearing. People suspicious about a sermon being preached in their parish church or chapel could check the documentation of the preacher, make a mental note of the content of the sermon, or pay attention to the manner in which the preacher was addressing them. Hypocrites, so the author of *Dives and Pauper* tells us, talk too much: 'It is a common prouerbe þat hoso speke vnwysly, and veynly or in euyl maner, he spekyt to mychil.'[53] For Knighton,

---

[50] Bodleian, MS Bodley 649, fo. 16ʳ: 'disgyset nuntios . . . wrappet in holines'; *Friar Daw's Reply*, 153.   [51] *Jacob's Well*, 73.
[52] *Three Middle English Sermons*, 65.   [53] *Dives and Pauper*, i. 220–1.

John Aston was a 'busy and contentious bee, always ready for argument', while the author of *Friar Daw's Reply* portrayed a heretic so full of malice that his venomous words were spat out all at once.[54]

Vanity, malice, and unwise speech are also common characteristics ascribed to condemned and penitent heretics in the public phases of trial and punishment. For example, the proclamation describing Oldcastle's trial characterizes his speech as excessive and foolish. After he had been condemned, at which point most heretics are rendered passive and defeated by the bureaucratic record, Oldcastle is said to have turned to the bystanders in the court and shouted that 'those who judge and wish to damn me are seducing you all and will lead you and themselves into hell, so beware of them'.[55] Putting these words into the mouth of the condemned Oldcastle makes them an impotent inversion of the biblical injunction to beware false prophets. His heresy is all the more strongly revealed because he rails against justice. William Taylor's teaching is similarly denigrated, described in his citation as 'vain and superstitious'.[56] The lollard was being constructed as an example of the false speaker, or 'ill-tongued' man, who, according to the pseudo-Aristotelian physiognomic work *Secretum secretorum*, could be recognized because his 'lower lippe lolle outward'.[57] The pride of heretics created in them an imbalance that led to anger and inconstancy in their speech and actions. Thomas Netter advised his readers to let their Wycliffite opponents 'rage and ridicule'. They would not prevail because 'truth was not in their mouths'.[58] In the same vein *Friar Daw* says to his Wycliffite interlocutor: 'in thi frensy thou fonnest more and more!' [59]

This image of the raging heretic was popular with polemicists, and was often expressed in extrapolations from the wolf in sheep's clothing

---

[54] Knighton, *Chronicle*, 284: 'apis argumentosus prompte ad dogmatizandum'; *Friar Daw's Reply*, 152: 'Thi malice is so michel thou maist not forhele, | But thi venym with vehemens thou spittest al at ones.'

[55] *Fasciculi zizaniorum*, 445: 'Isti qui judicant et volunt damnare me, seducent vos omnes, et seipsos, et vos ducent ad infernum; ideo caveatis ab eis.'

[56] Reg. Arundel (Canterbury), ii. fo. 118ᵛ: 'vanum et supersticiosam doctrinam'.

[57] *Secretum secretorum: Nine English Versions*, ed. M. A. Manzalaoui, EETS 276 (Oxford, 1977), 106.

[58] Thomas Netter, *Doctrinale antiquitatum fidei catholicae ecclesiae*, ed. B. Blanciotti, 3 vols. (Venice, 1757–9; repr. Farnborough, 1967), i. 6: 'saeviant, et rideant', and ii. 142: 'Sancti patres de haereticis exclamaverunt, quod non sit in ore eorum veritas.'

[59] *Friar Daw's Reply*, 166.

metaphor. Dymmok described how the wolf throws back his head and howls at the sky, whereas the lamb softly bleats.[60] For Richard Lavynham, the wolf was wrath, who wreaked a stealthy vengeance on all who had offended him. When in sheep's clothing the wolf was torn between the natures of the two animals, creating a chimerical harpy 'not in good twne . . . for þe contrariowste of kendis betwene boþe'.[61] This physiological and psychological imbalance, leading to unhealthy extremes of behaviour, was alluded to in the *Book of Vices and Virtues*, in which the wrathful man 'haþ werre wiþ hymself, for whan wraþþe is ful in a man, he turmenteþ his soule and his body so þat he may haue no sleep ne reste; and oþerwhile it bynemeþ hym mete and drynke, and makeþ hym falle in-to a feuere, or into suche a sorwe þat he takeþ his deþ'.[62] Linking extreme behaviour with sexual hypocrisy and heresy, Knighton told how after he had been spurned by a woman, William Smith 'affected the outward forms of sanctity so extravagantly that he despised all earthly desires'.[63] The possibility of using visual signs of internal strife to identify heretics was not beyond reason in late medieval England. For Thomas Gascoigne heretics continually turned from one thing to another, and for the author of *Friar Daw's Reply* they were 'Wanderynge wedercokkes with every wynd waginge'.[64] The impression of the heretic as inconstant and indecisive was communicated to the people of Norwich on Palm Sunday 1405 in the abjuration made by John Edward. In a passage that merges the wolfish, wrathful, and vacillating stereotypes with the parable of the wheat and the tares and the idea of heresy as a crime hidden in the heart, Edward was made to 'publicly say and confess that that ravening and roaring wolf my heart, which was fickle in the faith, learned to sow weeds amongst the Christian faithful'.[65] Once fierce and contrary, however, in penitence he was presented as meek and certain.

---

[60] Dymmok, *Liber*, 309: 'Ouis inclinando deorsum balat, lupus capud conuertit sursum contra celum et ululat.'   [61] Lavynham, *Seven Deadly Sins*, 10.

[62] *The Book of Vices and Virtues*, ed. W. N. Francis, EETS 217 (London, 1942), 25.

[63] Knighton, *Chronicle*, 292: 'Qui cupiens ducere in uxorem iuuenticulam quandam set ab ea spretus, in tantam prorupit sanctitatis ostentacionem quod omnia mundi concupiscibilia despexit.'

[64] Thomas Gascoigne, *Loci e libro veritatum*, ed. J. E. T. Rogers (Oxford, 1881), 117; *Friar Daw's Reply*, 153.

[65] Reg. Arundel (Canterbury), i. fo. 390ᵛ: 'publice dico et confiteor quod dudum ille lupus rapax et rugiens cor meum quod in fide flexibile esse nouit ad seminandum zizaniam inter christi fideles.'

As soon as he began to bother the authorities in Leicestershire in 1381, Swinderby was described in similar terms. Buckingham's register records that 'a certain William, a hermit living in the chapel of St John near the town of Leicester, calling himself a priest, tried to seduce our flock like a ravening wolf disguised in the simplicity of a sheep, running about various places in the archdeaconry like a vagabond'.[66] Swinderby's movements, hither and thither, prompted Knighton to conclude that 'he proved to be of inconstant life and morals, having tried many styles of life, and he fidgeted from one to another, never finding one satisfactory to himself'. Just like the 'inconstant scholar' in a popular pseudo-Boethian exemplum, Swinderby went through an undulating pattern of enthusiasm, disillusionment, and change of lifestyle, before his imbalanced character caught up with him. The inconstant scholar was turned into an ass, while Swinderby was arrested and tried for heresy.[67]

Observations on the speech, behaviour, and lives of heretics naturally led to, and were in part derived from, opinions about where they might be found. Two assumptions about the location of heretics predominate, and yet it is not clear whether either was meant to act as a definitive topographical guide to their whereabouts. The first, already alluded to above, was the itinerant cleric, probably unlicensed, who upon coming to a village might preach in a public place such as church, chapel, cross, market place, or street. William Woodford had this figure in mind when he contrasted the friars, who travelled in pairs to guard each other's morality, with the lollard who travelled alone and fell into every kind of vice.[68] All legislation against unlicensed preaching thus played upon a suspicion of strangers that was endemic in medieval England. Especially to those in authority, the vagabond, pedlar, pilgrim, mendicant, alms collector, and heretic represented a challenge to settled society. The second assumption was that heretics would gather in secret groups to pass on their ideas and perform their rituals. Netter located the heretic in the dens of thieves and the dark

---

[66] Reg. Buckingham (Lincoln), fo. 236ᵛ: 'quidam Willelmus hermita in capella sancti Johannis prope villam Leycestro habitans presbiterum se asserens gregem nostrum lupina rapacitate sub ouina simplicitate palliata seducere nititur per loca varia dicti archidiaconatus vagabunde discurrens.'

[67] Knighton,*Chronicle*, 306: 'inconstans uita et moribus repertus est. Nam multos gradus uiuendi temptauit, et de gradu in gradum saltauit. Nullusque ei placibilis repertus est status'; for comparison see Pseudo-Boethius, *De disciplina scolarium: Édition critique, introduction et notes*, ed. O. Weijers (Leiden, 1976), ch. 3.

[68] Doyle, 'Woodford', 163.

corners of the city.[69] So it is that legislation against them lists conventicles, confederacies, assemblies, and congregations as the social forms that heresy might take. Anne Hudson has shown that the peculiarly educational aims of some Wycliffites were empirically observed by the authorities and the term *scolas*, schools, was added to that list around 1392.[70] Undoubtedly, Wycliffites did meet together, and activities consonant with schooling did take place in some cases, but this catalogue of terms was not primarily intended to describe social reality; rather it was meant to make the heretic a familiar figure for the people who would have to report him or her.

At several points I have already mentioned that canon lawyers and ecclesiastical administrators did not possess a language with which to discuss the contribution made to their work by the laity. When the laity did feature in the documents produced by this class it was as seditious rebels, violators of holy places, despoilers of church rights and liberties. For the local clergy, any gathering of the laity was suspicious. It was upon these suspicions that the anti-lollard language of conventicles and congregations played, even when it was consciously being copied from older pieces of anti-heresy legislation. Activities as diverse as the illegal sale of benefices in 'conuenticula' and the liturgical parodies of the 'Glotonmesse' in Leicester were evoked when bishops used words like conventicle and confederacy.[71] Interestingly the advent of concern about heresy coincided with a chronological peak in concern over all kinds of illicit gathering, due to the nerve-jangling effects of the 1381 revolt on both church and crown. By 1388 Richard II felt the need to demand assurances from all guilds and fraternities that their purposes and members were peaceful and obedient.[72] Such organizations were perhaps distrusted because they cut across the judicial structures of county, manor, and parish, although there was arguably no good reason to suspect their members of fomenting sedition. The pressure for the guild returns may in fact have come from a local level, where parish priests were especially sensitive to public gatherings outside their control. For example, in April 1386 the bishop of Exeter complained that 'meetings, councils, public parliaments, vanities, and profanities' were being conducted in the

---

[69] Netter, *Doctrinale*, iii. 865–6.   [70] Hudson, *Premature Reformation*, 175–8.

[71] Reg. Clifford (London), fos. 148ᵛ–149ʳ; *Reg. Repingdon (Lincoln)*, iii. 252–3.

[72] *English Gilds: The Original Ordinances of More than One Hundred Early English Gilds*, ed. L. T. Smith, EETS 40 (London, 1870).

chapel at Bosham, a prebend of Exeter within Chichester diocese. In July the same year, merriment and suspicious gatherings in the cemetery of Exeter cathedral were causing concern, and in December tumultuous activity was reported at Tiverton church in Devon.[73] The frequency of such entries in Brantyngham's register suggests that once he had begun to do so, a prelate was liable to see illegal and threatening gatherings everywhere.

5. MIXED MESSAGES ON THE REPORTING OF HERESY?

This chapter has presented evidence for two seemingly contradictory impulses in anti-heresy propaganda. According to the parable, humanity is divided into good and evil persons who are revealed by their deeds:

> Beware of false prophets, who come to you in sheep's clothing but inwardly are ravenous wolves. By their fruits you will know them. Are grapes gathered from thorns, or figs from thistles? In the same way, every good tree brings forth good fruit, but a bad tree brings forth bad fruit. A good tree cannot bear bad fruit, nor can a bad tree bear good fruit.[74]

This understanding formed the basis of the message that the evil of heresy was located in a distinct social group, capable of being identified. However, much judicial display, including abjuration, purgation, and readmission to the church, was calculated to communicate the message that heresy was a diffuse category of crime and not the activity of a sect.[75] Was this a case of mixed messages? Were the laity, as one scholar has recently suggested, not meant to play a part in the detection of heresy?[76]

First of all we have to acknowledge that reports of heresy, or of suspicions of heresy, were necessary and without them we would not have any judicial records of lollardy at all. Clearly someone was reporting heresy. Secondly we need to accept that the laity were not excluded from this through any lack of education or clerical status. The use of inquisitorial

---

[73] *Reg. Brantyngham (Exeter)*, ii. 610–11, 616–17, 631–2.   [74] Matt. 7: 15–18.

[75] M. Aston, 'Were the Lollards a Sect?', in P. Biller and B. Dobson (eds.), *The Medieval Church: Universities, Heresy, and the Religious Life. Essays in Honour of Gordon Leff*, SCH Subsidia, 11 (Woodbridge, 1999), 163–91.

[76] F. Somerset, ' "Mark him wel for he is on of þo": Training the "Lewed" Gaze to Discern Hypocrisy', *English Literary History*, 68 (2001), 315–34.

and visitatorial procedures assumed the involvement of the laity, and communicative procedures such as processions, interdicts, public abjurations, and citations were predicated on the assumption that significant information on heresy had to come from the laity. The necessity of making reports was regularly communicated to a very wide public through the mouths of penitent heretics, such as the promise made by Thomas Hellis in 1431 that 'if I know ony heretikys or of heresey ony man or wemmen suspekt or of thaim fautors consilloris or defensores or eny men or wymene makyng preve conventicules or assembles or holdyng ony singler or diverse opineouns frome the commyn doctryne of the churche I schall let yow worschypful fadyer or your vicar generaill in yowr absens or the diocesanes of suche men haue sone and redi knowyng'.⁷⁷ Besides being evidence of a successfully concluded heresy trial, these words instructed the assembled clergy and laity themselves in the detection of heresy. Suspicions roused by communication with known heretics, private meetings, or singular opinions were to be speedily reported to the diocesan or provincial authorities.

These clear instructions reflect the optimism of one strand of propaganda that held heresy to be recognizable. The sin hidden in the heart would be made manifest in the world, which would allow it to be seen or heard by people properly alert to such things. The phrase 'by their fruits you will know them' indeed became a well-known text around which many writers developed the theme of discernment and recognition. Reflecting on his own appearance after a period of illness, the Privy Seal clerk and poet Thomas Hoccleve wrote that 'Man by his deedes and nat by his lookes | Shal knowen be as it is write in bookes.' Beside this in the margin he appended the Latin tag 'a fructibus eorum cognoscetis eos', linking his self-examination with the discernment of heresy, which, although not revealed by appearances, was revealed by deeds or the fruit of sin.⁷⁸ John Audelay adapted the same phrase to serve in several contexts: the discernment of sinful priests, wicked friars, and heretics. The assertion 'Lef þou me, a loller his dedis þai wyl hym deme' expresses his confidence that heresy would be manifested and revealed.⁷⁹

---

⁷⁷ Reg. Langdon (Rochester), fo. 75Xᵛ.
⁷⁸ Thomas Hoccleve, *Complaint and Dialogue*, ed. J. A. Burrow, EETS 313 (Oxford, 1999), 17.
⁷⁹ *Poems of John Audelay*, 34; for sinful priests see 13, and for wicked friars, 29.

On the other hand, Hoccleve also expressed doubts about the possibility of knowing what was hidden in the heart. Writing about John Oldcastle he said that 'Many man outward seemeth wondir good, | And inward is he wondir fer ther-fro: | No man be Iuge of þat but he be wood [mad] | To god longith þat knowleche, & no mo.'[80] The familiar canonical claim that certain knowledge belongs only to God had the potential to confound the discernment of any inward deviance. For Hoccleve, hypocrisy was an effective cloak for vice, rather than a manifest sign of heresy itself. His words do go some way to explaining the contradiction presented here. 'No man may judge because final knowledge is God's alone' is a warning connected to judgement rather than the reporting of suspicion. However, if a judge was to proceed cautiously, always with equity in mind as Hostiensis had advised, then were not the parish clergy and laity expected to help detect heresy even more at risk of making false deductions?

Warnings about the inconclusive nature of any temporal justice were ubiquitous in anti-heresy propaganda. To begin with the church was supposed to be merciful to all who would 'torn wyth gode wyl and hert to the onhede of the chirche consideryng that holy churche schetteth not her bosom to hym that will torn ageyn, ne god will not the deth of a synner but rather and [*sic*] live wyth a pure hert'.[81] Mercy was extended to heretics on grounds of age, as in the case of Thomas Mone who was condemned to be burnt at Norwich in 1430 but was spared 'because of his age and feebleness', and in order to rehabilitate offenders.[82] In 1433 John Woodhulle abjured heresy 'to the help of myn owne soule, restorynge of myn owne name, and that nought by me mennes sowles sholde be hyndred either empeired', and in 1420 the physician William James had been given leave to practise medicine again having been incarcerated as an infamous heretic and lollard.[83] This mercy was necessary because temporal justice was limited.

If judgement was limited, then reported suspicion was even less certain. Dymmok cast doubt on the reliability of sensory perception when he distinguished between looking and considering in the discernment of heresy, while Netter argued that the identification of heretics was

[80] *Hoccleve's Works: The Minor Poems*, ed. F. J. Furnivall, EETS extra ser. 61 (London, 1892), 19.   [81] Reg. Langdon (Rochester), fo. 75X^r.
[82] *Norwich Heresy Trials*, 181.
[83] *Reg. Spofford (Hereford)*, 153; *Reg. Chichele (Canterbury)*, iv. 203–4.

not to be achieved 'by the fruits of their living, which are external and able to be coloured equally as sincere or false'.[84] There are echoes of this in the 'sly coloured arguments' that Hoccleve ascribed to heretics.[85] In order to be effective, spiritual discernment had to be preceded by virtue and self-knowledge, and this further restricted its execution by the laity. Even the ecclesiastical judge was admonished to 'understand himself first and cleanse in himself what he judges must be cleansed in others', and so how could this level of pure insight be achieved by those untrained and unpractised in law, theology, and meditative prayer?[86]

This impasse may be breached if we consider that the reporting of suspicions by the laity was only a preliminary stage in the prosecution of heretics. Detected signs of heresy need not be watertight to be transmitted to the bishop because the procedure most commonly applied, inquisition, did not require the written accusations, prior admonitions, and trustworthy eyewitnesses of procedure by accusation or denunciation. Nor was the accuser required to submit himself to punishment if the accusation proved to be false. Actual guilt, so far as that existed under canonical equity, would be tested by a qualified judge. In this light the frequency of warnings about the dangers and difficulties of detection are not evidence of lay involvement being 'displaced and directed elsewhere' as Fiona Somerset argues, but rather the fact that the laity, as well as the clergy, were indeed reporting heretics.[87] Neither should the claims of Bishop Pecock, that the hierarchy coerces the laity too much and trusts it too little, be taken to reflect the practice or attitudes of the episcopate.[88] The warnings are an attempt to manage rather than obstruct the detection of heresy through clerical and lay reporting.

Similarly, complaints about the misidentification of people as lollards should not be read as evidence of the failure of heresy reporting, but as evidence of the active engagement of people with this new aspect of public life. When Audelay protested that 'Yif þer be a pore prest and

---

[84] Dymmok, *Liber*, 308: he urged 'attendite' rather than 'aspicite'; Netter, *Doctrinale*, i. 621: 'non operibus conversandi, quae extrinsecus colorare possunt aequaliter sinceros et fictos.' [85] Hoccleve, *Minor Poems*, 17.
[86] *Fasciculus morum: A Fourteenth-Century Preacher's Handbook*, ed. S. Wenzel (Philadelphia, 1989), 404: 'Cognoscat ergo seipsum primo et purget quod ab aliis iudicat purgandum.' [87] Somerset, 'Training the "Lewed" Gaze', 316.
[88] J. H. Landman, ' "The Doom of Resoun": Accommodating Lay Interpretation in Late Medieval England', in B. A. Hanawalt and D. Wallace (eds.), *Medieval Crime and Social Control* (Minneapolis, 1999), 90–123.

spirituale in spiryt, | And be deuoute, with deuocion his seruyse syng and say, | Þay likon hym to a lollere and to an epocryte', he was commenting on a few specific failures of detection he had heard of, rather than illustrating a universal problem.[89] A passage from the devotional treatise *The Fyve Wyttes*, which has incorrectly been taken as proof that its author was a lollard sympathizer, may be read in the same way. 'Videte ne scandalizetis vnum ex pusillis istis, þough þey be called heretykes or lollardes. Bot be war, consente þou nouȝt to calle hem so ne leue nouȝt lyȝtly to þe commune sclaundre or clamour of fooles, yf þey preche trewely Crist and his gospel.'[90] The author of this was not saying that lollards preached truly, but that if someone did so and yet was called a heretic, one should not necessarily accept that identification. The fact that some reports may amount to no more than 'common slander or the clamour of fools' shows that rumour and hearsay were seen as distinct from reliably reported suspicion. This will be further explored in the next chapter.

Anti-heresy propaganda presented a range of outward signs that could be considered evidence of possible heresy. It is important to note that even when 'the heretic' was the subject of propaganda, the proper object of suspicion was heresy. This allowed bishops and preachers to engineer their communications to encourage a focused but restrained reporting of suspicions, and, perhaps more importantly, to encourage people to look within themselves for signs of heresy. The picture of heresy built up from propaganda is not one of an easily distinguished, discrete sect, but rather one of a diffuse crime whose seeds lay dormant in every human being. The boundaries of heresy were therefore not defined by sociological criteria, and to have done so would have been counterproductive for the church. Christian society was instead delineated by moral boundaries common to all and drawn by authority. From this it follows that the study of heresy detection will not allow definitive statements on the social contours of heresy, but it will allow the social contours of the reporting of heresy to be described.

---

[89] *Poems of John Audelay*, 15.
[90] *The Fyve Wyttes: A Late Middle English Devotional Treatise*, ed. R. H. Bremmer (Amsterdam, 1987), 19.

PART III

IMPLEMENTATION

7

Reporting Heresy

Previous chapters have developed the idea of two apparently competing impulses in the anti-heresy campaign conducted by the late medieval English church. Heresy was a danger that could only be defeated by widespread public involvement in the detection process, but detection was fraught with difficulties relating to knowledge and authority. These impulses did not make the system unworkable because heresy detection was a dialogue, between the knowledge and attitudes of *fidedigni* on the one hand, and episcopal vigilance and receptiveness on the other. One party made reports of heresy, and the other managed and interpreted them. The first stage was open to educated and uneducated alike, in a variety of jurisdictional contexts, and depended on trustworthiness before the law. The second stage was confined to the episcopal and inquisitorial courts, where the information in reports[1] was tested to see whether a charge of heresy was justified. This chapter will look at both sides of the coin, asking how in practice reports were made, whose suspicions were legally valid, what aspects of the statutes and polemic they found most useful, and how suspicion was dealt with as evidence in court.

1. MAKING REPORTS

Heresy came before the church courts via one of three procedural routes: accusation, denunciation, or inquisition, the details of which were outlined in Chapter 3. In most cases we do not know the name of the person

[1] A report in this context could include the reception of a secular indictment, under the terms of the 1414 parliamentary statute.

whose suspicion first raised the possibility of heresy, because most of our records represent much later stages in the judicial process. However, in a sizeable minority of cases we have a fairly good idea of who had reported the suspect and in others we can identify a group of jurors or *fidedigni*. In addition, the process of reporting heresy and the information received often leave clear traces in documents from the later stages of trial and punishment.

The social history of heresy detection would be much easier to write if more cases had begun with a formal accusation, the process requiring a named accuser, named witnesses and a written summary of the charge. However, the condition that the accuser bear the punishment if the accusation was unproven made this a very unattractive course of action. When accusation was the method of reporting, it was usually not the only procedure used, and our knowledge of it tends to come from later stages of the trial process. For example, when John Burgh of Kent made his abjuration of heresy in 1426, the preamble recited summary details of his trial, including the comment that he had been 'accused and indicted'. This was repeated in English in the text of the abjuration as 'I have be accusyde ande desclawnderyde'.[2] One year earlier Thomas Halle had stood before the bishop of Rochester 'being and having frequently been accused and reported of the same crime before several of his ordinaries'.[3] In the latter case the apparent mixture of procedure by accusation and by inquisition, of private and public prosecution, may be explained by Halle's repeated offending. In the former, Burgh seems to have come to the notice of the bishop by some form of mixed process. Trials begun in response to anonymous public reporting were sometimes promoted, that is moved through the judicial process, by named persons appointed by the bishop, giving the appearance of having begun at the instance of a private individual, *per accusationem*.[4]

It was also possible for a case to begin by inquisition and then proceed according to other criteria. This happened in the search for the accomplices, favourers, and defenders of Thomas Compworth of Kidlington

---

[2] Reg. Langdon (Rochester), fo. 58ʳ: 'accusatus et impetitus'.

[3] Ibid., fo. 69ᵛ: 'frequenter fuit et est de eodem crimine coram diuersis suis ordinariis accusatus et detectus.'

[4] This is probably how the phrase 'accused *ex officio*' in the trial of William Ramsbury, *Reg. Waltham (Salisbury)*, 169, should be understood.

in 1385.[5] The archdeacon of Oxford, a canon of Osney abbey, and the diocesan sequestrator were instructed to proceed on behalf of the bishop, *or* as promoters of a case on behalf of a denouncer or an accuser.[6] The implication of this was either that they should search for possible accusers, or that they should act as accusers themselves if that were the only feasible means of securing a trial. If this were the case, they would have to find two eyewitnesses to the alleged heresy, which was likely to have been easier in cases of assisting a known heretic than it was in cases of holding heretical opinions. It is possible that the abbot of Osney, from whose house Compworth had been preaching the withdrawal of tithes, was approached as a potential accuser, since he could be considered the injured party. Corporate bodies such as religious houses were in a stronger position to proceed by accusation than were private persons, as it would be harder to force punishment upon them in the event of a false or failed accusation. This seems to have been behind Arundel's receipt of 'an accusatorial bill' from the Dominican order, detailing charges of heresy against a professor of theology, John Whitehead, in 1410.[7] If the accusation failed, then it would be very difficult to force a whole religious order to undergo punishment for heresy. Similarly it was only the powerful who undertook procedure by denunciation in crimes as serious as heresy, because the requirement to admonish the suspect before reporting him or her to a judge was likely to make one vulnerable to a personal vendetta. So John Bagworth, the vicar of Wilsford in Lincoln diocese, was warned by Bishop Repingdon about communicating with heretics before being 'denounced and detected for the harbouring and sustaining of lollards and heretics'.[8]

Two rare examples of accusation by individuals point to the circumstances in which this was possible. Walter Brut was accused by several 'faithful Christians and zealots of the catholic faith', whom we may

[5] On Compworth see M. Jurkowski, 'Lollardy in Oxfordshire and Northamptonshire: The Two Thomas Compworths', in Somerset et al. (eds.), *Lollards and their Influence*, 73–95.

[6] Reg. Buckingham (Lincoln), fo. 310ᵛ: 'in forma iuris quatinusque canonice procedendum cognoscendum et diffiniendum ex officio nostro mero seu ad partis cuiuscumque promocionem denunciacionem seu instanciam.'

[7] Reg. Arundel (Canterbury), ii. fo. 16ʳ: 'quandam billam accusatoriam'.

[8] *Reg. Repingdon (Lincoln)*, iii. 69: 'super fomento et sustentacione lollardorum et hereticorum denunciatos et detectos, monuerimus . . . et contra monicionem nostram . . . dictus dominus Johannes vicarius aluit et fovit [hereticos].'

cautiously identify as the witnesses from Hereford and St David's
dioceses listed in the trial documents. They were Reginald de Wolstone,
a canon of Hereford, Philip Dilesk, the rector of Llanwrin in Powys,
Thomas Guldesfeld, the rector of English Bicknor in Gloucestershire,
John Cresset, the rector of Whitbourne in Herefordshire, and Thomas
Wallewayn esquire.[9] The accusers produced documents consonant with
the privately initiated criminal procedure of the church courts, including
a libel beginning: 'First we present, show and intend to prove . . .', but we
cannot tell whether this accusation represented the initial report, or
whether it had been prepared at the instruction of Bishop Trefnant on the
basis of information from an unnamed party.[10] It sometimes happened,
as in the case of William Russell in 1428, that promoters were appointed
to act as judicial accusers, what we might call public prosecutors. Once
Chichele had ordered two prominent London clerics, Richard Collyng
and Robert Felton, to prepare the case against Russell, they presented
libels and the positions and articles, and produced witnesses.[11] Russell
and Brut were both susceptible to formal accusations because they were
known individuals of whose heretical preaching there were many suitable
eyewitnesses. The use of accusatory procedure by a private individual
against someone not already suspected of heresy is far less common.

One notable example of this, which in its exceptional nature proves the
rule that accusation was an unpopular route to the detection of heresy,
was the case against Margery Baxter of Martham in Norfolk. Baxter was
brought before Bishop Alnwick on 7 October 1428 'noted for lollardy
and heresy', and several aspects of her case suggest that it was conducted
according to the rules of accusation. Her accuser is named, as Joan
Clifland of Norwich; in accordance with canon law two eyewitnesses
were produced, both servants of Clifland; and they all attested to events
rather than reporting their suspicions.[12] These events took place in
Clifland's house, where Baxter was alleged to have propounded numerous
heterodox opinions at some length. Baxter then asked Clifland whether
she would go with her to hear her (i.e. Baxter's) husband William read

[9] *Reg. Trefnant (Hereford)*, 278: 'Cristi fideles fideique catholice zelatores'; and 285.
[10] Ibid. 279: 'In primis damus et exhibemus et probare intendimus . . .' On the stages
and documentation of instance procedure, see D. M. Owen, 'Ecclesiastical Jurisdiction
in England 1300–1500', in D. Baker (ed.), *The Materials, Sources and Methods of
Ecclesiastical History*, SCH 11 (Oxford, 1975), 209–10.
[11] *Reg. Chichele (Canterbury)*, iii. 126–7.   [12] *Norwich Heresy Trials*, 41–51.

from the Gospels. Clifland looked dubious, possibly because William had at some point in the past been convicted of heresy,[13] and Baxter guessed she had spoken rashly, saying, 'Joan, it seems from your face that you intend and propose to reveal this advice I have given you to the bishop.' Clifland replied that she would not reveal it unless Baxter gave her cause to do so.[14] Truly scared now, Baxter threatened Clifland that if she were to accuse her, she would make a counter-accusation against her or have her killed. To back up her threat, Baxter told Clifland that in the past she had counteracted an accusation of heresy made against her by a Carmelite from Yarmouth priory by accusing him of carnally desiring her.[15] Whether or not that exchange ever took place, the threat to Clifland shows that Baxter had some knowledge of the stipulation in the *ordo iudiciarius* allowing a defendant to object to a witness if some crime, in this case implied rape or abduction, were imputed against him or her.[16] In the face of such intimidation, it is all the more remarkable that this case came to court at all.[17]

In addition to William Baxter's record, what acted in Clifland's favour was the fact that she was able to persuade her two servants, Joan Grymle and Anges Bethom, who had witnessed the conversation and the threats, to testify against Baxter. Any fear of reprisals from Baxter was perhaps outweighed by their economic ties to Clifland. In this complex and unusually well-documented case, a definitive account of what actually happened may not be possible, given the propensity of lawyers and notaries to order testimony and narrative in accordance with the legal procedure. Clearly there was some form of co-operation between sections

[13] Ibid. 39. This detail is mentioned in the trial of John Midelton, the vicar of Halvergate, on 5 October 1428, two days before the hearing of Clifland's testimony, but it is not clear when he had been convicted.

[14] Ibid. 48: 'Dixit insuper dicta Margeria isti iurate sic: "Johanna, apparet per vultum tuum quod tu intendis et proponis revelare istud consilium quod dixi tibi episcopo." Et ista iurata iuravit quod ipsa nunquam voluit revelare consilium suum in hac parte nisi ipsa Margeria dederit sibi occasionem hoc faciendi.'

[15] Ibid.: 'Et tunc dixit dicta Margeria eidem iurate, "et si tu accusaveris me dicto episcopo, ego faciam tibi sicut feci cuidam fratri Carmelite de Jernemuth, qui fuit doctissimus frater tocius patrie" . . . audiens quod dictus frater ipsam accusavit sic, ipsa Margeria accusavit ipsum fratrem quod ipse voluit eam carnaliter cognovisse.'

[16] Baxter was referring to the procedure known as *exceptio criminis*, for which see X 2.25.1.

[17] See J. A. Brundage, *Medieval Canon Law* (London, 1995), 93, on the difficulty of accusing someone of heresy.

of Norfolk society and the bishop's inquisition, and Baxter's case was initiated by the relatively unusual route of accusation, but whether this went as far as engineering the entrapment of a notable suspect is impossible to tell from the evidence.[18]

The bulk of extant heresy cases, however, resulted from inquisitions which could either be regular and proactive or irregular and reactive. The former category was capable of uncovering previously unknown instances of suspected heresy, while the latter usually relied upon information gleaned from previous prosecutions, the presentments of secular juries, and reports about persons already suspected of, or condemned for, heresy. Formally at least, this procedure was initiated by the ordinary or metropolitan bishop or an inquisitor, and so the names of individual informants are recorded even more rarely than in accusations. Where we do have names, their identification as the initiator of the case is not always straightforward. For example, when William Colyn of South Creake in Norfolk was tried before Alnwick in 1429, three local husbandmen are noted simply as being present. Their economic status may indicate that they were 'viri fidedigni' of their parishes who had reported Colyn, but they may equally have been witnesses or the constables of their villages.[19] Where we do have names, we often find that they belonged to quite substantial local persons. Concurrent with the trials in Norwich, Alnwick was also pursuing heresy in Bury St Edmunds. In October 1428 he ordered William Curtis, the abbot of Bury, to cite 'six priests and six laymen unsuspected of heresy, from the more notable living within your jurisdiction, to appear before us and our commissaries'.[20] The laymen who appeared, John Maggys, John Nottingham, John Edward, William Rycher, John Regges, and Edward Goldsmith, were model *fidedigni*. Maggys was the current alderman, Nottingham the previous incumbent, while Edward, Rycher, and Regges would all hold the same office at some point over the next twenty years.

Such sociological evidence for trustworthy reporters of heresy cannot always be taken at face value, however. A group of London citizens, to all

[18] For this suggestion see M. Aston, 'Lollard Women', in D. Wood (ed.), *Women and Religion in Medieval England* (Oxford, 2003), 173–4.

[19] *Norwich Heresy Trials*, 89.

[20] Reg. Alnwick (Norwich), fo. 108ᵛ: 'sex presbiteros et sex laicos de notabilioribus infra vestram jurisdiccionem commorantibus super heretica prauitate non suspectos quod compareant et quilibet eorum compareat coram nobis nostrisve commissariis.'

intents and purposes no different from their Bury counterparts, testified in the same year that one Ralph Mungyn was a heretic. Mungyn had allegedly aired his heretical opinions at a dinner hosted by the elderly mercer John Shadworth, a former alderman, sheriff, and mayor of London. The witnesses against him were all Shadworth's guests: William Estfield, a mercer who had been sheriff in 1422–3 and would be mayor for the first of two stints in 1429–30; John Russell, also a mercer, who had held the office of Common Hunt in 1423; and someone called William Drax.[21] Their status suggests a group of respectable men, scandalized by what they had heard, but there may well be another side to the story. Part of the evidence against Mungyn was that when asked by one of the dinner guests whether he thought papal indulgences were beneficial to the soul, he replied that they were not because the pope had more no power to issue them than he did himself.[22] The trial gives no indication that this was a hostile question designed to entrap Mungyn, and it seems quite possible that the guest asked out of sympathy with the expected response. This possibility is made more likely by the fact that David Pryce, presiding in this case, had established that Mungyn had long been suspected of heresy in London and Oxford. The conclusion that he was the invited guest of sympathizers who knew his reputation is quite plausible.[23]

If there were even a grain of truth in this, Shadworth and his dinner guests would have placed themselves in grave danger of being reported for heresy themselves, as sustainers and favourers of a suspected heretic. It is possible that in reporting Mungyn for heresy they hoped to escape the same charge, a tactic tried by Robert Bert of Bury St Edmunds in 1430. Bert was charged with owning a suspicious book, *Dives and Pauper*, which he claimed had been annotated by Robert Dykkes of Bury who had been tried for heresy in 1428. By giving information about someone publicly known to have been investigated, Bert convinced Alnwick to

---

[21] On Shadworth, Estfield, and Russell, see C. Barron, *London in the Later Middle Ages: Government and People 1200–1500* (Oxford, 2004), 144, 335–6, 339–41, 368; S. Thrupp, *The Merchant Class of Medieval London 1300–1500* (Ann Arbor, 1962), 338, 366.

[22] *Reg. Chichele (Canterbury)*, iii. 204: 'eodem tempore unus de discumbentibus in loco predicto interrogavit a dicto Radulpho an indulgencie per summum pontificem . . . valerent seu proficerent animabus . . . Ad quam questionem respondebat dictus Radulphus quod dicte indulgencie in nullo valebant quia papa in ea parte non habuit majorem potestatem concedendi indulgencias quam ipsemet habuit.'

[23] Ibid. 202–3.

admit him to purgation.[24] In this instance we do not know whether Dykkes was reinvestigated, but in other cases information from lollards 'just lately captured' proved invaluable to investigators.[25] Suspects arrested and tried in groups, such as those at Norwich 1428–31 or Coventry 1511–12, were particularly vulnerable to mutual incrimination, making heresy suspects themselves the most common reporters of persons suspected of heresy.[26] Once a cycle of denunciations had begun, it was possible that two people could be tried whose only reason to be suspected was statements they had made against one another. Clearly the system of fear upon which this rested benefited the anti-heresy campaign, but a judge would need a key to unlock these networks, turning them from circles of concealment into cycles of mutual incrimination. This key may well have been provided by Joan Clifland in Norwich, who was the only reporter of heresy in that series of prosecutions not also reported for heresy, and Baxter's was the only case brought by accusation. In early sixteenth-century Coventry the only two witnesses who escaped prosecution themselves may have played this role. The editors of those trials have commented that 'it is remarkable how infrequently non-Lollards testified against Lollards', a feature of canonical procedure that is explained by the difficulties of proceeding in any other way.[27] Continental inquisitors of the fourteenth century, who dealt with large numbers of witnesses and suspects, regularly initiated an investigation by soliciting confessions of heresy in return for leniency. These depositions were then used against the more recalcitrant, and presumably more dangerous, suspects in the area.[28]

When *fidedigni*, clerics, secular juries, episcopal staff, and suspected heretics made reports of heresy to a bishop, they did so on the basis of suspicion that someone either held heretical opinions, or was behaving in a manner redolent of heresy. The latter was more common, but on occasion we have evidence that an initial report was made because certain beliefs were recognized as unorthodox. Most lists of heretical opinions in legal records come from much later stages in the judicial process, once

[24] *Norwich Heresy Trials*, 98–102; Reg. Alnwick (Norwich), fo. 109ᵛ; Hudson, *Premature Reformation*, 207.

[25] PRO, C 54/263, m. 6d (*CCR 1413–19*, 114–15): 'lollardi vulgariter nuncupati iam tarde capti.'

[26] M. Aston, 'William White's Lollard Followers', in *Lollards and Reformers*, 71–99, gives details of the group relationships of the Norwich suspects.

[27] *Lollards of Coventry*, 122, 240.   [28] Given, *Inquisition*, 42.

the suspect had been questioned at length and the answers systematized into a catalogue of condemned beliefs. Only occasionally in ecclesiastical sources do we have witnesses describing the beliefs of suspects. For instance, Margery Baxter's accuser quickly recognized the heterodoxy of all that she said, and Ralph Mungyn was reported to Chichele for asserting that it was not licit to fight or kill the Bohemian heretics, and that all goods should be held in common.[29] Public preaching exposed Wycliffite and other radical preachers to the possibility that their ideas would be judged heretical by a member of their audience. Where the audience contained persons conversant with doctrinal boundaries, such as the better-educated clerics or friars, the risk grew. In 1420, for example, Thomas Drayton and William Taylor were arrested in Bristol by the mayor, James Cokkes, and the sheriff, David Buddock, because of 'certain heretical, erroneous and false propositions, opinions, and conclusions, and determinations repugnant to the holy canons and holy mother church . . . as told by many faithful Christians'.[30] One of the many witnesses to their preaching had been a Bristol Carmelite, John Walton, perhaps better qualified than most to recognize unorthodox ideas when he heard them. With some prompting, the content of William Swinderby's preaching was remembered by the rector of Kinnersley in Herefordshire and chaplain of Bettwsclyro just over the border in Radnorshire who attested that they had heard his sermon from beginning to end, and that the articles now written out in Latin had indeed been those he had preached in English.[31]

Most reports of heretical doctrine in ecclesiastical records stress the contingency of such qualitative judgements. This was provided for in the thirteenth of Arundel's 1409 constitutions, which ordered the citation of anyone defamed, detected, or vehemently suspected of any heretical acts

---

[29] *Reg. Chichele (Canterbury)*, iii. 204: 'dominus Radulphus expresse tenuit et affirmavit quod non est licitum impugnare seu occidere hereticos de Bohemia . . . omnia bona quorumcumque essent omnibus communia.' On Mungyn's pacifism see Hudson, *Premature Reformation*, 369.

[30] Reg. Morgan (Worcester), p. 36: 'certas proposiciones, opiniones et conclusiones . . . hereticas, erroneas atque falsas et determinacionibus sacrorum canonum sancteque matris ecclesie repugnantes . . . ut dicebatur quamplures christi fideles.'

[31] *Reg. Trefnant (Hereford)*, 255: 'dixit quod contenta in articulo sunt vera, videlicet quod idem Willelmus Swynderby predicando tenuit et affirmavit in omnibus et per omnia in effectu, excepto quod idem Willelmus predicavit in Anglicis verbis et articulus est in Latinis, causam sciencie reddens qui tunc ibidem interfuit et sermonem dicti Willelmi prout articulatur a principio usque ad finem audivit.'

or words, or of anyone preaching 'any article whatsoever sounding evilly against the catholic faith or good morals'.[32] In practice this meant that people reported words 'sounding like lollardy', and persons who 'spoke words sounding of heresy'.[33] The language in which such insights were described by diocesan notaries was designed to be inconclusive, as the orthodoxy of words could only be judged by bishops and inquisitors assisted by theologians. However, this did not prevent heretical doctrine being identified and reported without ambiguity in other jurisdictions.

The secular panels and juries created by county commissioners in the wake of the Oldcastle revolt of 1414, and the juries of the 1417 royal investigations into heresy and insurrection, frequently presented reports of heretical beliefs in a very straightforward manner. On 6 February 1414, a jury of men from north Leicestershire reported that William Warde, William Smith, John Parlibien, and Thomas Novery 'are lollards and they maintain heretical opinions contrary to the catholic faith, not worshipping the sacraments of the church, saying that no one ought to confess to a priest, but only to God, and also that it is not meritorious to go on pilgrimage and it is equally good to be buried outside holy ground as inside, and many other heresies'.[34] The contrast with ecclesiastical reports that someone is suspected of being a lollard and reputed to have held certain opinions sounding like heresy is vivid. Similarly in 1417 jurors in Warwickshire presented John Ewyk as a lollard, saying that 'he holds various lollard opinions contrary to the faith of holy church and its determinations, and these opinions he maintains, preaches, and supports'.[35] In presentments of this kind the figure of the lollard is easily recognized and his beliefs identifiable as self-evidently heretical. No circumspection or mere suspicion is felt necessary, but on occasion, the

---

[32] Reg. Arundel (Canterbury), ii. fo. 12ᵛ: 'alio articulo quocumque in fide catholica aut bonis moribus male sonante.'

[33] *Reg. Bubwith (Bath & Wells)*, i. 284: 'in lollardiam sonantibus'; *Visitations in the Diocese of Lincoln, 1517–1531*, ed. A. H. Thompson, 3 vols., Lincoln Record Society, 33, 35, 37 (1940–7), i. 113: 'Johannes Conyngton seruiens Melton est locutus verba quedam sonantia in heresim.'

[34] PRO, KB 9/204/1, m. 130: 'sunt lollardi et sustinent oppiniones hereticas contra fidem catholicam non honorando sacramenta ecclesie, dicendum quod nullus debet se confiteor alicui sacerdoti nisi soli deo et eciam quod non est meritorium peregrinare, et tam bonum sepeliri extra sanctuarium quam infra sanctuarium ac multas alias hereses.'

[35] PRO, KB 9/209, mm. 47, 50: 'tenet diuersas oppiniones lollardrie contra fidem sacrosancte ecclesie et determinacionem eiusdem, et oppiniones huiusmodi manutenet predicat et sustentat.'

language of the church courts does seep into jurors' presentments. When this happens, probably as a result of a canonical or curial education on the part of someone connected to the commission, it stands out against the legal certainty and moral clarity of all other secular reports of heresy. One such example is the presentment made by a Northamptonshire jury on 16 February 1414, 'that John [name erased], fuller, Thomas Seyton and John Tukley, weavers, were defamed that they were of the sect of the lollards'.[36]

The normal practice of secular juries was akin to accusatory procedure in canon law, in that facts were stated and events related, but the dominant anti-heresy procedure, by inquisition, elicited much less certainty and much more circumspection. Even the most positive and assured secular presentment would have to be tested by an episcopal or inquisitorial judge before a suspect could be declared a heretic, and information passed to bishops by the justices of King's Bench would be treated in the same way as information acquired in the church's own investigations. For example, Thomas Novery was not made a heretic by his presentment in 1414, and Repingdon eventually allowed him to proceed to purgation. It is significant that within the framework of ecclesiastical justice the *facts* of the royal investigation became 'infamy said to exist against Thomas', and subject to the equity of canon law rather than the black and white judgements of royal justices.[37]

As discussed in Chapters 3 and 6, actions were thought to be indicators of belief, and in their abjurations penitents had to promise to report 'anyone known or suspected of heresies or errors, or anyone taking part in secret meetings, or anyone differing in life and morals from the usual behaviour of the faithful and the determinations of the church'.[38] Was this too general to be of any practical use? A variation on the 'differing in life and morals' clause made by Bishop Alnwick's notary during the 1428 investigation in Bury suggests how it might have been interpreted. The appointed *fidedigni* and clerics were asked to report 'heretics and their

[36] PRO, KB 9/204/1, m. 99: 'quod Johannes [*erasure*], fuller, Thomas Seyton et Johannes Tukley, weuer, diffamati fuerunt quod ipsi essent de secta lollardorum.'
[37] *Reg. Repingdon (Lincoln)*, iii. 70–1: 'contra ipsum Thomam super premissis infamia dicitur laborare.' See also PRO, KB 9/204/1, m. 139, and Lincolnshire Archives, Episcopal Register 15B (royal writs addressed to Repingdon), fo. 13ᵛ.
[38] *Reg. Morgan (Worcester)*, p. 87: 'aliqui super heresibus seu erroribus notati vel infamati, seu occulta conuenticula celebrantes seu a communi conuersacione fidelium et ecclesie determinacione vita et moribus discrepantes.'

believers and their receivers, favourers, and defenders, besides anyone who holds private meetings or withdraws himself from church on feast days or from the usual behaviour of men'.[39] Here the sense of differing is expressed by the word 'subtrahentes', withdrawing, instead of the more usual 'discrepantes' or 'dissidentes'. If differing from the behaviour of the faithful was understood as withdrawal from the regular course of parochial observances, rather than the more sensational rejection of all social norms implied in the usual rendition, then reporting offenders would have been almost second nature.

This narrow conception of deviant behaviour is evident in Joan Clifland's deposition against Margery Baxter, who was reported to have said that no child of Christian parents should be baptized in water 'according to the usual practice', because they were sufficiently baptized in the womb.[40] It seems likely that 'secundum usum communem' was added to Margery's actual words by Clifland or by the notary recording the testimony. Further on in Clifland's deposition, she alleges that Baxter had falsely confessed to the dean of a secular college in Norwich, so that he would believe her to be a person of good life.[41] This suggests that Baxter herself recognized the practical requirements for membership of the community of the faithful, despite being prepared to subvert them, and Clifland saw the danger in her deception. The religious practice that stands out in the Norwich trials as a marker of heresy is eating meat on Fridays and at other prohibited times. However, this, together with absence from church, false confessions, and so on, could never be a definitive guide to the detection of heresy, since many people were weak, negligent, forgetful, or even rebellious, but very few merited condemnation as heretics. For example, when John Fyllys was reported in 1430 for eating meat on the vigil of St Thomas the Apostle, Alnwick inquired amongst his neighbours and nothing untoward was detected in his life or morals.[42] One Norwich case of non-attendance at church did lead to

---

[39] Reg. Alnwick (Norwich), fo. 108ᵛ: 'hereticos et eis credentes ac eorum receptatores et fauctores [*sic*] atque defensores, necnon quoscumque priuata conuenticula facientes aut se diebus festiuis ab ecclesiis vel a communi hominum conuersacione subtrahentes.'

[40] *Norwich Heresy Trials*, 46: 'nullus puer siue infans natus habens parentes Christianos debet baptizari in aqua secundum usum communem quia talis infans sufficienter baptizatur in utero matris.'

[41] Ibid. 48–9: 'fuit sepius ficte confessa decano de Campis ad finem quod ipse decanus reputaret eam esse bone vite.'   [42] Ibid. 104.

suspicion of heresy, but elsewhere no such link was made.[43] While proving useful to would-be reporters of heresy, the practical guidelines drawn around deviant observance did not constitute positive and final identifications of heretics. Lists such as Lyndwood's were merely the framework within which laity and episcopacy could communicate with one another about potential heresy.

The first sign of heresy given in Lyndwood's list was the ownership of heretical books, which has become for historians the defining feature of Wycliffite dissent. Aston for example argues that it was as a 'vernacular literate movement that Lollardy had gathered momentum and it was as a vernacular literate movement that it was suspected and persecuted'. Similarly Hudson writes that 'the readiest way . . . in which suspected Lollards might reveal themselves was by their ownership of books.'[44] Although the importance of writing, both vernacular and Latinate, to religious dissent of all kinds in late medieval England cannot be disputed, there is reason to question the centrality of books and writing to the detection of heresy. As a marker of heresy, literacy has perhaps been overestimated by historians and literary scholars, because ours are literate disciplines relying upon literate sources, and we naturally privilege them in our interpretations. Because the written word is by its very nature recorded for posterity while the spoken word is not, legislation such as the constitutions issued by Arundel in 1409 have elicited greater excitement for the censorship of writing than for the restrictions on preaching and speaking.[45] The key to understanding the place of writing in the detection of heresy, however, is to examine how the authorities saw the *use* of books, bills, and libels within the context of oral communication.

The realization that written words as well as spoken words would have to be controlled if heresy were to be defeated came in 1388 with the series of commissions described in Chapter 2. They recognized the multiple forms that the written word communicating heresy could take, referring to 'many books, libels, schedules and pamphlets containing manifest heresies and errors'. Written in English and Latin, such writings were said to be compiled, published, and shared by Wyclif, Hereford, Aston, and

---

[43] Ibid. 102–3; *Reg. Waltham (Salisbury)*, 114–15, 138, 141, 158–9, for examples of non-attendance and working on fast days not eliciting suspicion of heresy.

[44] M. Aston, 'Lollardy and Literacy', in *Lollards and Reformers*, 207; Hudson, *Premature Reformation*, 166.

[45] Watson, 'Censorship and Cultural Change in Late Medieval England', 830–40.

their followers.[46] The sale of such writings is also mentioned.[47] From the outset then, heretical writings were understood within the contexts of their use: composition was described in the same breath as publication, sharing, buying, and selling. By 1407 heretical writing was at the centre of Arundel's concern about unorthodox education and proselytizing. The sixth and seventh of his constitutions deal with the ownership and copying of Wyclif's works, the translation of the Bible, in its entirety or parts, and indeed the composition of any unauthorized works of commentary or simplification.[48] But these constitutions should not be seen in isolation from others dealing with preaching (numbers 1–4) and teaching (numbers 5, 8, and 9), activities which the written word was thought to facilitate.

The only forms of writing that seem to have directly elicited reports of suspected heresy were those that achieved a wide public distribution, either through multiple copying or prominent display. For example, in 1413 Richard Devenish was excommunicated for posting a bill allegedly written by lollards onto the choir stalls of the church of the Holy Cross of the Temple in Bristol, and in 1414 Thomas Ile of Braybrooke was said to be a distributor and carrier of bills that urged support for Oldcastle.[49] When people mentioned bound books in their reports, it was rarely as the sole piece of incriminating evidence, and the use to which they were put was all-important. Consider for example Margery Baxter's invitation to her accuser that she should come to hear her husband read from the Gospel. This gives us a domestic setting for a communal and oral use of the written word. It is not merely the presence of the Bible in English that makes this report savour of heresy, but also the context. Similarly when

---

[46] PRO, C 66/325, m. 26d (*CPR 1385–89*, 468): 'ex insana doctrine magistorum Johannis Wyclyf dum vixit Nicholi Hereford, Johannis Aston et suorum sequacium quamplures libri, libelli, cedule et quaternum hereses et errores manifestos continentes . . . compilantur, publicantur, communicantur et conscribuntur tam in anglico quam latino.'

[47] PRO, C 66/325, m. 26d (*CPR 1385–89*, 468): the commission orders that anyone who presumes to buy or sell [euiare vel vendere presumat] such things is to be investigated.

[48] A. Hudson, 'Lollardy: The English Heresy?', in *Lollards and their Books*, 148–9.

[49] *Reg. Bubwith (Bath & Wells)*, i. 142: 'quemdam libellam famosum vicarii dicte ecclesie Sancte Crucis scandalum et infamium gravia valde continentem a certis satellitibus, Lollardis nuncupatis quin verius heresiarchis, scienter accepit et in stallo dicti vicarii in choro ecclesie predicte maliciose posuit et ibidem dimisit'; PRO, KB 9/204/1, m. 141: 'Thomas Ile est lollardus et compartitor ac asportator billarum Johannis Oldecastell militis in fauorem ipsius Johannis Oldecastell.' On bills and libels see W. Scase, ' "Strange and Wonderful Bills": Bill-Casting and Political Discourse in Late Medieval England', *New Medieval Literatures*, 2 (1998), 225–47.

William Harry of Tenterden in Kent was captured in London in 1428, he admitted to reading proscribed books, attending secret gatherings, and conversing with men suspected of being lollards. The record goes on to specify that it was because of his communication with suspect men that he was declared vehemently suspect of heresy and error.[50] Reading was important to the case, but alone it was not grounds for suspicion. This is also shown in the case of John Claydon of London, who was initially suspected because of his communication with men also suspected of heresy. It was only the depositions of witnesses that revealed this illiterate's taste for hearing heretical books, among them the *Lanterne of Liȝt*, read out to him, and his private discussion of their contents with other persons suspected of heresy. Only after suspicion had been aroused in this way were his books scrutinized.[51] Similarly the citation of books such as *Dives and Pauper* and the *Canterbury Tales* in heresy trials suggests that it was not vernacular or even Wycliffite books *per se* that were signs of heresy, but the context in which they were used.[52] How else are we to account for the possession of Wycliffite Bibles by powerful men and women of undoubted orthodoxy?[53]

There were exceptions to the rule that possession of books alone did not make one suspect of heresy but they do not add up to much of a counter-argument. For example, when the bailiff of Rochester, the constable of Shamell, and others were commissioned to search for books in the houses of John and Robert Boyden in 1436, that was the only instruction given, suggesting that the books had prompted the initial suspicion.[54] However, following Chichele's redefinition of the investigative spheres of church and crown in 1416, books were all that secular officers could legitimately investigate. The one thing that seems to have been guaranteed to arouse suspicion was any attempt to keep books hidden from the investigating authorities. When Richard Herberd

[50] *Reg. Chichele (Canterbury)*, iii. 190: 'recognovit se legisse diversos libros in vulgari de sacra scriptura, et sepius fuisse in conventiculis occultis cum hominibus diversis suspectis de hujusmodi secta lollardie; et idcirco dominus propter fugam suam in hac parte ac communicacionem suam cum hujusmodi hominibus suspectis et propter alia que ipsum movebant in ea parte reputabat et declarabat ipsum de heresi et errore fore vehementer suspectum.' [51] Ibid. iv. 134–5.

[52] Hudson, *Premature Reformation*, 167, and 'Lollardy: The English Heresy', 142, 149; Thomson, *Later Lollards*, 243–4; Aston 'Lollardy and Literacy', 208.

[53] R. Hanna, 'English Biblical Texts before Lollardy and their Fate', in Somerset et al. (eds.), *Lollards and their Influence*, 148–53; Hudson, *Premature Reformation*, 233–4.

[54] Reg. Brouns (Rochester), fo. 5ᵛ.

abjured in 1431, he did so 'well knowing in my self that I have wetyngly and wilfully ikept coverid and hid certeyn bokys of englysh contenyng perverse doctrine ageynst the determination of the chyrche of rome, and so be this suspekt of errour and heresey'.[55] These words put into his mouth suggest that the suspicion against him was a result of his concealment of books containing errors, not merely his possession of them. Adduced in conjunction with other evidence, the discovery of hidden books could be a decisive influence on a case. This was demonstrated when John Galle, tried for heresy before Chichele in 1428, persistently denied the charges against him, but was confounded and unable to deny his guilt when confronted with a copy of the New Testament in English that had been found in his home.[56] We can only say that hiding books *seems* to have been considered sufficient grounds for suspicion of heresy because the words uttered by Herberd and the trial of Galle were *post facto* reconstructions of the reporting process, representing the agenda of the prosecutors. As instances of propaganda, as well as moments in a judicial process, their cases suggest the fabrication of a link between the revelation of heresy hidden in the heart, and the revelation of books hidden under the floorboards.

The other main ingredient in reports of proscribed books and libels was communication with known heretics, an important part of Lyndwood's list of suspicious activities. Reports of secret meetings, conversations with suspected persons, and help or audience given to heretical preachers were always alarming enough to trigger a swift investigative response from church and crown. This was because heresy was most frightening in its movement and multiplication, more so than in its incubated and hidden existence. The most frightening Wycliffites were those who were most mobile and most active in converting people to their opinions, and so the anti-heretical campaign focused on them. Reports of conversations, meetings, and travelling should be seen as the first steps taken towards tracking the spread of heresy. However, the language used in them must be taken to reflect the formulaic conventions of legal idiom, as well as empirical observations of new phenomena. In particular 'conventicle' need not indicate a fixed or uniform type of heretical meeting: we should try to appreciate that suggestion and imprecision were as important to the anti-heresy message as factual accuracy.

---

[55] Reg. Langdon (Rochester), fo. 74X[v].
[56] *Reg. Chichele (Canterbury)*, iii. 190.

In the Norwich trials of 1428–31 great store was set by communication had with known heretics, and it was Alnwick's main task to identify the people that had come into contact with William White, the Wycliffite evangelist.[57] It was communication with White and Hugh Pye, 'condemned heretics', that formed the substance of the charge against John Wardon, for example. Richard Clerk was 'repeatedly suspected of communication and conversation with heretics' and charged with receiving heretics in his house, supporting, sustaining, and hiding them, and giving them encouragement, help, and favour in their opinions.[58] White was originally from Kent and so his movements were of especial concern to an episcopate keen to minimize the spread of heresy. This image of the itinerant heretical preacher roaming the country from one safe house to another is exemplified in the charge against John Bagworth and an anonymous associate that they communicated with a named heretic, John Bond, 'in the street, the house, and various other places'.[59] Reports that they gave Bond food and drink were enough to justify episcopal attention. It is striking that no one charged with these offences tried to use the ignorance and innocence defence employed by parishes subject to interdict. Presumably it would be hard to deny that visits from a condemned heretic had taken place if there were witnesses, and to feign ignorance of that person's legal status would be a risky strategy. For example, in 1414 Thomas and Agnes Tickhill of Derbyshire were presented for harbouring William Ederyk, a condemned heretic, 'knowing him to be a lollard holding, speaking and preaching various opinions contrary to the ordinances and determinations of the catholic church'.[60] In 1417 Richard Fuller of Northamptonshire was presented for receiving Laurence Fuller (possibly a relation) and Robert Taillour despite 'knowing and recognizing them to be lollards'.[61] A condemnation for heresy was assumed to be public knowledge, and ignorance was no defence for fraternizing.

---

[57] Aston, 'William White's Lollard Followers', 83, for a tabulation of the relationships within the group of suspects.

[58] *Norwich Heresy Trials*, 32–4 (Wardon); 191–2 (Clerk): 'ipse Ricardus habuit sepius suspectam communicacionem et conversacionem cum hereticis, et quod recepit hereticos in domos suas et eos supportabat, sustentabat et concelabat ac eisdem in eorum opinionibus prebuit consilium, auxilium et favorem.'

[59] *Reg. Repingdon (Lincoln)*, iii. 69: 'in via in mansa et aliis diversis locis communicabant.'

[60] PRO, KB 9/204/1, m. 59: 'scientes ipsum esse lollardum et diuersas opiniones contra ordinacionem et determinacionem ecclesie catholice tenentem, dicentem et predicantem.'

[61] PRO, KB 9/209, mm. 57, 62: 'sciens et cognoscens ipsos fore lollardos.'

Reporters of heresy also informed ecclesiastical judges of the locations of abnormal social or religious activity, as if it were an important facet of the suspicion against offenders. Although, as Hudson and Gradon note, we know very little about the contexts in which Wycliffite sermons were preached or read, suspicious speech was reported as having been heard in private houses and in public places such as churches and taverns.[62] The dangers of speaking freely to friends and neighbours on subjects of theological controversy are well illustrated in the case of Margery Baxter. Other examples of suspicious words heard in private houses are rare, although two witnesses did testify against William Wakeham of Wiltshire in 1434, saying that they had been in the house of one William Duke when Wakeham had asserted the earth to be above the sky, and that it was no better for a layman to say the Lord's Prayer in Latin than to say 'bibul babul'.[63]

The public realm was most dangerous for religious dissenters during periods of heightened awareness of heresy, in particular just before and after the Oldcastle revolt, and after the nationwide scares of 1428. For example, in 1429 William Colyn of Norfolk was charged with having expressed an erroneous opinion on the Trinity to the vicar of his parish, John Goleth, while in a tavern.[64] It is reasonable to assume that Goleth was then the person who reported this to one of Alnwick's officials. A morality of social space may also have informed the report against John Anneys of Leicestershire, who in 1413 was charged with preaching and teaching erroneous and heretical opinions 'in taverns and other public places'.[65] Taverns also featured in reports of heresy as places where the insurgents of 1414 had arranged to meet before rising against the king.[66] Because they were sites of public congregation outside immediate church control, taverns were regarded with some suspicion

[62] *English Wycliffite Sermons*, iv. 33–6.

[63] Reg. Nevill (Salisbury), part 2, fo. 52ᵛ: 'dicit iste deponens quod xxi die mensis Septembre Anno Domini Mᵒ CCCCᵒ xxxvijᵒ in domo Willelmi Duke, weuer de Marleburgh presens fuit iste deponens vbi fuit et audiuit dictum Willelmum Wakeham dicentem quod terra est supra celum et . . . non est melius laicus dicere pater noster qui es in celis etc. latino sermone, quam dicere bibull babull.'

[64] *Norwich Heresy Trials*, 90.

[65] Lincolnshire Archives, MS Vj/0, fo. 14ᵛ: 'in tabernis et aliis locis publicis'.

[66] See for example PRO, KB 9/204/1, m. 58, which tells how William Ederyk and John Grene set out from Derbyshire to rendezvous in Smithfield at an inn called 'Lez Wrastelers on the Hope'.

by the clergy, even if, like John Goleth, they frequented the places themselves.[67]

Even more feared than public places with negative associations were private places where heresy could be hidden and yet spread. The late medieval church and crown were very used to dealing with secret gatherings and meetings, and this familiarity was shared by the clergy and laity who reported their suspicions of heretical meetings. From the rather terse reports in legal records, we cannot learn much about the size or nature of many such gatherings, although the imprecision of the terms 'conventicle' and 'congregation', should alert us to the probability that by no means all such reports describe heretical schools or reading groups. Many reports allude to suspicious gatherings in 'unlawful places', and presentments for holding 'congregations and other unlawful meetings' were common.[68] For these to have any meaning, some concept of what constituted an illegal gathering must have pre-dated the advent of heresy in England. Naturally the idea of a specifically heretical gathering had entered the public consciousness after two generations of anti-heresy propaganda, but it was in the interests of the authorities to keep any definition vague. The crown investigations of 1417 were indeed predicated on the assumption that one illegal gathering was much like any other, with juries being instructed to inquire into lollardy and heresy alongside any other insurrection, congregation, or conventicle.[69] The implication here is that information gained in pursuit of one kind of assembly might yield information about another.

This possibility may have been behind the report made in 1428 by the convent of Bonhommes (Augustinian canons) at Edington in Wiltshire, that at least nineteen of their parishioners had gathered at a cross in the hamlet of Tinhead and formed a combination to withhold offerings for the sacraments above the level of 1d. until agreement had been reached in

---

[67] The literature on taverns is growing fast. See J. M. Bennett, *Ale, Beer, and Brewsters in England: Women's Work in a Changing World 1300–1600* (Oxford, 1996), 122–44; B. A. Hanawalt, 'The Host, the Law and the Ambiguous Space of Medieval London Taverns', in Hanawalt and Wallace (eds.), *Medieval Crime and Social Control*, 204–23; B. A. Kümin and B. A. Tlusty (eds.), *The World of the Tavern: Public Houses in Early Modern Europe* (Aldershot, 2002).

[68] PRO, KB 9/204/1, m. 139; KB 9/205/1, m. 83. When the latter case was tried in 1417, *Reg. Bubwith (Bath & Wells)*, i. 283–90, there was no mention of conventicles. It seems that this information was deemed unnecessary to the trial.

[69] PRO, KB 9/209 *passim*.

a dispute. The dispute in question had been simmering for several generations, and involved the claims of a dependent chapel to parochial status,
the role of the canons as rectors of the parish, and the economic demands
being placed on the laity.[70] The report made to Bishop Nevill of Salisbury
asserted that the protesters were lollards, although its wording was a very
close paraphrase of the description of illegal assemblies in the *Memoriale
presbiterorum*, a fourteenth-century confessor's manual.[71] It seems clear
that the canons interpreted this latest incident in a long-running dispute
as part of a long history of parochial disobedience and proscribed communal activity, but also in terms of the newer concept of the heretical
meeting or conventicle. When Nevill investigated the case, he swiftly
dropped the charge of lollardy and the disruptive parishioners were
punished only for conspiring to withdraw the revenues of the church.
There are two possible explanations for the initial description of the protesters as lollards: either the canons were trying to attract the attention of
the bishop, who would be obliged to investigate a report of heresy, or they
were responding to the national propaganda campaign that associated all
illegal assemblies with potential heresy. Both possibilities suggest that
well-established notions of moral danger and limitations on collective
action were being applied to the detection of heresy.

There was a danger, of course, in encouraging reports of heresy on the
merest hint of suspicious activity, but the reports that we have examined
so far all contained a range of information, on doctrine, unlicensed
preaching, illicit gatherings, the location of and contacts with known
heretics; and the tests and safeguards of canonical process barred the
unfounded or malicious report. No single detail was sufficient in itself for
a prosecution to proceed. In a strictly linguistic sense, reports of heresy
were narratives that presented observed reality within the conceptual
framework provided mainly by the propaganda of judicial *acta* and

---

[70] *The Edington Cartulary*, ed. J. H. Stevenson, Wiltshire Record Society, 42 (Devizes,
1987), 12, 17–19, 165–7.

[71] Reg. Nevill (Salisbury), part 2, fo. 32^r: the suspects were cited 'de et super certis ac
variis opinionibus Lollardicis et contra vniuersalis ecclesie determinacionem erroneis
quas tenent et predicant aliosque ad hoc faciendum sub penis grauibus nequiter
inducebant . . . confessi sunt quod ipsi, vna cum aliis parochianis quampluribus de
Edyngton . . . fuerunt adiunctem congregati iuxta crucem in villula de Tened . . . ibique
tractarunt ac confederarunt adiunctem statuentes et ordinantes quod ipsi ac alii parochiani
ibidem deuociones suas solitas et consuetas . . . subtraherent'; W. A. Pantin, *The English
Church in the Fourteenth Century* (Cambridge, 1955), 210.

sermons. This is especially evident when we consider references in reports and charges of heresy to the analogous crimes discussed in the last chapter. Allusions to sexual sin, defamation, sorcery, and treason are relatively common in reports, and given the polemical climate in which heresy was discussed in late medieval England, we would do well to interpret these as serious attempts on the part of heresy reporters to understand and represent the crime they were helping to detect, and not as salacious and superfluous additions to information on wrong doctrine.[72] Grado Merlo's distinction between the legalistic and polemical sections of heresy trial records is therefore too simplistic. The legal is frequently polemical and the polemical frequently necessary for legal purposes.

The connection between heresy and sexual offences frequently manifested itself in reports which attributed crude, libertine, or blasphemous views to persons suspected of heresy. In 1424, when John Russell OFM was reported to Chichele for heretical preaching, it was because he had publicly asserted that 'a religious was allowed to lie with a woman and not commit mortal sin'.[73] Reports in which sexual allegations feature prominently may have been made because a witness to a sermon or a conversation was shocked by and remembered what he or she had heard. In 1430 William Colyn was charged with having said that he would rather see a woman's vagina than the sacrament of the altar, but at his trial he corrected the judge, asserting that he had said he would rather *touch* a woman's vagina than the Eucharist.[74] How should this charge be understood in relation to his reported heresy? Colyn's words were a rejection of the Eucharist on two levels: the crude blasphemy of his preference, and the implication that he did not care whether he was unready to receive communion because of sexual contact.[75] Given the ubiquity of sexual warnings in sermons and homilies, it is not unreasonable to suggest

[72] Merlo, *Eretici e inquisitori*, 12.

[73] *Reg. Chichele (Canterbury)*, iii. 91: 'Religiosus potest concumbere cum muliere et non mortaliter peccare.'

[74] *Norwich Heresy Trials*, 91: 'Item quod tu asseruisti te malle videre secretum membrum mulieris quam sacramentum altaris. Ad istum articulum idem Willelmus dixit et fatebatur iudicialiter quod ipse dixit se velle libencius tangere secretum membrum mulieris quam sacramentum altaris.'

[75] On the prohibition of sex before communion see M. Rubin, *Corpus Christi: The Eucharist in Late Medieval Culture* (Cambridge, 1991), 149; P. J. Payer, *The Bridling of Desire: Views of Sex in the Later Middle Ages* (Toronto, 1993), 98–102.

that the clerics or lay people who reported him were aware of the link of concupiscence between sex and heresy. Edmund Archer and John Pert both admitted they had eaten meat on fast days 'as ofte as Y had luste to ete alle suche days and tymes'.[76] In what may be a trace of the original report against them, these words present lust, or concupiscence, as fundamental to the crime of heresy.

People suspected of heresy could also be suspected of sexual sins themselves. William Ramsbury for example, was said to have acted upon his belief that it was licit for priests to have sex 'with any woman, even nuns, virgins, and wives, to increase mankind'.[77] In one quite striking case dealt with by Alnwick, lechery was a key constituent in a report. Chichele had conducted a visitation of Redlingfield priory in Suffolk in January 1425 when the see of Norwich was vacant, and two years later Alnwick was left to follow up infractions of the injunctions that the archbishop had issued. His inquisition heard that Isabella Hermit, the prioress, had been sleeping in a private room, had assaulted one of the nuns, had been 'in societate' with her bailiff Thomas Langelond, once in private and once 'sub heggerowes et sub boscis' (she claimed to have been gathering herbs), had entered false accounts, alienated goods belonging to the priory, encouraged a nun to commit fornication, made erasures in the priory's court rolls, and committed 'crimen lollardie'. This consisted of telling the nuns that it was less of an evil to commit the vice of incontinence than to disobey her orders, and giving them permission to receive men so that they would not murmur against her own sins.[78] Many are the polemical texts that accuse Wycliffites of lechery, but this example shows that some people, in this case nuns, really did understand lollardy to mean the encouragement of sexual sin.

The link between heresy and defamation was also reflected in reports. John Belgrave was a thorn in the side of church and crown officers in Leicester for almost twenty years. In 1396 he was the subject of a writ sought in Chancery by the archdeacon of Leicester for his arrest on a charge of slander. That the archdeacon was not acting within his own

[76] *Norwich Heresy Trials*, 165, 170.   [77] *Reg. Waltham (Salisbury)*, 169.
[78] Reg. Alnwick (Norwich), fo. 104ᵛ: 'Priorissa commisit crimen lollardie informando moniales sibi subditis quod minus malum est eisdem vicium incontinencie committere quam ad sui preceptum ipsam non sequi, ac eciam ipsa Priorissa dedit licenciam generalem monialibus suis vt acciperent viros vel maritos et sic contra ipsam Priorissam non amplius murmurarent.'

jurisdiction suggests that he had tried that route already and secular aid was needed because ecclesiastical censures had not had any effect. Belgrave was said to have posted a notice in St Martin's parish church in Leicester on the eve of a session of the diocesan consistory court to be held there. The notice claimed that ecclesiastical judges made incorrect judgements and oppressed the innocent, comparing them to the corrupt elders who had judged Susannah, an apocryphal figure from a continuation of the Book of Daniel who had been wrongly accused by judges whose sexual advances she had refused.[79] At this stage there was no mention of suspicion of heresy against Belgrave, but in 1413 a similarly slanderous attitude to the church on his part did lead to a report of heresy. Belgrave was said to 'disparage and slander all religious estates in the church militant, namely the dignity of priests and bishops'.[80] Despite swearing never to preach any heresies again, Belgrave was reported only the following year for being 'a lollard and a great speaker against the pope and his power, and against all prelates of the church'.[81]

Another repeat offender was William Swinderby, whose preaching in 1382 was said to be 'heretical, blasphemous, and schismatic'. In 1391 when he was cited by the bishop of Hereford, 'defamatory' was added to this list.[82] This seems to have been meant simply in the sense that his preaching defamed the church. More oblique links between heresy and defamation can also be found in judicial records. For instance, in 1510, Thomas Morpath and Thomas Moberly were brought together by their neighbours to settle a dispute that had arisen between them. However, reconciliation was forgotten when Morpath said to Moberly, 'Thomas Moberly thou art a heretic and I will not be agreed with thee.' Moberly brought a suit of defamation against Morpath and won.[83] Just as defamation was a constituent of heresy, so a false accusation of heresy opened the accuser to a charge of defamation. Because the two crimes were so closely linked, it is possible that suspicion of one was sometimes translated into suspicion of the other. In 1436 John and Robert Boydon of Strode in Kent were arrested for heresy and their homes searched for heretical

---

[79] *Select Cases in Chancery 1364–1471*, ed. W. P. Baildon, Selden Society, 10 (1896), 106.

[80] Lincolnshire Archives, MS Vj/0, fo. 10ʳ: 'detrahit et deprauat omnem statum in ecclesia militante religiones, videlicet sacerdocium et dignitatem episcopalem.'

[81] PRO, KB 9/204/1, m. 141: 'est lollardus et excellens loqutor [*sic*] versus papam ac potestatem eius et prelatos tocius ecclesie.'

[82] Reg. Buckingham (Lincoln), fo. 243ᵛ; *Reg. Trefnant (Hereford)* 232: 'heretica, blasphemia, scismatica, ac diffamatoria'.   [83] *Select Cases on Defamation*, 12–14.

literature. One year later a relation of theirs, Agnes Boydon of Strode, was called to appear before the Rochester consistory for defaming one Robert Stodefold and his wife. It is possible that a recent conviction for heresy exposed a whole family to suspicion regarding other sins of speech.[84] In another case from Kent, the obverse relationship is suggested. In 1422 Thomas Halle was subject to a charge of defamation because he had objected to John Denys's purgation on charges of murder and forgery. Halle claimed that the forgery charge was true, but failed to prove this assertion, leaving himself open to the counter-charge from Denys. Then in 1425 Halle was tried for heresy by the bishop of Rochester.[85] The connection between these cases is either that someone with a loose tongue was likely to commit both defamation and heresy, or that once reported for defamation, a report of heresy was more credible. Either way, there seems to have been a link in the public mind between the two crimes.

The case of John Raynald, an Irish Dominican prosecuted by justices of gaol delivery at York in 1448 for scandalizing the Franciscan order, is notable for its claim that he had preached heresies and 'lollardies'. In addition to the charge of defamation or slander, his indictment for heresy and lollardy seems to have been compounded by his mendicancy, an allegation that he had falsified his letters of ordination, and the implication that he had sold false indulgences. Cases such as this suggest that suspicion of heresy attracted supplementary accusations very easily. A whole range of social menaces might then be embodied in a single offender, whatever the contradictions involved in a Wycliffite friar selling indulgences.[86]

In the wake of the Oldcastle revolt the link between heresy and treason, so fundamental to secular involvement in the detection of heresy, became for a time even stronger. The commissions issued in the days following the suppression of the rising suggest that the two crimes are in fact one, calling for the arrest of 'many of our subjects commonly known as lollards, and others, who have treacherously, against their allegiance, imagined our death and planned the destruction of many other things

---

[84] Reg. Brouns (Rochester), fo. 5ᵛ; Centre for Kentish Studies, MS DRb/Pa1, fo. 31ʳ.

[85] Canterbury Cathedral Library, Act Book Y. 1. 3, fos. 209ᵛ, 218ʳ; Reg. Langdon (Rochester), fo. 69ᵛ.

[86] R. L. Storey, 'Malicious Indictments of Clergy in the Fifteenth Century', in M. J. Franklin and C. Harper-Bill (eds.), *Medieval Ecclesiastical Studies in Honour of Dorothy M. Owen* (Woodbridge, 1995), 221–2.

both in the faith and the estate of temporal and spiritual lords of our realm of England'.[87] The returns to the commissions made in February 1414 almost always refer to lollardy and treason in the same breath, but there are compelling grounds for arguing that this was more than an analogous link based on the alleged coincidence that some lollards were behaving treacherously. For a time, in the royal courts at least, lollardy came to be understood as meaning treason rather than heresy: heresy was in effect subsumed within the crime of treason. This is best exemplified in presentments such as that of John Asser of Daventry, whose indictment as a lollard is explained by the allegation that he rose against the king in insurrection, rather than the more common formula giving heretical opinions as the explanation for a charge of lollardy.[88] In 1414 treason made one a lollard.

Connections made between heresy and other crimes were clearly a useful means of encouraging reports, but there is nevertheless a question over the motivation behind reports which seem to link heresy with another crime rather too readily. The charge of lollardy made by the canons of Edington is a case in point. If we believe the canons were using the heresy charge tactically, as a way of ending a long-running dispute, we must also accept that the bishop declined to be party to such heavy-handedness, reserving heresy charges for heresy cases. Similarly in Swinderby's trial before Trefnant, one witness used his testimony of seeing the suspect celebrate mass to comment on the parlous state of the chapel where this took place, which was being used for keeping pigs.[89] Again the subversion of a heresy investigation for other ends was a private decision and not official policy.

The case which best exemplifies the private use of the new laws against heresy is a complicated tangle of crime and local politics in

---

[87] PRO, C 66/393, m. 30d (*CPR 1413–16*, 175): 'quamplures subditi nostri lollardi vulgariter nuncupati ac alii mortem nostram contra ligeancie sue debitum, proditorie imaginauerunt ac quam plura alia tam in fidei catholice quam status dominorum et magnatum regni nostri Anglie tam spiritualem quam temporalem destruccionem proposuerunt.'

[88] PRO, KB 9/204/1, m. 105: 'Johannes Asser est lollardus et die memorie proximum ante festum Epiphanie domini anno supradicto apud Dauentre fuit consenciens et existens ad insurrexcionem versus dominum Regem.'

[89] *Reg. Trefnant (Hereford)*, 256: 'Rogerus Newton . . . dixit quod pluries interfuit in capella de Newton, et audivit missas dicti Willelmi Swynderby . . . scit quod antequam idem Willelmus veniret ad celebrandum in eadem et post recessum eiusdem porci solebant pernoctare et in estu dierum jacere in eadem.'

Huntingdonshire, involving charges of heresy, sorcery, defamation, and theft. In chronological order, this is what seems to have happened. Sometime before 25 June 1417, when the case came before Ralph Louth acting as Repingdon's commissary, John Smith of Alconbury broke into the parish church in neighbouring Buckworth and despoiled the contents. He tried to pin the blame for this on Roger Boucher, a parishioner of Buckworth, who was arrested and imprisoned. However, this deception was challenged by Boucher, who began a defamation suit against Smith. Boucher claimed that Smith had imputed the theft and despoliation to him by the practice of nefarious arts, upon which Smith admitted that he had indeed conspired to create the impression of Boucher's involvement and acknowledged that he was himself the guilty party. Louth's investigation noted that Smith had used necromancy, sorcery, and magic, invoking evil spirits using bread. Thus it would seem that Smith was a professional diviner who took advantage of his reputation for finding stolen objects to commit theft himself and direct the blame elsewhere.[90] It was not unknown for people wrongly accused by divination to seek revenge against the diviner, but Boucher's response was particularly effective: he reported it to a general inquisition being conducted by Ralph Louth under the terms of Chichele's 1416 statute on heresy.[91] Sorcery was not strictly speaking heresy, despite their similarities, and inquisitors had been barred from investigating it since the thirteenth century.[92] This had not prevented English bishops from trying heresy alongside sorcery, since they usually acted within their ordinary jurisdiction, which did of course allow them to try sorcerers.[93] In this instance, however, sorcery is said actually to be heresy whereas in normal circumstances it is unlikely that mundane cases of divination would concern episcopal officials investigating heresy. Boucher cleverly raised the stakes by saying that Smith had preached that Saints Peter and Paul

---

[90] *Reg. Repingdon (Lincoln)*, iii. 195: 'artem nigromancie ac sortilegium et coniuraciones illicitas et prohibitas invocacionem spirituum malignorum cum panibus . . . excercuisset.' On divination and theft see S. Clark, *Thinking with Demons: The Idea of Witchcraft in Early Modern Europe* (Oxford, 1997), 463–4.

[91] For revenge against diviners see *Calendar of Plea and Memoranda Rolls for the City of London 1364–1381*, ed. A. H. Thomas (Cambridge, 1929), 188, and A. H. Thompson, *The English Clergy and their Organisation in the Later Middle Ages* (Oxford, 1947), 221.

[92] VI 5.2.8.

[93] See for example Reg. Alnwick (Lincoln), fo. 75; *Reg. Stafford (Bath & Wells)*, ii. 225–7.

had themselves been sorcerers.[94] In the same way that the withdrawal of tithes was not in itself heresy, but became so when one preached that others should do so, public advocacy of divination coupled with blasphemy against the saints pushed it into the realm of heresy. Knowing that heresy investigators were approaching, Boucher took the opportunity to exploit the canonical requirement that all reports containing the merest hint of heresy must be carefully examined.

2. RECEIVING REPORTS

The fact that malicious reports of heresy were an occasional eventuality but not provincial policy underlines the point that reporters of heresy did not identify heretics (however certain the language of presentments to royal justices); they identified suspicion of heresy. The identification of heretics was done by ecclesiastical judges. In order that those judges had before them serviceable information which met the standards imposed by the canonical rules on inquisitorial procedure, reports had to be managed. The criteria for suspicion of heresy were communicated through the propaganda described in Chapters 5 and 6 and applied to actual cases in the examples dealt with so far in this chapter. When a suspect came to court, that suspicion, however strong, was insufficient to condemn him or her without further evidence. This evidence was sought in answers given in interrogation, the statements of witnesses, and the discovery of proscribed texts; but the true test of orthodoxy was the suspect's willingness to submit to episcopal correction and discipline.[95]

The bridge between report and courtroom must be explained in terms of the different concepts of knowledge that pertained to each stage of the process. In order to do this, a rather confusing problem needs to be explained. Evidence gathered after a report had been made, or after a series of corroboratory reports, was used by judges to prove what they often called 'vehement suspicion'. This suspicion was qualitatively

---

[94] *Reg. Repingdon (Lincoln)*, iii. 195: 'palam et publice asseruit et predicavit quod licitum est uti coniuraciones et sortilegium nam hoc fecerunt sanctus Petrus et sanctus Paulus.'

[95] Hostiensis, *Summa aurea*, 1532: 'Ergo sola praesumptione, vel suspicione quamuis vehementi non tamen probabili de tanto crimine non condemnatur quis, ex quo negat, et paratus est ecclesie obedire.'

different from that which stimulated reports of heresy, being something established by legal process rather than asserted by untrained lay helpers. In Roman and canon law this distinction was sometimes described as being that between 'formal' and 'informal' fame. Fame was a person's standing either in law (formal) or in fact (informal), and could be good or bad. Someone whose fame was bad was said to be infamous, and this could similarly come about by legal proclamation or social reputation.[96] Fame and suspicion are often used synonymously. Informal fame, or infamy of fact, was widespread belief in a person's guilt, and could lead to a judicial investigation if the suspicion resulted from frequent reports or utterances and was not based on just one occurrence.[97] This is the theory underlying instructions such as that from Robert Nevill to his commissary Robert Beaumont, asking him to investigate William Wakeham who, 'as we have learnt from *fama*, held, preached and told the people in the town of Marlborough in our diocese and neighbouring areas heresies, opinions and articles contrary to the faith'.[98]

Once fame had been reported to a judge and confirmed by inquisition, it acquired a formal status and became a legal fact, capable of being adduced in a trial as firm evidence, although on its own it did not constitute grounds for a condemnation.[99] Formal fame could also be pronounced if a heresy suspect remained contumacious for one year, since it was 'probable because of infamy' that he or she was guilty.[100] However, if the informal fame of a report was not upheld by inquisition, the suspect would be allowed to proceed to purgation.[101] Opinion or rumour was not sufficient to secure a condemnation, but it was necessary in order to instigate an inquisition. Coming to the subject admittedly with interests other than legal and social history in mind, scholars such as Anne Hudson and Paul Strohm have arguably underestimated the evidential value

---

[96] F. Migliorino, *Fama e infamia: Problemi della società medievale nel pensiero giuridico nei secoli XII e XIII* (Catania, 1985), 73–83; *Select Cases on Defamation*, pp. xxxiv–xxxv; *DDC*, v. 1358–9; A. H. J. Greenidge, *Infamia: Its Place in Roman Public and Private Law* (Oxford, 1894), 38–9.

[97] Durandus, *Speculum iuris* (Basel, 1574), book 3, De notoriis criminibus, § 4: 'fama est communis uiciniae acclamatio'; Tancred, *Ordo iudiciarius*, 153.

[98] Reg. Nevill (Salisbury), part 2, fo. 52ʳ: 'prout ex fama didicimus in villa de Marleburgh dicte nostre diocesis et locis conuicinis, hereses opiniones et articulos fidei antedicte contrarias tenuit, predicauit et populum . . . informauit.'

[99] *Reg. Chichele (Canterbury)*, iii. 168.

[100] *Glos. ord.* to X 5.7.13, v. *condemnentur*: 'probabilus fuerit propter infamiam.'

[101] X 5.7.13.

of *fama*. For Strohm the basis of justice was corrupted by evidence which was 'a quantity of hearsay and supposition about presumed or rumoured activities' and Hudson describes the contents of court-books as 'unsystematic and for any legal purpose unsatisfactory: hearsay is reported, personal opinions and experiences retailed, unsubstantiated and possibly spiteful suspicions of heterodoxy passed on.'[102] The kind of information they mean by these comments was in fact vital to legal process and admissible in court. That does not mean that it could form the basis for a verdict without corroboration. Lay participation, as I have argued, was not an abuse in canon law, even if it was little discussed.

Nonetheless the distinction between informal or organic fame, and formal, judicially tested fame, was not always easy to maintain.[103] For example, the legal pronunciation of an individual's formal ill fame would have an effect on his or her informal fame among the wider public, and conversely, when a suspect was successfully purged of suspicion, the judge would formally restore his or her good fame. When he did this, the judge expected that it would have a real effect on the suspect's public standing. These assumptions present a theoretical problem in that the two categories of fame could not be kept separate and yet be expected to influence one another. Because of this difficulty Thomas Halle, whose propensity to criminous speech has been noted above, found it impossible to shake off the 'notoriety of infamy' after purging himself of heresy in September 1425. On the basis that formal infamy of heresy had been cancelled by his purgation, subsequent persistent infamy of fact was regarded as evidence of *new* suspicions. Halle was rearrested and made to abjure, but he still had in his possession the letters testimonial certifying his original purgation. He was once again formally restored to 'pristine bone fame'.[104]

Testing fame or suspicion by further investigation and interrogation was thus the prime method by which the episcopate managed the reports of the laity and lower clergy. In a number of extant trial records we can observe the process of confirming rumour by securing either the testimony of two eyewitnesses or a confession from the suspect. In 1393 Bishop Buckingham of Lincoln heard the case of Agnes, a nun from Northampton. She had been reported 'by the repeated noise of the

---

[102] Strohm, *England's Empty Throne*, 73; Hudson, *Premature Reformation*, 36.
[103] Migliorino, *Fama e infamia*, 73.   [104] Reg. Langdon (Rochester), fo. 69ᵛ.

clamour against her', and this popular suspicion was then 'sufficiently clearly proved before us'.[105] More detail of what might constitute proof is given in the trial of William Taylor, who was found guilty by Chichele on the basis of 'things done, things not done, things deduced and things proved before us in this matter, and also things confessed, recognised and written by you, as well as things exhibited before us'.[106] Written proofs appear in the trial of Thomas Hellis, although it is not exactly clear what they were. Bishop Langdon had asked him whether he wished to object to any of the witnesses against him, a safeguard designed to allow cross-examination, but Hellis declined, perhaps sensing the weakness of his position. The bishop then produced legal proofs, among them 'legitimate documentation that the said Thomas had held, taught and affirmed heresy and error'.[107] When witnesses were called by a judge, the shift in the standard of evidence and proof becomes very clear. As in the 1382 trial of William Swinderby, the widely held suspicion that brought someone to court was insufficient to reach a verdict. Bishop Buckingham had called for anyone who objected to Swinderby's purgation to come forward and testify whether he had broken his oath not to preach without a licence. Far from being asked to report general and unsubstantiated suspicions, people were now being asked to attest to specific facts. This is a crucial difference.[108]

Suspects were in a fairly strong position in properly conducted heresy trials, as the requirement to test fame against evidence bound both judge and defendant to the outcome of a rational procedure. Indeed testing fame could be expressed as an obligation on the suspect, as implied by the citation of John Burrell in 1430 to respond personally to the suspicion against him.[109] As in the case of Thomas Hellis, suspects had the opportunity to draw the bishop's attention to potential bias or malice on the part of the prosecution witnesses. William Smith of Corby in Northamptonshire, for example, was asked to confirm that the bishop's

---

[105] Reg. Buckingham (Lincoln), fo. 406ᵛ: 'Ex frequenti insinuacione clamosa pulsante'; 'satis clare coram nobis probatur.'

[106] *Reg. Chichele (Canterbury)*, iii. 171: 'acta, inactitata, deducta et probata coram nobis in negocio antedicto ac per te confessata, scripta et recognita, exhibita eciam coram nobis in eodem.'

[107] Reg. Langdon (Rochester), fo. 75Xʳ: 'legitima documenta coram eo ministrata dictam Thomam heresym et errores tenuisse, docuisse et affirmasse.'

[108] Reg. Buckingham (Lincoln), fo. 243ʳ.

[109] *Norwich Heresy Trials*, 77: 'ad iudicium evocatus personaliter responsurus'.

'trustworthy witnesses' were acceptable to him.[110] This was not any mere show of due process, but a legal requirement to which judges genuinely adhered. When in 1421 Henry Taylor was charged with holding an erroneous opinion and repeatedly asserting it to his neighbours, he was able to deny the charge, saying that the report was malicious and he had fallen foul of his enemies. No one was to be convicted solely on the basis of evidence given by their friends, family, enemies, creditors, or debtors.[111]

The people called as witnesses to this later stage of the trial process had the same social and legal profile as reporters of heresy, ranging from the *fidedignus* to the condemned heretic. There was also a quantitative aspect to testing fame by witnesses, with Durandus asserting that the agreement of the 'greater part' of the people about the articles in question was required.[112] In practice 'the people' under consideration were just the eyewitnesses called, for which the minimum was two, or a panel of visitation *fidedigni* numbering six or eight. For example, when the bishop of Exeter wished to investigate reports of unlicensed preaching in Lanner and St Neots, he ordered the official of the peculiar jurisdiction of Cornwall to inquire 'through trustworthy men . . . as to the reports and into the names and surnames of those preaching and those admitting and authorizing them'.[113] These men could be drawn from whatever area the bishop thought necessary, and need not all come from precisely the parish where a suspected heretic had preached. In 1437 Robert Nevill investigated William Wakeham 'through trustworthy men of his village and neighbouring places'. The aim of distinguishing between these two areas was to strike a balance between reliable local knowledge and disinterested testimony.[114]

Despite reliance on the canonical standards of evidence, the polemical and stereotypical could not be totally erased from legal proceedings, and various constituents of the vague suspicion found in reports of heresy made their way into trials for heresy. Especially persistent was the idea

---

[110] *Reg. Repingdon (Lincoln)*, iii. 197.

[111] Reg. Morgan (Worcester), p. 87: 'hoc devenit ex suorum relatibus emulorum.' See X 5.1.7, X 5.1.21.   [112] Durandus, *Speculum iuris*, lib. 3, 46.

[113] Reg. Stafford (Exeter), ii. fo. 246: 'per viros fidedignos . . . super premissis ac de nominibus et cognominibus sic predicancium eosque admittencium et auctorizancium.'

[114] Reg. Nevill (Salisbury), part 2, fo. 52ʳ: 'per viros fidedignos eiusdem ville et locorum vicinorum.'

that guilt and innocence could be revealed by visible signs, in either the person or the environment. For example, in order to persuade a judge to allow purgation a suspect had to convince him that he or she was contrite, which was partly achieved by a formal abjuration, but also involved an assessment of appearance. There was wide agreement among canonists that contrition was to some extent perceptible, and they instructed judges to assess the signs of penance.[115] For example, when John Jordan, John Colchester, and John Ruell of Bristol were questioned by Bubwith in 1417, they are said to have replied 'in a catholic manner as it appeared'.[116] Negative manifestations of character were conversely taken as confirmation of heresy, as in the case of Edmund Frith who tore down Oldcastle's citation from the doors of Rochester cathedral 'with temerity and in anger', and William Sawtry who mocked Arundel's authority 'as if scornful or laughing'.[117] William Taylor was similarly described in terms of his 'arrogant appearance', which, although not a legal proof, was taken to be a manifestation of his sinfulness.[118] Reactions of the natural environment, or divine providence, also made their way into trial records. In a story that caught the imagination of the chronicler Walsingham and the theologian Netter, the notary recording John Badby's trial in 1410 describes the miraculous appearance of an allegorical serpent in the form of a very real spider on Badby's lips, just as he was giving heretical responses to questioning on the Eucharist.[119] Such manifestations of heresy in trials attested to its self-evident depravity.

By no means all trials went so smoothly. Suspects such as William Browne in 1419 and William White in 1422, who freely admitted they were vehemently suspected before 'good and serious persons', were easy to

---

[115] VI 5.2.4: 'taliter deprehensis, etiamsi sine ulla penitus audientia relinquendi sint iudicio saeculari, si tamen postmodum poeniteant, et poenitentiae signa in eis apparuerint manifesta, nequaquam sunt humiliter petita sacramenta poenitentiae ac eucharistiae deneganda'; Hostiensis, *Summa aurea*, 1531: 'Si confitetur vocatus timore probationis et iudex videat ipsum contritum, et speret de conuersione sua, potest ei parcere.' See also Innocent IV, *Apparatus super quinque libros decretalium*, De sententia excommunicacionis, c. *a nobis*; Paul, *Summa summarum*, V. X. q. 27 (Bodleian, MS Bodley 293, fo. 178ᵛ).

[116] *Reg. Bubwith (Bath & Wells)*, i. 288: 'sicut apparuit, responderunt se catholice.'

[117] *Reg. Chichele (Canterbury)*, iv. 139: 'temere abstraxerat et in frusta cominuerat'; Reg. Arundel (Canterbury), ii. fo. 183ʳ: 'quasi ridendo siue deridendo'.

[118] Reg. Arundel (Canterbury), ii. fo. 118ᵛ: Taylor appeared 'fronte indomita'.

[119] The original account is in Reg. Arundel (Canterbury), ii. fo. 18ʳ. Strohm, *England's Empty Throne*, 151n., recounts the episode from Thomas Walsingham, *Historia Anglicana*, ed. H. T. Riley, 2 vols., Rolls Series, 28 (London, 1863–4), ii. 282; and Hudson, *Premature Reformation*, 151n., from Netter, *Doctrinale*, ii. 387.

deal with.[120] Frequently, however, fame or suspicion was difficult to verify, and in some cases the defendant simply refused to accept the grounds of the prosecution. These difficult cases reveal the division between formal and informal *fama*, in law and in society, and show how the detection of heresy was determined by categories of knowledge with which we are no longer familiar. If, as happened during the investigation into Henry Good of Earsham in Norfolk, neighbours had been asked to confirm the suspicion against a suspect but were unable or unwilling to do so, a judge had no choice but to abandon the case.[121] Even when a bishop was so convinced of a suspect's guilt that possible objectors to his purgation were sought far and wide, as in the case of Thomas Novery, and yet none came forward, the rules governing the proof of suspicion had to be upheld.[122]

Just as judges were bound by the higher standards of evidence required once a case moved from reported suspicion to tried and tested suspicion, so defendants had to accept the change in their legal position once suspicions had been confirmed. However, some were so brazen or so confident of outwitting their judges that they simply refused to admit the suspicion or fame against them, even after it had become a matter of legal fact. The defences mounted by two prominent Wycliffites, Robert Hooke and Ralph Mungyn, are particularly interesting in this regard. The contest over reputation, formal and informal fame, and suspicion of heresy is revealed in their answers to the questions put to them. On 6 June 1425 Hooke appeared before Chichele in Convocation, where it was put to him that in 1405 he had been cited to respond to allegations of heresy by Bishop Repingdon, that he had abjured, and that he had then neglected to carry out the penance enjoined upon him. This was all a matter of record and so Hooke sensibly admitted everything. Chichele went on to allege that for a long time before his 1405 appearance Hooke had been publicly defamed and vehemently suspected of heresy and lollardy, and publicly held to be a sower of heresy and error. The defendant was a little more wary this time, admitting the article but denying the early existence of vehement suspicion against him. Questioned again on his previous trial, Hooke admitted it had taken place but continued to deny the suspicion. Chichele then brought the interrogation more up to date, asking him about his 1419 appearance at Lambeth, where he was said to have

---

120 *Reg. Chichele (Canterbury)*, iii. 56, 84–5.   121 *Norwich Heresy Trials*, 210–14.
122 *Reg. Repingdon (Lincoln)*, iii. 170–1.

confessed the existence of suspicion against him. Confidently, Hooke admitted making the confession, but denied the existence of the suspicion to which he had confessed, in effect saying that he had made a false confession on that occasion. He then denied that he had received proscribed books despite admitting to writing books that contravened the 1409 constitutions, and then he even denied any knowledge of those constitutions. As he began to realize the evidence against him was too strong, this line of defence collapsed and he admitted the vehement suspicion, before 1405, before 1419, and in the present.[123]

Some of his defence was reasonably well thought out. The claim to ignorance of Arundel's constitutions for instance, had it not been contradicted by the admission of writing books in contravention of them, might well have been accepted, since assertions of educational deficiency were fairly common among suspects who wished to avoid answering incriminating questions.[124] John of Bath, tried by Bishop Chaundler of Salisbury in 1418, for example, had declined to respond to one article against him, saying that he believed what the church told him to.[125] In 1428 Katerina Dertford made a similar defence, saying that she would not respond because she had only been taught the creed and the ten commandments, and if we are to believe his account, William Thorpe deliberately prevaricated when asked to state his position on transubstantiation and asked Arundel for instruction.[126] In his denials of suspicion however, Hooke was on much shakier ground. While it might have been possible at his original 1405 trial to deny that he was suspected, the fact that he then abjured heresy implies an acknowledgement of suspicion on his part. Without suspicion he would have gone on to purgation not abjuration. His ill fame prior to 1405 was then not a matter to be contested, but a matter of legal fact. This in turn meant that the suspicion prior to his 1419 trial would have been enough to make him a relapsed heretic,

[123] *Reg. Chichele (Canterbury)*, iii. 105–7.

[124] On the point that no one may knowingly bury a heretic, Johannes Andreae had surmised, in *Glos. ord.* to VI 5.2.2, that ignorance would be a defence. See also C. 24 q. 1 c. 34 and *Summa summarum*, V. X. q. 2 (Bodleian, MS Bodley 293, fo. 178ʳ).

[125] Reg. Chaundler (Salisbury), ii. fo. 18ʳ: 'Ad istum articulum nescit dictus Johannes respondere. Credit tamen, ut dicit, secundum discripcionem sancte et vniuersalis ecclesie.'

[126] *Reg. Chichele (Canterbury)*, iii. 188: 'dixit se nescire respondere ad talia, pro eo quod non erat instructa ut asseruit nisi solomodo in cimbolo et decalogo'; *Two Wycliffite Texts*, 53–5.

since it merely confirmed previously admitted suspicion.[127] If the 1405 suspicion had never been admitted, it would have remained a report of informal ill-fame and the onus would have been on Chichele in 1419 and 1425 to prove the subsequent reports of suspicion.[128] Hooke failed to appreciate the difference between informal and formal fame. One could deny informal fame, but not formal fame.

A similar mistake was made by Ralph Mungyn, who appeared before Chichele in November and December 1428, determined to pursue a very odd and risky line of defence. The prosecution rested on Mungyn's association with a condemned heretic, Peter Payne, which, if acknowledged in even the slightest degree, was enough to convict him. However, Mungyn denied he had anything to abjure. He said that he did know Payne, and knew him to be an infamous Wycliffite. He admitted having been taught by him and to owning some of Wyclif's works himself, but he then claimed that he did not believe the contents of those books, nor what Payne had taught him, which he said was mere sophistry. Although disingenuous in the extreme, he had to say these things in order to deny the article he knew was coming: did he recognize that he had been infamous and suspected of heresy for the last twenty years? Mungyn replied that he did not know he was defamed, for he believed himself to be, and have been, a man of good fame.[129] What he did not realize, or perhaps would not admit to himself, was that his own assertions of good fame were meaningless unless corroborated by the sworn testimony of *fidedigni* or *boni et graves*, and even then his association with Payne was quite enough justification for Chichele to continue the case. Like Hooke, Mungyn had not fully grasped the differences between the fluid arena of public opinion where reputations were malleable, and the rigid structures of canon law, within which recorded fame became legal fact.

This chapter has illustrated the character and the limits of reports of heresy, which were necessary to the judicial process whilst presenting

---

[127] The category of relapsed heretic, although known from the decretals, was clarified for Convocation in 1423 by Lyndwood; *Reg. Chichele (Canterbury)*, iii. 168–9, and Jacob, *Chichele*, 70–1.

[128] VI 5.2.8; *Summa summarum*, V. X. q. 62 (Bodleian, MS Bodley 293, fo. 179ʳ).

[129] *Reg. Chichele (Canterbury)*, iii. 199: 'Item quod occasione premissorum et aliis ex causis per xx annos proxime jam elapsos et continue citra idem dominus Radulphus fuit et adhuc est de et super secta, ritu et opinionibus eorum quos in regno Anglie lollardos nuncupamus suspectus et publice infamatus et pro tali comuniter dictus, tentus, habitus et reputatus. Super quo articulo interrogatus dixit quod non novit se in aliquo casuum hujusmodi diffamatum, set credidit se fuisse et esse virum bone fame.'

challenges to bishops and inquisitors. The detection of heresy was not a free-for-all of unsubstantiated gossip and rumour, but a carefully managed process in which reports were encouraged from certain groups among the laity and from the clergy. The challenge for the ecclesiastical courts was to avoid being exploited by persons pursuing private vendettas, giving credence to malicious charges, or perpetuating mistaken identifications of heresy. Instead they were to uphold the canonical definition of heresy as a choice presented to the defendant between return to the church or disobedience. Because suspicion, reputation, fame, rumour, and notoriety are not admissible as evidence in most modern judicial systems, it is necessary to remind ourselves that these categories of social knowledge were admissible, if subjected to the appropriate tests. Our remaining task is to examine how that social knowledge was generated, and to do this the last chapter will consist of a detailed local case study in the detection of heresy.

8

The Social Contours of
Heresy Detection

The procedure most frequently used to gather reports of suspected heresy was inquisition, and in England, especially after 1413, this usually meant some form of episcopal visitation. That is to say, reports of heresy were not initially dealt with separately from all the other offences and defects subject to a bishop's ordinary jurisdiction. However, in most cases our knowledge is based on a later stage of the judicial process, once heresy suspects had been isolated in procedural terms so as the better to deal with the complex problem they presented. This chapter will focus on a visitation of Leicester archdeaconry carried out by Repingdon in 1413, whose proceedings and findings were recorded in a slim paper volume of thirty-two folios, now Lincolnshire Archives, MS Vj/0. This was arguably the pioneering use of ordinary visitation against heresy, something which soon became provincial policy, as noted in Chapter 2. A number of the reports of heresy in this visitation book have previously been extracted from the manuscript and studied for the information they provide on Wycliffite history.[1] This chapter will look at heresy within the context of all the crimes reported to the visitor, as it was this broad judicial framework which gave heresy reports their legal and social character.

1. POINTS OF CONTACT

Visitation was an administrative tool for gathering information about the state of religion in a diocese and for exercising canonical justice. It was

---

[1] J. Crompton, 'Leicestershire Lollards', *Transactions of the Leicestershire Archaeological and Historical Society*, 44 (1968–9), 11–44, includes transcriptions of some heresy cases; Jurkowski, 'Lawyers and Lollardy', 155–82.

also one of the means by which centre and periphery were linked together in diocesan government, verifying the qualifications and authorization of the clergy, involving people in justice, and reinforcing the values and norms of canon law. Matters dealt with at visitation included administrative questions concerning benefices and religious houses, as well as those raised by the parish clergy and their parishioners, not necessarily in concert, in response to questions distributed by the visitor. Indeed, the visitor, whether bishop, commissary, official, or archdeacon, could shape the agenda of a visitation by the questions put in the original citation. Sometimes he might be concerned simply with the general correction of abuses and the improvement of pastoral care, but sometimes he might have a particular reform agenda in mind.[2] Jean Gerson's ideal of the reforming bishop, who dealt with heresy alongside the other offences within his jurisdiction, seems to have found an especially strong English expression in Repingdon.[3]

The main logistical task of the visitor was to ensure the efficient organization of the itinerary and the presence of reported offenders in the right place at the right time, along with the requisite witnesses, proctors, and parochial representatives. In an initial two-week circuit, repeated over a further two weeks by Thomas Brouns and David Pryce, Repingdon visited 180 parishes at six deanery centres, and heard the cases of 575 individual and corporate offenders.[4] These offenders were between them responsible for 784 crimes, defects, and excesses, which may be categorized as follows: there were 306 charges of defective rights and titles to benefices, tithes, and so on (39 per cent), 138 of non-appearance at the hearings (17 per cent), 115 of sexual incontinence (15 per cent), 69 of lay persons deviating from proper observances (9 per cent), 56 pastoral failings on the part of the clergy (7 per cent), 53 instances of church dilapidations (6 per cent), 22 testamentary cases (3 per cent), 22 separate charges of heresy (3 per cent), 2 of sorcery, and 1 of infanticide.

---

[2] L. Binz, *Vie religieuse et réforme ecclésiastique dans le diocèse de Genève pendant le grand schisme et la crise conciliaire 1378–1450* (Geneva, 1973), 200–4; N. Coulet, *Les Visites pastorales* (Turnhout, 1977), 34–6; W. H. Frere, *Visitation Articles and Injunctions of the Period of the Reformation*, 3 vols. (London, 1910), i. 87–93.

[3] *Œuvres complètes*, ed. Glorieux, viii. 50; *DDC*, vii. 1522.

[4] The 1413 itinerary (Lincolnshire Archives, MS Vj/0, fo. 1ʳ) was the same as that made in 1416 (*Reg. Repingdon (Lincoln)*, iii. 156–9), even if a little more or less time was taken depending on the complexity of the business, suggesting that routes were fixed but timings were not.

The offenders or their legal representatives had to be cited in person or in public, during the course of which episcopal officers or locally co-opted clergy would have to travel not only to every parish to be visited, but also to many outlying hamlets and farms as well. Once cited, offenders and witnesses would have to be presented at the deanery centre, with someone being assigned to make sure they appeared. After each hearing the more recalcitrant might be required to make an additional appearance, either at a different centre further into Repingdon's itinerary, at the same centre during Brouns's and Pryce's circuit, or at one of the episcopal palaces of Sleaford in Lincolnshire, St Neots in Huntingdonshire, or Lincoln itself. Twenty-seven per cent of the offenders in 1413 had to make a second appearance, and we have evidence for these summonses being honoured and being ignored.[5] Follow-up hearings were recorded in spaces left under the initial entry in the visitation book, and when the complexity of a case had been poorly estimated by the scribe these additions extended into the margins.

Some offenders would acknowledge their fault and be dismissed; others would be fined, excommunicated, whipped, or given penance. In a number of cases the offender was committed to the care or observation of a local clergyman, or sometimes a group of parishioners, to ensure that he or she did not slide into recidivism.[6] In particularly serious cases the intervention of a higher authority might be required, as when Roger Ippon of Scraptoft was surrendered to the observation of the official of the court of Canterbury on account of his non-attendance at the hearing in Gartree deanery.[7] Journeys to distant Sleaford may be considered as punishment in themselves. All these sentences were labour-intensive, especially those that generated additional written documents, and all the efforts of the episcopal household, archidiaconal staff, parochial clergy, rural deans, and lay assistants would be required. Considering the progression from citation to final hearings, which often took over a year, we can see that visitation was much more than a momentary point of contact

---

[5] The proctor of the prior of Belvoir, John Castle, and the rector of Walton, Thomas Bond, both failed to honour their second summonses: MS Vj/0, fos. 2[r], 7[v]. The proctor of the prior and convent of Sempringham, William Philypp, did honour a second summons to Sleaford to answer charges about a dilapidated church: MS Vj/0, fo. 7[r].

[6] MS Vj/0, fos. 23[v] (Ashby Magna), 2[v] (Eaton), for examples of parishioners appointed. When a cleric was the offender, as in the case of the vicar of Barkby who had left an infant unbaptized and did not say divine services, a diocesan officer was appointed to observe his behaviour, MS Vj/0, fo. 6[v].   [7] Ibid., fo. 27[v].

between the bishop and the laity. In its long-running and often complex processes, dissimilar offences were dealt with in a judicial setting that brought together clergy and laity, governors and governed, offenders and reports of crime.

Visitation began with citation, which was carried out by criers or heralds ('precones') under the supervision of rural deans, with ultimate responsibility belonging to John Boney, the bishop's apparitor. For example, when John Milner of Shackerstone was reported for prostituting his wife to John Jakes of Odstone we are told that 'the rural dean certified that he had been cited by the crier'.[8] This was no guarantee of the suspect's presence before the visitor, and in fact Milner failed to appear and had to be excommunicated by Pryce in writing. In addition to the single suspect who 'said that he did not wish to appear', several fled across diocesan boundaries before they could be summoned.[9] That this occurred mainly in heresy and lechery cases suggests that flight was driven by fear of physical punishment. Citation was only effective if suspects remained in the place where they had been reported, and indeed if they remained alive. When William Aleyn of Cold Overton was ordered to answer charges that he had abandoned his wife Alice, he duly appeared, but Alice had died, and did not.[10] Citation could also fail if the dean or crier were subject to threats, as in the case of William Shirlock of Stoughton Grange, who was not cited for fornication because the crier feared death or a broken body if he executed the summons.[11] Walter Ruskyn, charged with failing to appear in his capacity as a parochial representative or *fidedignus*, later swore that he had in fact not been cited to appear in that visitation at all and so was released.[12] Clearly correct information and fearless officials were the backbone of successful visitation.

In order to ensure that suspects did appear, each report was assigned between one and five promoters, or presenters, who would see the case from beginning to end. In this visitation these officers were a mixture of laymen and clerics, including Lincoln episcopal staff such as the suffragan bishop of Meath, the registrar Robert Stretton, the sequestrator

---

[8] MS Vj/0, fo. 20ʳ: 'decanus loci certificauit virum citatum quem preconatum.'

[9] Ibid., fo. 16ᵛ: 'dixit se nolle comparare.' [10] Ibid., fo. 18ʳ.

[11] Ibid., fo. 26ʳ: 'decanus loci certificauit quod non audebat citari dictos virum et mulierem propter metum mortis et cruciatum corporis eius.'

[12] Ibid., fo. 4ᵛ: 'Walterus Ruskyn parochianus ecclesie ibidem non comparuit in visitacione ideo excommunicatus. Excusatur se per iuramentum quod non fuit citatus de comparendo in visitacione et sic dimissus est.'

Laurence Blakesby, the apparitor John Boney, and the notaries Thomas Hill, Edmund Langeford, and William Aylyf. The local clergy were represented by Richard Killum, a canon lawyer who was rector of Asfordby and had been commissary to Bishop Buckingham during the Chipping Warden heresy investigation of 1388, besides the rectors of Belton, Bottesford, and Nailstone.[13]

The most active presenters of cases however, were John Oudeby and John Ernesby, who were neither diocesan staff nor archdeaconry clergy. Their surnames suggest local origins in Oadby and Arnesby respectively, and each acted as proctor for religious houses during the visitation, but the basic legal training this implies does not seem to have been gained at university.[14] Ernesby, who was a notary public, was bailiff of Leicester in 1406 and by 1417 had become mayor, offices which placed him at the centre of local politics and justice and made him an ideal choice for the coercive role of a presenter of visitation cases.[15] Oudeby was a native of Oadby just south of Leicester, where in 1398 he had founded a chantry in the parish church. In 1413 he was archdeacon of Derby in the neighbouring diocese of Coventry and Lichfield, and perhaps was asked to participate on account of his knowledge of heresy suspects just across the diocesan border who were responsible for some of the offences reported to Repingdon in Leicester archdeaconry.[16]

The absence of the archdeacon of Leicester, Richard Elvet, from the 1413 visitation may be explained by his dispute with Repingdon over testamentary jurisdiction that lasted from 1408 until 1417. Episcopal government was apparently flexible enough to allow the co-opting of outsiders if it proved impossible to work with local officials, although the sidelining of Elvet in his own backyard cannot have helped resolve his dispute with the bishop.[17] In addition to Ernesby another powerful layman who presented offences was Sir Robert Moton, the lord of several

---

[13] For Killum see Reg. Buckingham (Lincoln), fo. 357ʳ; MS Vj/0, fo. 13ʳ (Thurcaston); *BRUC*, 338.

[14] Ernesby represented the abbot and convent of Leicester, MS Vj/0, fo. 28ʳ, and Oudeby the master of St Leonard's Hospital in Leicester, Ibid., fo. 10ᵛ.

[15] *A Calendar of Charters and Other Documents Belonging to the Hospital of William Wyggeston at Leicester* [hereafter *Wyggeston Hospital Records*], ed. A. H. Thompson (Leicester, 1933), 328–9; J. Nichols, *The History and Antiquities of the County of Leicester*, 4 vols. (Leicester, 1815), vol. i, part 2, 368–72; *List of Early Chancery Proceedings*, i: *Lists and Indexes*, 12 (London, 1901), 21. [16] Reg. Beaufort (Lincoln), fo. 8ᵛ.

[17] Reg. Arundel (Canterbury), i. fo. 150ʳ; *Reg. Repingdon (Lincoln)*, iii. 190–3.

manors in the county, a regular commissioner and juryman on royal inquests, and in 1422 a knight of the shire.[18] The basic requirement to assist the church in this way was literacy, or at least a familiarity with the written forms used in the church courts. John Horningwold, who presented one case of fornication and one of unpaid tithes, was elsewhere described as 'a literate man of Leicester'.[19] Laymen of Moton's stature were more than conversant with legal and documentary culture, and their political and economic might was very useful to ecclesiastical investigators across the country, not only in Leicestershire.

The parishioners with whom these officers and helpers interacted during the course of visitation were not a heaving mass of chaotic humanity, clamouring to have their grievances heard, nor were they a democratically elected group of representatives. The people who in this instance are described simply as 'the parishioners', but who are more usually called the *fidedigni*, were representative of the parish in the sense that they presented communal and personal grievances and reported offences in response to the visitor's questions, but they were not representative of the parish in a demographic sense. They were drawn from a fairly narrow pool of oligarchic families, who regularly held not only the office of parochial representative, but also constable, juror for manor, hundred, and county, and other secular offices.[20] Many of the 'parishioners' in 1413 were pressed into service again in 1414 as panellists on the inquests into the Oldcastle rising, such as William Lussel of Misterton, Thomas Wistow of Foston, and Walter Ruskyn of Melton Mowbray.[21] Duplication of offices is highly suggestive of an oligarchic representation, as is the use here of the familiar canonist's allusion to the 'greater part' of a parish, which meant the most important and trustworthy men, and was not a statistical description.[22] As discussed in earlier chapters, the lay persons qualified to

---

[18] MS Vj/0, fo. 20ʳ; PRO, KB 9/204/1, mm. 136, 138; E. Acheson, *A Gentry Community: Leicestershire in the Fifteenth Century c.1422–1485* (Cambridge, 1992), 241–2.   [19] MS Vj/0, fos. 10ᵛ–11ʳ, 26ᵛ; *Reg. Repingdon (Lincoln)*, iii. 127.

[20] *Lower Ecclesiastical Jurisdiction*, p. lxii: roles in different jurisdictions were 'alternative facets of local responsibility for which certain parishioners were especially likely to be selected'; see also A. Musson, 'Sub-Keepers and Constables: The Role of Local Officials in Keeping the Peace in Fourteenth-Century England', *EHR* 117 (2002), 4.

[21] MS Vj/0, fos. 2ᵛ, 22ʳ, 23ʳ; PRO, KB 9/204/1, mm. 138, 143. Continuing influence of certain families over time is suggested by the presence of a John Wystowe of Foston as 'chief-taxer' there in 1377; *The Poll Taxes of 1377, 1379 and 1381*, ed. C. C. Fenwick, Records of Social and Economic History, NS 29 (Oxford, 2000), i. 588–9.

[22] MS Vj/0, fo. 6ᵛ: In Hungerton the 'maior pars' of the parish reported on the state of the church building.

deal with the ecclesiastical courts were those who possessed good informal fame amongst their neighbours, who were not suspected of any crime, and who were trusted to witness charters, execute testaments, and speak on behalf of others. It was within this context that social knowledge of heresy or suspected heresy was forged, and it will provide the framework for our examination of the heresy suspects of 1413 and the people who reported them.

2. THE HERESY SUSPECTS

The offenders fall into two categories: named individuals reported for holding heretical opinions or displaying behaviour considered to make them suspect of heresy, and unlicensed preachers for whose admission the relevant clergy and parishioners were held responsible. The first two individuals to be reported for holding suspected opinions were William Tryvet and John Belgrave. Tryvet was reported in Twyford for publicly preaching on the Gospels in taverns and for being absent from church at Easter and Christmas, lying in his bed until the services were over, and setting a bad example to other Christians.[23] This is a good example of a report based on a combination of suspicious words and behaviour, without any specifically heretical content. At the visitation stage there does not seem to have been any verifiable evidence against him, as he was assigned a date to appear at Sleaford to purge himself with twelve compurgators. However, when he appeared without compurgators the strength of the suspicion against him began to harden into formal infamy, and he was challenged to say why he should not be convicted. He made no defence, was convicted, and swore to perform penance. Since the visitation had failed to uncover any substantial proofs, *and* Tryvet had failed to produce compurgators, the quality of his fame in Twyford remains unclear. In these circumstances judicial procedure was bound by the evidential standards of the *ordo iudiciarius* and by the compassionate imperative of *equitas canonica* to find a middle way, which was a conviction on the basis of vehement suspicion followed by a lenient sentence.

---

[23] Ibid., fo. 6ʳ: 'iacebat in lecto suo usque post altas missas decantatas, et predicat aperte de euangelis in tabernis publicis, et quamplurea consimilia enormia committit in detestabile exemplum ceterorum Cristianorum.'

John Belgrave's appearance before the visitors was based on much
stronger suspicion. He had been indicted of blasphemous and slanderous
offences before, as discussed in Chapter 7, and so was familiar to the
authorities of the archdeaconry. As in the 1390s he was reported for
attacking the reputations of local ecclesiastics, but by 1413 he had
become widely suspected of heresy and whoever reported him was able to
list in some detail four other opinions he had allegedly preached. This
would suggest that the report had been drawn up after careful consideration and information gathering by the Leicester clergy. However,
Belgrave denied the charges and no one in the town was willing or able to
provide the crucial eyewitness account, and so he was allowed to proceed
to purgation. His compurgators were all members of Leicester's *Corpus
Christi* guild, who it appears could not be gainsaid, even if the suspicions
against Belgrave ran deep.[24] It was perhaps because Belgrave was so
prominent in Leicester's affairs that Repingdon found it hard to secure
a conviction. We have evidence for his involvement in the local land
market, granting property to John Randolf, one of the more prosperous
men of the county, in 1412, and he appears as a witness to charters from
the 1380s to the 1420s.[25] A William Belgrave was farmer of the benefice
of Belgrave in Leicester in 1413, and the receiver of the honour of
Leicester in 1414. A generation earlier, a Roger Belgrave had been
a burgess of Leicester and responsible for reporting heresy to Archbishop
Courtenay's metropolitan visitation in 1389.[26] However, these creden-
tials did not prevent John being indicted before the royal justices in 1414,
alongside one of his 1413 compurgators, Ralph Friday, and another man
related to one of the compurgators, Roger Barbour. One of Belgrave's
1413 compurgators, John Wynger, stood on the other side of the heresy
divide in 1414, acting as one of the jurors responsible for Belgrave's
presentment for lollardy.[27] The circles within which social knowledge of
the kind that informed heresy reports was produced were circles which

[24] MS Vj/0, fo. 10ʳ: 'Vir comparuit personaliter in ecclesia Sancte Martini Leycestre, et
negat omnes istos articulos simpliciter prout articulantur, unde habet limitum post nonam
ad purgandum se cum xiiᵐᵃ manu, presentibus Oudeby et Ernesby.' On his compurgators
see Rubin, *Corpus Christi*, 243, and Hudson, *Premature Reformation*, 77–8.

[25] *Wyggeston Hospital Records*, 318–19, 337, 507.

[26] MS Vj/0, fo. 6ᵛ; Acheson, *Gentry Community*, 217; *The Metropolitan Visitations of
William Courtenay, Archbishop of Canterbury 1381–1396: Documents Transcribed from the
Original Manuscripts*, ed. J. H. Dahmus (Urbana, Ill., 1950), 165.

[27] PRO, KB 9/204/1, m. 141.

could close against the intrusion of outside authority from time to time, but their members were not bound to a single set of allegiances or a single religious outlook. John Wynger may well have sympathized with Belgrave in 1413 but by the early months of 1414 he was decidedly more in tune with the anti-heresy agenda.

In Wigston Magna, 4 miles to the south of Leicester, another of the men indicted with Belgrave in 1414, William Smith, was reported for suspected heresy along with John Hutte junior, Peter Herrick, and John Friday, the brother of Ralph Friday, one of Belgrave's compurgators. Hutte, Smith, and Herrick had been found in possession of many suspect English books, and were suspected of spreading the opinion that any priest could preach anywhere, notwithstanding Arundel's recent constitutions promulgated at Oxford.[28] Even though they denied the charges, such was the strength of the fame against them and so horrible the offences, that they were not allowed to purge themselves, but were forced to abjure and were surrendered to the observation of their rector, William Newport.[29] In addition Hutte was said to have harboured suspect persons and Friday was reported for contact with the other three. In terms of social status, all these men may be said to have belonged to the law-worthy section of society that enjoyed good reputation and informal fame. Hoskins, whose study of the midland peasantry focused on Wigston, described them all as free tenants, while Jurkowski comments on their membership of 'prominent families'.[30] The Friday family was particularly well connected, since both Ralph and the third brother, Richard, were men of law retained by clients in the local area and in London. John Friday is recorded as a witness to twenty charters centring on Wigston in the late fourteenth and early fifteenth centuries, while his

---

[28] MS Vj/0, fo. 22ʳ: 'habent quamplures libros anglicos suspectos et sunt publice diffamati super nephanda doctrina vocata lollardia nam cum personis super huiusmodi doctrina multum suspectis multum confabulantur et communicant et tenent opinionem quod non obstantibus constitucionibus nouellis Oxonie nuper editas possit et potest quilibet presbiter indifferenter predicare.'

[29] Ibid., fo. 22ʳ: 'propter famam in hac parte laborantem et abhominacionem et horribilitatem et detestandam nominacionem doctrine huiusmodi ipsi omnes iurarunt simpliciter tactis euangeliis quod ipsi numquam ab hac hora in antea nullam opinionem conclusionem siue articulum . . . tenebunt . . . Et pro contemplacione magistri Willelmi Neuport rectoris de eadem tunc presentis dimissi sunt.'

[30] W. G. Hoskins, *The Midland Peasant: The Economic and Social History of a Leicestershire Village* (London, 1957), 31–55; Jurkowski, 'Lawyers and Lollardy', 162.

brothers Ralph and Richard witnessed a further five.[31] Being held in high esteem by one's neighbours was no guard against being reported or indicted for heresy, however, and even Richard was soon indicted before the royal justices and handed over to Repingdon alongside Thomas Novery of Ilston-on-the-Hill in Leicestershire in 1415.[32] Hutte is recorded as a witness to land transactions twelve times, Smith nine times, and the Herrick family is mentioned three times.[33]

One other man, a tailor called John Anneys from Castle Donington, was reported for holding heretical opinions. Anneys was said to have preached in taverns and other public places that he would not confess fully and honestly to a single priest, although he would rather not confess at all, and that all doctors and bishops of the church were stupid and were widely thought to be stupid. He was also said to be a disciple of a lollard called William and was reputed to be a known lollard himself.[34] When he appeared before the visitation hearing at Rothley he denied the articles and so was given the opportunity to produce compurgators. Since the record then states that he proceeded straight to a simple abjuration of the articles and of all heresies and errors, we may assume that his denial did not stand for long. Anneys is unfortunately a suspect whose social status cannot be ascertained from other sources, but we do know more about the lollard called William whose presence in Castle Donington seems to have stimulated the suspicion against him.

William 'Tykelprest' is described as a false chaplain who had been admitted to preach in the parish at Easter by the parishioners, from whose ranks twelve *fidedigni* were cited to answer the charge. The vicar of Donington appeared later in the visitation at Breedon, and by the time

---

[31] *Wyggeston Hospital Records*, 494–514 *passim*; Ralph Friday also owned land in Stoughton, 3 miles to the north-east of Wigston: R. H. Hilton, *The Economic Development of Some Leicestershire Estates in the Fourteenth and Fifteenth Centuries* (Oxford, 1947), 47; John Friday had become a knight by 1442: F. Bickley, *Report on the Manuscripts of the Late Reginald Rawdon Hastings*, 4 vols., Historical Manuscripts Commission (London, 1928), i. 96.
[32] Lincolnshire Archives, Episcopal Register 15B (royal writs addressed to Repingdon), fo. 13ᵛ.　　　　　[33] *Wyggeston Hospital Records*, 494–514 *passim*.
[34] MS Vj/0, fo. 14ᵛ: 'Johannes Anneys sutor discipulus ut asseritur ipsius Willelmi lollardi, tenet et affirmat ac in publico utpote in tabernis et aliis locis publicis predicat . . . et reputatur pro publico lollardo. Idem dicit se nolle vni sacerdoti integre et plenarie una et eadem vice confiteri, sed si quid sibi placuerit reservare, non confessurum. Idem dicit quod omnes doctores et episcopi in ecclesia militante iuste breve essent fatui et pro fatuis reputabuntur.'

the court had reached Ulverscroft, Repingdon had relaxed the interdict.[35] We may identify the preacher as William Ederyk, a chaplain who was supported by the family of Thomas Tickhill in Chaddesden, Derbyshire.[36] His name is clearly a reference to this patronage, but may also be a pun suggestive of the irritation he caused the authorities. He seems to have made a preaching circuit close to the county and diocesan borders as he was reported again in Kegworth 3 miles to the east, and the 'chaplain from Derbyshire' reported in Sibson 27 miles south-south-west near the Warwickshire border, is likely to have been the same person.[37] The Donington report on Ederyk is lightly scored out, apparently by the original scribe, which may indicate that inquiries had to cease once the suspect crossed back into Coventry and Lichfield diocese. This was not a complete dead end, however, since Ederyk and Tickhill were both indicted by secular juries in Derbyshire the following year, probably on the basis of information copied down in 1413 by John Oudeby, the archdeacon of Derby, and passed on to Henry V's Derbyshire commissioners.[38]

Ederyk may also have been one of the 'utterly unknown' chaplains reported in Thurcaston and Wigston under the terms of the 1409 constitutions, but there are other named preachers reported elsewhere who may fit this bill.[39] In Sproxton John Beuley was reported for preaching without the bishop's licence.[40] In Seagrave a chaplain from nearby Quorndon called John was admitted without a licence at the will of the parishioners.[41] In Barrow-on-Soar John Edward, the chaplain of Lincoln diocese who had abjured before Bishop Despenser in Norwich eight years

---

[35] Ibid., fo. 14ᵛ: 'Citentur xij de fidedignis ipsius parochia super eo quod admiserunt quendam dominus Willelmus Tykelprest capellanum pretensum ad predicandum in ecclesia ibidem in die Pasche vltimo preterito contra tenorem constituciones nuper Oxonie celebrate. Apud Bredon vicarius fecit fidem quod dominus relaxauit huius interdictum apud Ulvescroft.'

[36] M. Jurkowski, 'Lancastrian Royal Service, Lollardy and Forgery: The Career of Thomas Tykhill', in R. Archer (ed.), *Crown, Government and People in the Fifteenth Century* (Stroud, 1995), 33–52.   [37] MS Vj/0, fos. 16ᵛ, 18ᵛ.

[38] PRO, KB 9/204/1, mm. 58, 59.

[39] MS Vj/0, fos. 13ʳ, 22ʳ: 'Quidam capellanus penitus ignotus'.

[40] Ibid., fo. 3ʳ: 'predicauit quamdam capellanum vocatus dominus Johannes Beuley in dicte ecclesie absque licencie diocesani.'

[41] Ibid., fo. 8ᵛ: 'Quondam dominus Johannes capellanus de Quernedon non licenciatus nec admissus per diocesanum predicandum in ecclesia ibidem de voluntate et consensu parochianorum et admissione eorundem. Remissus et relaxatur fuit interdictum huiusmodi apud Syleby.'

earlier, was reported for preaching without a licence in Woodhouse, a dependent chapel within the parish. Edward was described as the priest of the chapel in Mountsorrel, and it seems as though this was a dispute over sub-parochial identities that became entangled with suspicions of heresy, as happened in the Wiltshire parish of Edington in 1428.[42] The final unlicensed preacher to be reported was William Brown, who preached after evening services in Wistow and Kibworth Harcourt, and is likely to have been a native of the latter parish.[43] The most detailed report of such an offence is that from Wigston, where an unlicensed and unknown preacher's arrival in the parish church is described to an unusual level of detail. 'A certain chaplain, utterly unknown, who distributed ten marks in alms among the parishioners of that place, preached in the parish church on the Sunday after the last feast of the Purification of the Blessed Virgin Mary [5 February 1413], without being admitted by licence, against the protestations of the parochial chaplain; for on that day he stood publicly in the parish church and said "The head man of the parish does not wish to permit me to preach in the church and therefore I am going to the cross to preach there", to which the parishioners then present responded "No, preach here, because it is cold." '[44] Ten parishioners appeared before the visitation and admitted to having been present. They were released under observation of their rector, William Newport, and an interdict that had been imposed upon Wigston was lifted. We do not

---

[42] MS Vj/0, fo. 13ᵛ: 'Dominus Johannes Edward capellanus in Mounsorell super eo quod presumit sibi officium predicandi infra diocesis Lincoln' non admissus per diocesanum contra effectum constitucione nuper Oxonie celebratur et presertim predicauit in capella de Wodehouse dependente ab ecclesie de Barwe'. For Edward's 1405 trial see Reg. Arundel (Canterbury), i. fo. 390, and for the Edington/Baynton chapel dispute see Chapter 7.

[43] MS Vj/0, fo. 26ʳ: 'Parochiani dicunt quod quidam dominus Willelmus Broune capellanus pretensus non admissus, predicauit in ecclesia ibidem quodam die festiualis post completorum contra tenorem constituciones nuper Oxonie celebrate.' For the Brown family in Kibworth Harcourt see C. Howell, *Land, Family and Inheritance in Transition: Kibworth Harcourt 1280–1700* (Cambridge, 1983), 45–6, and *Poll Taxes*, i. 158. A William Brown was a pledge at the manor court in 1412 and 1413; Merton College Oxford, Muniment 6417.

[44] MS Vj/0, fo. 22: 'Quidam capellanus penitus ignotus qui in elemosinam X marcas distribuit inter parochianos ibidem quadam diem dominicam post festam Purificacionis Beate Marie ultimo preterito predicauit in ecclesia ibidem non admissus licencia, eciam contra reclamacionem capellani parochia, nam ipso die stetit publice in ecclesia et dixit, Caput vir parochia non vult permittere me predicare in ecclesia et ideo vadam ad crucem ut predicare ibi, cui [qui *crossed out*] responderunt parochiani tunc presentes non, sed predica hic quia frigus est.'

know, however, what happened to the preacher, whether he was William Ederyk or one of the other named preachers discussed here. He seem to have been a rich chaplain or to have enjoyed substantial patronage, distributing ten marks in alms to parishioners who were then no doubt only too happy for him to preach in their church, whatever the head man of the parish or the parochial chaplain had to say about the matter.[45] The decision of the preacher to repair to the village cross shows the wisdom of Lyndwood's clarification of the 1409 constitution on interdict, which he made to apply to the total extent of the geographical parish, rather than just the church. Itinerant preachers were apparently used to dealing with objections and obstructions, and were practised at gaining the support of the laity. The real interest of this report, however, lies in its illustration of the self-evident, but rarely visible, fact that anti-heresy and support for heresy could cut across the social grain of the parish, pitting neighbour against neighbour before the church courts.

3. THE HERESY REPORTERS

Attainment of the status of a *fidedignus* did not depend on wealth or economic superiority within the parish: it depended on trustworthiness, familiarity, and reliability assessed over time by all the persons and authorities with whom an individual enjoyed social and legal relations. Membership of a family in whose hands various offices were concentrated seems to have added to the law-worthiness of some individuals, but oligarchy was never so rigid, especially in the late medieval period of increased geographical mobility, that newcomers could not enter into it. For example, in Kibworth Harcourt, where the unlicensed preacher William Brown was reported, the names of Saunders, Polle, and Heyne occur again and again in lists of jurors, reeves, and supervisors of lands and tenements, and sometimes several members of the same family appear on the same tribunal. Howell describes these as the 'managerial families' of the manor, but notes that many others who were less well established came and went as local office holders.[46]

---

[45] The 'caput vir parochia' may well be an example of a parish master, officers whom Clive Burgess has identified as being the 'chief executives' of parish affairs, who had already served as churchwardens; Burgess, 'Pre-Reformation Churchwardens' Accounts', 306–32.

[46] Merton College Oxford, Muniments 6412–20; see nos. 6413 and 6419 for supervisors of lands and tenements packed with Saunders men; Howell, *Land, Family and Inheritance*, 34–5.

We have already seen that families who provided jurors and constables also provided parochial representatives at visitation, but how did they behave in this office; and what does that tell us about the relationship between reported crime and the social contours of the actual reporting? The single most striking fact about offences reported at visitation is that they involved other law-worthy persons far more frequently than their numbers in the population should merit. Men who sat on the panels of inquiry in the 1414 lollardy and treason commissions were especially prominent as defendants in two categories of offence: sexual crimes and reneging on financial obligations to the church. In the latter category John atte Vykars of Belton, who was a juror in an inquisition post mortem in 1413 and became a hundred juror in 1414, was reported for failing to maintain a light in his parish church, which he had presumably sworn to do.[47] Thomas Oadby of Diseworth, also a hundred juror in 1414, was similarly reported for 'withholding from the church two quarters of grain which he was bound by ancient custom to give'.[48] The constable of Foxton, John Chapman, was reported for failing to maintain a light in the church which he was bound to do under the terms of a last will and testament. Not only was he considered trustworthy enough to act as an executor and to be constable, but he also became a hundred juror in 1414 and was a witness to several charters in Leicester in the 1380s.[49]

This pattern of prominent local office holders reported for spiritual offences continues when we turn to the sexual crimes of adultery, fornication, concubinage, and incest. John of Loughborough, for example, was reported for spiritual incest (committed with his god-daughter) in Leicester during the 1413 visitation, and yet the following year he was a juror for the borough in the Oldcastle inquiries.[50] Michael Joy of Stathern deanery was reported for incontinence with his own servant Joan, and was a juror for his hundred in 1414.[51] One of the most

---

[47] MS Vj/0, fo. 14ʳ; *Quorndon Records*, ed. G. F. Farnham (London, 1912), 129; PRO, KB 9/204/1, m. 129.

[48] MS Vj/0, fo. 16ʳ: 'Thomas Oudeby subtrahit ab ecclesia ibidem ij quarteria granorum [frumenti *crossed out*] que tenetur dare dicte ecclesiae ex consuetudine antiqua'; PRO, KB 9/204/1, m. 129.

[49] MS Vj/0, fo. 27ʳ; PRO, KB 9/204/1, m. 139; *Wyggeston Hospital Records*, 319.

[50] MS Vj/0, fo. 10ʳ; PRO, KB 9/204/1, mm. 140–1.

[51] MS Vj/0, fo. 2ᵛ; PRO, KB 9/204/1, m. 143; *Poll Taxes*, i. 599, records a mason called Simon Joy and his wife Matilda at Stathern in 1381, who were assessed at 2s., placing them above the lowest rungs of manorial society.

incorrigible offenders in 1413 was William Odynell of Harby, only a mile or so from Stathern. His crimes covered both the sexual and the fiscal, being reported for adultery (a case which dragged on well into the next year, with extra entries squeezed into the margins of the visitation book in a tiny script), and a long-running dispute over withheld offerings. Despite this apparent criminality he was selected as a juror for the hundred in 1414.[52] John Jakes of Odstone, who was reported in 1413 for committing adultery with Anna Milner from nearby Shackerstone, had in the past been a reporter of crime himself, when in 1391 his wife Amicia was assaulted by one William Madoc. Jakes sat on the 1414 Oldcastle panel for his hundred like so many other men reported at the 1413 visitation, but his case has additional interest because one of the men responsible for bringing his adultery to the bishop's notice in 1413 was the local landholder Robert Moton, who was a fellow juror in 1414.[53] The impression gained from these examples of responsibility for crime and for the reporting of crime is that law-worthiness was double edged. If one was law-worthy in the sense of being reputable and trusted, it was more likely that one's own offences would be deemed worthy of being dealt with at law than the offences of people outside this self-referential circle. Indeed it often seems as though sexual immorality cases were reported because of the status of the husband who was cuckolded, or the master whose servant had brought shame on his household. We may well ask why the adultery of a lowly servant called Henry Mason was reported in Leicester instead of the other sexual infidelities of a busy county town: a possible answer is that his master was John Howet, a juror for the borough in 1414 and a regular witness to land transactions between prominent local citizens from 1402 to 1416.[54]

It seems that frequent access to the machinery of local justice, whether in ecclesiastical or secular jurisdictions, led to a moral interest being taken in the behaviour of other members of that law-worthy network. That sexual morality was only dealt with by legal means within a certain section of society is also suggested by Howell's analysis of the Kibworth Harcourt court rolls, which record payments known as marriage fines, a tax levied

---

[52] MS Vj/0, fos. 1ᵛ–2ʳ; PRO, KB 9/204/1, m. 143.
[53] MS Vj/0, fo. 20ʳ; G. F. Farnham, *Leicestershire Medieval Village Notes*, 6 vols. (Leicester, 1933), iv. 90; PRO, KB 9/204/1, m. 136.
[54] MS Vj/0, fo. 10ʳ; PRO, KB 9/204/1, m. 140; *Wyggeston Hospital Records*, 334, 440–1.

on couples when they wed. According to Howell '[a]ll the persons concerned came from the leading families in the village and thought of themselves as free.'[55] The fines were not levied upon, or not recorded for, those of a lower legal status. Although this record may have been the creation of the more wealthy fathers with dowries to protect, we cannot assume that interest in sexual morality and marriage was confined to the leading families. Those outside the office-holding networks surely cared about such issues, but on this evidence it seems that their concerns were more seldom dealt with in processes that left written records than were the concerns of the leading, prominent, or managerial families. Participation in the administration of justice led to a familiarity with the law that perhaps encouraged people to seek formal legal redress, whereas those not regularly exposed to legal culture were more likely to deal with such issues in other ways. It also seems to denote a particular set of social attitudes, prompting a moral interest in the lives of people similarly belonging to law-worthy and office-holding networks.

This excursus into sexual immorality and the law was prompted by more than the appeal of the salacious. In Chapter 6 the preponderance of sexual imagery and analogues in anti-heresy propaganda was discussed, with the conclusion that although lechery was not intended to be a direct sign of heresy, it was a useful facet of polemic because the people used to reporting sexual offences in an inquisitorial system were now being asked to report heresy. A brief examination of the analysis of visitation reporting in 1413 will show the perceptiveness of the ecclesiasts and polemicists who made that link. In all the parishes visited by Repingdon the average proportion of sexual morality cases was 13 per cent of all reported offences. In those parishes where heresy was reported, sexual morality accounted for 19 per cent of offences. Whilst by no means conclusive in statistical terms, this supports and is supported by the association of heresy and lechery in anti-heretical propaganda, and the use of sexual charges against some heresy suspects, illustrated in the last chapter. Heresy was more likely to be reported, it seems, in those places where the *fidedigni* or office-holding network had developed a more acute sensitivity towards the sexual mores of their fellows. Of course, the same may be said of heresy itself, which was likely to flourish in parishes that had developed a sharp moral awareness, perhaps through the experience of

---

[55] Howell, *Land, Family and Inheritance*, 33–4.

having to deal with a negligent priest, or through the more positive stimulus of critical and original minds. Although we are left with a chicken-and-egg situation with regards to their effect upon one another, it is clear that both heretical and anti-heretical zeal were products of the same socially and geographically delineated moral networks. From this position it is possible to argue both that heresy happened to exist in places where the corresponding enthusiasm of the orthodox ensured it was detected, and that heresy was a phenomenon constructed in the minds of people most committed to defending the faith. Since this study's primary concern is to understand anti-heresy, I will not at this point dismiss heresy as a figment of the zealous imagination, nor shall I accord it the sectarian and corporate status it has enjoyed in some histories. The two possible arguments are not in fact incompatible, and keeping both in mind may lead to more fertile conclusions.

One of the most striking details of the 1413 visitation book is that John Hutte junior, reported for heresy in Wigston, was not only part of a family who regularly witnessed charters, but his uncle or father, John Hutte senior, was one of the parish representatives responsible for making those reports to the visitor in the first place. Hutte senior was reprimanded for failing to appear in this capacity along with one William Cook, another regular witness to local charters alongside Ralph and John Friday, two of the other Wigston heresy suspects.[56] It is not clear whether Hutte senior was personally responsible for reporting his younger relation, and several plausible explanations suggest themselves why he did not appear at the visitation hearing. It is possible that he had heeded the biblical injunction that if a family member was known secretly to worship false gods 'you shall have no pity on him, you shall not spare him nor shield him . . . your own hand shall be the first raised against him and then all the people shall follow'. There was also a danger, expressed in the thirteenth-century canons, that if Hutte junior's heresy were not reported, suspicion would eventually fall on his family as well.[57] Cases of heresy and anti-heresy splitting a family are not uncommon and Leicestershire examples include John and Roger Belgrave in Leicester, Simon and Robert Polle in Kibworth Harcourt, and Nicholas and

[56] MS Vj/0, fo. 22ʳ; *Wyggeston Hospital Records*, 494–514 *passim*. John and Henry Cook also acted as regular witnesses. In 1384 one Thomas Cook of Wigston was reported for spilling blood in the churchyard: Reg. Buckingham (Lincoln), fo. 280ᵛ.
[57] Deut. 13: 7–10; X 5.7.5, X 5.7.6.

Robert Gilbert, also in Kibworth Harcourt.[58] Whatever the case, the heresy of the Wigston suspects had become a matter of common repute and fame, and it is difficult to see how Hutte senior could not have been aware of his relative's involvement. Given the tendency of serious crimes reported at visitation to concern the families of the people doing the reporting, we may conjecture that Hutte junior was reported because of Hutte senior's position within the parish. Heresy within the community of the law-worthy was worthy of being dealt with by that community.

The relationship between heresy, heresy reporting, fame, and office holding was a close one, and had been so since the Roman idea of infamy as a public disability attached itself to the new public crime of heresy in the late imperial period. In the thirteenth century a great deal of effort went into elucidating the social basis of suspicion, which casts a very revealing light on heresy reporting in late medieval England, and the material presented in this chapter. To be capable of becoming infamous and being barred from public office, one had first to have been in possession of good fame and have been capable of holding office. The same is true of heresy. In the statement that no heretic, no believer of heretics, and no son of a heretic may be admitted to any ecclesiastical benefice or any public or elected office lies the key to the social proximity of reporter and reported observable in the 1413 visitation book.[59] One had to have been capable of holding office for the deprivation of that capability to be a serious deterrent against support for heresy. Heretics were also to be treated as insane for testamentary purposes, and therefore assumed to be intestate.[60] We have seen in the Leicester evidence that acting as an executor to last wills and testaments was one facet of the law-worthiness that qualified people to report heresy. It seems then that bishops and canonists saw heresy as a problem of the office-holding and law-worthy classes, which adds to our understanding of why reporters of the crime identify other members of those classes as suspects. Part of the explanation for this comes from the familial and local outlook of the heresy reporters themselves, and part comes from the canonical concept of heresy as applied to Wycliffism and other forms of dissent in late medieval England. There was some disagreement as to whether penitent heretics

---

[58] PRO, KB 9/204/1, m. 132; Merton College Oxford, Muniment 6417.

[59] VI 5.2.1; BL, MS Royal 6 E VII, fo. 200^r; Tancred, *Ordo iudiciarius*, 154.

[60] VI 5.2.3.

could shake off the infamy that prevented them from holding office, but the evidence of actual cases shows that unless actually condemned and burnt, the abjured, purged, and penitential could advance in society.[61] The Wigston suspects went on witnessing charters, Repingdon became a bishop, and so on. When an abjuration of heresy was not followed by the restoration of the penitent's ability to hold public office, as in a case dealt with by Cardinal Beaufort at Rouen in 1431, it was treated as an abuse of canonical process.[62]

As persons qualified to hold public office, reporters of heresy may be assumed to have had at the very least a rudimentary knowledge of documentary culture, and even many illiterate manorial officers would have understood the mechanisms and significance of various types of written record.[63] How far we may extrapolate from this an understanding of and familiarity with anti-heresy legislation is another question. The categories of person we have been concerned with in this chapter were undoubtedly the target audience for much of the anti-heresy propaganda detailed in Chapters 5 and 6, but what more can we tell about the quality of their comprehension of it, particularly with regard to the meaning of new legislation? The reports of unlicensed preaching in the visitation book all invoke Arundel's constitutions promulgated only four years earlier. However, we cannot tell whether these references were independently made by the parochial representatives, added to their reports by the visitor's notary, or had been included in the original citation and were therefore repeated by the *fidedigni* at the bishop's prompting. The third of these possibilities is the most probable, but that does not mean that the parishioners did not understand the legal framework within which their reported suspicions were expressed. It is likely that they had quickly assimilated Arundel's legislation to their knowledge of licences, charters, and contracts by which the church was administered, and in which the laity were frequently expected to participate. In addition to lay participation, the parochial clergy were indispensable to the processes of reporting and citing suspected heretics. Despite occasional silences in the records, we must ascribe some role to rectors like William Newport in Wigston,

---

[61] In one of his harsher comments, Hostiensis, *Summa aurea*, 1540, argues that even a penitent heretic should be called a rebel and treated as infamous, intestate, and not eligible for public office. The opposite point of view is held by William Paul, *Summa summarum*, V. X. q. 108 (Bodleian, MS Bodley 293, fo. 180ʳ).   [62] *CPL 1427–47*, 342.

[63] Clanchy, *Memory to Written Record*, 46–51.

and parochial chaplains in many other places.[64] With some rudimentary education common to nearly all parish priests, a local familiarity with checking written documents may be taken for granted.

The smooth day-to-day functioning of the church was facilitated by documents that recorded the bearer's obligations and rights. By checking the provisions of a chaplain's letter of title, or a layman's right to receive the fruits of a church, the visitor could discern who was in breach of his or her 'contract'. The range of ecclesiastical administration and reform that was achieved through written documentation is illustrated by the character of the offences reported to Repingdon's visitation. If we look more closely at the categories of offences listed near the beginning of this chapter, we see that he heard 156 cases of written titles to benefices not exhibited, 79 cases of parochial incomes collected on the basis of unknown rights, 48 cases of a benefice being farmed without a licence, 31 cases of clerical non-residence without written dispensation, 24 instances in which clerics had defective letters of title or ordination, 22 in which the provisions of a last will and testament were queried, 7 of admitting an unlicensed preacher, 6 of the failure to provide a chaplain in breach on a priest's letter of ordination, 6 of failing to distribute alms in the same circumstances, 4 of unlicensed preaching itself, and 2 of a broken marriage contract. The total number of offences that relied upon documentation, or the lack of it, was 385, or just under 50 per cent of all reported offences. In this context it is unimaginable that new legislation on a topic high on the visitor's agenda would not have been both strenuously publicized and intelligently received.

The documentary awareness demanded from parochial representatives matched the moral awareness that characterized those parishes where more heresy and sexual immorality was reported. However, the reduction of moral offences such as heresy to documentary criteria widened the moral community over which the *fidedigni* could exercise vigilance to include itinerant and unknown persons whose trustworthiness was assessed by their possession of the correct document. Although this suggests a social disjunction between the 'local community' and the wider world, such a division is purely formal, since the networks of law-worthiness, land transactions, local office holding, and religious observance always

---

[64] Given, *Inquisition*, 198–204, and Hamilton, *Medieval Inquisition*, 43, on parochial clergy reporting heresy; Merlo, *Eretici e inquisitori*, 129, on collaboration in citation process.

stretched much further afield than the edge of the parish or manor. In the records created by a central judicial authority we do not see the horizontal social links between people from different parishes, along which information and news could travel. Indeed, the fear that heretical ideas could spread independently of vertical hierarchies is proof that such horizontal routes for knowledge transfer were known to contemporaries, and poor documentation should not blind us to the certainty of their existence. We may expect that news about unlicensed preachers and news about anti-heresy legislation also spread independently of episcopal propaganda efforts.

That parishioners were expected to take responsibility for breaches of the 1409 constitutions is shown by the contrasting involvement of the laity in the unlicensed preaching cases in Thurcaston, Sibson, and Wigston. In Thurcaston it was the rector, John Mersedeum, who was held responsible for admitting the preacher, and it was a group of parishioners whose testimony ensured that the interdict could be lifted.[65] At Sibson and Wigston, however, it was the parishioners who were held responsible for the unlicensed preaching and had to appear before Repingdon, while the reports seem to have been made by parochial chaplains in both cases.[66] Spiritual vigilance was imagined not only as the preserve of clergymen watching over their flocks, but as the responsibility of all Christians over each other. Just because an offender came from outside the geographical community with whose politics a *fidedignus* might be expected to be familiar, that did not mean he or she was not part of the universal community of the faithful and so liable to Christian correction.

The key to the identification of suspicions of heresy by the laity and the parochial clergy was social and moral vigilance of a kind that was by no means unusual. The *fidedigni* were not only the voice of their parish; they were its eyes and ears, exercising a communal responsibility over many aspects of life. Watching the weather, looking out for signs of murrain in sheep and tares in the wheat crop, were all practical measures against famine and starvation as well as being metaphors for the detection of heresy. At the human level, vigilance was exercised over the proper func-tioning of social relationships, particularly those governed by custom and contract. In the same way that suspicion of heresy was determined by deviation from the norms of parochial observance as well as by deviant

---

[65] MS Vj/0, fo. 13ʳ.   [66] Ibid., fos. 18ᵛ, 22ʳ.

doctrine, so deviation from the proper provision of religious services was a common concern of the *fidedigni* within each parish. The rector of Barkby was reported for failing to say divine services and leaving a child unbaptized for three days, while the rector of Seagrave was reported for non-residence and ordered to mend his ways.[67] Cases of this kind demonstrate that lay awareness of religious obligations and responsibilities was not confined to the habits of their fellow laymen and women. Since heresy was often found in the clerical class, this kind of lay vigilance over the clergy was vital, but it could not be turned into effective action without the co-operation of the visitor. In the case of Thomas Darley, the rector of Belton, a report for fornication and fathering a child was compounded when he could not show the proper letters of title to his benefice. Between them the visitor and the parishioners forced his misdeeds into the open. Interestingly, Darley was reported despite, or perhaps because of, the probable fact that he was a rural dean, presenting a series of cases to Repingdon at Diseworth, Kegworth, and Ashby-de-la-Zouch.[68] The parishioners were most often called upon to verify or deny claims made at visitation in cases that turned on the memory of local custom, of which they were seen as custodians. In Barwell and Kirkby Mallory for example, the rectors were reported for failing to distribute a quantity of wheat, which by custom should have been given to the parishioners.[69] The parishioners of Arnesby complained when the prior of Caldwell in Bedfordshire, to which the church was appropriated, failed to give a sixpenny loaf of white bread to each unmarried man at Easter as he was bound to do by custom, and in Shackerstone the rector was admonished for failing to provide a deacon for the parish as his predecessor had done.[70]

In the absence of legal documents such as licences, the vigilance of the parishioners over customary relationships and obligations could serve the same purposes, measuring practice against legally binding expectations. This vigilance over custom and social practice could be exercised internally within the parish or externally against outsiders. Despite the artificiality of the division between local and global in late medieval society, some habits of mind among the law-worthy did differentiate between the

[67] MS Vj/0, fos. 6ᵛ, 8ᵛ.
[68] Ibid., fos. 17ʳ (his offences); 15ʳ–16ʳ (his activities as rural dean).
[69] Ibid., fo. 19.   [70] Ibid., fos. 20ʳ, 22ᵛ.

danger within and the danger without. To some extent social responsibility was understood in terms of vigilance against outsiders, and the fear of heretical infection or invasion was only a part of this. In Kibworth Harcourt, for example, immigrants had to pay a fine to the manor court at least until 1349, after which time the mobility of the peasant labour force was discouraged at a national level.[71] The failure of the labour laws of the fourteenth century to inhibit geographical mobility may have actually increased sensitivity towards this distinction. In 1414 a thief presented to royal justices by a North Kibworth jury was additionally described as a vagabond, suggesting that the concept of insider and out-sider was still potent at this time.[72] Indeed expulsion from the village may be behind some of the cases of defendant absenteeism during the 1413 visitation. In heresy cases the self-imposed exile of the suspect, or his temporary removal across the diocesan border, is usually seen as a tactic to avoid arrest, but in some sexual immorality cases, such as that of John Maybroke of Whitwick who suffered his sentence of sixteen lashes of the whip while his lover Alice returned to her native village in the 'High Peak', coercion may have been involved.[73] The case of the unlicensed preacher barred from the church in Wigston reminds us that coercion on the part of powerful elements within parish society did not preclude opposition from others who did not agree with the choices made by those office holders and parish representatives. It also reminds us that outsiders could be welcomed as well as suspected, although the rhetoric of vagrancy and foreignness was controlled by those who co-operated with the record-keeping officers of church and crown, and so we seldom hear that undertone.

Outsiders also began at a disadvantage to locals when suspicions of heresy were raised. Not being familiar to large numbers of reputable local people, a stranger would find it difficult to establish the kind of good informal fame that many heresy suspects relied upon to steer them towards purgation and freedom from suspicion. If already suspected of heresy, the stranger could only grow to be notorious the more recognized he became, which seems to have happened in the case of William Ederyk

---

[71] Howell, *Land, Family and Inheritance*, 35; see also C. Dyer, *Lords and Peasants in a Changing Society: The Estates of the Bishopric of Worcester 680–1540* (Cambridge, 1980), 359.
[72] PRO, KB 9/206/1, m. 36.
[73] MS Vj/0, fo. 14ᵛ; coercion certainly did feature in a case of expulsion described in R. H. Hilton, *The English Peasantry in the Later Middle Ages* (Oxford, 1975), 57.

in the years 1413 to 1414. The itinerant preacher was subject to the attentions of the *fidedigni* in a slightly different way from the local person suspected of heresy, whose behaviour and communications could be observed over a longer period of time. However, both were reported to the bishop by the same group within society, whose role it was to keep the peace in their locality and co-operate with the central bureaucracies of church and crown.[74] This was a role for which they had been primed not only by anti-heresy propaganda, but also by an engagement with ecclesiastical justice that went much deeper and extended further back in time than that single-issue campaign. The overlapping and oligarchic nature of local office holding is in part explained by the need for persons well versed in documentary forms and legal norms, but also by the need for persons whose business meant that they regularly intruded upon other people's lives. In this context it is only natural that the people whose beliefs and religious behaviour they intruded upon were those with whom they dealt in other capacities. The evidence of Repingdon's 1413 visitation is that heresy was seen by bishop and parishioner alike to be an abuse of the trust that characterized the *fidedigni*.

[74] On keeping the peace see Davies, 'Kinship, Neighbours and Communities', 181, and C. Herrup, *The Common Peace: Participation and the Criminal Law in Seventeenth-Century England* (Cambridge, 1987), 193–8.

Conclusion

A large part of this book has been devoted to the decisions made by persons in authority as to the best way of detecting heresy. Theirs were the decisions of policy makers and, at a lower administrative level, the implementers of policy. Such are the traditional subjects of institutional and legal history, but what of the other, socially inferior, decisions that shaped the detection of heresy and the character of the records studied in these pages? What are we to make of the decision to report suspicions of heresy taken by a parochial representative before the bishop's official at visitation? What significance should we attribute to the decision of the head man of Wigston Magna to block the way of an unlicensed preacher, defying some of his own neighbours in the process? And where, one might well ask, do these and similar decisions stand in relation to the decision, or choice, with which we began: heresy?

Heresy was considered the manifestation of man's perennial disobedience towards God, which had blighted human history since the fall from grace in the garden of Eden. Reflecting personal desire and spiritual pride, heresy was a result of choice, concupiscence, the root of all sin. But we have seen that reporting heresy also required choices, often quite courageous ones, sometimes tinged with social responsibility or concern for the peace of one's parish, sometimes coloured by more self-interested motivations born of disputes that were otherwise, or so it seemed to the participants, insoluble. Choices were necessary to the detection of heresy, but the concept of choice as the exercise of personal preference was also central to the medieval understanding of heresy. It is to this contradiction that all the problems surrounding the detection of heresy may be distilled: questions of authority, discernment, judgement, and equity may all be posed in terms of the regulation of choice.

At one level this means that the phenomenon of heresy and anti-heresy, taken as a whole and dispassionately viewed, can be seen to have performed a didactic role in society. It formed arguably the clearest and most condensed cultural expression of the relationship between Christians and sin, presenting opportunities for those in authority to illuminate the psychological sources of sin and emphasize mankind's universal suscept-ibility to it. This didactic function did not, of course, mean that heresy was encouraged rather than suppressed, but that occasions of anti-heresy propaganda could provide opportunities for the reiteration of deeper messages than the headline news that a heretic was a danger to the community of the faithful. The return of so many suspects to the church, after undergoing the rituals of purgation and penance, served not only to advertise the danger of heretics as a category of criminals and indicate the provisional nature of temporal justice, but also to remind every witness to such events that they themselves were susceptible to heresy simply because they were humans living after the fall. This reaffirmation of what it meant to be a Christian living in the world was continued in the actual detection of heresy, since reporting one's suspicions of heresy was a good, obedient choice that provided a channel for the heightened aware-ness of sinfulness and social decay that was stimulated by anti-heresy propaganda.

However, those condemned as heretics did not see themselves as agents of concupiscence, and prosecutors were for the most part not concerned with the wider social utility of anti-heresy propaganda; they were more worried about solving the problem itself. They saw heresy as the present manifestation of a historical and eschatological curse, and the fire of heresy was to be extinguished, not stoked in order to illuminate moral failing. The temptation to use heresy and anti-heresy as vehicles for a general call to moral reformation or national unity did exist, and it would be naive to eliminate it from our analysis; but that was a strategy to be used sparingly, so that fear of heresy did not cause moral panic. As noted in Chapter 6 for example, the detection of neither heresy nor lechery would have benefited if the link between these crimes had been too mech-anistic. Social danger and suspicion had to be managed carefully to avoid indiscriminate and purely political accusations. Nonetheless, heresy and anti-heresy had social effects that need to be borne in mind when consid-ering their historical significance. In particular, the fundamental fact that the detection of heresy forced an engagement between the learned law and social realities raises the question of what effect the application of that law had upon society. Did the detection of heresy, and the choices it entailed, aid social formation or hinder it: did inquisition make or break communities?

Some historians of heresy and inquisition have assumed, or been convinced of, the socially destructive effects of the inquisitorial process, turning neighbour against neighbour, father against son, and class against class. In this vein James Given has written that the inquisitor's techniques 'were designed to break existing social relations among men and women; they did not form new ties or reorganize old ones so that they could be put to use to serve the interests of the rulers . . . The inquisitors incapacitated individuals by cutting them out of the social networks in which they were embedded.'[1] There are three points here: that the destruction of relationships was essential to inquisition, that no new relationships were forged by inquisition, and that persons suspected of heresy were forcibly exiled from their communities. By contrast, the argument of this book has been that while a culture of suspicion was necessary to inquisition, it required the cultivation and management of social relations rather than their destruction. Relations between local society and the state were given a new outlet, and familiar forms of communal peace-keeping and legal representation were given a national focus. In addition, ecclesiastical justice strove to maintain and repair social unity and inclusion wherever possible, even if this meant forcible inclusion. Persons hauled before inquisitors had every chance to rejoin the legal and religious communities in which they had been detected, and the individual was only cut adrift in the most serious cases.

A similar attitude to Given's informs the work of Grado Merlo, who, consciously or unconsciously, has inverted the medieval adage that heretics tore the fabric of holy mother church, applying it instead to inquisitorial procedure. He argues that inquisition had a profound effect on social and religious life, contributing to the growing laceration and fracture of the medieval social fabric, and, implicitly, hastening the convulsions of the reformation period.[2] Of course, there is a tendency in all kinds of writing about inquisition to deplore abuses of medieval papal power, and for present-day catholics to apologize for the past behaviour of their church; but these reactions bear more relation to the persistent myth of inquisition than to the historical evidence.[3]

The social effect of inquisitorial procedures on the societies in which they were applied has yet to be studied systematically, and the present

---

[1] Given, *Inquisition*, 216.   [2] Merlo, *Eretici e inquisitori*, 121.
[3] On the myth and the historiography see E. Peters, *Inquisition* (Berkeley, 1989).

book has really only scratched the surface of what is possible given modern historical techniques and the availability of sources, especially for England. On the basis of the material presented here, this much can be said. Inquisition and the detection of heresy provided opportunities for the individual to become more involved in public action than he, or to a lesser extent she, had been before. The process of reporting one's suspicions within a legal framework that had universal application across Christendom, and was administered by the most powerful people in society, helped to make the parish *fidedigni* part of the state. In this sense heresy detection was one of a number of areas in which the persons defined as trustworthy or substantial members of various legal communities— parish, manor, vill—were increasingly being drawn into much larger political and conceptual communities—diocese, county, province, and realm—as active participants.[4] In the new world of social and geographical mobility created by recurrent pestilence, this creation of imagined communities was a welcome side effect of participation in a new, national law enforcement campaign of such high importance.

It would be possible to take this argument much further, and suggest that the experience of anti-heresy created an orthodox community in opposition to a heterodox one. A conclusion of this kind would support the impression created by Duffy and others of a late Middle Ages characterized by a dominant majority orthodox community that enjoyed widespread internal unity and harmony. It would also support the impression formed by many historians and literary scholars of a distinct heretical community, enjoying a high degree of sectarian coherence and exclusivity. On the basis of the conclusions presented in each of the preceding chapters, however, neither of these pictures seems a fair representation of social reality. While Wycliffism proved to be an intellectual movement capable of lending some coherence to otherwise disparate groups and individual dissenters, these people were not homogeneous and did not form communities that excluded other, equally binding, communal identities. The boundaries of attraction to Wycliffite ideas were also shaded with great varieties of belief, both orthodox and heterodox. Rather than simply being the social category implied in some studies, I have sought to show that heresy was also a legal and mental

---

[4] Musson and Ormrod, *Evolution of English Justice*, 116–38.

category defined by personal choices and judicial decisions. This is not to say that Wycliffism was not an important factor in the formation of social identity, merely to assert that it was only one of many influences on the late medieval experience of religion, and that in those cases when it is applicable it was not exclusive of other influences.

As such the creation of a new community of the orthodox in the fifteenth century did not primarily mean new social alignments, but the creation of a new way of thinking about belief and one's place within the Christian community. Orthodoxy was a moral rather than a demographic community. The advent of anti-heresy as a public discourse altered the relationships between a great variety of cultural commonplaces, such as the image of the sinful priest and the parochial community, in effect shuffling the mental cards on which late medieval people's ideas about the world were written. In any circumstances, but most noticeably in a situation of rapid cultural change, the imagining of identity cannot be satisfactorily defined in statistical terms, asking who was in and who was out, because identity was, and is, idealized and always changing. Individual heretics might symbolize the boundaries of this moral community at particular moments, but orthodoxy was not the clearly contained city of God or ship of souls familiar from sermons. The feeling of orthodox community arguably impinged most strongly on the individual in terms of the regulation of behaviour. He or she was encouraged to use the concept of heresy to regulate his or her own actions and beliefs, and the actions and beliefs of others. Reporting heresy was then both the social consequence of orthodox identity, and one of the most important means of its creation.

So in terms of its social effects, heresy and anti-heresy created new ways of thinking and feeling, and gave people an extra contact point with the apparatus of the ecclesiastical and royal government. What of the social causes of these phenomena? Of course there is another book in this, but some observations can be made on the basis of the present study. It was suggested in Chapter 8 that parishes where the relationship between clergy and laity was more critical, and where a greater moral interest was taken in the sexual offences of one's neighbours, were more likely to recognize certain beliefs and behaviour as potentially heretical than less morally aware parishes. At the same time such a tradition of criticism and habitual moral scrutiny may also be posited as the source of the reasoned rejection of orthodoxy that became heresy once it was proscribed by the church, the 'attitude of intellectual questioning and criticism' described by Kantik Ghosh.[5] The suggestion that heresy and anti-heresy were produced co-dependently in the same circumstances is supported by the evidence in Chapter 8 of the close social connections between the reporters and the reported. What characterized the social stratum in which heresy seemed to thrive was religious zeal and contact with the written word, whether in Wycliffite reading circles or in discharging the legal duties of a *fidedignus*. As a component of religious zeal, we may also consider the propensity of individuals to make choices about religious observance.

In their relationship to choice, heresy and orthodoxy had common roots. A discontented parishioner, influenced by the message of a Wycliffite preacher or questioning the ecclesiastical hierarchy from first principles, might choose to confess to a trusted friend or sympathetic lay person rather than to a priest. In a similar way, a wealthy layman or woman might choose his or her own confessor. The action and the impulses behind this choice are similar to those in the dissenting example, in that they seek to satisfy a personal preference. The only substantial difference is that one could qualify for episcopal authorization under canon law, whilst the other could not. Similarly the erection of a private chapel in a noble household is not very different from the appropriation of a disused chapel by the followers of William Swinderby; membership of a recognized religious guild was prompted by the same desire for additional spiritual community outside the parish church as membership of a lay reading circle such as that apparently run by Margery and William Baxter; and attendance at a sermon preached by a mendicant friar (suspected by large sections of the population) was determined by the same kind of interest in the spoken word of God that brought people out to hear a Wycliffite preacher (suspected by some of the same sections of the population). Of course, a line was crossed when the individual in question knew that what he or she was doing was likely to make him or her suspect of heresy, but the spiritual motivations began in the same place; and that is something we may too easily forget.

[5] Ghosh, 'Bishop Reginald Pecock and the Idea of "Lollardy" ', 264; see also J. A. F. Thomson, 'Orthodox Religion and the Origins of Lollardy', *History*, 74 (1989), 39–55.

Given such a similarity in the motivations of dissenters and conformists, it seems that we should consider those beliefs and actions labelled as heretical in concert with those we label orthodox rather than in simplistic opposition to them. Sceptical readers may object at this point that my argument obscures real differences and issues of clear contemporary disagreement: Wycliffites and their opponents were obviously different and recognized each other as such. The existence of a body of texts produced collectively in a well-funded scriptorium, the community of outlook perceptible in a significant number of people broadly opposed to the material church, and the impressively penetrating and long-lasting influence of an academic theologian on people very far from the universities in every sense make the denial of a basically Wycliffite dissenting position impossible.

And yet if heresy was not a socially discrete sect but a dissenting position, and orthodoxy a moral rather than a demographic community, the evidence of Wycliffism need not preclude an appreciation that religious differences overlaid structural similarities. The exercise undertaken in Chapter 8 sought to show what can be learnt from locating the people we call heretics within the judicial and social contexts in which suspicion against them had been generated. Normal historical practice, by contrast, is to isolate examples of a single phenomenon such as heresy, and then group all these examples together in a conceptual class or category. Although this kind of classification and grouping is necessary if we are to make sense of society, we must remain aware that if our categories are too rigid we risk seeing medieval society in a way that makes individuals difficult to understand, and change, such as the influence of new ideas, hard to accommodate. Thinking about issues of common concern allows us to question the heresy–orthodoxy polarity that is often imposed on late medieval religion in England; a polarity which conceals too many anomalies to be viable.

Besides similarities in the exercise of pious preference, common concerns may be found in the late medieval interest in church reform. Movement towards parochial participation and the 'Christianization' of the social and moral order had gained pace in the thirteenth century as the reforms of the Fourth Lateran Council were introduced to England. Generally speaking the aim of the episcopate during the succeeding two centuries was to create a more Christian society by making available a greater volume of fairly closely controlled information relating to the basics of the faith.[6] In response, various sections of the laity and clergy initiated new structures into which their piety could be channelled, from private reading to guild membership, chantry foundation to new feasts and cults.[7] In addition, as direct manorial authority waned, the parish increasingly became the focus of local public life. Put simply, people increasingly wanted to get involved, and to take some personal responsibility for their salvation.[8]

As noted in Chapter 5, the Wycliffites were themselves located firmly within this tradition in their continuation of the Pechamite programme of preaching and pastoral instruction. The aim of the hierarchical church in the late Middle Ages, and even the aim of Wycliffites, was not to create a nation of free-thinking individuals, but to achieve Christian unity. The information and ideas that were to achieve this were transmitted via preaching, pastoral instruction, proclamations, and so on: in fact all of the channels described in Chapter 5. However, any project of cultural homogenization based on the reception of information by individuals cannot be expected to produce only conformists. Dissenters are a natural by-product of such exposure to information relating to the fundamental questions of life, and the best that the church could have hoped for, if indeed any ecclesiast ever imagined the question in these terms, was to create more conformists than dissidents. This seems to have been accomplished in later medieval England, although not without some difficulty.

The big problem, as we have seen, lay in determining who were the dissidents and who the conformists, given the possibility of being a natural conformist who had been led astray, or a dissident only in certain

[6] Gibbs and Lang, *Bishops and Reform*; Haren, *Sin and Society*, 1–5; Boyle, *Pastoral Care*; J. Hughes, *Pastors and Visionaries: Religion and Secular Life in Late Medieval Yorkshire* (Woodbridge, 1988), 143–61; S. Powell, 'The Transmission and Circulation of *The Lay Folks' Catechism*', in A. J. Minnis (ed.), *Late-Medieval Religious Texts and their Transmission* (Woodbridge, 1994), 67–84.

[7] M. Rubin, 'Small Groups: Identity and Solidarity in the Late Middle Ages', in J. Kermode (ed.), *Enterprise and Individuals in Fifteenth-Century England* (Stroud, 1991), 132–56; G. Rosser, 'Parochial Conformity and Voluntary Religion in Late-Medieval England', *TRHS* 6th ser. 1 (1991), 173–89; V. Bainbridge, *Gilds in the Medieval Countryside: Social and Religious Change in Cambridgeshire c.1330–1558* (Woodbridge, 1996); Hughes, *Pastors and Visionaries*, 298–347.

[8] L. Poos, *A Rural Society after the Black Death: Essex 1350–1525* (Cambridge, 1991), 271–3, describes an 'activist stance towards parochial affairs'; see also P. D. A. Harvey, 'Initiative and Authority in Settlement Change', in M. Aston, D. Austin, and C. Dyer (eds.), *The Rural Settlements of Medieval England: Studies Dedicated to Maurice Beresford and John Hurst* (Oxford, 1989), 42–3.

matters. There was also, of course, a long tradition of dissidence and radicalism *within* the church. Indeed a reform Christianity, which is essentially what the late medieval church strove to represent, had to be radical and self-critical. Heresy was defined as the disobedient persistence in views and practices so radical that the balance of authoritative opinion deemed them to have gone beyond acceptable criticism. At times of fear and crisis, this imaginary but significant dividing line naturally contracted and more people found themselves on the outside, some purposefully and some unwittingly.

The modalities of suspicion and status within the community might then combine to cause their detection to the bishop, and they would find themselves before a judge who sought to ascertain their willingness to step back inside the community of the obedient and faithful. Everything about the detection of heresy, from the doubt, circumspection, and safeguards, to the extraordinary measures, the co-operation between church and crown, and the threat of severe punishment, reflects the difficulty of the exercise and the close relationship between orthodox and heterodox religious enthusiasm. Managing that enthusiasm, and channelling the choices it required into acceptable forms of expression and participation, was the challenge faced by the late medieval church in the detection of heresy.

Detection was organized from above but required collaboration from below. The framework for this collaboration existed in a general sense in 1382 in the shape of a quite widespread familiarity with the inquisitorial process, gained from participation in visitations and the prosecution of other occult crimes such as clerical concubinage. By 1428, two generations later, the framework for detection was more specifically geared to the problems raised by heresy, with the machinery in place for proactive as well as reactive investigations, a uniform mode of questioning suspects, a uniform text for public abjurations, and a central record of the most serious investigations and prosecutions. The development of a legal response to heresy was not, however, a simple or uncritical reception of the major thirteenth- and fourteenth-century canons on heresy, but an adaptation of general principles and specific remedies to the particular circumstances of the English experience. This adaptation occurred through the deliberations of Convocation and the royal council, the decisions made by diocesans as to what procedures were most suited to their local needs, and their reactions to the relative success or failure of those procedures. Just as popular engagement with church, crown, and community was changed for ever by anti-heresy activity, so policy making at the highest level found a new focus in the decades following the condemnation of Wyclif.

Heresy and anti-heresy made a massive impact on the political life of the nation, whatever the numbers of the dissidents or the level of their social organization. This is unsurprising given the centrality of heresy to medieval conceptions of social and ecclesiastical unity. The fact that the English experience of heresy and anti-heresy was peculiar is equally unsurprising, since the adaptation of canon law that was involved took place within a society that was very different from that in which *Excommunicamus* and *Ad abolendam* had been framed. However, the same was true of all late medieval anti-heresy campaigns, whether in England, Bohemia, or the Low Countries. There was nothing unusual in being exceptional: it was only the character of the peculiarity that differed from region to region. Despite these differences, the detection of heresy drew on a legal framework that was common to all of Latin Christendom, and the production of our evidence of heresy suspects, condemned heretics, and networks of Wycliffite influence needs to be understood in that international context.

The legal records that attest to this international stage connect matters of European significance with events in the humblest English parish. We learn that medieval systems of government and justice relied upon the co-operation and participation of the parochial clergy and the trust-worthy laity, as well as upon the training and dedication of the bureau-cratic class. The relationship between those in authority and those over whom authority was exercised is shown to have used communication channels that were well established, yet capable of reconfiguration and revivification in light of a new threat to the order it represented. Historians on the whole have tended to invert the inquisitorial view of heresy as threat and anti-heresy as order, seeing the former as a sign of vitality in the church and the latter as an instrument of repression having a negative impact on society. Eschewing such value judgements, I have sought to show that heresy was the natural product of the church's aspiration to create a unified Christian society, while the detection of heresy through inquisi-tion contributed to that unification. Without condescension to the people suspected of heresy, I have tried to cast those responsible for their detection in a more sympathetic light, since there was much vitality in the response to heresy as well. Held up to the mirror of inquisitorial method and canonical circumspection, historiographical assumptions about who heretics were and what their significance was seem too rigid and monochrome. Heresy was nebulous and a transitory legal state, not a sectarian church. That made it more, not less, dangerous, and its significance in our understanding of late medieval society has, if anything, been underestimated.

Bibliography

1. MANUSCRIPTS

Cambridge University Library

MS Gg. 6. 21 [Ecclesiastical statutes].
MS Mm. 4. 41 [Canon law miscellanea].
Ely Diocesan Registry, MS F/5/32 [Formulary].
Ely Diocesan Registry, MS G/1/2 [Register of Thomas Arundel (Ely), 1374–88].
Ely Diocesan Registry, MS G/1/3 [Register of John Fordham (Ely), 1388–1425].

Canterbury

Canterbury Cathedral Library, Act Book Y. 1. 3 [Consistory Court Act Book].

Exeter

Devon Record Office
MSS Chanter 8 and 9 [Register of Edmund Stafford (Exeter), 1395–1419].

Hereford

Hereford Cathedral Library, MS P. ii. 2 [Richard Rudhale's canon law collection].
Hereford Cathedral Library, MS P. vii. 7 [Ecclesiastical statutes].

Lincoln

Lincolnshire Archives
Episcopal Register 12 [Register of John Buckingham (Lincoln), 1363–98, volume 3].
Episcopal Register 13 [Register of Henry Beaufort (Lincoln), 1398–1404].
Episcopal Register 15B [Royal writs addressed to Philip Repingdon (Lincoln), 1405–19].
Episcopal Register 16 [Register of Richard Fleming (Lincoln), 1420–31].
Episcopal Register 17 [Register of William Gray (Lincoln), 1431–6].
Episcopal Register 18 [Register of William Alnwick (Lincoln), 1435–49].
MS Vj/0 [Visitation book].

London

British Library
MS Additional 6157 [Henry Chichele's pontifical].
MS Additional 35205 [Roll of writs].
MS Additional Charter 12794 [Verse fake papal bull].
MS Cotton Cleopatra B 1 [Miscellaneous].
MS Cotton Cleopatra E II [Ecclesiastical documents].
MS Cotton Faustina C VII [Formulary].
MS Cotton Julius D XI [Bérengar Frédol].
MS Harley 335 [Ecclesiastical statutes].
MS Harley 644 [Royal statute book].
MS Harley 670 [Formulary].
MS Harley 862 [Formulary].
MS Harley 1197 [*The Pore Caitif*].
MS Harley 1777 [JPs' register].
MS Harley 2179 [Formulary].
MS Harley 2276 [Homilies].
MS Harley 3705 [Ecclesiastical statutes].
MS Lansdowne 470 [Royal statute book].
MS Royal 6 E VI and VII [*Omne bonum*].
MS Royal 8 A XVIII [Bérengar Frédol].
MS Royal 9 A VIII [*Decretum*].
MS Royal 9 E X [Bartholomeus Pisano].
MS Royal 10 B IV [Third Lateran Council].
MS Royal 10 D X [*Summa summarum*].
MS Royal 11 A II [*Liber extra*].
MS Royal 11 A XIV [Bérengar Frédol].
MS Royal 11 C XI [*Clementines*].

Corporation of London Record Office
Journals of the Court of Common Council, 2 (1425–8).

Guildhall Library
MS 9531/3 [Register of Robert Braybroke (London), 1382–1404].
MS 9531/4 [Registers of Richard Clifford (London), 1407–22, and John Kempe (London), 1422–5].

Lambeth Palace Library
Register of William Courtenay (Canterbury), 1381–96.
Register of Thomas Arundel (Canterbury), 1396–1414.

Public Record Office
C 54 [Close rolls].

C 66 [Patent rolls].
KB 9/204/1 [Commissions of inquiry, panels, and indictments, 1414].
KB 9/205/1 [Commissions of inquiry, panels, and indictments, 1414].
KB 9/206/1 [Trailbaston indictments, 1414].
KB 9/209 [Commissions of inquiry, panels, and indictments, 1417].

Maidstone

Centre for Kentish Studies
MS DRb/Ar5 [Register of William de Bottlesham (Rochester), 1389–1400].
MS DRb/Ar6 [Register of John de Bottlesham (Rochester), 1400–4].
MS DRb/Ar7 [Register of Richard Young (Rochester), 1404–18].
MS DRb/Ar8 [Register of John Langdon (Rochester), 1422–34].
MS DRb/Ar9 [Register of Thomas Brouns (Rochester), 1435–6].
MS DRb/Pa1 [Composite Act Book].

Norwich

Norfolk Record Office
MS DN Reg/4/8 [Register of John Wakeryng (Norwich), 1416–25].
MS DN Reg/5/9 [Register of William Alnwick (Norwich), 1426–36].
MS DN Reg/5/10 [Register of Thomas Brouns (Norwich), 1436–45].

Oxford

Bodleian Library
MS Bodley 293 [*Summa summarum*].
MS Bodley 649 [Sermons].
MS Douce 312 [Royal statute book].
MS e. Musaeo 86 [*Fasciculi zizaniorum*].
MS New College 179 [Edmund Stafford's civil law texts].
MS New College 204 [Thomas Chillenden].
MS Rawlinson C 100 [Ecclesiastical statutes].

All Souls College
MS 42 [Ecclesiastical statutes].
MS 63 [Pastoral collection].

Balliol College
MS 158 [Ecclesiastical statutes].

Exeter College
MS 41 [Ecclesiastical statutes].

Merton College
MS 223 [Peter Quesnel].

Muniments 6412–20 [Kibworth Harcourt court rolls].
Muniments 6590–2 [Barkby court rolls].

Trowbridge

Wiltshire and Swindon Record Office
MS D1 2/4 [Register of Ralph Erghum (Salisbury), 1375–88].
MS D1 2/6 [Registers of Richard Mitford (Salisbury), 1395–1407, and Nicholas Bubwith (Salisbury), 1407].
MS D1 2/8 [Register of John Chaundler (Salisbury), 1417–26].
MS D1 2/9 [Register of Robert Nevill (Salisbury), 1427–38].

Winchester

Hampshire Record Office
MS A 1/12 [Register of Henry Beaufort (Winchester), 1405–47].

Worcester

Worcestershire Record Office
Register of Philip Morgan (Worcester), 1419–26.
Register of Thomas Polton (Worcester), 1426–33.

2. PRINTED PRIMARY SOURCES

(NB Bishops' registers are all alphabetized under 'R' for register, and then by name.)

Acta Concilii Constanciensis, ed. H. Finke, 4 vols. (Regensburg, 1896–1928).
ADAM of Usk, *The Chronicle of Adam Usk*, ed. C. Given-Wilson (Oxford, 1997).
Andreas von Regensburg: Sämtliche Werke, ed. G. Leidinger (Munich, 1903).
Die Anfänge einer ständigen Inquisition in Böhmen: Ein Prager Inquisitoren-Handbuch aus der ersten Hälfte des 14. Jahrhunderts, ed. A. Patschovsky (Berlin, 1975).
AUDELAY, JOHN, *The Poems of John Audelay*, ed. E. K. Whiting, EETS 184 (London, 1931).
BALBUS, JOHANNES, *Catholicon* (Lyon, 1492).
The Black Death, ed. R. Horrox (Manchester, 1994).
BOETHIUS (Ps.-), *De disciplina scolarium: Édition critique, introduction et notes*, ed. O. Weijers (Leiden, 1976).
The Book of Vices and Virtues, ed. W. N. Francis, EETS 217 (London, 1942).
A Calendar of Charters and Other Documents Belonging to the Hospital of William Wyggeston at Leicester, ed. A. H. Thompson (Leicester, 1933).

Calendar of Plea and Memoranda Rolls for the City of London 1364–1381, ed. A. H. Thomas (Cambridge, 1929).

Concilia Magnae Britanniae et Hiberniae, a synodo Verolamiensi, A.D. 446 ad Londinensem, A.D. 1717, ed. D. Wilkins, 4 vols. (London, 1737).

The Council of Constance: The Unification of the Church, ed. L. R. Loomis, J. H. Mundy, and K. M. Woody (New York, 1961).

Councils and Synods with Other Documents Relating to the English Church, ii: *1205–1313*, ed. F. M. Powicke and C. R. Cheney, 2 vols. (Oxford, 1964).

The Coventry Leet Book or Mayor's Register, ed. M. D. Harris, 4 vols., EETS 134, 135, 138, 146 (London, 1907–13).

Dives and Pauper, ed. P. H. Barnum, 2 vols., EETS 275, 280 (Oxford, 1976–80).

DOYLE, E., 'William Woodford O.F.M. (c.1330–c.1400): His Life and Works together with a Study and Edition of his *Responsiones contra Wiclevum et Lollardos*', *Franciscan Studies*, 43 (1983), 17–187.

DURANDUS, *Speculum iuris* (Basel, 1574).

DYMMOK, ROGER, *Rogeri Dymmok Liber contra XII errores et hereses Lollardorum*, ed. H. S. Cronin (London, 1922).

Early Treatises on the Practice of the Justices of the Peace in the Fifteenth and Sixteenth Centuries, ed. B. H. Putnam, Oxford Studies in Social and Legal History, 7 (Oxford, 1924).

The Edington Cartulary, ed. J. H. Stevenson, Wiltshire Record Society, 42 (Devizes, 1987).

English Gilds: The Original Ordinances of More than One Hundred Early English Gilds, ed. L. T. Smith, EETS 40 (London, 1870).

English Wycliffite Sermons, ed. A. Hudson and P. Gradon, 5 vols. (Oxford, 1983–96).

Fasciculi zizaniorum, ed. W. W. Shirley, Rolls Series (London, 1858).

Fasciculus morum: A Fourteenth-Century Preacher's Handbook, ed. S. Wenzel (Philadelphia, 1989).

FRÉDOL, BÉRENGAR, *Le* Liber de excommunicatione *du Cardinal Bérengar Frédol*, ed. E. Vernay (Paris, 1912).

Friar Daw's Reply, in *Six Ecclesiastical Satires*, ed. J. Dean (Kalamazoo, Mich., 1991).

The Fyve Wyttes: A Late Middle English Devotional Treatise, ed. R. H. Bremmer (Amsterdam, 1987).

GASCOIGNE, THOMAS, *Loci e libro veritatum*, ed. J. E. T. Rogers (Oxford, 1881).

GERSON, JEAN, *Œuvres complètes*, ed. P. Glorieux, 10 vols. (Paris, 1960–73).

GUY DE CHAULIAC, *The Middle English Translation of Guy de Chauliac's Treatise on 'Apostemes'*, ed. B. Wallner (Lund, 1988).

Heresy Trials in the Diocese of Norwich, 1428–31, ed. N. P. Tanner, Camden Society, 4th ser. 20 (London, 1977).

HOCCLEVE, THOMAS, *Hoccleve's Works: The Minor Poems*, ed. F. J. Furnivall, EETS extra ser. 61 (London, 1892).

—— *Complaint and Dialogue*, ed. J. A. Burrow, EETS 313 (Oxford, 1999).

HOSTIENSIS, *Summa aurea* (Venice, 1605).

—— *In decretalium libri commentaria* (Venice, 1591).

INNOCENT IV, *Apparatus super quinque libros decretalium* (Rome, 1511).

Jacob's Well: Part One, ed. A. Brandeis, EETS 115 (London, 1900).

Kent Heresy Proceedings 1511–1512, ed. N. Tanner, Kent Records, 26 (Maidstone, 1997).

KNIGHTON, HENRY, *Knighton's Chronicle 1337–1396*, ed. G. H. Martin (Oxford, 1995).

The Lanterne of Liȝt, ed. L. M. Swinburn, EETS 151 (London, 1917).

LAVYNHAM, RICHARD, *A Litil Tretys on the Seven Deadly Sins*, ed. J. P. W. M. van Zutphen (Rome, 1956).

Liber exemplorum ad usum praedicantium, ed. A. G. Little (Aberdeen, 1908).

List of Early Chancery Proceedings, i: *Lists and Indexes*, 12 (London, 1901).

Lollard Sermons, ed. G. Cigman, EETS 294 (1989).

Lollards of Coventry, 1486–1522, ed. N. Tanner and S. McSheffrey, Camden Society, 5th ser. 23 (Cambridge, 2003).

Lower Ecclesiastical Jurisdiction in Late-Medieval England: The Courts of the Dean and Chapter of Lincoln, 1336–1349 and the Deanery of Wisbech, 1458–1484, ed. L. R. Poos, Records of Social and Economic History, NS 32 (Oxford, 2001).

LYDFORD, JOHN, *John Lydford's Book*, ed. D. M. Owen, HMC, Joint Publications, 22 (London, 1974).

LYNDWOOD, WILLIAM, *Provinciale seu constitutiones Angliae* (Oxford, 1679).

Memoriale credencium: A Late Middle English Manual of Theology for Lay People, ed. J. H. L. Kengen (Nijmegen, 1979).

The Metropolitan Visitations of William Courtenay, Archbishop of Canterbury 1381–1396: Documents Transcribed from the Original Manuscripts, ed. J. H. Dahmus (Urbana, Ill., 1950).

MIRK, JOHN, *John Mirk's Instructions for Parish Priests*, ed. G. Kristensson, Lund Studies in English, 49 (Lund, 1974).

Monimenta Medii Aevi, ed. C. Walch (Göttingen, 1757).

Monumenta historica Carmelitana, ii, ed. R. P. B. Zimmerman (Îles de Lérins, 1906).

NETTER, THOMAS, *Doctrinale antiquitatum fidei catholicae ecclesiae*, ed. B. Blanciotti, 3 vols. (Venice, 1757–9; repr. Farnborough, 1967).

PECOCK, REGINALD, *The Repressor of Over Much Blaming of the Clergy*, ed. C. Babington, Rolls Series, 19 (London, 1860).

—— *The Donet*, ed. E. V. Hitchcock, EETS 156 (London, 1921).

Pillii, Tancredi, Gratiae libri de iudiciorum ordine, ed. F. Bergmann (Göttingen, 1842).

The Poll Taxes of 1377, 1379 and 1381, ed. C. C. Fenwick, Records of Social and Economic History, NS 29 (Oxford, 2000).

Quorndon Records, ed. G. F. Farnham (London, 1912).

Reading Abbey Cartularies, ed. B. R. Kemp, 2 vols., Camden Society, 4th ser. 31, 33 (London, 1986–7).

The Register of Thomas de Brantyngham, Bishop of Exeter 1370–1394, ed. F. C. Hingeston-Randolph, 2 vols. (London, 1901–6).

The Register of Nicholas Bubwith, Bishop of Bath and Wells 1407–1424, ed. T. S. Holmes, 2 vols., Somerset Record Society, 29, 30 (London, 1914).

The Register of John Chandler, Dean of Salisbury 1404–1417, ed. T. C. B. Timmins, Wiltshire Record Society, 39 (Devizes, 1984).

Registrum Thome de Charlton, Episcopi Herefordensis 1327–1344, ed. W. W. Capes, CYS 9 (London, 1913).

The Register of Henry Chichele, Archbishop of Canterbury 1414–1443, ed. E. F. Jacob, 4 vols., CYS 44–7 (Oxford, 1941–5).

The Register of John de Grandisson, Bishop of Exeter 1327–1369, ed. F. C. Hingeston-Randolph, 3 vols. (London, 1915).

The Register of William Greenfield, Lord Archbishop of York 1306–1315, ed. A. H. Thompson, 5 vols., Surtees Society, 145, 149, 151–3 (Durham, 1931–40).

Registrum Roberti Hallum, Diocesis Saresbiriensis 1407–1417, ed. J. M. Horn, CYS 72 (London, 1982).

Registrum Edmundi Lacy, Episcopi Herefordensis 1417–1420, ed. J. H. Parry, CYS 22 (London, 1918).

The Register of Edmund Lacy, Bishop of Exeter 1420–1455, ed. G. R. Dunstan, 5 vols., CYS 60, 61, 67, 69, 71 (London, 1963–71).

Registrum Simonis Langham, Cantuariensis Archiepiscopi, ed. A. C. Wood, CYS 53 (London, 1955).

Registrum Roberti Mascall, Episcopi Herefordensis 1404–1417, ed. J. H. Parry, CYS 21 (London, 1917).

The Episcopal Register of Robert Rede Ordinis Predicatorum, Lord Bishop of Chichester 1397–1415, ed. C. Deedes, 2 vols., Sussex Record Society, 8, 11 (London, 1908–10).

The Register of Bishop Philip Repingdon 1405–1419, ed. M. Archer, 3 vols., Lincoln Record Society, 57, 58, 74 (Hereford and Norwich, 1963–82).

Registrum Thome Spofford, Episcopi Herefordensis 1422–1448, ed. A. T. Bannister, CYS 23 (London, 1919).

The Register of Edmund Stafford, Bishop of Exeter 1395–1419, ed. F. C. Hingeston-Randolph (London, 1886).

The Register of John Stafford, Bishop of Bath and Wells 1425–1443, ed. T. S. Holmes, 2 vols., Somerset Record Society, 31, 32 (London, 1915–16).

Registrum Johannis Trefnant, Episcopi Herefordensis 1389–1404, ed. W. W. Capes, CYS 20 (London, 1916).

Registrum Johannis Trilleck, Episcopi Herefordensis 1344–1360, ed. J. H. Parry, CYS 8 (London, 1912).

The Register of Henry Wakefield, Bishop of Worcester 1375–1395, ed. W. P. Marett, Worcestershire Historical Society, NS 7 (Worcester, 1972).

The Register of John Waltham, Bishop of Salisbury 1388–1395, ed. T. C. B. Timmins, CYS 80 (Woodbridge, 1994).

The Register of William Wykeham, Bishop of Winchester 1367–1404, ed. T. F. Kirby, 2 vols. (London, 1899).

RICHARDSON, H. G. (ed.), 'An Oxford Lawyer's Notebook', in *Formularies which Bear on the History of Oxford c.1204–1420*, ed. H. E. Salter, W. A. Pantin, and H. G. Richardson, 2 vols., Oxford Historical Society, NS 4, 5 (1942), ii. 453–69.

Rotuli Parliamentorum ut et petitiones et placita in parliamento, ed. J. Strachey, 6 vols. (London, 1767–77).

Secretum secretorum: Nine English Versions, ed. M. A. Manzalaoui, EETS 276 (Oxford, 1977).

Select Cases in Chancery 1364–1471, ed. W. P. Baildon, Selden Society, 10 (London, 1896).

Select Cases on Defamation to 1600, ed. R. H. Helmholz, Selden Society, 101 (London, 1985).

Select English Works of John Wyclif, ed. T. Arnold, 3 vols. (Oxford, 1869–71).

Selections from English Wycliffite Writings, ed. A. Hudson (2nd edn., Toronto, 1997).

Snappe's Formulary and Other Records, ed. H. E. Salter, Oxford Historical Society, 80 (Oxford, 1924).

Statutes of the Realm, ed. J. Raithby and A. Luders, 9 vols. (London, 1766–1826).

THOMAS of Chobham, *Summa de arte praedicandi*, ed. F. Morenzoni, Corpus Christianorum Continuatio Mediaevalis, 82 (Turnhout, 1988).

Three Middle English Sermons from the Worcester Chapter Manuscript F. 10, ed. D. M. Grisdale (Leeds, 1939).

Two Wycliffite Texts: The Sermon of William Taylor 1406, The Testimony of William Thorpe 1407, ed. A. Hudson, EETS 301 (1993).

Visitations in the Diocese of Lincoln, 1517–1531, ed. A. H. Thompson, 3 vols., Lincoln Record Society, 33, 35, 37 (1940–7).

WALSINGHAM, THOMAS, *Historia Anglicana*, ed. H. T. Riley, 2 vols., Rolls Series, 28 (London, 1863–4).

The Westminster Chronicle 1381–1394, ed. L. C. Hector and B. F. Harvey (Oxford, 1982).

The Works of a Lollard Preacher, ed. A. Hudson, EETS 317 (2001).

3. SECONDARY SOURCES

ACHESON, E., *A Gentry Community: Leicestershire in the Fifteenth Century c.1422–1485* (Cambridge, 1992).

AERS, D., 'Altars of Power: Reflections on Eamon Duffy's *The Stripping of the Altars*', *Literature and History*, 3rd ser. 3 (1994), 90–105.

ALATRI, M. d'., *Eretici e inquisitori in Italia: Studi e documenti*, 2 vols. (Rome, 1987).

ANAYA HERNÁNDEZ, L. A., *Judeoconversos e inquisición en las Islas Canarias (1402–1605)* (Las Palmas, 1996).

ARNOLD, J. H., 'Lollard Trials and Inquisitorial Discourse', in C. Given-Wilson (ed.), *The Fourteenth Century*, ii (Woodbridge, 2002), 81–94.

ASTON, M., *Thomas Arundel: A Study of Church Life in the Reign of Richard II* (Oxford, 1967).

—— *Lollards and Reformers: Images and Literacy in Late Medieval Religion* (London, 1984).

—— 'William White's Lollard Followers', in *Lollards and Reformers*, 71–99.

—— 'Devotional Literacy', in *Lollards and Reformers*, 101–33.

—— 'Lollardy and Literacy', in *Lollards and Reformers*, 193–217.

—— *Faith and Fire: Popular and Unpopular Religion, 1350–1600* (London, 1993).

—— 'Bishops and Heresy: The Defence of the Faith', in *Faith and Fire*, 73–94.

—— 'Were the Lollards a Sect?', in P. Biller and B. Dobson (eds.), *The Medieval Church: Universities, Heresy, and the Religious Life. Essays in Honour of Gordon Leff*, SCH Subsidia, 11 (Woodbridge, 1999), 163–91.

—— 'Lollard Women', in D. Wood (ed.), *Women and Religion in Medieval England* (Oxford, 2003), 166–85.

—— and RICHMOND, C. (eds.), *Lollardy and the Gentry in the Later Middle Ages* (Stroud, 1997).

BAILEY, T., *The Processions of Sarum and the Western Church* (Toronto, 1971).

BAINBRIDGE, V., *Gilds in the Medieval Countryside: Social and Religious Change in Cambridgeshire c.1330–1558* (Woodbridge, 1996).

BALL, R. M., 'Thomas Cyrcetur, a Fifteenth-Century Theologian and Preacher', *JEH* 37 (1986), 205–39.

—— 'The Opponents of Bishop Pecok', *JEH* 48 (1997), 230–62.

BARBER, M., *The Trial of the Templars* (Cambridge, 1978).

BARRELL, A. D. M., 'The Ordinance of Provisors of 1343', *Historical Research*, 64 (1991), 264–77.

BARRON, C., *London in the Later Middle Ages: Government and People 1200–1500* (Oxford, 2004).

BARTON, J. L., 'The Legal Faculties of Late Medieval Oxford', in J. I. Catto and R. Evans (eds.), *The History of the University of Oxford*, ii: *Late Medieval Oxford* (Oxford, 1992), 281–313.

BELLAMY, J. G., *The Law of Treason in England in the Later Middle Ages* (Cambridge, 1970).

BELLOMO, M., *The Common Legal Past of Europe, 1000–1800* (Washington, DC, 1995).

BENNETT, J. M., *Ale, Beer, and Brewsters in England: Women's Work in a Changing World 1300–1600* (Oxford, 1996).

BETHENCOURT, F., *L'Inquisition à l'époque moderne: Espagne, Italie, Portugal XVe–XIXe siècle* (Paris, 1995).

BICKLEY, F., *Report on the Manuscripts of the Late Reginald Rawdon Hastings*, 4 vols., Historical Manuscripts Commission (London, 1928).

BILLER, P., 'William of Newburgh and the Cathar Mission to England', in D. Wood (ed.), *Life and Thought in the Northern Church c.1100–c.1700: Essays in Honour of Claire Cross*, SCH Subsidia, 12 (Woodbridge, 1999), 11–30.

—— 'The Earliest Heretical Englishwoman', in J. Wogan-Brown et al. (eds.), *Medieval Women: Texts and Contexts in Late Medieval Britain. Essays for Felicity Riddy* (Turnhout, 2000), 363–76.

—— *The Waldenses, 1170–1530: Between a Religious Order and a Church* (Aldershot, 2001).

BINZ, L., *Vie religieuse et réforme ecclésiastique dans le diocèse de Genève pendant le grand schisme et la crise conciliaire 1378–1450* (Geneva, 1973).

Biographical Register of the University of Oxford to A.D. 1500, ed. A. B. Emden, 3 vols. (Oxford, 1989).

Biographical Register of the University of Cambridge to 1500, ed. A. B. Emden (Cambridge, 1963).

BOLTON, B., 'The Council of London of 1342', in G. J. Cuming and D. Baker (eds.), *Councils and Assemblies*, SCH 7 (Cambridge, 1984), 147–60.

BORST, A., *Die Katharer* (Stuttgart, 1953).

BOSE, M., 'Reginald Pecock's Vernacular Voice', in Somerset et al. (eds.), *Lollards and their Influence*, 217–36.

BOSSY, J., *Christianity in the West 1400–1700* (Oxford, 1985).

BOYLE, L. E., *Pastoral Care, Clerical Education and Canon Law, 1200–1400* (London, 1981).

—— 'The *Summa summarum* and Some Other English Works of Canon Law', in *Pastoral Care*, essay XV, 415–56.

—— 'Canon Law before 1380', in J. I. Catto and R. Evans (eds.), *The History of the University of Oxford*, i: *The Early Oxford Schools* (Oxford, 1984), 531–64.

BRAMBILLA, E., *Alle origini del Sant' Uffizio: Penitenza, confessione e giustizia spirituale dal Medioevo al XVI secolo* (Bologna, 2000).

BRAND, P., 'Courtroom and Schoolroom: The Education of Lawyers in England Prior to 1400', in *The Making of the Common Law* (London, 1992), 57–75.

BRUNDAGE, J. A., *Medieval Canon Law* (London, 1995).

BRUNDAGE, J. A., 'The Canon Law Curriculum in Medieval Cambridge', in J. A. Bush and A. Wijffels (eds.), *Learning the Law: Teaching and Transmission of Law in England 1150–1900* (London, 1999), 175–90.

BRUSCHI, C., and BILLER, P. (eds.), *Texts and the Repression of Medieval Heresy* (York, 2003).

BURGESS, C., 'Pre-Reformation Churchwardens' Accounts and Parish Government: Lessons from London and Bristol', *EHR* 471 (2002), 306–32.

—— 'A Hotbed of Heresy? Fifteenth-Century Bristol and Lollardy Reconsidered', in L. Clark (ed.), *The Fifteenth Century*, iii: *Authority and Subversion* (Woodbridge, 2003), 43–62.

CATTO, J. I., 'Wyclif and Wycliffism at Oxford 1356–1430', in J. I. Catto and R. Evans (eds.), *The History of the University of Oxford*, ii: *Late Medieval Oxford* (Oxford, 1992), 173–261.

CHADWICK, H., *The Early Church* (Harmondsworth, 1967).

CHENEY, C. R., *English Synodalia of the Thirteenth Century* (Oxford, 1941).

—— *English Bishops' Chanceries 1100–1250* (Manchester, 1950).

—— 'William Lyndwood's *Provinciale*', in *Medieval Texts and Studies* (Oxford, 1973), 158–84.

—— *Episcopal Visitation of Monasteries in the Thirteenth Century* (2nd edn., Manchester, 1983).

CHIFFOLEAU, J., 'Les Processions parisiennes de 1412: Analyse d'un rituel flamboyant', *Revue historique*, 284 (1990), 37–76.

CHURCHILL, I. J., *Canterbury Administration: The Administrative Machinery of the Archbishopric of Canterbury Illustrated from Original Records*, 2 vols. (London, 1933).

CLANCHY, M. T., *From Memory to Written Record: England 1066–1307* (2nd edn., Oxford, 1993).

CLARK, S., *Thinking with Demons: The Idea of Witchcraft in Early Modern Europe* (Oxford, 1997).

CLOPPER, L. M., 'Franciscans, Lollards, and Reform', in Somerset et al. (eds.), *Lollards and their Influence*, 177–96.

COLE, A., 'William Langland and the Invention of Lollardy', in Somerset et al. (eds.), *Lollards and their Influence*, 37–58.

COPELAND, R., *Pedagogy, Intellectuals and Dissent in the Later Middle Ages: Lollardy and Ideas of Learning* (Cambridge, 2001).

COPSEY, R., 'The Carmelites in England 1242–1539: Surviving Writing', *Carmelus*, 43 (1996), 175–224; and *Carmelus*, 44 (1997), 188–202.

COULET, N., *Les Visites pastorales* (Turnhout, 1977).

CROMPTON, J., '*Fasciculi zizaniorum*', parts I and II, *JEH* 12 (1961), 35–45; and *JEH* 11 (1960), 155–66.

—— 'Leicestershire Lollards', *Transactions of the Leicestershire Archaeological and Historical Society*, 44 (1968–9), 11–44.

D'ALTON, C., 'The Suppression of Heresy in Henrican England', D.Phil. thesis (Melbourne University, 1999).

DAVIES, R. G., 'Martin V and the English Episcopate, with Particular Reference to his Campaign for the Repeal of the Statute of Provisors', *EHR* 92 (1977), 309–44.

—— 'The Episcopate', in C. H. Clough (ed.), *Profession, Vocation and Culture in Later Medieval England* (Liverpool, 1982), 51–89.

—— 'Lollardy and Locality', *TRHS* 6th ser. 1 (1991), 191–212.

DAVIES, R. R., 'Kinsmen, Neighbours and Communities in Wales and the Western British Isles, c.1100–c.1400', in P. Stafford, J. L. Nelson, and J. Martindale (eds.), *Law, Laity and Solidarities: Essays in Honour of Susan Reynolds* (Manchester, 2001), 172–87.

DAVIES, W., and FOURACRE, P. (eds.), *The Settlement of Disputes in Early Medieval Europe* (Cambridge, 1986).

D'AVRAY, D., *Medieval Marriage Sermons: Mass Communication in a Culture without Print* (Oxford, 2001).

DENTON, J. H., and DOOLEY, J. P., *Representatives of the Lower Clergy in Parliament 1295–1340* (Woodbridge, 1987).

DERENS, J.-A., 'Pouvoir consulaire, espace urbain et cérémonies religieuses à Montpellier à la fin du Moyen Âge', in G. Cholvy (ed.), *Espaces religieux et communautés méridionales* (Montpellier, 1994), 73–83.

Dictionnaire de droit canonique, ed. R. Naz et al., 7 vols., (Paris, 1935–65).

DOBSON, R. B., 'The Residentiary Canons of York in the Fifteenth Century', in *Church and Society in the Medieval North of England* (London, 1996), 195–224.

DOIG, J. A., 'Political Propaganda and Royal Proclamations in Late Medieval England', *Historical Research*, 71 (1998), 253–80.

DONAHUE, C., Jr., 'Roman Canon Law in the Medieval English Church: Stubbs vs. Maitland Re-examined after 75 Years in the Light of Some Records from the Church Courts', *Michigan Law Review*, 72 (1974), 647–716.

—— *The Records of the Medieval Ecclesiastical Courts, Part II: England, Reports of the Working Group on Church Court Records*, Comparative Studies in Continental and Anglo-American Legal History, 7 (Berlin, 1994).

DUFFY, E., *The Stripping of the Altars: Traditional Religion in England c.1400–1580* (New Haven, 1992).

DYER, C., *Lords and Peasants in a Changing Society: The Estates of the Bishopric of Worcester 680–1540* (Cambridge, 1980).

ESCAMILLA, M., *Synthèse sur l'inquisition espagnole et la construction de la monarchie confessionnelle, 1478–1561* (Nantes, 2002).

FARNHAM, G. F., *Leicestershire Medieval Village Notes*, 6 vols. (Leicester, 1933).

FERME, B. E., *Canon Law in Late Medieval England: A Study of William Lyndwood's Provinciale with Particular Reference to Testamentary Law* (Rome, 1996).

FLETCHER, A. J., *Preaching, Politics and Poetry in Late Medieval England* (Dublin, 1998).

FORDE, S., 'Social Outlook and Preaching in a Wycliffite *Sermones dominicales* Collection', in I. Wood and G. A. Loud (eds.), *Church and Chronicle in the Middle Ages: Essays Presented to John Taylor* (London, 1991), 179–91.

FORREST, I., 'Anti-Lollard Polemic and Practice in Late Medieval England', in L. Clark (ed.), *The Fifteenth Century*, iii: *Authority and Subversion* (Woodbridge, 2003), 63–74.

FRAHER, R. M., 'Preventing Crime in the High Middle Ages: The Medieval Lawyers' Search for Deterrence', in J. R. Sweeny and S. Chodorow (eds.), *Popes, Teachers and Canon Law in the Middle Ages* (Ithaca, NY, 1989), 212–33.

FRASER, C. J., 'The Religious Instruction of the Laity in Late Medieval England with Particular Reference to the Sacrament of the Eucharist', D.Phil. thesis (Oxford, 1995).

FRERE, W. H., *Visitation Articles and Injunctions of the Period of the Reformation*, 3 vols. (London, 1910).

GALLAGHER, C., *Canon Law and the Christian Community: The Role of Law in the Church According to the* Summa aurea *of Cardinal Hostiensis* (Rome, 1978).

GHOSH, K., *The Wycliffite Heresy: Authority and the Interpretation of Texts* (Cambridge, 2002).

—— 'Bishop Reginald Pecock and the Idea of "Lollardy" ', in H. Barr and A. M. Hutchison (eds.), *Text and Controversy from Wyclif to Bale: Essays in Honour of Anne Hudson* (Turnhout, 2004), 251–65.

GIBBS, M., and LANG, J., *Bishops and Reform, 1215–1272: With Special Reference to the Lateran Council of 1215* (Oxford, 1934).

GIOS, P., *L'inquisitore della Bassa Padovana e dei Colli Euganei, 1448–1449* (Candiana, 1990).

GIVEN, J. B., *Inquisition and Medieval Society: Power, Discipline and Resistance in Languedoc* (Ithaca, NY, 1997).

GREENIDGE, A. H. J., *Infamia: Its Place in Roman Public and Private Law* (Oxford, 1894).

GRUNDMANN, H., 'Ketzerverhöre des Spätmittelalters als quellenkritisches Problem', *Deutsches Archiv für Erforschung des Mittelalters*, 21 (1965), 535–50.

HAINES, R. M., *The Administration of the Diocese of Worcester in the First Half of the Fourteenth Century* (London, 1965).

—— ' "Our Master Mariner, our Sovereign Lord": A Contemporary Preacher's View of King Henry V', *Mediaeval Studies*, 38 (1976), 85–96.

HAMILTON, B., *The Medieval Inquisition* (London, 1981).

HANAWALT, B. A., 'The Host, the Law and the Ambiguous Space of Medieval London Taverns', in Hanawalt and Wallace (eds.), *Medieval Crime and Social Control*, 204–23.

—— and WALLACE, D. (eds.), *Medieval Crime and Social Control* (Minneapolis, 1999).

HANNA, R., 'English Biblical Texts before Lollardy and their Fate', in Somerset et al. (eds.), *Lollards and their Influence*, 148–53.

HAREN, M., *Sin and Society in Fourteenth-Century England: A Study of the Memoriale presbiterorum* (Oxford, 2000).

HARRISS, G., *Cardinal Beaufort: A Study of Lancastrian Ascendancy and Decline* (Oxford, 1988).

HARVEY, M., *The English in Rome 1362–1420: Portrait of an Expatriate Community* (Cambridge, 1999).

HARVEY, P. D. A., 'Initiative and Authority in Settlement Change', in M. Aston, D. Austin, and C. Dyer (eds.), *The Rural Settlements of Medieval England: Studies Dedicated to Maurice Beresford and John Hurst* (Oxford, 1989), 31–43.

HELMHOLZ, R. H., 'Excommunication as a Legal Sanction: The Attitudes of the Medieval Canonists', *ZRG Kan. Abt.* 68 (1982), 202–18.

—— *The Spirit of Classical Canon Law* (Athens, Ga. 1996).

—— 'The Canon Law', in L. Hellinga and J. B. Trapp (eds.), *The Cambridge History of the Book in Britain*, iii: *1400–1557* (Cambridge, 1999), 387–98.

—— *The* Ius Commune *in England: Four Studies* (Oxford, 2001).

—— *The Oxford History of the Laws of England*, i: *The Canon Law and Ecclesiastical Jurisdiction from 597 to the 1640s* (Oxford, 2004).

HERRUP, C., *The Common Peace: Participation and the Criminal Law in Seventeenth-Century England* (Cambridge, 1987).

HILL, R. M. T., 'Public Penance: Some Problems of a Thirteenth-Century Bishop', *History*, 36 (1951), 213–26.

HILTON, R. H., *The Economic Development of Some Leicestershire Estates in the Fourteenth and Fifteenth Centuries* (Oxford, 1947).

—— *The English Peasantry in the Later Middle Ages* (Oxford, 1975).

HORNER, P. J., 'Preachers at Paul's Cross: Religion, Society and Politics in Late Medieval England', in J. Hamesse et al. (eds.), *Medieval Sermons and Society: Cloister, City, University* (Louvain-la-Neuve, 1998), 261–82.

HOSKINS, W. G., *The Midland Peasant: The Economic and Social History of a Leicestershire Village* (London, 1957).

HOWELL, C., *Land, Family and Inheritance in Transition: Kibworth Harcourt 1280–1700* (Cambridge, 1983).

HUDSON, A., *Lollards and their Books* (London, 1985).

—— 'The Examination of Lollards', in *Lollards and their Books*, 125–40.

—— 'Lollardy: The English Heresy?', in *Lollards and their Books*, 141–63.

—— *The Premature Reformation: Wycliffite Texts and Lollard History* (Oxford, 1988).

—— 'Lollard Book Production', in J. Griffiths and D. Pearsall (eds.), *Book Production and Publishing in Britain 1375–1475* (Cambridge, 1989), 125–42.

HUDSON, A., 'Notes of an Early Fifteenth-Century Research Assistant, and the Emergence of the 267 Articles against Wyclif', *EHR* 118 (2003), 685–97.

—— '*Hermofodrita or Ambidexter*: Wycliffite Views on Clerks in Secular Office', in Aston and Richmond (eds.), *Lollardy and the Gentry*, 41–51.

HUGHES, J., *Pastors and Visionaries: Religion and Secular Life in Late Medieval Yorkshire* (Woodbridge, 1988).

HYAMS, P. R., 'Deans and their Doings: The Norwich Inquiry of 1286', in S. Kuttner and K. Pennington (eds.), *Proceedings of the Sixth International Congress of Medieval Canon Law* (Vatican, 1985), 619–46.

JACOB, E. F., *Archbishop Henry Chichele* (London, 1967).

JAMES, E., *The Origins of France from Clovis to the Capetians, 500–1000* (London, 1982).

JANSEN, K. J., 'Mary Magdalen and the Mendicants: The Preaching of Penance in the Late Middle Ages', *Journal of Medieval History*, 21 (1995), 1–25.

JENKS, S., 'Die Rolle von König und Klerus bei der Häretikerverfolgung in England', *Zeitschrift für Kirchengeschichte*, 99 (1988), 23–46.

JONES, W. R., 'Relations of the Two Jurisdictions: Conflict and Co-operation in England during the Thirteenth and Fourteenth Centuries', *Studies in Medieval and Renaissance History*, 7 (1970), 77–210.

JURKOWSKI, M., 'New Light on John Purvey', *EHR* 110 (1995), 1180–90.

—— 'Lancastrian Royal Service, Lollardy and Forgery: The Career of Thomas Tykhill', in R. Archer (ed.), *Crown, Government and People in the Fifteenth Century* (Stroud, 1995), 33–52.

—— 'Lawyers and Lollardy in the Early Fifteenth Century', in Aston and Richmond (eds.), *Lollardy and the Gentry*, 155–82.

—— 'The Arrest of William Thorpe in Shrewsbury and the Anti-Lollard Statute of 1406', *Historical Research*, 75 (2002), 273–95.

—— 'Lollardy in Oxfordshire and Northamptonshire: The Two Thomas Compworths', in Somerset et al. (eds.), *Lollards and their Influence*, 73–95.

KAEPPELI, T., *Scriptores ordinis praedicatorum Medii Aevi*, 4 vols. (Rome, 1970).

KEDAR, B. Z., 'Canon Law and Local Practice: The Case of Mendicant Preaching in Late Medieval England', *Bulletin of Medieval Canon Law*, NS 2 (1972), 17–32.

KELLY, H. A., 'Lollard Inquisitions: Due and Undue Process', in A. Ferreiro (ed.), *The Devil, Heresy and Witchcraft in the Middle Ages* (Leiden, 1998), 279–303.

KENDALL, R. D., *The Drama of Dissent: The Radical Poetics of Nonconformity 1380–1590* (Chapel Hill, NC, 1986).

KIECKHEFER, R., *Repression of Heresy in Medieval Germany* (Liverpool, 1979).

KIGHTLY, C., 'The Early Lollards: A Survey of Popular Lollard Activity in England 1382–1428', D.Phil. thesis (University of York, 1975).

KÜMIN, B. A., and TLUSTY, B. A. (eds.), *The World of the Tavern: Public Houses in Early Modern Europe* (Aldershot, 2002).

KURZE, D., *Quellen zur Ketzergeschichte Brandenburgs und Pommerns* (Berlin, 1975).

—— 'Anfänge der Inquisition in Deutschland', in P. Segl (ed.), *Die Anfänge der Inquisition im Mittelalter* (Cologne, 1993), 131–93.

KUTTNER, S., *Repertorium der kanonistik (1140–1234): Prodromus corporis glossarum*, Studi e Testi, 71 (Vatican, 1937).

LAMBERT, M., *Medieval Heresy: Popular Movements from the Gregorian Reform to the Reformation* (3rd edn., Oxford, 2002).

LANDMAN, J. H., ' "The Doom of Resoun": Accommodating Lay Interpretation in Late Medieval England', in Hanawalt and Wallace (eds.), *Medieval Crime and Social Control*, 90–123.

LEA, H. C., *A History of the Inquisition in the Middle Ages*, 3 vols. (London, 1888).

LEFF, G., *Heresy in the Later Middle Ages: The Relation of Heterodoxy to Dissent, c.1250-c.1450* (2nd edn., Manchester, 1999).

LE NEVE, J., *Fasti ecclesiae Anglicanae 1300–1541*, ed. T. D. Hardy (Oxford, 1954); revised and expanded (London, 1962–).

LEPINE, D., ' "A Long Way from University": Cathedral Canons and Learning at Hereford in the Fifteenth Century', in C. M. Barron and J. Stratford (eds.), *The Church and Learning in Later Medieval Society: Essays in Honour of R. B. Dobson. Proceedings of the 1999 Harlaxton Symposium* (Donington, 2002), 178–95.

LERNER, R. E., *The Heresy of the Free Spirit in the Later Middle Ages* (Berkeley, 1972).

LOGAN, F. D., *Excommunication and the Secular Arm in Medieval England: A Study in Legal Procedure from the Thirteenth to the Sixteenth Century* (Toronto, 1968).

LUNT, W. E., *Financial Relations of the Papacy with England 1327–1534* (Cambridge, Mass., 1962).

McCLURE, J., 'Handbooks against Heresy in the West, from the Late Fourth to the Late Sixth Centuries', *Journal of Theological Studies*, NS 30 (1979), 186–97.

McFARLANE, K. B., *Lancastrian Kings and Lollard Knights* (Oxford, 1972).

McHARDY, A. K., 'Bishop Buckingham and the Lollards of Lincoln Diocese', in D. Baker (ed.), *Schism, Heresy and Religious Protest*, SCH 9 (Cambridge, 1972), 131–45.

—— 'Liturgy and Propaganda in the Diocese of Lincoln during the Hundred Years War', in S. Mews (ed.), *Religion and National Identity*, SCH 18 (Oxford, 1982), 215–27.

—— '*De heretico comburendo* 1401', in Aston and Richmond (eds.), *Lollardy and the Gentry*, 112–26.

MADDICOTT, J., 'The County Community and the Making of Public Opinion in Fourteenth-Century England', *TRHS* 5th ser. 28 (1978), 27–43.

MANSFIELD, M. C., *The Humiliation of Sinners: Public Penance in Thirteenth-Century France* (Ithaca, NY, 1995).

MARTIN, G. H., 'Wyclif, Lollards and Historians, 1384–1984', in Somerset et al. (eds.), *Lollards and their Influence*, 237–50.

MASSCHAELE, J., 'The Public Space of the Marketplace in Medieval England', *Speculum*, 77 (2002), 383–421.

MERLO, G. G., *Eretici e inquisitori nella società Piemontese del trecento* (Turin, 1977).

MICHAUD-QUANTIN, P., *Sommes de casuistique et manuels de confession au Moyen Âge* (Louvain, 1962).

MIGLIORINO, F., *Fama e infamia: Problemi della società medievale nel pensiero giuridico nei secoli XII e XIII* (Catania, 1985).

MOORE, R. I., 'Heresy as Disease', in D. W. Lourdaux and D. Verhelst (eds.), *The Concept of Heresy in the Middle Ages* (Louvain, 1976), 1–11.

—— *The Formation of a Persecuting Society: Power and Deviance in Western Europe, 950–1250* (Oxford, 1987).

MÜLLER, W. P., *Huguccio: The Life, Works, and Thought of a Twelfth-Century Jurist* (Washington, DC, 1994).

MUSSON, A., 'Sub-Keepers and Constables: The Role of Local Officials in Keeping the Peace in Fourteenth-Century England', *EHR* 117 (2002), 1–24.

—— 'Law and Text: Legal Authority and Judicial Accessibility in the Late Middle Ages', in J. Crick and A. Walsham (eds.), *The Uses of Script and Print, 1300–1700* (Cambridge, 2004), 95–115.

—— and ORMROD, W. M., *The Evolution of English Justice: Law, Politics and Society in the Fourteenth Century* (Basingstoke, 1999).

NEDERMAN, C. J., and LAURSEN, J. C. (eds.), *Beyond the Persecuting Society: Religious Toleration before the Enlightenment* (Philadelphia, 1998).

NICHOLS, A. E., 'Lollard Language in the Croxton *Play of the Sacrament*', *Notes and Queries*, 36 (1989), 23–5.

NICHOLS, J., *The History and Antiquities of the County of Leicester*, 4 vols. (Leicester, 1815).

NIRENBERG, D., *Communities of Violence: Persecution of Minorities in the Middle Ages* (Princeton, 1996).

NISSÉ, R., 'Staged Interpretations: Civic Rhetoric and Lollard Politics in the York Plays', *Journal of Medieval and Early Modern Studies*, 28 (1998), 427–52.

NUTTON, V., 'The Seeds of Disease: An Explanation of Contagion and Infection from the Greeks to the Renaissance', *Medical History*, 27 (1983), 1–34.

ORMEROD, P., and ROACH, A. P., 'The Medieval Inquisition: Scale-Free Networks and the Suppression of Heresy', *Physica A*, 339 (2004), 645–52.

ORMROD, W. M., *Political Life in Medieval England, 1300–1450* (Basingstoke, 1995).

OWEN, D. M., 'Ecclesiastical Jurisdiction in England 1300–1500', in D. Baker (ed.), *The Materials, Sources and Methods of Ecclesiastical History*, SCH 11 (Oxford, 1975), 199–221.

—— *The Medieval Canon Law: Teaching, Literature and Transmission* (Cambridge, 1990).

PANTIN, W. A., *The English Church in the Fourteenth Century* (Cambridge, 1955).

PAYER, P. J., *The Bridling of Desire: Views of Sex in the Later Middle Ages* (Toronto, 1993).

PEDERSEN, F., *Marriage Disputes in Medieval England* (London, 2000).

PETERS, E., *Inquisition* (Berkeley, 1989).

PHYTHIAN-ADAMS, C., 'Ceremony and the Citizen: The Communal Year at Coventry 1450–1550', in P. Clark (ed.), *The Early Modern Town: A Reader* (London, 1976), 57–85.

POLLOCK, F., and MAITLAND, F. W., *The History of English Law before the Time of Edward I*, 2 vols. (2nd edn., Cambridge, 1968).

POOS, L., *A Rural Society after the Black Death: Essex 1350–1525* (Cambridge, 1991).

POWELL, E., *Kingship, Law, and Society: Criminal Justice in the Reign of Henry V* (Oxford, 1989).

POWELL, S., 'The Transmission and Circulation of *The Lay Folks' Catechism*', in A. J. Minnis (ed.), *Late-Medieval Religious Texts and their Transmission* (Woodbridge, 1994), 67–84.

REX, R., *The Lollards* (Basingstoke, 2002).

RICHARDSON, H. G., 'Heresy and the Lay Power under Richard II', *EHR* 51 (1936), 1–28.

RICHARDSON, M., *The Medieval Chancery under Henry V*, List and Index Society, Special Series, 30 (Kew, 1999).

ROBERTSON, C. A., 'The Tithe Heresy of Friar William Russell', *Albion*, 8 (1976), 1–16.

ROSSER, G., 'Parochial Conformity and Voluntary Religion in Late-Medieval England', *TRHS* 6th ser. 1 (1991), 173–89.

RUBIN, M., *Corpus Christi: The Eucharist in Late Medieval Culture* (Cambridge, 1991).

—— 'Small Groups: Identity and Solidarity in the Late Middle Ages', in J. Kermode (ed.), *Enterprise and Individuals in Fifteenth-Century England* (Stroud, 1991), 132–56.

—— *Gentile Tales: The Narrative Assault on Late Medieval Jews* (New Haven, 1999).

SANDLER, L. F., *Omne bonum: A Fourteenth-Century Encyclopaedia of Universal Knowledge*, 2 vols. (London, 1996).

SAYERS, J. E., *Papal Judges Delegate in the Province of Canterbury, 1198–1254: A Study in Ecclesiastical Jurisdiction and Administration* (Oxford, 1971).

SCARISBRICK, J. J., *The Reformation and the English People* (Oxford, 1984).

SCASE, W., ' "Strange and Wonderful Bills": Bill-Casting and Political Discourse in Late Medieval England', *New Medieval Literatures*, 2 (1998), 225–47.

SCHULTE, J. F. VON, *Die Geschichte der Quellen und Literatur des canonischen Rechts, von Gratian bis auf Papst Gregor ix*, 3 vols. (Stuttgart, 1875–80).

SMITH, D., *Guide to Bishops' Registers of England and Wales* (London, 1981).

—— *Supplement to the Guide to Bishops' Registers of England and Wales*, CYS (2004).

SOMERSET, F., ' "Mark him wel for he is on of þo": Training the "Lewed" Gaze to Discern Hypocrisy', *English Literary History*, 68 (2001), 315–34.

—— HAVENS, J. C., and PITARD, D. G. (eds.), *Lollards and their Influence in Late Medieval England* (Woodbridge, 2003).

SOUTHERN, R. W., *Robert Grosseteste: The Growth of an English Mind in Medieval Europe* (Oxford, 1986).

SPENCER, H. L., *English Preaching in the Late Middle Ages* (Oxford, 1993).

STOREY, R. L., 'Malicious Indictments of Clergy in the Fifteenth Century', in M. J. Franklin and C. Harper-Bill (eds.), *Medieval Ecclesiastical Studies in Honour of Dorothy M. Owen* (Woodbridge, 1995), 221–40.

STROHM, P., *England's Empty Throne: Usurpation and the Language of Legitimization, 1399–1422* (New Haven, 1998).

SWANSON, R. N., 'The "Mendicant Problem" in the Later Middle Ages', in P. Biller and B. Dobson (eds.), *The Medieval Church: Universities, Heresy and the Religious Life*, SCH, Subsidia, 11 (Woodbridge, 1999), 217–38.

—— *Treasuring Merit/Craving Indulgence: Accounting for Salvation in Pre-Reformation England* (Birmingham, 2003).

TANNER, N., 'Penances Imposed on Kentish Lollards by Archbishop Warham 1511–12', in Aston and Richmond (eds.), *Lollardy and the Gentry*, 229–49.

THOMPSON, A. H., *The English Clergy and their Organisation in the Later Middle Ages* (Oxford, 1947).

THOMSON, J. A. F., 'John Foxe and Some Sources for Lollard History: Notes for a Critical Reappraisal', in G. J. Cuming (ed.), *Papers Read at the Second Winter and Summer Meetings of the Ecclesiastical History Society*, SCH 2 (London, 1965), 251–7.

—— *The Later Lollards, 1414–1520* (Oxford, 1965).

—— 'Orthodox Religion and the Origins of Lollardy', *History*, 74 (1989), 39–55.

THRUPP, S., *The Merchant Class of Medieval London 1300–1500* (Ann Arbor, 1962).

Trusen, W., 'Der Inquisitionsprozess: Seine historischen Grundlagen und frühen Formen', *ZRG Kan. Abt.* 74 (1988), 168–230.

Vodola, E., *Excommunication in the Middle Ages* (Berkeley, 1986).

Walsham, A., *Providence in Early Modern England* (Oxford, 1999).

Watson, N., 'Censorship and Cultural Change in Late Medieval England: Vernacular Theology, the Oxford Translation Debate and Arundel's Constitutions of 1409', *Speculum*, 70 (1995), 822–64.

Watt, J. A., *The Theory of the Papal Monarchy in the Thirteenth Century: The Contribution of the Canonists* (London, 1965).

Watts, J., *Henry VI and the Politics of Kingship* (Cambridge, 1996).

Wickham, C., *Courts and Conflict in Twelfth-Century Tuscany* (Oxford, 2003).

Wilks, M., '*Reformatio Regni*: Wyclif and Hus as Leaders of Religious Protest Movements', in D. Baker (ed.), *Schism, Heresy and Religious Protest*, SCH 9 (Cambridge, 1972), 109–30.

Winroth, A., *The Making of Gratian's Decretum* (Cambridge, 2000).

Zeleny, R., 'Councils and Synods of Prague and their Statutes (1343–1361)', *Apollinaris*, 45 (1972), 471–532.

Index